ECONOMIC HISTORY
OF THE JEWS

ECONOMIC HISTORY OF THE JEWS

SALO W. BARON, ARCADIUS KAHAN and others

Edited by NACHUM GROSS

SCHOCKEN BOOKS • NEW YORK

First published by SCHOCKEN BOOKS 1975

First SCHOCKEN PAPERBACK edition 1976

Copyright © 1975 by Keter Publishing House Jerusalem Ltd.

Library of Congress Catalog Card No. 75-534

Manufactured in the United States of America

CONTENTS

The Introduction was written by Dr. Nahum Gross. The other articles, which were prepared originally for Encyclopaedia Judaica, were written by:

Part One: Chaps. 1—7, Prof. Salo W. Baron; Chaps. 8—10, Prof. Arcadius Kahan.

Part Two: Chap. 1, J. Goldberg, Dr. S. Tapuach, Dr. J. Brandes, Dr. H. Avni; Chap. 2, A. Wein; Chap. 3, H. Wasserman; Chap. 4, Prof. H. H. Ben-Sasson.

Part Three: Chaps. 1, 4, 5, 8, 10, editorial staff, Chap. 2, Prof. H. H. Ben-Sasson; Chap. 3, Dr. Gedalia Yogev; Chap. 6, M. Lamed; Chap. 7, J. Kaplan; Chap. 9, Dr. M. Graetz; Chap. 11, H. Pohl; Chap. 12, H. Wasserman, Dr. V. D. Lipman, I. Yellowitz; Chaps. 13, 14, H. Wasserman.

Part Four: Chaps. 1, 4, 13, Dr. H. Kellenbenz; Chaps. 2, 5, 10, 11, H. Wasserman; Chap. 3, J. Kaplan; Chap. 6, I. Levitats; Chap. 8, D. M. Friedenberg; Chap. 9, Prof. H. H. Ben-Sasson; Chap. 12, T. Oelsner, Rabbi B. W. Korn; Chap. 14, editorial staff.

INTRODUCTION

This volume is in its own way a pioneer — an overall survey of the economic aspects of Jewish history and a consideration of major trends and developments within the most important spheres of economic activity. For many decades much has been said about examining the economic motivations and facts of Jewish life throughout the centuries and a number of specialized studies have appeared, but not enough has been achieved in the direction of an overall synthesis. One reason for this is the relative scarcity of mature scholars versed in history *and* economics *and* Jewish studies. The field remains largely unplowed and this book is a first attempt at opening it up both for laymen and for future scholars. It reflects the state of knowledge of the subject at the present time. The reader will find here the colorful story of the economic life of the Jews throughout the ages, the impact of internal and external factors and chapters describing how the Jews have played key roles in a great variety of occupations in all parts of the world. The potential specialists will find here many topics that have still not been adequately studied and will discover topics and directions for future research. The contents of this book will be an invaluable complement to the standard Jewish histories.

The various directions in which the future study of Jewish economic history can proceed are in fact supplementary rather than exclusive alternatives, as, indeed, are their underlying philosophies and methods. One major line of division runs between regarding the subject primarily as an aspect of Jewish history and viewing it as part of "general" economic history, — irrespective of whether the framework for both approaches be a region, a country, or the international economy. The choice and formulation of problems, the direction and tools of investigation, and the interpretative emphasis on specific results will all vary with the approach — but it is this variety that engenders the richness of history. In the case of our subject, in particular, it is probably true that the integration of a Jewish community within the surrounding society was most advanced in the economic sphere. The economic life of Jews in a particular country is thus of prime importance for an understanding of their life and development in all its aspects, but it is also an integral part of the history of that country. This far-reaching interaction is, at the same time, the source of one of the major pitfalls for the economic historian — that of deviating into an apologetic line of reasoning, such as a simplistic "explanation" of Jewish occupations, or a laudatory exposition of Jewish "contributions" to an economy.

Interpretation must be built upon a foundation of data. These have to be collected according to selective criteria, but frequently the information most desired by the historian is either not accessible or even nonexistent. Genuine economic history has to be based on information as comprehensive as possible and as quantitative as possible — it is first of all the story of the "common man" and of society as a whole, and only secondly concerned with leading figures. We want to know the occupational structure of a Jewish community, i.e., how its members made a living; its industrial structure, i.e., their distribution among sectors and branches of the economy; its composition by economic status, such as the classification into employees, self-employed, and employers; and, last but not least, composition by levels of wealth, income, and standard of living in the broader sense. In general, such data are hard to come by, but for our purposes this difficulty is aggravated by a well-known paradox of Jewish history — the fact that the achievement of equal civic status for the Jews involves also the end of their specific identification in legal and official sources. Thus, just when the development of the social sciences is followed by a growing recognition of the need to collect and preserve information, and as the increasing orientation toward welfare policies and economic planning turns the modern state into the chief producer of economic statistics and surveys — the consequences of emancipation cause the Jews, as such, to be nonexistent in this wealth of source material. In most Western-type democracies even the number of Jewish inhabitants becomes a subject of guesswork. These difficulties result not only from the non-inclusion of religious and ethnic identification in censuses and other official sources, but also — and no less seriously — from the abolition of compulsory membership in Jewish communal organizations, whose records could serve as the prime internal source of comprehensive information.

The collection of data will therefore be determined both by each scholar's desiderata and by the limitations of his sources. Analysis will be founded on interpretative questions, some of which are already well established. Can one legitimately speak of a specific Jewish economic structure? If so, we want to determine its characteristic elements as well as its causes and effects, to observe their development in time, and to test their similarities in different political systems and at various stages of economic development. As such an analysis proceeds, to a large extent by comparative research, further historiographical questions evolve. Which is the relevant frame of reference — the economic structure of the total surrounding society or that of its urban population? And even more fascinating are questions leading to and resulting from comparison with other minority groups — an approach which on the one hand establishes Jewish economic history within a special, and nowadays even topical, branch of the social sciences, and on the other hand is bound to bring into sharper focus the problem of specifically Jewish economic structures and behavioral patterns.

For an understanding of the patterns of Jewish economic behavior, such as consumption and saving habits or degrees of risk aversion, quantitative data must be supplemented by qualitative, descriptive material, even more than for the above-mentioned structural analyses. Of particular interest, for both the Jewish and "general" historian, are the issues of business organization and entrepreneurial behavior. How valid and general are accepted views as to typically Jewish preferences for certain business structures, for risky ventures, for economic innovation? True, investigation of such problems may soon digress into the more specific discipline of business and entrepreneurial history. The economic historian proper will be more interested in the generalizations inferred from a larger number of studies on individual firms and businessmen than in details. He will be even wary of an excessive concern with atypical, extraordinary cases. This reservation, however, applies to various sectors and industries with unequal force. If, for instance, we find in the present volume a particularly large number of family and business names in the essays on banking and on spices, this reflects much more than a certain style of historiography. Clearly, colonial trade in the early modern period and brokerage and banking, especially investment banking, in recent times are highly oligopolistic industries, and their history is indeed the story of a rather small number of leading firms. The delineation of family ties and alliances among them is therefore also strictly relevant; and at least the Jewish historian will be curious to know who of these leading entrepreneurs were Jews.

This line of thought leads back to the fundamental issue of economic integration and interaction between the Jews and their social environment. In particular, how deep was the integration? We have already suggested that it went furthest in the economic sphere. Even when cultural segregation and organizational autonomy of the Jewish community were most developed, at least some of its members were economically part of the host society. But, on the other hand, even when economic integration appears to be complete, and discriminative barriers nonexistent, there remain some individuals who make their living exclusively or mainly within the Jewish community, such as rabbis and kosher butchers. No less important and interesting are the issues of what may be termed economic tribalism. To what degree do Jews prefer each other in trade, employment, lending? Are there not only economic positions and sectors from which Jews are, at least informally and incompletely, excluded, but also certain occupational or industrial branches in which Jews predominate and furthermore endeavor to exclude others? These are, probably, still debatable questions; but there can be no doubt as to the existence of specifically or predominantly Jewish formal organizations, such as cooperatives and trade unions, which deserve further study.

This discussion has concentrated on suggested lines of research on the economic life of the Jews as individuals. However, Jewish economic history must also encompass the sphere of Jewish public finance: Taxes and contributions, on the one hand, both mandatory and voluntary, and their allocation between the state and the Jewish community; and public services and institutions, on the other hand, partly or entirely self-financed, providing for the community exclusively or also for the public at large. This type of economic activity has to be studied at the local and at the country-wide level, but its specific Jewish character is perhaps most pronounced when international. As this implies particular concern with the financial institutions and policies of the Zionist movement, and with the economic history of Erez Israel and its *Yishuv*, we are considering a very special, and methodologically separate chapter of Jewish economic history.

* * * * * *

The contributions to this volume were originally published in the *Encyclopaedia Judaica.* By their very nature, they offer different approaches and employ different methodologies; in this, as well as in the exclusion of a number of important topics, the collection reflects the present state of research in the field.

Credit is due to the editorial staff of *Encyclopaedia Judaica*, and, above all, to Professor H. H. Ben-Sasson, who took upon himself the tasks of divisional and departmental editor for all articles on economic history. Textual changes for the purpose of this collection have been kept to a minimum. In particular, the bibliographies of the individual articles were kept intact, although relocated at the end of the volume; in this way they should best serve the needs of various readers, even if as a result certain items recur several times. For non-specific surveys on Jewish economic history in modern times the reader must, at present, be referred to works on Jewish history in general and by countries. (But cf. also Simon Kuznets, "Economic Structure and Life of the Jews," in Louis Finkelstein (ed.), *The Jews*, 3rd ed. (New York, 1960), II, 1597–1666 and sources mentioned there.).

Nahum Gross

Part One
GENERAL SURVEY

1

THE FIRST TEMPLE PERIOD

Reconstruction of ancient Jewish economic conditions is greatly hampered by the paucity of available documentation. The main source of information still is the Bible; but its general orientation is either normative in the legal sections, exhortatory in the prophetic enunciations, or romanticizing in some of the historical descriptions. Thus a great deal may be learned of what the leaders believed the economic conditions ought to be rather than what they really were. Archaeology, on the other hand, which has greatly enriched our knowledge about such *realia* as the utensils employed in agricultural and industrial production, the size and shape of buildings, sudden devastations by earthquakes or wars, and the like, has proved wholly inadequate in reflecting the daily economic relationships or the dynamics of economic evolution. More informative have been the documents found in archaeological mounds. But these documents are too few and limited to certain localities which may not warrant generalization from them to other areas and periods. However, much can also be learned from the vaster accumulation of materials in the neighboring civilizations (including the more recently explored Mari, Nuzi, and Ugaritic collections), provided one does not lose sight of the great differences prevailing between the respective countries and the many unique features which characterized ancient Israel's economy as it did Israelite society and culture at large. Utilizing these and other sources, as well as the combined results of many generations of intensive research by scholars, often of high competence, one may perhaps obtain some approximation of the actual economic evolution of ancient Israel after its entry into Canaan and the formation of its monarchy.

One conclusion which seems clearly to emerge from the state of our knowledge today is that we must abandon the long-held assumption of both traditionalists and critical scholars that the historic evolution of ancient Israel must be explained in terms of a gradual emergence of a nomadic people into an agricultural society which was later combined with an urban civilization characterized by an increasing division of labor. This evolution, it was believed, required several centuries of slow growth. Such gradualism was used to explain not only the changing economic trends but also the general societal and religious transformations; it supposedly proved helpful even in the dating of biblical sources. However, it is now known that the ancient Middle East, including the land of Canaan, had a fairly advanced civilization more than 2,000 years before the appearance of Israel on the historical scene. Even according to the biblical narratives, the first patriarch, Abraham − now widely accepted as an historic personality of prime magnitude − combined in his career an intimate acquaintance with his native Babylonian city of Ur, the excavation of which has revealed its rich and ramified social stratification at the beginning of the second millennium B.C.E., with that of Egypt, which he visited for a time and of Canaan, in which he settled. The segment of the Canaanite people which appears under the name of Phoenicians was soon drawn into the orbit of a maritime empire extending all the way to Spain. Hence even a primitive, nomadic tribe conquering one Canaanite city after another could quickly learn its methods of production and adopt its mode of living, skipping many stages of the accepted economic evolution.

It may be assumed, therefore, that Israel very early replaced nomadic cattle raising by agriculture as its dominant source of livelihood. Settlers in the formerly Canaanite cities also turned to crafts and even commerce as their primary occupation. With the establishment of a monarchy and the building of the Temple in Jerusalem there also arose a substantial royal and priestly bureaucracy. The new capitals of Jerusalem and Samaria, especially, revealed many characteristics of major urban centers whose upper classes indulged in considerable luxuries in dwellings and personal attire, such as are described by Isaiah in his censure of the ladies of Jerusalem (Isaiah 3:18 ff.). At the same time, the old occupations of cattle raising and even the still more "primitive" activities of fishing and hunting − the latter was never a mere sport even among the Israelite kings − were never completely given up. They flourished particularly in the peripheral areas of the south and Transjordan.

This great diversity of pursuits was aided by both climatic and hydrographic conditions in the country. Despite its relatively small size, ancient Palestine consisted of no less than 40 distinct geographic units, each with a different set of natural conditions, which not only affected the type of production but also colored the entire system of political and social life by promoting local independence, even tribalism. That is also why throughout the First Temple Period Israel continued to share its land with Edomites, Moabites, Ammonites, Philistines, and some Arameans, while, beginning with a sort of "amphyctionic" alliance, its own 12 tribes gradually built up whatever unity was to exist later in their divided kingdom.

Although the country was dotted with many localities called cities *(arim)*, these settlements did not resemble, as has often been assumed, the medieval and modern cities in being primarily centers of industry and commerce. While no less than 400 such "cities" existed in the territory of Israel and Judah, their population, as a rule, numbered no more than a 1,000 persons and consisted principally of farmers who had banded together to live behind city walls for protection against raiders. Their livelihood was derived from cultivating their fields, vineyards, and orchards, for the most part located outside the city walls, to which they proceeded in the morning and from which they returned in the evening (note this sequence in Ps. 121:8; II Kings 19:27). Outside their fields and vineyards there also were some pastures where the farmers could maintain some sheep and goats, particularly for the purpose of producing milk.

Nutrition of the ancient Palestinian population was about equally divided between grain and fruit. Barley was a particularly important staple which, if we may deduce the prices from better known Babylonian parallels, was at times more in demand, and even more costly, than dates. Among the fruits grapes, dates, olives, and figs loomed very large in the popular diet. Meat was always considered a luxury and was consumed by the majority of the population only on festive occasions. The cultivation of vineyards and orchards often required intensive irrigation — already practiced in the pre-Israelite period — and years of waiting for actual production, further aggravated by certain ritualistic taboos and imposts. This system presupposed investment of much capital and human labor. But the ultimate returns were quite rewarding in produce yielded by small plots of land. The quality of some ancient Israel fruits seems to have been as high as that of similar products of the Second Temple era (see below).

Industrial production, on the other hand, was usually in the hands of artisans, who were often organized in clans or guilds or both. We know of villages dedicated to single crafts (I Chronicles 4:14). Entire families or clans served as scribes. While there is no evidence of guild monopolies, it appears that admission to certain crafts depended on a fairly long apprenticeship and hence was beyond the reach of ordinary laborers. At the same time we also learn about royal enterprises employing, for instance, numerous potters. The frequent occurrence of potsherds bearing the imprint of *la-melekh* ("to the king") suggests that it might have been a trademark of royal potteries. Some scholars, however, interpret that mark as a fiscal receipt for a certain quantity of wine or oil delivered to the royal treasury in payment of taxes. No final decision can be made on this score, since the entire subject of ancient Jewish taxation is shrouded in obscurity, deepened by many unresolved controversies.

A certain number of Israelites also entered mercantile occupations. Some of them did this as "king's merchants," especially in the days of King Solomon (I Kings 10:28). At that time ancient Israel's international trade made rapid strides both because it was fostered by the concentrated royal power and

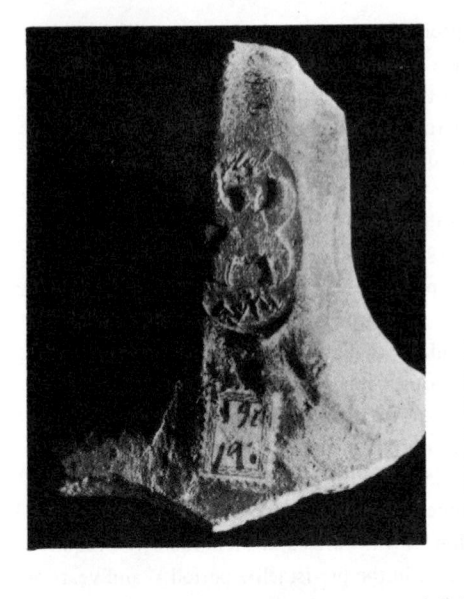

Jar handle from Lachish, c. 7th century B.C.E., engraved with winged scarab seal with royal stamp, *lmlk* ("to the king"), and the place name, Soco. The legend *lmlk* may represent weights and measures standardized by the royal administration.

because, ever since David's conquest of Edomite territory, Israel had gained access to Ezion-Geber-Eloth on the Red Sea (I Kings 9:26). The new open route to the Indian Ocean made Israel a very welcome ally to Hiram, king of Tyre. Even earlier some northern Israelites seem to have hired themselves out as sailors to Phoenician shipowners (this seems to be the meaning of "Dan, why does he sojourn by the ships?" in the Song of Deborah; Judges 5:17). But now the two kings could collaborate in sending ships both to the Indian Ocean and the western Mediterranean, where the Phoenicians had long been exploiting the copper mines of Sardinia and were ultimately to establish a colony in Tartessus, Spain. A combined Phoenician-Israelite expedition to Ophir, probably located on the west coast of India or even further east, was a landmark in the history of eastern navigation.

This condition did not last, however. After Solomon's death and the ensuing partition of the country into two kingdoms, Israel lost its overlordship over the Edomites, not to regain it except for a short time under Jehoshaphat. Nor could Israel any longer exploit the copper mines and use the refinery built by Solomon in Ezion-Geber. These losses contributed to the overall decline in both the commercial and political activities of Northern Israel and Judah, which often became tributary to foreign monarchs and occasionally indulged in internecine struggles. As a result, most of the country's mercantile activities were now conducted by strangers, mainly Phoenicians and other Canaanites. The term *Kena'ani* ("Canaanite") became a synonym for merchant in popular parlance.

All through that period Israelite commerce was abetted by a more or less stable system of weights and measures which the country shared with other Middle Eastern nations. There was also an increasing demand for money to facilitate mercantile transactions, and even in his day Abraham purchased the cave of Machpelah for "four hundred shekels of silver, current money with the merchant" (Genesis 23:16). At first the currency circulated in the form of silver bars which had to be weighed, but soon their weight was standardized and officially marked. By the end of the First Temple era regular coins, whether first introduced in Lydia or in Babylonia, gained the ascendancy. Curiously, gold never became the main instrument of exchange; down to the Roman period it was often considered a mere commodity, valued at so-and-so many silver shekels, although its price was steadily gaining.

Another effect of the political weakness of the two kingdoms was the relative absence of slaves from the productive processes in the country. Even Solomon's ambitious public works, including the building of the royal palace and the Temple, required more manpower than could be supplied by slaves. Hence the royal imposition of corvée labor on hundreds of thousands of free Israelites. After Solomon's death the supply of unfree labor must have further dried up, since the country now was rarely victorious in battle and thus could recruit only a small number of slaves from among prisoners of war. On the other hand, to purchase slaves in the Phoenician slave markets became increasingly unremunerative. As early as the early days of the Book of the Covenant (ninth century B.C.E. or before) the indemnity for a male or female slave was set at 30 shekels of silver (Exodus 21:32). Later on the price seems to have gone up to 50 or more shekels. With the prevailing high rates of interest throughout the ancient Middle East, which ranged from a minimum of 20–25% on cash loans and of $33\frac{1}{3}\%$ on grain loans, up to 100% and more for more risky credit or in periods of scarcity of capital, it simply did not pay a landowner or craftsman to acquire a slave and maintain him to the end of his life while free day laborers were readily available at very low cost. "Hebrew" slaves probably originated only from debt bondage or a condemned criminal's inability to pay the fine. But the legal restrictions on the treatment of Hebrew slaves, the enforced manumission at the end of a six-year term, and the (probably utopian) demand of the Deuteronomist that a manumitted slave should be provided by his master with means for earning a living (Deuteronomy 15: 13–14), made the possession of a Hebrew slave very irksome. It was, therefore, not for productive purposes but rather for domestic service or concubinage that a few slaves were acquired by better situated masters. However, unemployment among free labor was often so great that one or another Hebrew slave may have chosen voluntarily to forego freedom and stay on after the expiration of the six-year term.

Surplus of free labor must have grown toward the end of the First Temple period as a result of the sharp inequalities which the prophets denounced. At that time many small farmers fell into debt and, unable to earn enough to pay the high rates of interest (probably collected under some subterfuge to avoid the even more far-reaching laws against usury), lost their land. Isaiah was not alone in exclaiming: "Woe unto them that join house to house, that lay field to field, till there be no room and ye be made to dwell alone in the midst of the land" (5:8; see also Hosea 5:10, Micah 2:1–2). The ensuing social unrest gave rise to the immortal calls for social justice by the great Israelite prophets. It also stimulated much idealistic social legislation (see below), the practical implementation of which left much to be desired. The rumblings of discontent among the masses helped to undermine the existing social order, particularly in Northern Israel with its constant revolts and assassinations of reigning monarchs. Of its ten ruling dynasties in the relatively short period of 931–721 B.C.E. all but two were replaced after the reign of one or two kings. Such instability was also ruinous for the country's economy and helped to bring about the disastrous fall of Samaria in 721 and of Jerusalem in 586 B.C.E. which spelled the end of the First Temple period.

2

EXILE AND RESTORATION

The fall of Jerusalem marked a turning point also in the economic history of the Jews. Not only was Palestine severely devastated — the reservations voiced by some modern scholars were disproved by the widespread desolation evidenced by archaeological diggings — but a large segment, perhaps the majority, of the Jewish population either perished during the war, was deported by the Babylonians, or emigrated voluntarily. The removal of the most active members of the community, including the royal house, the priests, the great landowners, and the artisans, further aggravated the effects of the depopulation and material destruction. Like the Philistine overlords of the early Israelite tribes, many ancient conquerors saw in the exile of smiths, the main suppliers of weapons as well as of industrial and agricultural tools, the best method of disarming the conquered population. Deprived of their leadership, the Israelites who remained behind were prone to adopt some of the more primitive ways of life and thought of their pagan neighbors.

On the other hand, the exiles to Babylonia joined the ever-growing Jewish dispersion. There are reasons to believe that a number of those deported from Northern Israel by the Assyrians in 733–719 B.C.E. had continued to profess their ancestral religion on the foreign soil. Their descendants, as well as those of the Judeans deported by Sennacherib in 702, now joined the groups of the new arrivals to form a powerful new community. (Only thus can we explain why those returning from the Babylonian Exile included descendants of families who had lived in northern Israelite localities before the fall of Samaria; see Ezra 2:2 ff. and the commentaries thereon.) They developed a new center in and around Nippur, the second largest city in Babylonia, which was located on the "river" Chebar, or rather the canal connecting the Euphrates and the Tigris. Here, both the new and old settlers now enjoyed the distinguished leadership of Ezekiel and many former Palestinian elders. They were also supported by surviving members of the royal family after Amel Marduk ("Evil-Merodach") had released the imprisoned king of Judah, Jehoiachin, and restored him to a high position at the royal court of Babel. This release, narrated in the Bible (II Kings 25:27 ff.) and confirmed also by Babylonian sources (E. F. Weidner in *Mélanges*

Dussaud (1939), II, 923–35), seems to have laid the foundation for the development of the exilarchate, a remarkable institution which lent the dispersed Jews a focus of leadership, with few interruptions, for the following 2,000 years.

Next to Babylonia Egypt accommodated a number of Jewish communities; the best known was the Jewish military colony of Elephantine in Upper Egypt, established perhaps as early as the seventh century by Psammetichus I to help defend the southern frontier of Egypt against Nubian raiders. Before long, Jewish settlers spread throughout the Middle East, especially after 549 B.C.E. when Cyrus and his successors founded the enormous Persian Empire, territorially exceeding in size even the later Roman Empire in its grandeur. The author of the Book of Esther did not hesitate to place in the mouth of Haman, the anti-Jewish courtier in the capital of Susa, the accusation against "a certain people scattered abroad and dispersed among the peoples in all the provinces of thy kingdom; and their laws are diverse from those of every people" (3:8). Nor was Deutero-Isaiah guilty of vast exaggeration when he prophesied that "I [God] will bring thy seed from the east and gather thee from the west; I will ... bring My sons from far and My daughters from the end of the earth" (Isaiah 43:5–6).

This multitude of Jewish settlers outside Judah appears to have been rather speedily integrated into the environmental economic structures. Despite their vivid messianic expectations, their majority followed Jeremiah's advice and built houses, took wives, and generally established themselves in their new countries on a semipermanent basis. In Babylonia, particularly, which at that time marched in the vanguard of a semicapitalistic civilization, Jews entered the stream of advanced mercantile exchanges. The people who at home had devoted itself largely to agriculture and small crafts now assumed an important role in banking and far-flung commerce. Whether or not Jacob, the founder of the leading banking house of Egibi, was Jewish – there is some support for this hypothesis in the fact that loans were formally extended without interest, though the bankers collected the revenues from the mortgaged properties including slaves and cattle – there is no question that some Jewish landowners and businessmen wrote significant contracts with leading Babylonian capitalists. In the archives of the House of Murashu, an important banking and warehousing firm, no less than 70 Jewish names have been identified. Some of the Jewish contracting parties, to be sure, merely undertook to raise sheep and goats in return for a specified annual delivery of cattle, butter, wool, and hides. Others obligated themselves to deliver to the firm 500 good fish within 20 days if they were provided with five nets and permits to fish in the firm's waters. But some major contracts were signed by wealthy Jewish landowners in their own right who traded with the Murashu Sons on a basis of equality.

In contrast, the Aramaic papyri of the Elephantine colony in Egypt include business contracts representing rather small amounts, as was to be expected from a typical soldiers' camp which derived its main livelihood from cultivating the soil. Other Egyptian localities, particularly Migdol, Tahpanhes, and Noph — mentioned by Jeremiah (44:1) and identified by scholars with Magdalos, Daphne, and Memphis in Lower Egypt — doubtless offered the Jewish settlers and other arrivals from the Asiatic mainland much wider business opportunities. We obtain certain glimpses of such "higher" activities from a number of other papyri which have come to light in recent decades.

In short, by acclimatizing themselves to their surroundings many Jews, especially those living in Babylonia, acquired considerable wealth and extensive political as well as business contacts with the ruling classes in the empire. They now could undertake the ambitious program of resettling thousands of their coreligionists in Palestine and to secure from the friendly Persian regime charters guaranteeing full autonomy to the reestablished community. In his original proclamation, Cyrus himself provided that the Jews remaining behind should equip the returning exiles "with silver, and with gold, and with goods, and with beasts, beside the freewill-offering for the house of God which is in Jerusalem" (Ezra 1:4). As a result some 50,000 Jews, including approximately 7,000 slaves, left with Zerubbabel and another 5,000 later on under Ezra.

Not surprisingly, the returning Jews found the country in a chaotic state; they also encountered considerable hostility on the part of their new neighbors. To begin with, those families which, on the basis of their excellently kept genealogical records, started reclaiming the landed possessions of their ancestors evoked, as has often been the case elsewhere, the staunch resistance of the new owners. Before very long their "theocratic" leadership (a term later coined by Josephus to describe the new form of government in the Second Temple period) had to fight a protracted battle to stave off both the hostile actions of neighbors and excessive assimilation to them. For several centuries the Jewish autonomous area covered no more than some 1,200 square miles in and around Jerusalem. Cut off from the coastal region occupied by Phoenicians, they engaged in small-scale farming and petty trade and crafts. The socioeconomic difficulties encountered in the First Temple period now returned with increased severity because of the greater yoke of taxation imposed by the Persian bureaucracy, made doubly burdensome by the numerous gifts, bribes, and other "voluntary" contributions extracted by the Persian officials.

Once again the economic shortcomings brought about a state of unrest which boded ill for the future of the country. The complaints of the masses to the new governor, Nehemiah, were eloquently restated by him in his memoirs. They claimed:

'We, our sons and our daughters, are many; let us get for them corn, that we may eat and live.' Some also there were that said: 'We are mortgaging our fields, and our vineyards, and our houses; let us get corn, because of the dearth.' There were also that said: 'We have borrowed money for the king's tribute upon our fields and our vineyards. Yet now our flesh is as the flesh of our brethren, our children as their children; and, lo, we bring into bondage our sons and our daughters to be servants, and some of our daughters are brought into bondage already; neither is it in our power to help it; for other men have our fields and our vineyards' (Nehemiah 5: 2–5).

We are told, to be sure, that Nehemiah succeeded in persuading the upper classes to renounce their claims, to restore the fields to their rightful owners, and thus to reestablish for a while the social equilibrium. But the activities of this disinterested high official, who emphasized that he "demanded not the bread of the governor, because the service was heavy upon the people" (5:18), undoubtedly could offer but temporary relief. The conditions in the city of Jerusalem were no more satisfactory. Nehemiah actually had to take measures to prevent the flight of Jerusalemites, particularly the Temple personnel, to the countryside. Yet, the prolonged era of peace within the borders of the Persian Empire made life more or less bearable in the long run, and the country could look forward to better times.

3

THE SECOND TEMPLE PERIOD

The boundaries of the autonomous Jewish state, as established under Ezra and Nehemiah, did not expand, but there was a possibility for some Jews to settle in other parts of the country on both sides of the Jordan. While fertile Galilee was still called the *gelil ha-goyim* ("the district of gentiles"), the Jewish minority there was becoming a substantial factor. Transjordan, too, had a growing number of Jewish settlers. Alexander the Great's conquest of western Asia and the replacement of the Persian domination by that of the Egyptian Ptolemies and Syrian Seleucids opened up vast new opportunities for both Palestinian and Diaspora Jews. The new pervasive Hellenistic civilization greatly encouraged exchanges between the various provinces, including those between the Jews of Palestine and their ever growing Diaspora. Legally, too, under Alexander, Ptolemy I, and Antiochus the Great, Jewish self-government, with its implied economic freedoms, received a favorable interpretation. If, in time, the new Hellenistic culture began attracting many Jewish individuals, fostered their assimilation to Greek ways of life, and thereby created deep internal cleavages within the Jewish people, the ultimate result was the Hasmonean revolt and the establishment of a new and enlarged sovereign Jewish state. In the century between 165 and 63 B.C.E. the Hasmoneans conquered all of Palestine and Transjordan, converted most of the subject population to Judaism, and established a strong and populous Jewish country with but a few enclaves of Samaritans and Hellenistic city states along the coast and in Transjordan.

Because the Temple of Jerusalem now served as a focal point for millions of dispersed Jews, the country benefited greatly from the influx of the half-shekels imposed annually upon all adult male Jews and from additional gifts voluntarily added by benefactors in various lands. A wealthy Egyptian Jew by the name of Nicanor, for example, provided the Temple with a brass gate named after him which allegedly required 20 men to open or close. In addition thousands upon thousands of pilgrims from all lands considered it a foremost religious duty to visit the Temple and offer their sacrifices there at least once in a lifetime. Even Egyptian Jewry which, for historic reasons, had built an independent Jewish "Temple of Onias" in the district of Leontopolis after the outbreak of the

Hasmonean revolt, continued to send to Palestine groups of pilgrims, including their spiritual leaders such as the Alexandrian philosopher Philo. Some pilgrims brought along with them substantial funds they had collected for Palestine in their home communities. Naturally, the coins collected by these cosmopolitan groups as well as those spent by them during their stay in the Holy Land greatly differed from one another in weight and value, at a time when many municipalities issued currencies of their own. To facilitate exchanges, the Palestinian authorities arranged for the opening of money-changing establishments in all parts of Palestine, including the Temple Mount, several weeks before Passover at the height of the pilgrim season. When Jesus "overthrew the tables of the money-changers" in the Temple precincts (Matthew 21:12), he merely removed a facility which the visitors from many lands greatly appreciated.

Not surprisingly some large collections aroused the cupidity of Roman officials. One of them, Lucius Valerius Flaccus, governor of Apamea, confiscated a local collection of 100 pounds of gold on the excuse that gold was not to be transferred to what in 59 B.C.E. still was a foreign country (despite Pompey's conquest of Palestine four years before). But in fact he merely sought to line his own pocket with the seized amount. However, he was promptly accused before the Roman senate of having committed a "sacrilege" on property belonging to a temple. He escaped severe punishment only after an effective defense by Cicero, whose eloquent plea, mixing Jew-baiting with purely legal arguments, still serves as a Latin text book in many schools today. Later Roman legislation, however, clarified the issue by placing all funds destined for the Jerusalem Temple, and later for the Palestinian patriarchs, under the protection of the laws governing sacrilege.

Domestically, too, the economy was surging upward. Agriculture still was the mainstay of the entire social structure. Benefiting from the accumulated energies of many generations, irrigation systems were installed in new areas, stimulating the annual output. True, in time the needs of a quickly expanding population forced the farmers to put many marginal lands under cultivation. Probably for this reason Rabbi Yose (second century) spoke of the seed yielding on the average a five-fold return in finished products (Ket. 112a), which contrasted with much higher yields in earlier periods. But some areas still produced the ten- or fifteenfold return characteristic of ancient Italy and even higher ones recorded both in the First Temple era and in the talmudic period (see the exaggerations cited, *ibid.*). Once again it was barley rather than wheat which was the mainstay of the bread diet. Dates, grapes, olives, and figs continued to furnish major ingredients for both domestic consumption and the export of surpluses. Remarkably, despite the growing population and the excessive costs of transportation, Palestine was able to export both cereals and fruits. Some of its choice fruits were served at the imperial tables in Rome, notwithstanding the competition of Italy, Spain, and Greece, all of which yielded similar products. A rarer plant was the papyrus grown in the Negev, the high price of which, however, maintained by the Egyptian state monopoly, made it noncompetitive as writing material with the far less expensive parchment, and still less costly ostracon. For its part Palestine had a sort of monopoly on the balsam tree, the production of which was largely limited to the "fat lands of Jericho." Balsam was often sold for its weight in gold. During the Roman-Jewish War of 66–70, Pliny informs us, the Jewish defenders cut down the balsam trees lest they fall into the hands of the enemy; and "there have been pitched battles in defense of a shrub" (*Historia naturalis*, 12, 54:113).

It is small wonder that plants were considered a vital social asset of the country and cutting them down wantonly was treated as a serious crime. The term for cutting down plants was extended metaphorically to cover infringement on the fundamentals of the Jewish law and religion. To be called a "cutter, son of a cutter" became a superlative insult. The vine, palm, and olive tree were often used as symbols of the Jewish people; they still adorn many extant Jewish graves in ancient cemeteries and catacombs. Compared with agriculture, cattle raising played a rather minor role. While sheep were still needed to provide wool and milk products, meat was a relatively minor article of consumption. According to a second-century rabbi, "a man who owns a 100 shekels shall buy a pound of vegetables for his stew; a 1,000 shekels, shall buy a pound of fish; 5,000 shekels, a pound of meat [it is later explained: for the Sabbath]. Only if he owns 10,000 shekels, he may put his pot on the stove every day" (Ḥul. 84a). A major consumer of cattle was the Temple with its sacrificial worship, particularly on Passover when thousands of families lined up to offer their paschal lambs. However, the total production could probably be provided by the outlying steppes in Transjordan and the south, where more intensive cultivation was impeded by the shortage of water. With this geographic differentiation also went a cultural disparity, since the cattle-raising areas were removed from the main centers of learning. As a result we may understand the transition from the high esteem of the shepherd in the First Temple period to the low status he held before and after the second fall of Jerusalem. Although conscious that in the Hebrew Bible God Himself was often compared to the "good shepherd," the rabbis now deprecated the shepherd not only as an illiterate person but also as a man untrustworthy to testify in court. Pigeon fanciers were likewise rejected as witnesses because they often engaged in aleatory games which were very popular throughout the Greco-Roman world.

In trade and industry the changes created by the new opportunities consisted in the main in the intensification of existing trends rather than in any change of direction or basic innovation. During most of the period the Jewish population remained cut off from the coastal area, the old Philistines and Phoenicians having been replaced by the Hellenistic city states. Josephus' observation, "Ours is not a maritime country; neither commerce nor the intercourse which it promotes with the outside world has any attraction for us" (*Against Apion*, I, 12.60) was generally true, in spite of the Maccabeans' determined drive to the sea, which was blocked by the Roman conquest; and the presence of substantial Jewish minorities in Jaffa and Caesarea, the harbor newly founded by Herod. Yet some Jews engaged in maritime commerce, owned ships, and even participated in Mediterranean piracy. During the Jewish War of 66–70, the pirates actually threatened to reduce the supplies to the Roman legions by blockading the port of Jaffa. But the majority of Jewish merchants consisted of shopkeepers, agents, and other petty traders.

Industry, too, was conducted on a very small scale. As before, Jews often organized guilds of their own. This movement was stimulated by the growth of Greco-Roman guilds which were often endowed with special privileges by the administration. As before, some crafts were concentrated in special villages or had assigned to them special quarters in the cities. In the battle for Jerusalem, the Romans stormed "that district of the new town, where lay the wool-shops, the braziers' smithies, and the clothes market" (Josephus, *Wars,* V, 8, 1.331). While the country was poor in metals, almost all of which had to be imported, it distinguished itself in the production of textiles, particularly linen. In the later price list of Emperor Diocletian the highest price was assigned to the linen produced at Beth-Shean (Scythopolis). The Dead Sea region supplied the country with a variety of minerals; it was renamed by the Romans the "Lacus Asphaltitis." Another series of industrial opportunities was created by the Temple. Because of its holiness and partial inaccessibility to laymen some tasks had to be performed by priests, so that we hear of 1,000 priests serving as skilled craftsmen at one time.

In general, the economic situation in the country might have been tolerable, were it not for the excessive fiscal exploitation by both Herodians and Romans and their corrupt bureaucracies. Ancient governments usually placed the main tax burdens on the farmers. As a major concession Caesar reduced the state's share in the farm produce from one-third to one-quarter. However, in actual practice the publicans, who farmed the taxes against lump sums, as a rule exacted more than their due. In Jewish Palestine, moreover, according to biblical law, the farmer was also expected to set aside a first tithe to the levite, a heave-offering averaging 2% to the priests, and an additional second tithe to be consumed in two out of three years in Jerusalem, and to be distributed among the poor every third year. Through the observance of the year of fallowness the farmer not only lost the crop of the seventh year but often had no incentive to cultivate the soil in the preceding year. There also was much chicanery in the collection of tithes. The total number of priests and levites seems not to have exceeded 3% of the population – it may not have exceeded 1% of the world Jewish population – and hence the 12% of the produce should have provided sufficient income for all of them. Yet the powerful priestly families used their political power to the disadvantage of their fellow priests. We are told by Josephus that the servants of High Priest Ananias (47–59 C.E.) "went to the threshing floors and took away tithes that belonged to the priests by violence and did not refrain from beating such as would not give these tithes to them . . . so that priests that of old were wont to be supported with those tithes died for want of food" (*Antiquities* 20, 8, 8:180–1; 9, 2:206–7).

As a result many farmers, crushed by these combined burdens and unable to resist the state-supported publicans, often disregarded the law of tithing altogether. In consequence, they appeared suspect to the orthodox leadership. Because of the prohibition on consuming untithed food there was practically no conviviality between observant Pharisees (or Sadducees) and the *am ha-arez* ("people of the land"), creating an almost unbridgeable class division (see Ber. 47b, and the exaggerations in Pes. 49b). Economically, too, the farmers were often unable to meet their obligations and lost their properties to better situated neighbors. Although Palestine never developed *latifundia* comparable with those existing in contemporary Italy, the number and size of "large estates" grew from generation to generation. The concomitant evils of absentee landlordism became even more manifest now, since after the Hasmonean expansion the capital, Jerusalem, was located at a considerable distance from those estates.

The great difficulties confronting the small farmer and his ensuing migration to the cities resulted in a rapid increase of the urban proletariat. Although many small towns continued to engage in a mixed economy in which agriculture still played a predominant role, the larger cities, especially Jerusalem, developed into centers of trade, industry, and governmental bureaucracy. Into such cities streamed thousands of landless peasants seeking employment as unskilled laborers at subsubsistence wages. Understandably, the role of slavery constantly diminished. Not being a conquering country Palestine had few prisoners of war, while purchasing slaves at the prevailing high prices was even less remunerative now that a vast army of underpaid free laborers was readily available. Hebrew slavery, in particular, hedged around by a variety of legal restrictions, to all intents and purposes disappeared completely. The rabbis phrased it metaphorically: "The Hebrew slave existed only when the Jubilee Year was in force" (Kid. 20a, 69a). Gentile slavery, too, played a small role in the agricultural and industrial production and was largely limited to domestic service.

Once again economic disarray combined with other socioreligious and political conflicts to bring about a social turmoil in the country which prepared the ground for its ultimate downfall. The great Roman-Jewish War of 66–70 C.E. was an almost unavoidable consequence. With it came the destruction of the Temple and the end of its hierarchy as well as of whatever residua of national independence had still remained after 6 C.E. when Judea was incorporated into the Roman Empire as a mere subdivision of the Syrian province. Thenceforth the center of gravity of the whole people shifted more and more to the Diaspora lands.

4

THE TALMUDIC ERA

Before the fall of Jerusalem the majority of the Jewish people had long lived outside Palestine. Yet the course of Jewish history was largely determined by the Palestinian leadership and society. Only Egypt acted in a more independent way and Alexandria, its great emporium of trade and culture, served as Jerusalem's counterpart, as it was designated by the Palestinian leaders in their letter to Rabbi Judah ben Tabbai (TJ, Ḥag. 2:2). Even Babylonia, upon which soon descended the mantle of leadership of the whole people, was rather inarticulate about its Jewish life until the third century C.E., when it came under the neo-Persian domination. Outside these two centers we have some information about the Jews of Rome, owing to the preservation of numerous catacomb inscriptions, as well as occasional references, mostly in an anti-Jewish vein, in contemporary Latin letters. As to the multitude of Jews inhabiting Syria, Asia Minor, the Balkans, and North Africa west of Egypt, we are limited to stray flashes of light thrown by a few surviving inscriptions, the Pauline Epistles, and other sporadic sources. Before long, the distinction between Palestine Jewry and those of other countries became increasingly blurred as the former gradually lost their position as a majority of the Palestinian population.

Minority status understandably affected also the Jewish economic structure. Many Mediterranean communities may have owed their origin to Jewish prisoners of war taken by the Romans and sold into slavery. This was particularly true of the capital itself. To be sure, the Jews did not long remain in bondage. Because many Jewish slaves insisted upon observing the Sabbath rest commandment and abstained from consuming ritually forbidden food, they must have been uncomfortable workers and domestic servants. On the other hand, Jewish families and communities bent every effort to redeem captives, a commandment placed high in the hierarchy of values by the ancient rabbis. Roman law facilitated manumission inasmuch as freedmen retained certain connections with their patrons — whose family names they usually assumed — and performed important economic services for them. According to law, moreover, freedmen enjoyed a limited Roman citizenship, while their descendants were treated as full-fledged citizens with rights far superior to those of other citizens in the complex political structure of the empire before 312 C.E. Economically, however, such privileged citizens at first joined only the vast group of landless proletarians. Especially in Rome many of them joined the estimated 200,000 welfare clients (about a fourth of the population). In fact, Augustus singled out the Jewish welfare recipients for special favors. Taking into account their religious scruples, he allowed them to demand a double portion of the grain due them on Friday so that they would not have to violate the Sabbath. He also gave them the option of refusing oil, the other major article of consumption given away free, and to ask for money instead. In this way the Roman emperor decided a question still controversial among Palestinian rabbis as to whether "the oil of gentiles" was prohibited for Jewish consumption.

Nevertheless some former slaves and many free immigrants found ultimate employment in agriculture. Most of them had been engaged in farming at home and, wherever given the opportunity, they tilled the soil either as small farmers or as hired hands. In the major countries of their settlement, particularly Egypt and Babylonia, many of them cultivated vineyards, which they and the Greeks seem to have introduced into Egypt, and olive groves, in the planting of which their ancestors appear to have pioneered in Babylonia. They also helped produce dates and other fruits, as well as grain. Dates were particularly plentiful and inexpensive. We are told about the Palestinian rabbi Ulla that, upon arriving in Babylonia, he exclaimed: "A whole basket of dates for a *zuz* [28 cents] and yet the Babylonians do not study the Torah!" But after overindulging in dates, which caused him a stomach upset, he varied his epigram by saying: "A whole basket of poison for a *zuz*, and yet the Babylonians study the Torah!" (Pes. 88a). To facilitate their coreligionists' agricultural pursuits in competition with non-Jewish farmers, the Babylonian sages quite early suspended the obligation of Diaspora Jews to observe the years of fallowness and even the payment of levitical tithes. They included these requirements among "commandments dependent on the land" of Israel, that is as being binding only for Palestine. Later on, under the pressure of Roman taxation and particularly after the reform of Diocletian — who instituted the collection in kind of the land tax from territorial groups (so-called *iugera*) regardless of the ethnic or religious differences among the owners of particular parcels of land — R. Yannai ordered even the Palestinian farmers, "Go out and sow during the sabbatical year because of the tax" (Sanh. 26a).

Connected with agriculture were certain industrial activities such as the brewing of beer. Unlike Palestine, whose population preferred table wines, Babylonia had from ancient times consumed much beer, one variety being brewed from a mixture of barley and dates. No less than three distinguished Babylonian rabbis, Huna, Ḥisda, and Papa, are recorded as having amassed considerable wealth from brewing. Jews were also active in many other crafts, and at times organized specific Jewish guilds. To be sure, the crafts of tanners, collectors of dog dung, and copper miners were considered so malodorous that the law permitted wives to sue for divorce on this ground; yet everybody knew that they were socially necessary and all that the patriarch Judah ha-Nasi could say was that "the world cannot get along without either a perfumer or a tanner. Happy is he whose occupation is perfuming. Woe unto him who must earn a living as a tanner" (Kid. 4:14; 82a-b). Nor were complaints of unethical practices by craftsmen rarely heard. An example of such prejudices was the popular adage that "the best of surgeons belongs to Hell, and the most conscientious of butchers is a partner of Amalek." Rabbi Judah bar Ilai, who reported this saying, also drew a line of demarcation between different types of transport workers. He contended that "most of the donkey drivers are evildoers, most of the camel drivers are honest, most of the sailors are pious." The latter's reputation may have been owing to the fact that shipping had now become an even more important occupation than in earlier centuries. The Alexandrian Jewish guild of *navicularii* had become so important that even the hostile Roman administration had to extend it important privileges in 390 C.E. (*Codex Theodosianus*, 13, 5, 8).

Perhaps the most significant economic change, resulting from the transfer of the center of gravity to the dispersion, occurred in the much larger Jewish participation in commerce. It is a well-known sociological phenomenon that alien immigrants often turn to mercantile endeavors because they have no attachment to the foreign soil, shun isolated living among native majorities, are familiar with two or more languages and cultures, and hence are able the better to mediate between distant localities. If, as seems to have been the case, a large number of former Phoenicians and Carthaginians had joined the Jewish community via conversion, they must have brought some of their commercial skills and contacts into their new communities. Jewish slaves, if employed in their masters' businesses, must also have acquired certain aptitudes which they put to good use upon obtaining freedom. For all these reasons the number of Jewish traders, ranging from peddlers to big merchants, must have greatly increased. Yet their ratio in the Diaspora's Jewish population need not have greatly exceeded the general mercantile ratios among the majority peoples.

Even banking began to assume a certain role in Jewish economic life. True, would-be Jewish moneylenders faced the tremendous obstacles of the traditional Jewish anti-usury laws. In fact, some rabbis tried, on segregationist grounds, to forbid their coreligionists to lend money with or without interest even to gentiles, unless they found absolutely no other means of earning a living (BM 70b). However, there were always certain legal subterfuges which made loans profitable, such as high conventional fines for missing the repayment date, intervening utilization of mortgaged properties, and the like (see, e.g., *The Tebtunis Papyri*, ed. by B.P. Grenfell *et al.*, 3, 315 ff., nos. 817–8; E.N. Adler, intro. to his ed. of *The Adler Papyri*, 5f.). In Alexandria Jewish banking may have played a certain role even in nurturing the anti-Jewish animus of the population. This is, at least, the interpretation given by some scholars to an Alexandrian merchant's warning to a friend "to beware of the Jews" recorded in a single papyrus dated in 41 C.E. (*Aegyptische Urkunden aus . . . Berlin, Griechische Urkunden*, 2, no. 1079). But this explanation has been cogently disputed. There is no question, however, that Philo's relatives, Alexander and Demetrius, holding the high position of *alabarchs* (the meaning of this term is still controversial) could enter banking on a large scale. For example, Alexander extended to Agrippa I the substantial loan of 200,000 *sestertii* (about $30,000), the bulk of which he paid out to the Jewish king from his Italian branch office in Puteoli-Dikaearchia (Josephus, *Antiquities*, 18, 6, 3:160). But these were exceptions confirming the rule that the majority of Jews were still very poor and eking out a living by hard work in various occupations.

On the other hand, in the talmudic age Jewish slavery played even less of a role than before. Jewish masters, rigidly circumscribed by law, did not enjoy employing coreligionists as slaves. A popular adage had it that "he who buys a Hebrew slave acquires a master unto himself" (Kid. 20a). Certainly, as aids in production, even gentile slaves could not compete with the readily available free laborers. Only toward the end of antiquity there developed the Roman *colonate* with half-free sharecroppers tilling the soil for the landlords. Characteristically, the new Christian empire after Constantine I, which totally outlawed Jewish ownership of Christian slaves and encouraged pagan slaves to obtain freedom by conversion to Christianity, nevertheless was prepared to tolerate the employment of Christian *coloni* by Jewish farmers (Gregory I, *Epistolae*, 4:21, 9:38). Even Jewish slave trading, which was to play a certain role in the early Middle Ages still, was quite insignificant.

In all these activities Jews depended even more than before on the general economic transformations which took place during the first centuries of the Christian era. The Roman Empire's semicapitalistic economy of the first two centuries increasingly gave way to a semifeudal system. The Sassanian Empire never reached the stage of relative economic freedoms of the early Roman Empire. Jews, as well as their intellectual leaders, had to make constant adjustments to both economic systems through the adaptation of traditional laws by way of interpretation. We shall see that, as a result of the pliability, rabbinic legislation proved quite useful to the Jewish communities in their medieval pioneering. One result of the growing state controls in both empires was a certain regimentation in occupations and price structures, which induced the

Jews, too, to organize their own zoning tariffs, in transportation, supervision of weights and measures, and even setting maximum prices. Even the unfriendly Theodosius I decreed in 396 that "no one outside the Jewish faith should fix prices for Jews" – a principle upheld by his successors (*Codex Theodosianus*, 16, 8, 10). On the other hand, because of the ensuing commercial restrictions, customs barriers, and innumerable official fees, the exchanges between the provinces of the Roman Empire were now severely hampered. This reduction in imperial and international commerce greatly stimulated the local and regional autarchy and helped to create in many parts of the empire highly diversified occupational structures, providing for most of the needs of the local populations. These developments account also for the greater diversity of occupations among Jews from the third century on.

Economically perhaps even more important was the sharp decline in the class struggle within the Jewish community. Confronted with indiscriminate hostility on the part of many neighbors, Jews, whether rich or poor, employers or employees, had to close ranks. Since the hostile state legislation often interfered with their ability to earn a livelihood, many Jews now depended on the ramified Jewish welfare system. The economic effects of anti-Jewish riots also were quite significant. Although far from resembling medieval massacres, the occasional anti-Jewish outbreaks in the Middle Eastern cities seriously interfered with Jewish business activities. The first major anti-Jewish riot, staged by the Alexandrian mob with the support of the Roman governor Avilius Flaccus, is well described by the philosopher Philo, an eye-witness. In this indictment of Flaccus, Philo wrote:

"But cessation of business was a worse evil than plundering. The provision merchants had lost their stores, and no one was allowed, either farmer or shipper or trader or artisan, to engage in his normal occupation. Thus poverty was brought about from both quarters, both from plunder, for in one day they were dispossessed and stripped of their property, and from inability to earn a living from their normal occupations" (*In Flaccum*, 7: 57).

Even in less stormy periods the Jewish masses required the intercession of their leaders to counteract inimical measures by unfriendly officials. Under these harsh conditions the old ritualistic animosities between the learned and the illiterate *am ha-arez* paled into insignificance. In any case, the main obstacle to rapprochement between the two classes was eliminated when the levitical tithes were discontinued in the Diaspora. Differences in the study of Torah were likewise toned down by the leading Palestinian rabbi Johanan's declaration (in the name of Rabbi Simeon b. Yohai) that the biblical commandment, "This book of the law shall not depart out of thy mouth" (Josh. 1:8), could be fulfilled by the mere recitation of the *Shema* in the morning and evening. If, because of fear that the disclosure of this statement might discourage study, the rabbis forbade its being given wide currency, the fourth-century Babylonian Raba insisted that it be divulged to the public (Men. 99b; see also the anecdote about Judah ha-Nasi's reconsideration in BB 8a). In short, even illiterate Jews could now fulfill their religious duties to the satisfaction of their more learned brethren.

5

THE MUSLIM MIDDLE AGES

After the rise of Islam and its speedy expansion from southern France to India, Jewish economic life took a drastic turn. Together with the simultaneous developments in Christian Europe, Islam's perennial antagonist, the new political and socioeconomic evolution for the first time converted a predominantly agricultural Jewish population into a people of merchants, moneylenders, and artisans. This lopsided economic stratification carried over into the modern period and was only slightly rectified in the emancipation era.

A major cause of this epochal change was the new treatment of Jews by the host nations as primarily an indispensable source of fiscal revenue for the respective governments and bureaucracies. In the declining Roman Empire and, still more, in Sassanian Persia Jews were often considered important objects of fiscal exploitation. But this was largely done by administrative chicanery within the generally oppressive taxation systems in the two empires. Jews and pagans in the Christian Roman Empire and Byzantium, Jews and Christians in Zoroastrian Iran may have been mere defenseless victims of arbitrary acts by rapacious officials. They may have, for special historic reasons, been forced after the fall of Jerusalem to pay for a time a special tax, the so-called *fiscus judaicus* (in lieu of the old Jewish Temple tax). But they were not singled out, as a matter of principle, as a separate class of taxpayers on whose shoulders was supposed to rest the main burden of financially maintaining the existing governmental structures.

It was left to the founder of Islam to enunciate the broad general commandment: "Fight those who do not practice the religion of truth from among those to whom the Book has been brought, until they pay the tribute by their hands, and they be reduced low" (*Qur'an* 9:29). Later Muslim jurists and statesmen, constantly invoking this injunction of their messenger, interpreted it to mean that Jews, Christians, and for a time also Zoroastrians, as "people of the book," that is as adherents of scriptural religions, be tolerated in Muslim countries, provided they pay "tribute," that is taxes of all kinds, and are kept in a low social status without exercising any control over faithful Muslims. The latter provision (similar to Christian Rome's denial to Jews of the *honos militiae et administrationis*) was supposed to entrust all responsibility for the defense of the country and its administration to the Muslims, while delegating the entire fiscal burden and the task of keeping the economy alive to the infidel or "protected" peoples. Though Muhammad himself left the details open, some extremists, such as Ash-Shafi'i, founder of one of the four influential schools of Muslim juris-prudence, contended that a Muslim state could exact tribute to the extent of two-thirds of all his possessions from a Jewish or Christian subject.

The prevailing practice was to collect from these religious minorities a land tax of 25% of the crops and a capitation tax from adult and able-bodied males. According to Abu Yusuf, Caliph Harun al-Rashid's chief fiscal expert, the Christians and Jews were divided into three income classes and paid 1 dinar, 2 dinars, and 4 dinars, respectively (*Kitab al-Kharaj*, 69 ff. (Arabic), 187 ff. (French); a dinar was valued at about $4 each by its weight in gold, but had many times that value in purchasing power). Despite the great inflationary changes in the following three centuries, Obadiah (Johannes), the Norman proselyte, recorded an increase by only half a dinar for each of these classes. He added that if a delinquent Jewish taxpayer died his body could not be buried unless his family or the Jewish community paid up all tax arrears (*Fragment*, ed. by A. Scheiber in KS, 30, 98). These basic imposts were augmented by a variety of local and individual taxes, enforced "gifts" and loans, and other services which made the life of the Jewish masses very difficult. But at least in periods of rapid economic progress, as in the ninth century, some Jews of the upper classes were able to amass sizeable fortunes.

Methods of tax collection aggravated the generally arbitrary and unpredict-able forms of fiscal exploitation. They were also designed to demonstrate the taxpayers' inferiority. A description preserved in an old papyrus gives us an inkling of the deliberately humiliating ceremony accompanying the delivery by a representative Jew or Christian of a sum collected from his community. "Then the emir," we are told, "gives him a blow on the neck, and a guard, standing upright before the emir, drives him roughly away . . . The public is admitted to enjoy this show" (J. Karabaček, in *Mitteilungen aus der Sammlung der Papyrus Erzherzog Rainer*, 2–3, 178). Occasionally, following an old Babylonian custom, the tax receipt was stamped on the taxpayer's neck in a more or less indelible form. Needless to say, the Jews resented such excesses. However, they realized that their special taxation was the main justification for their being allowed to live in Muslim countries altogether. A Jewish family chronicle informs us that the prominent Baghdad Jewish banker, Netira, on being told by Caliph Al-Mu'tadhid (c. 892), that the administration wished to eliminate all special Jewish taxes, allegedly dissuaded the ruler from such drastic action. He agreed that a reduction of the tax to its original size would be a blessing for his community, but he added, "Through the tax the Jew insures his existence. By eliminating it, you would give free rein to the populace to shed Jewish blood" (A. Harkavy in *Festschrift Berliner*, 36 (Arabic), 39 (Hebrew)). In the back of Netira's mind may also have loomed the danger that one of Al-Mu'tadhid's successors might not only reinstate the taxes but also demand from the Jews the instantaneous repayment of all arrears thus accrued.

One effect of this discriminatory fiscal pressure was the constant diminution of the Jewish share in agriculture. Even after the extension of the land tax to the growing Muslim majority, many farmers were unable to meet their obligations to the state. Jewish farmers had the additional burden of the heavy capitation tax paid in produce at a price arbitrarily set by the tax collector. The requirements of Jewish law, too, particularly the Sabbath rest commandment, which was much more stringent than the rest requirements of the Muslim Friday and Christian Sunday, generally made Jewish agricultural endeavor less competitive. We have evidence that in the days of Harun al-Rashid (766–809) the land flight of Palestinian farmers was so severe that the government was forced to appeal for their return under the promise of permanent tax abatement. The chances are that fewer Jews returned after having found shelter in one or another urban Jewish community. The growing disorders in the great caliphate from the tenth century on must also have induced many Jewish villagers, whose defenselessness invited attacks by marauders, to leave their landed properties – despite their attachment to their ancestral soil attested by some geonic sources – and settle in a somewhat more secure urban Jewish quarter. Beginning in the 12th century the increasingly powerful trends toward semifeudalism throughout the Middle East further militated against Jewish farming as they did, on a larger scale, in contemporary Christian Europe.

On the other hand, new opportunities beckoned to Jews in the commercial area. The general upsurge of the Middle East economy during the first centuries of Muslim rule, the rise of great metropolitan areas such as Baghdad and Cairo, and, for a time, uniformity and stability of currency and relative security in travel and transportation, all stimulated the expansion of mercantile activities on the part of merchants of various nationalities. Commerce was generally held in higher esteem than agriculture among Middle-Eastern Muslims, Christians, and Jews. The Arab thinker Al-Farabi voiced the prevailing notions that "villages are in the service of cities." While in the internal exchanges within the caliphate the Jews encountered severe competition on the part of several equally gifted mercantile groups, including Greeks, Armenians (increasingly muslimized), Syrians, and even Arabs – a popular Middle-Eastern adage was to state later that one Greek could cheat two Jews, and one Armenian could cheat two Greeks – Jewish merchants had certain advantages in domestic and, even more, in international trade.

In the first place their competitors often came from regions of diverse legal systems. Most of the Christian merchants followed deep-rooted customs and traditions of the former provinces of the Byzantine Empire. The Muslims, too, were divided in their mercantile and other civil laws through the disparate teachings of their four major schools of Muslim jurisprudence and the great variations of local and regional customs. These factors were far less pronounced in the case of Jews. Although the Babylonian and Palestinian laws often differed in many significant details, a growing majority of Jews, settled in the great caliphate and adjoining countries, increasingly came under the sway of the Babylonian Talmud and its official interpretation by the geonic academies of Babylonia. At the same time the presence of Jewish communities throughout the far-flung empire and in many neighboring countries, both east and west, assured Jewish merchant travelers a brotherly reception and help in emergencies wherever they went. They could also readily establish branch offices, and engage a number of dependable local agents. Examples like those recorded in the documents preserved in the Cairo *Genizah* have shown the vast geographic extension of the mercantile dealings of certain Cairo-Fostat firms. In 1115–17 one Abu Imram gave a power of attorney to an agent surnamed "the candle maker" to look after all his business undertakings in Sicily, Morocco, and other localities, as well as to manage his houses in Spain and Sicily. Another businessman, Ḥalfon ben Nethanel, after returning to Aden in 1134 from a prolonged stay in India, soon thereafter traveled to Cairo. In the following year we find him in Morocco and Spain before his return home (H. Hirschfeld, in *JQR*, 16, 280 f.; S. D. Goitein, *Speculum*, 29, 186 f.).

An even greater advantage accrued to Jewish merchants in the burgeoning international trade with Western Europe. Although the Carolingian Empire and its successor states were still economically quite backward, their growing landed aristocracy furnished many customers for the luxury articles imported from eastern lands. Here Jewish traders served as important mediators in a world divided between Islam and Christendom. Few western merchants traveled to the Middle East, despite occasional Christian pilgrimages to the Holy Land, while even fewer Arabs dared to enter the hostile Christian countries for any length of time. Jews were tolerated under both civilizations. The legal advantages arising from the uniformity of their law were even greater in this area, since Christian and Muslim laws diverged very greatly and familiarity with each other's legal systems was extremely rare. The Jews also had a linguistic advantage in being able to communicate with one another, whereas few Christians knew Arabic and still fewer Arabs could converse in Latin or any local dialect. But a few polyglot individuals could occasionally serve as interpreters. We hear of a ninth-century Jewish linguist named Sallam, apparently a native of Spain or Khazaria, who in

845 reached the "wall of Gog and Magog" in China and who allegedly was able to converse in 30 languages. Multilingual documents were also found in the Cairo *Genizah*. When Charlemagne decided to send an embassy to Harun al-Rashid he had to add a Jewish interpreter, named Isaac, to the mission. It turned out that the chief noble envoys died on the journey and Isaac alone returned from Baghdad, bearing gifts from the eastern potentate to the western emperor. In general, however, Hebrew could easily serve as the regular medium of communication among Jewish merchants under both Islam and Christendom, and by the ninth century it had become a leading international language.

In his oft-cited *Kitab al-Masalik* ("Book of Routes"), written in 846 and revised some 40 years later, Ibn Khurdadhbah, who held in the caliphate an office approximating that of a modern postmaster general, described the routes taken by the Jews known as Radhanites from northern France and southern Morocco to India and China. There is some reason to believe that western Jewish merchants quite early reached even Korea and Japan.

Ibn Khurdadhbah's statement helped support what soon became a Christian ecclesiastical myth adopted by some modern historians, about an extensive Jewish slave trade in the Middle Ages. From St. Agobard, archbishop of Lyons, onward, medieval and modern controversialists often pointed a finger at the medieval Jews as the main slave traders who transported Christian slaves, especially from Slavonic countries, to the ever more manpower-hungry Middle East and Muslim Spain. They readily overlooked the staggering legal barriers erected against that trade by both Jewish and gentile laws. Islam and Christendom severely outlawed the possession by Jews of Muslim or Christian slaves respectively. On its part, the Talmud had long demanded that a slave acquired by a Jewish master should be circumcised, made to observe the seven Noachide commandments, and live an essentially Jewish life. If a slave refused to be converted within 12 months, he was to be freed or sold to a gentile master. Female slavery, mainly intended to serve sexual purposes, was made difficult for Jewish slaveholders by the strict prohibition on sexual relations with slave girls. Typical of the provisions of Jewish law was the following statement by the ninth-century Babylonian teacher, Natronai Gaon: "If a son of Israel is caught with his slave . . . she is to be removed from him, sold, and the purchase price distributed among Israel's poor. We also flog him, shave his hair, and excommunicate him for 30 days" (*Sha'arei Zedek*, fol. 25a, attributed to Amram Gaon). The trade in eunuchs, so much in demand for oriental harems, depended on whether the Jewish slave trader could acquire castrated males. Otherwise talmudic law had long included castration among the physical mutilations which entitled the slave to seek immediate release. Responsibility for a slave's hidden blemishes, both mental and physical, was greatly delimited by talmudic law and hence anyone acquiring a slave ran considerable risks. If some Jews, defying these legal difficulties, were attracted to this extremely lucrative commercial branch, they must have constituted but a minority among the international slave traders and doubtless played an even smaller role in the various domestic slave markets throughout the world of Islam. It is not surprising, therefore, to find that in the vast, populous, and affluent North African lands, hardly any reference to Jewish slave traders appears in the extant Muslim and Jewish sources of the time.

Under the rule of medieval Islam Jews also entered the money trade in all its ramifications in an important way. Some of them played a considerable role in the very minting of coins. For example, one Sumeir helped set up the very important monetary reform under Caliph 'Abd al-Malik (695–696). That reform so impressed a Jewish homilist that he placed it among the signs of the approaching Messiah (PDR, xxix, ed. by Michael Higger in *Horeb*, 10, 193 f.; in G. Friedlander's English trans., p. 221). Other Jewish minters are recorded in various Muslim and Christian countries, though not in Byzantium where minting was an effective state monopoly. Some of the first coins issued by Poland in the 11th and 12th centuries bore inscriptions in the Hebrew alphabet, probably because the minter was most familiar with that script.

Money changing likewise became a very widespread and profitable trade, particularly after the dissolution of the caliphate when diverse coins from various lands began appearing in all large mercantile centers; it required considerable expertise to recognize defects, whether inflicted by coin clippers or by the admixture of undue amounts of alloy. Here, too, internationally experienced Jewish dealers were often in a favored position. Deposit banking also assumed a major economic role. Unlike the ancient temples and medieval churches, neither mosques nor synagogues ever served as important depositories of funds. Because of the relative absence of expulsions and large-scale massacres of Jews, Jewish bankers were considered a fairly secure outlet for surplus funds which, if profitably invested, could yield substantial profits to both depositors and depositaries. To be sure, in unstable periods an arbitrary official (for instance, Al-Baridi, governor af Al-Ahwaz) could seize the bankers' possessions, including deposits held by them for other accounts, without compensation. But the depositors running afoul a dignitary's personal greed or whim found keeping their funds at home no less risky. In general, however, the frequency and usefulness of the new methods were so great that the rabbis had to relax some ancient restrictions and alter the areas of responsibility on the part of the depositaries in order to facilitate their operations.

Similarly, the transfer of large amounts from one province to another in the vast empire and beyond its boundaries became the more imperative as carrying cash to a distant locality by land or sea became increasingly hazardous. Gangs of robbers on land were far exceeded in number and efficiency by both Mediterranean and Indian Ocean pirates. The North African coast, and the extended coastline of the Arabian Peninsula, served as particularly useful hideouts for corsairs. If the Talmud had objected to the method of transferring money through a deed called *dioqni* (derived from sign), and some medieval rabbis still opposed the bearer instrument called *suftaja* in Arabic (which Jews apparently helped develop jointly with the Arabs), the economic realities were such that the *geonim* had to yield and recognize its employment as a legitimate mercantile usage, "lest the commercial transactions of the people be nullified" (*Teshuvot ha-Geonim*, ed. by A. E. Harkavy, nos. 199, 423, 467). Ultimately, Samuel ben Hophni, head of the academy of Sura, felt impelled to write a special legal monograph on "Letters of Authorization" *(Sefer ha-Harsha'ot)*. Nor did the distinguished Kairouan scholar, Nissim ben Jacob, hesitate to use a *suftaja* in forwarding a gift for the support of the Babylonian academies.

Even more important, of course, was the large-scale Jewish participation in the increasingly vital credit system. Although all three major denominations tried to outlaw usury, the Muslim *ribah* being even more broadly defined than the Christian *usura* or the Jewish *ribbit*, the economic needs of credit became overwhelming. Since most loans were now extended not to impoverished farmers but rather to businessmen or government officials for use in trade or public administration, the outlawry of any kind of increment over the amounts lent lost its moral justification. Jews were in a strategic position to overcome the legal obstacles, as they were the relatively smallest group in the population and, even if observing the prohibition of charging interest to coreligionists, could engage in profitable moneylending with the large majority of borrowers of other denominations. All sorts of legal evasions, moreover, were conceived by jurists of all groups, although this system was never quite so refined as it was to become in medieval Europe. One of the simplest expedients appeared to be a fictitious sale of income-producing property with the right of repurchase which gave the lender the opportunity of collecting the revenue of that property during the interim The widespread *commenda* contract, in which the investor appeared as a partner in the enterprise, likewise offered him the opportunity of exacting the pledge that he would participate in the ultimate sale with a specified profit regardless of possible losses. It was this form of purported silent partnership with a guaranteed revenue which was most widely used to secure for the lender an income agreed upon in advance. Until today, some pious Jews still enter on a bond of indebtedness the words *al ẓad hetter iska* (often in abbreviated form) to indicate their mental reservation against the transgression of the biblical commandment.

In quiescent periods profits derived from banking could be enormous. As a result there emerged a number of wealthy Jewish bankers, especially in the metropolitan areas of Baghdad, Cairo, Alexandria, Kairouan, Fez, and Córdoba. These banking firms did not limit their activities to loans but usually engaged in related businesses such as trade in jewelry and precious metals, investment in real estate, and the like. They often had at their disposal large funds deposited with them by high government officials secreting away illicit income from briberies. Ibn al-Furat, a leading vizier of early tenth-century Baghdad, admitted having had large deposits with the two Jewish bankers Aaron ben Amram and Joseph ben Phineas. In return, to be sure, the bankers had to perform services for these officials which went much beyond ordinary business risks. For example, 'Ali ibn 'Isa, Ibn al-Furat's more virtuous rival, did not hesitate to force his Jewish banker to advance him monthly the equivalent of $40,000 in gold for the wages of the imperial infantry. This loan was to be covered by the banker's revenue from tax farming in the province of Al-Ahwaz. Another Jewish tax farmer, Ibn 'Allan al-Yehudi of Basra, who had lent both the sultan and the famous Persian statesman Nizam al-Mulk the equivalent of $100,000, was assassinated in 1079. Sometimes the whole Jewish community was held responsible for a banker's refusal to lend money to a dignitary. In one such case in 996 the mob attacked the entire Jewish quarter.

Less dramatic, but equally significant, was the expansion of Jewish activities in the traditional fields of handicrafts and professions. Needless to say, these occupations offered vast opportunities to many more Jews than did commerce and banking. Regrettably no exact occupational statistics can be offered, but a few extant lists show that the proportion of craftsmen considerably exceeded that of merchants, even including the petty shopkeepers and peddlers. Three such *Genizah* lists show percentages ranging from 38.4 to 52.1 for industrial occupations, compared with 17.3 to 37.5 for commerce and banking. According to Al-Jahiz Jews predominated in the industries of dyeing and tanning in Egypt, Syria, and Babylonia and formed the majority among the Persian and Baby-lonian barbers, cobblers, and butchers. Another contemporary Arab observer, Muqaddasi, contended that "for the most part the assayers of corn, dyers, bankers, and tanners are Jews; while it is usual for physicians and scribes to be Christian" (J. Finkel, ed., in *Journal of the American Oriental Society*, XLVII, 311–34; Muqaddasi, *K. Ahsam at-taqasim*, p. 183; in Le Strange's English trans. in his *Description of Syria*, p. 77). In fact no less than 265 different crafts are mentioned in the *Genizah* records, showing both the extensive Jewish partici-pation in industrial occupations and their great specialization. Gradually Jews also penetrated the medical profession, some of them achieving considerable fame as medical theorists and writers (Asaph, Israeli, Maimonides, and others). One must add, of course, a considerable number of Jews employed by their own

Jewish artisan weaving a belt on a bow-shaped loom, southern Morocco.

communities as rabbis, teachers, cantors, ritual slaughterers, sextons, and in administrative capacities, forming a sort of Jewish civil service.

This occupational diversification was greatly facilitated by the openness of Muslim society and the relatively large measure of economic equality for subjects of all faiths. The latter included much freedom of movement, except in Egypt, where the traditional state-capitalistic order presupposed governmental controls over the influx of foreigners and the exit of natives. Only Egypt enacted strict regulations concerning passports. In industry, too, there was much freedom of choice. Even where industrial guilds existed, they were neither so monopolistic nor so discriminatory in the admission of Jewish members as their counterparts in Europe. It was also possible for the autonomous Jewish communal organs to use considerable discretion in enforcing their own price controls whenever needed, supervising weights and measures, and generally policing the markets in the Jewish quarters.

It was unfortunate for the Jews and non-Jews alike that this flourishing commercial-industrial civilization sharply declined after the tenth century as a result of the caliphate's dissolution and its constant foreign and civil wars. By the time of the 13th-century Mongolian invasions much of the grandeur of that great civilization had given way to a slow process of decay. Coming on top of the

Christian Crusades, these invasions dealt further severe blows to both the international and local commerce of the eastern lands. While Christian Europe was marching ahead on the road toward a flourishing economic structure, the eastern lands began stagnating. Among the numerous departures were Jews, fleeing from foreign invaders as well as domestic enemies and seeking whatever uncertain shelter they could secure in the western lands. The center of world commerce now began shifting westward, with the various Italian merchant republics taking over the offensive, establishing colonies in the eastern Mediterranean and later in the Indian Ocean, and ultimately displacing the East even in the Levantine trade.

MEDIEVAL CHRISTENDOM

At first, to be sure, far fewer Jews lived under Christendom. Only from the 13th century on, as a result of the general upsurge of the western nations, the Spanish reconquest, and the simultaneous sharp decline of the eastern countries, did the center of gravity of the Jewish people slowly move to the European area. Here the far better accumulation and preservation of archival materials and the concerted efforts of generations of scholars have yielded much reliable and detailed information about general and Jewish economic developments. Jewish documents, too, such as the "starrs" of England, the records of the Laurenz parish in Cologne, the vast collection of Arabic and Hebrew documents in Toledo and other parts of Spain, the numerous notarial records, and even occasional private archives of Jewish firms, have made the study of economic Jewish history much more reliable and concrete.

Clearly, the existing trends toward the alienation of Jews from agriculture were much stronger in Europe than in the Muslim Middle East and North Africa. In certain areas the insecurity of Jewish life and the ever-present danger of massacres, expulsions, and forced conversions made landholdings far less attractive for Jews. Whenever a landowner had to depart suddenly or was otherwise obliged to dispose of his property within a very short time, forced liquidation, if not total confiscation, resulted in enormous losses. For example, two years after the expulsion of Jews from France in 1306 a Christian landlord was able to acquire 50 Jewish houses in the old and venerable community of Narbonne for the mere pittance of 3,957 livres. This transaction so aroused the ire of both the viscount and the archbishop, each of whom had special feudal rights in the city, that, to appease them, the purchaser gave an additional 5,000 livres, two houses, and a plot of land to the viscount and an unspecified, but undoubtedly large, amount to the archbishop (S. Luce in REJ, II, 50 ff. no. lxi). Of course, the Jewish exiles received nothing. Similarly, according to the court historian Andrés Bernáldez, after the promulgation of the Spanish decree of expulsion in March 1492, anyone could acquire a Jewish vineyard for a piece of cloth or linen (*Historia de los Reyes Católicos*, Seville (1870) I, 338 f.). In addition to such country-wide expulsions, there were local and regional forced exiles of varying frequency. For instance, the city of Speyer, to which Jews had originally been admitted in 1084 by Bishop Ruediger-Huozmann "in order to enhance the city's honor," subsequently often ousted them on short notice. To mention only the events of the 15th century, Jews were expelled from Speyer in 1405, to be readmitted in 1421; they were banished again in 1430, and allowed to return in 1434, to be once more evicted a year later. Yet we find them there again in 1465. They became objects of renewed episcopal legislation in 1468–72.

The first major blow of this kind came to the Jews of Byzantium as a result of Emperor Heraclius' decree of 632 forcing all Jews to become Christians. Although incompletely carried out even in the areas which remained Byzantine after the expansion of Islam soon after, such Byzantine decrees were repeated once in each of the following three centuries. It was truly amazing, therefore, that during his visit to the Balkans in the 1160s Benjamin of Tudela found an entire Jewish community of 200 families in the village of Crissa who "sow and reap on their own land" (*Travels*, pp. 12 (Heb.), 10 (Engl.)). Similar forced conversions occurred in Visigothic Spain, Merovingian Gaul, and Langobard Italy in 613–661, and were replaced in Spain by many sharply discriminatory laws against the Jews who survived or were allowed to return before the Muslim conquest of 711–712. To all intents and purposes these hostile actions put an end to all forms of organized Jewish life there, only a small Jewish remnant remaining under Catholic domination in central and southern Italy. Even if not all Jews left these countries, their ownership and cultivation of land must have practically ceased, while returning Jews may have had little incentive or opportunity to acquire new agricultural property. Similar effects were later produced by the successive expulsions of Jews from royal France, England, Spain, Portugal, various Italian states, and other parts of Christian Europe between 1182 or 1290 and 1600.

An equally important factor was the growth of European feudalism. Land now not only became the source of economic power but also the mainstay of political and military force. He who owned land exercised dominion over a multitude of peasants whether they tilled the soil as half-free sharecroppers so long as the Roman *colonate* persisted, or as villeins furnishing part of their produce and corvée labor to their masters. While since Gregory the Great the Church allowed Jews to maintain Christian *coloni* on their land, it became increasingly awkward for Jews to be either vassals taking oaths of fealty to Christian lords or seigneurs administering such oaths to Christian barons. Remarkably, this system persisted in Provence up to the 12th century and beyond. In Angevin England, too, kings protected Jewish feudal holdings through decrees such as that issued by Richard the Lion Heart in 1190 in favor of one Isaac, son of R. Joce, and his sons or, more broadly, through the generic decree by John Lackland in 1201. It was in the royal interest to protect the Jewish holding of a "baronial state, claiming for themselves wardships, escheats, and advowsons," as did Henry III. Even the antagonistic Edward I had to allow Jews to acquire feudal possessions if their noble owners defaulted on the payment of their debts. But the antagonisms aroused in such cases contributed to the baronial revolt against the crown in 1264–66. The barons argued that the kings selfishly promoted feudal acquisitions by Jews because through the royal overlordship over Jews noble property was thus indirectly transferred to the royal domain. Ultimately, beginning in 1269 the kings themselves had to oblige Jewish creditors to dispose of such foreclosed estates to Christian owners within a year. In short, feudalism and Jewish landholdings appeared incompatible in the long run and it was the weaker Jewish side which had to yield ground.

On the other hand, unlike under Islam, Jewish landowners were not subjected to a special land tax. "In our entire realm," declared Meir b. Baruch of Rothenburg, "[Jews] pay no tax on land. Sometimes capitalists have tried to change this system, but when the matter was brought before us, we disallowed it" (Responsa (Prague 1607) fol. 50c no. 452). In other areas, however, the general land taxes became so burdensome that the Barcelona rabbi Solomon ibn Adret complained that "frequently the very best fields yield insufficient harvests to pay the royal taxes" (Responsa, 3 (Leghorn, 1778), no. 148). More universal and irksome was the ecclesiastical drive to force the Jews to pay tithes on property they acquired from Christian owners, lest the parish priests or monasteries lose the income from such lands. Finally, the Fourth Lateran Council of 1215 insisted that these contributions be universally collected from Jews, riding roughshod over the religious scruples of some Jewish pietists who saw in such payments subsidies for the erection of churches and monasteries devoted to the worship of another faith.

Employment of Christian agricultural workers by Jews became another important issue, Jew-baiters of all kinds clamoring that Jews be forced to cultivate the land with their own hands. The nobles, on the other hand, even in Mediterranean countries, often tried to eliminate Jewish landholdings altogether. Such a proposal was advanced, for instance, by the Castilian Cortes in 1329. These opponents readily overlooked the early medieval Jewish pioneering contributions to European agriculture. Coming from the more advanced eastern countries, Jewish groups settling in the West are often still remembered in such names as Terra Hebraeaorum, Judendorf, Żydaczów, and the like. Even a Spanish name like Aliud is probably a derivative of *Al-Yahud*. As late as 1138 three Jews of Arles bought from Abbot Pontius of Montmajour the entire output of *kermes* of the district of Miramar, thus stimulating the farmers to produce that dyestuff. They were also very active in introducing the silkworm into Sicily and other Mediterranean countries.

Yet it was only the opposition of the crown which prevented general prohibitions of Jewish landownership. Wherever such were enacted, they usually bore a local character and even there were not always fully implemented. Even in fervently anti-Jewish Germany after the Black Death of 1348–49, the assertion of the author of the *Rechtsbuch nach Distinctionen* (iii.17, 1) that "Jews are not allowed to own real property in this country" was a clear exaggeration. In the Mediterranean lands, especially, Jews continued to own and cultivate landed properties; this they did to the very end of their sojourn in Spain, Portugal, Provence, Sicily, and Naples. Their endeavors were particularly flourishing in those areas where extensive orchards and vineyards, located in the neighborhood of towns, enabled them to combine fruit production with other occupations. Queen Maria of Aragon was not wrong when in 1436 she upheld the right of Huesca Jewry to dispose of the grain and wines produced on its property, "since the Jews of the said city for the most part live as workers and cultivators of fields and vineyards and derive a living from the latter's produce" (Y. F. Baer, *Die Juden im christlichen Spanien*, 1, part 1, 858 f. no. 535). The city council of Haro (Faro), close to the Navarrese border, complained that Jewish and Muslim landowners in the district had in 1453 signed a covenant not to sell any land to Christians. In the council's opinion this created a threat that before long the entire land of the area would fall into the hands of infidels (N. Hergueta in *Boletím de la Real Academía de Historia*, 26, 467 ff.). Less exaggeratedly, a modern scholar of the rank of F. de Bofarull y Sans claimed (in his *Los Judíos en el territoria de Barcelona*) that between the tenth and 12th centuries one-third of all the land around Barcelona was owned by Jews. In short, Jewish agriculture never completely disappeared from the European scene and the alleged complete outlawry of Jewish landholdings throughout medieval Europe is another example of a widely accepted historical myth.

Jewish landownership was particularly frequent in urban settlements, particularly in Jewish quarters. Understandably, wherever the Jewish population grew rapidly and its quarter could not enlarge its area the real estate owned by a family was often subdivided into small parcels by the large progeny. In the Laurenz parish of Cologne a Jewish couple sold in 1322 a one-eighth and one-96th portion of "a large house" in which two other coreligionists owned another quarter and one-16th part. Thirteen years later another Jewish couple acquired a share of one-third and one-60th minus one-700th of a house from a Christian neighbor. For the most part, however, in Europe north of the Alps and the Loire Jews were rarely allowed to live long enough to create many such subdivisions over several generations.

In Europe, too, Jewish industrial occupations were far more significant. In this area early Jewish immigrants from the Middle East and North Africa, often in possession of an advanced technology, could perform many pioneering services. In 1147 Roger II of Naples attacked Byzantine Thebes, a major center of the silk industry, and evacuated "all" Jews to southern Italy, where they helped establish a flourishing silk industry. Another trade in which Jews played a considerable role since ancient times was that of dyeing. When Benjamin of Tudela arrived in Brindisi he found there ten Jewish dyers. A particular "Jewish" dye existed in the Neapolitan kingdom. Weaving, too, had long been a prominent Jewish craft. It was partly stimulated by the biblical prohibition of *sha'atnez* (mixing wool and linen) which, carried down through the ages, became an important factor in preserving Jewish tailoring and other branches of the clothing industry in many lands. Another religiously stimulated industrial craft was that of slaughtering animals according to the Jewish ritual. Even where, as in most German areas, the Christian guilds tried to suppress Jewish competition, they had to make some exceptions in favor of Jewish butchers and tailors who were permitted to produce such ritually restricted goods for the Jewish customers. Many Jewish crafts were stimulated by Jewish pawnbroking. Since most pledges consisted of articles of clothing, furniture, or jewelry which, upon the debtor's default, became the property of the pawnbroker, it was natural for him to try to refurbish the pawns for sale to the public at a higher price. In fact, many restrictive ordinances inspired by Christian merchants made a special allowance for Jewish trade in used articles. For instance, in Counter-Reformation Rome Jews performed a major service by acquiring second-hand clothing from the luxury-loving high clergy and nobility for resale to the masses of the population. Indirectly, such business furnished employment also to tailors, dyers, and other craftsmen.

Beyond these specially Jewish areas we find Jewish craftsmen in almost all domains of industry, although specialization here was far less developed than in the contemporary Islamic world. In Cologne, for example, where the guilds succeeded in ultimately barring Jews from almost all industrial occupations, they still allowed them to become glaziers, probably because no other qualified personnel was available. This exception was reminiscent of the Greek glassblowers in seventh-century France who claimed to be able to produce glass as well as the Jews did. The few extant Spanish occupational statistics are very enlightening indeed. For example, the 20 Jewish families in the small town of Valdeolivas near Cuenca embraced, in 1388, 6 shoemakers, 3 tailors, 1 weaver, 1 smith, and 1 itinerant artisan. Some of the wealthiest of the 168 Jewish taxpayers in Talavera de la Reina shortly before the expulsion in 1492 consisted of 13 basket-makers and 3 goldsmiths. Jewish cobblers, tailors, blacksmiths, and harness makers also seem to have made a reasonable living there. True, in 1412–13 Castile and Aragon, in sharply anti-Jewish decrees, forbade Jews to serve as veterinarians, ironmongers, shoemakers, tailors, barbers, hosiers, butchers, furriers, rag pickers, or rag dealers for Christians. Yet the very man who inspired that legislation, Antipope Benedict XIII, himself employed a Jewish bookbinder, two Hebrew scribes, and even a Jewish seamstress-laundress for his ecclesiastical vestments. A Roman list of 1527 recorded the presence of 1,738 Jews in a population of 55,035 in the city. The more than 80 Jewish families whose occupations were recorded included 40-odd Jewish tailors and a substantial number of other craftsmen. Twelve years earlier Cardinal Giulio de' Medici had urged his cousin Lorenzo to attract some of the Jewish manufacturers of saltpeter from Rome to Florence or Pisa, since "such opportunities do not occur every day." Although similar detailed data are not readily available elsewhere, it appears that wherever Jews lived in larger numbers their majority derived a livelihood from one or another craft.

In some Spanish cities there were enough Jewish craftsmen to form independent guilds. The statutes of the Jewish cobblers' guild in Saragossa, approved by Pedro IV in 1336, offer mute testimony to the continuity of Jewish craftsmanship from the ancient associations of Jewish master artisans. When the Spanish decree of expulsion was extended to Sicily on June 18, 1492, the Christian leaders of Palermo and other cities protested that "in this realm almost all the artisans are Jews. If all of them will suddenly depart there will be a shortage of many commodities, for the Christians are accustomed to receive from them many mechanical objects, particularly iron works needed both for the shoeing of animals and for cultivating the soil; also the necessary supplies for ships, galleys, and other maritime vessels." In the north, of course, there was no opportunity for Jews to organize guilds of their own, whereas the Christian guilds in their constant drive for monopolistic control of their trades and political power in their municipalities not only sought to suppress Jewish competition but, if possible, to get rid of the Jews completely.

At the same time Jewish commercial activities played an ever increasing role in Western Europe. We have relatively few records of Jewish peddlers. Apart from the insecurity of roads in most European countries, aggravated by the hostility toward Jews on the part of many peasants and townsfolk — even hostile legislators often freed Jews from wearing their badges on journeys for this reason — the majority of the villeins had little cash available to purchase goods from itinerant merchants. Most of their needs were provided for by their own agricultural production and the home work of their wives and daughters in spinning, weaving, and tailoring. But Jewish shopkeepers increased in number with the growth of the urban centers, wherever Jews were tolerated at all. Of course, there was a constant struggle with the growing burghers' class which wanted to monopolize whatever trade was available locally or regionally. In many cities these commercial rivals sooner or later succeeded in ousting Jews completely and even in obtaining from the royal power, whose self-interest dictated protection of Jewish tradesmen, special privileges *de non tolerandis Judaeis.* In England, for instance, where Henry III's exorbitant fiscal exploitation depended on the presence of a prosperous Jewry, there was a wave of such enactments in favor of many cities in the 1230s and 1240s. In many continental localities the law restricted Jewish shopkeeping to the Jewish quarter and often forced the Jewish merchants to abstain from displaying their wares on Sundays and Christian holidays — a major burden indeed for observant Jewish shopkeepers who kept their stores closed on the Sabbath and Jewish festivals. Nevertheless economic necessity forced Jews to use all means at their disposal to earn a living from merchandising.

Jewish international trade, which in the Carolingian age had been a major incentive for Christian regimes to invite Jewish settlers, later suffered greatly from the competition of the Italian merchant republics, the prevalence of Mediterranean piracy, highway robbery on land routes, discriminatory tolls at the multitude of feudal boundaries, and special Jewish taxation. Nevertheless, many rulers still tried to maintain freedom of movement and trading for their Jewish "serfs." The major imperial privileges for German Jewry often repeated, with minor variations, the provision in Emperor Henry IV's 1090 privilege for the Jews of Speyer, that they "should have the freedom to trade their goods in just exchange with any persons, and that they may freely and peacefully travel within the confines of Our kingdom, exercise their commerce and trade, buy and sell, and no one shall exact from them any toll or impost, public or private" (J. Aronius, Regesten, 71 ff., no. 170, etc.). Similar sweeping provisions were enacted by John I of England in 1201 and other monarchs (J. M. Rigg, *Select Pleas,* 2). If in practice Jews often suffered from attacks and despoliation by local barons and arbitrary officials, this was the effect of the poorly organized governmental systems in most European countries rather than of the rulers' intent. In this respect Jews had plenty of fellow sufferers among their gentile competitors.

International fairs in particular offered many opportunities for Jewish traders profitably to exchange goods with other merchants, Jewish and non-Jewish. Even in the less hospitable northern lands they played a considerable role in the famous Champagne fairs and those of Cologne. When in the last three medieval centuries most of these fairs lost their international character and catered more to regional needs, Jews still appeared as welcome visitors even in areas from which they were generally excluded. They enjoyed the special protective devices developed by many communities seeking to attract foreign trade without discriminating among the visitors according to their faith or country of origin. One important concession generally granted at fairs was the suspension of the group responsibility of merchants of the same origin for each other's misdeeds or insolvency. Such mutual responsibility affected non-Jewish burghers as well as Jews, but the process of generalization in blaming all Jews for the misconduct of any coreligionist was generally much more prevalent. Even in Mediterranean commerce, where group responsibility was less strongly stressed, Pedro III of Aragon felt obliged to intervene in 1280 on behalf of many Jewish Levant traders, when one of their coreligionists, Isaac Cap of Barcelona, had been accused of unethical business dealings in the Middle East. The main argument advanced by the king in his epistle addressed to the Templars and Hospitalers in Jerusalem, the consuls of Pisa and Venice, and the representative of the king of Cyprus was not that other Jews should not be held responsible for Cap's actions, but that Cap had long since left Aragon. It so happened that in time Cap was able to return to Barcelona, settle his debts, and again become an honored member of his community.

Another major concession to Jewish traders was the acceptance by many regimes of the prevailing Jewish practice with respect to the so-called law of concealment. In the talmudic age the rabbis had already come to the conclusion that a merchant who had unwittingly acquired some stolen object was not to suffer complete loss in returning that object to its legitimate owner. They provided, "for the benefit of the market," that if the acquisition was proved to have been made in good faith, the owner had to compensate the merchant to the full amount of his investment. The more primitive Teuton laws, which dominated many European legislative systems, had made no such provisions in favor of the *bona fide* merchant. Jews, expecially in areas where they were largely restricted to dealing in second-hand merchandise or lending on used pledges, could not carefully investigate the title of each seller or borrower. At times fraudulent borrowers might actually scheme to offer, through impecunious intermediaries, pledges for loans and subsequently as owners reclaim these objects without paying their debts. There were antecedents for such protection of legitimate merchants in other laws. Yet Jewish traders were in the vanguard of those clamoring for redress. Ultimately, this provision, which German anti-Semites often denounced as a *Hehlerecht* (privilege for "fences"), became a widely accepted principle in most modern mercantile laws.

Despite these and other legal safeguards, the general insecurity of Jewish life affected the Jewish merchants as well. A remarkable illustration is offered by the business ledgers kept during the years 1300–18 by the important mercantile firm of Héliot (Elijah) of Vesoul in Franche-Comté. These extant ledgers reveal both the firm's effective method of bookkeeping and its far-flung business interests. Principally a banking establishment endowed with vast resources, it also bought and sold merchandise of all kinds either through *commenda* agreements with Christian or Jewish traders, or by direct shipment of its own. It dealt in cloth, linen, and wine produced in its own vineyards. Héliot also served as a tax collector for the government. Characteristically, the ledgers also include entries relating to horses and carriages used by members of the firm for business travel as far as Germany and Flanders. Héliot was also very precise in delivering the ecclesiastical tithes to the churches, notwithstanding scruples he may have had in thus contributing to the upkeep of non-Jewish religious institutions. His career was cut short, however, when in 1322 Philip the Tall extended his decree of expulsion of the Jews from France to Burgundy as well. Two years later Héliot's house was given away to a lady-in-waiting of the queen.

In spite of all these difficulties Jewish commerce, particularly in the more friendly Mediterranean lands, frequently flourished and became another mainstay of the Jewish economy. In the 12th century a German rabbi, Eliezer ben Nathan, could assert that "nowadays we are living on commerce only" (*Sefer Even ha-Ezer* (Prague, 1610), fol. 53d no. 295).

Commerce included money trade in its various ramifications, particularly moneylending. Because of their general insecurity and frequently enforced mobility Jews under Christendom were not good risks for deposits. Unlike under Islam, they could not compete with the stability of deposits in churches or such major banks as the Banco di San Giorgio in 12th-century Genoa. Their rabbis, therefore, fell back on the talmudic regulation that treasures should be buried in the soil, which was not always feasible in the crowded Jewish quarters. Burying them out of town subjected the owner to the risk of some stranger accidentally discovering the place of burial and appropriating the treasure trove. Moreover, even accumulations of savings by Jewish communal bodies were subject to seizure by unfriendly rulers. In 1336 King John of Bohemia not only confiscated the communal "treasure trove" kept in the old synagogue of Prague but also fined the Bohemian elders for concealing its presence from him. Minting could occasionally help support a Jewish individual, especially in backward areas. But generally the manufacture of coins was a governmental enterprise, even if exercised by some local baron or city council (there were, indeed, many kinds of coins and even scrip circulated by such local rulers). On the other hand, coin clipping, whether for the purpose of reminting or for that of using the gold or silver in the fabrication of some industrial objects, was considered a major crime if indulged in by private individuals, although it was accepted as a perfectly legitimate performance on the part of governments. One such accusation of coin clipping, real or alleged, supposedly resulted in 1278–79 in the execution of 293

English Jews and was partially responsible for the decree of expulsion of 1290 (H. G. Richardson, *English Jewry*, 218 ff.). Finally, notwithstanding the great variety of coins in circulation, money changing likewise seems to have been only a minor sideline of Jewish banking, if we are to judge from the paucity of references thereto in the extant sources.

Moneylending, however, increasingly became the lifeblood of the Jewish economy at large. It was abetted by the increasing Christian prohibition on usury which was broadly defined by Richard, son of Nigel, as "receiving, like the Jews, more than we have lent of the same substance by virtue of a contract" (*Dialogus de Scaccario*, trans. by C. Johnson, 99 f.). It was an uphill struggle for the Church because, down to the 12th century, the clergy themselves often indulged in moneylending on interest, a practice surreptitiously pursued by some priests even later. Jews also encountered stiff competition from Lombards and Cahorsins, often styled the papal usurers for their major services in transferring ecclesiastical dues to Rome. However, Jews had the advantage of being able openly to engage in this legally obnoxious business; as a matter of fact they did it as a rule with considerable governmental support.

In fact, kings considered Jewish gains via moneylending as an increase of their own resources. This was basically the meaning of such terms as that Jews "belong to the imperial chamber," a stereotype phrase in many imperial privileges in Germany, that they were the "king's treasure," as they were designated in Spanish decrees, and the like. When in 1253 Elias of Chippenham left England and took along his own bonds, Henry III prosecuted him because he had "thievishly carried off Our proper chattels." This nexus did not escape the attention of hostile observers who often blamed the princes for the excesses of their Jewish usurers. In his letter of 1208 to the count of Nevers the powerful Pope Innocent III complained that while certain princes "themselves are ashamed to exact usury, they receive Jews into their hamlets [*villis*] and towns and appoint them their agents for the collection of usury" (S. Grayzel, *The Church and the Jews in the XIIIth Century*, 126 f.). Although in a special pamphlet *De regimine judaeorum* Thomas Aquinas tried to appease the conscience of Princess Aleyde (or Margaret) of Brabant for deriving benefits from Jewish taxation largely originating from usurious income, one of his most distinguished commentators, Cardinal Tommaso Vio Cajetan, sweepingly declared that "the gain accruing to a prince from a usurer's revenue makes him an accessory to the crime." The better to control Jewish revenues, the English administration introduced in 1194 the system of public chests *(archae)* into which all bonds had to be deposited, supposedly to avoid controversies between lenders and debtors. Philip II in France tried in 1206 and 1218 to emulate the English example, as did Alfonso IV of Aragon in 1333, and in a somewhat different way Alfonso XI of Castile in

1348. But outside of England this system broke down, apparently because neither lenders nor debtors wished to comply. In any case, the Protestant clergy of Hesse was not wrong when, in its memorandum of 1538 to the landgrave, it compared the role of Jewish moneylending with that of a sponge, used by the rulers to suck up the wealth of the population via usury ultimately to be squeezed dry by the treasury.

Despite all opposition, Jewish moneylending was an imperative necessity in many areas. Because of the prevailing high rates of interest it also was a lucrative business. Emperor Frederick II's Sicilian constitution of Melfi of 1231 restricting the permissible interest rate to 10% remained a dead letter even in his own kingdom. Somewhat more effective were the maximum rates of 20% set by certain Aragonese kings and Italian republics. But for the most part the accepted rates ranged between $33\frac{1}{3}$% and $43\frac{1}{3}$%, although sometimes they went up to double and treble those percentages, or more. Upon their readmission to France in 1359–60, Jews were specifically allowed to charge up to 86%. Even some Silesian princes are recorded to have paid 54% to their Jewish moneylenders. In the case of the innumerable small loans by petty pawnbrokers these high rates were justified by the lenders' overhead in receiving weekly interest payments, slow amortization, and much bookkeeping. But the Lombards who, for the most part, dealt in larger credit transactions nevertheless likewise charged what the trade could bear.

So long as the economy was on the upswing the resentment against these high rates of interest was moderate. But when the European economy entered a period of deceleration in the late 13th century, further aggravated by recurrent famines and pestilences, such exorbitant charges, though economically doubly justified because of the increased risks, created widespread hostility. They were an important factor in the growing intolerance aimed at the English, French, and German Jews. Of course, expelling the Jews from the country, as England did in 1290 and France in 1306, merely meant replacing one set of moneylenders by another. Christian creditors, as a rule, charged even higher rates, partly to compensate for the increased opprobrium and sinfulness connected with their trade. As a result, Philip IV's successor, Louis X, in 1315 revoked the decree of expulsion and called the Jews back to the country as he claimed, in response to "the clamor of the people." Yet when the Jews returned under the royal pledge that they would be tolerated for at least 12 years, the popular outcry became so vehement that Philip the Tall broke his predecessor's promise and banished the Jews again in 1322.

At the same time in neighboring Italy, where the grandeur of the Florentine and Genoese bankers was on the decline, Jews began to be invited by various republics to settle in their midst and to provide credit "to the needy population." These *condottas*, resembling formal treaties between the governments and groups of Jewish bankers, extended to the latter a variety of privileges for specified periods of time, subject to renewals. The city of Reggio (Emilia) went so far as to guarantee to the incoming Jewish bankers that, if they ever were to sustain losses from a popular riot, the city would fully indemnify them. This significant chapter in Jewish economic history, however, began drawing to a close in the latter part of the 15th century on account of the emergence of the new, rivaling institution of *monti di pietà*. These charitable loan-banks were supposed to extend credit to the poor without any interest and thus make Jews wholly expendable. In itself this was a laudable idea and spread quickly into countries such as France from which Jews had long disappeared. At times the *monti* were supported by Jewish bankers themselves (for instance, by Isaac ben Jehiel of Pisa). But most of them assumed from the outset a strongly anti-Semitic character. They were propagated by outspoken Jew-baiters and rabble rousers, especially the Italian Franciscan friar Bernardino da Feltre Only in Venice, which refused admission to da Feltre, did the Serenissima reach a compromise with the Jews by persuading them to establish so-called *banchi del ghetto* which, financed entirely by Jews, were to serve an exclusively Christian clientele at nominal rates of interest. These institutions lasted until the Emancipation era when, upon the entry of the French army into Venice in 1797, the Jewish community voluntarily transferred the assets of its five banks to the new republic.

Connected in many ways with banking was Jewish public service. As under Islam, the Christian rulers could not scrupulously adhere to the demands of their religious leaders to keep "infidels" out of any public office lest they exercise dominion over the faithful. Governments often had to rely on the religious minorities to provide fiscal experts whose specific experiences as taxpayers as well as businessmen could be put to good use by the treasuries for tax collection and necessary cash advances. In his petition to Alfonso IV of Aragon (before 1335), requesting the king's assistance in the collection of loans from Hospitallers, the Navarrese Jewish banker, Ezmel ben Juceph de Ablitas, boasted that Alfonso "had never received so great a service from either a Christian or a Jew as you have received from me at a single stroke" (M. Kayserling, "Das Handelshaus Ezmal in Tudela," *Jahrbuch für Israeliten*, 5620, 40–44).

Most widespread was the Jewish contribution to tax farming. The medieval regimes, as a rule, aided by only small, inefficient, and unreliable bureaucracies, often preferred to delegate tax collection to private entrepreneurs who, for a specified lump sum they paid the treasury, were prepared to exact the payments due from the taxpayers. Of course, the risks of undercollection were, as a rule, more than made up by considerable surpluses obtained, if need be, by ruthless methods. So indispensable were the Spanish Jewish tax farmers that the Catholic Monarchs signed such four-year contracts with Jewish entrepreneurs as late as 1491, only a year before the expulsion. Among their most prominent collectors was Abraham Seneor, officially the "rabbi of the court" or chief rabbi of Castilian Jewry, and the courtier and scholar Don Isaac Abrabanel. In the early days of the Christian reconquest the services of able Jewish financiers and administrators were even more indispensable. Members of the Cavalleria and Ravaya families were particularly prominent in 13th-century Aragon. For one example, Judah ben Labi de la Cavalleria served from 1257 on as bailiff of Saragossa, from 1260 on as chief treasurer to whom all royal bailiffs had to submit regular accounts, and finally in 1275 also as governor of Valencia. Jews were also active in diplomatic service, for which their familiarity with various lands and languages made them especially qualified. In vain did Pope Honorius III address a circular letter to the kings of Aragon, Castile, Navarre, and Portugal, warning them against dispatching to Muslim courts Jewish envoys who were likely to reveal state secrets to the Muslim enemies, since "you cannot expect faithfulness from infidels." Yet his successor Gregory IX, generally even more insistent on the observance of all canonical provisions, conceded in 1231 and 1239 that the Portuguese and Hungarian monarchs had no workable alternative.

In other countries Jews exerted political influence more indirectly. Even in some antagonistic German principalities of the 14th and 15th centuries, some Jews were called upon to provide the necessary funds for raising mercenary forces as well as to supply them with food, clothing, and other necessities. Such a combination of large-scale financing and contracting was performed, for example, by a Jewish banker, Jacob Daniels, and his son Michael for the arch-bishop-elector Baldwin of Trier in 1336—45. This adumbration of the future role of Court Jews in helping build up the modern German principality was cut short, however, by the recurrent waves of intolerance which swept over Germany in the last medieval centuries and resulted in the expulsion of Jews from most German areas.

ECONOMIC DOCTRINES

Notwithstanding these constant changes in the Jewish economic structure and the vital role played by the Jewish economic contributions for the general society, no ancient or medieval Jewish scholar devoted himself to the detailed interpretation of these economic facts and trends. No Jew wrote economic tracts even of the rather primitive kind current in Hellenistic and early Muslim letters. All Jewish rationales must therefore be deduced indirectly from the legal teachings. Even Maimonides who, in his classification of sciences, recognized the existence of a branch of science styled domestic economy, or rather the "government of the household" (a literal translation of the Greek *oikonomía*), did not feel prompted to produce a special monograph on the general or Jewish economic life. Speaking more broadly of political science which included that branch of learning, he declared: "On all these matters philosophers have written books which have been translated into Arabic, and perhaps those that have not been translated are even more numerous. But nowadays we no longer require all this, namely the statutes and laws, since man's conduct is [determined] by the divine regulations" (*Treatise on Logic [Millot ha-higgayon]*, Arabic text, with Hebrew and English translations, by Israel Efros, 18 f.). In consonance with this conception, the great codifier devoted the last three sections of his *Mishneh Torah* to economic matters regulated by civil law; he also often referred to economic aspects in the other 11 books, following therein the example of both Bible and Talmud. None of these normative sources, however, which always emphasized what ought to be rather than what is or was, can satisfactorily fill the lacuna created by the absence of dispassionate, analytical, theoretical, and historical economic studies. From the outset we must, therefore, take account of the idealistic slant of our entire documentation. The emphasis upon ethics and psychology far outweighs that of realistic conceptualism. Only indirectly, through the use of the extant subsidiary factual source material, can we balance that normative slant by some realistic considerations.

Typical of such idealistic approaches is the biblical legislation. For example, the commandment of a year of fallowness may have resulted from the practical observation that land under constant cultivation was bound to deteriorate and to yield progressively less produce. Similar experiences led other agricultural systems to adopt the rotation of crops and other methods. But there is no hint to such a realistic objective in the biblical rationales. The old Book of the Covenant justifies the commandment by stating that in this way "the poor of the people may eat" (Exodus 23:11). The more religiously oriented Book of Leviticus, on the other hand, lays primary stress on the land keeping "a Sabbath unto the Lord" (25:2) so that it provide "solemn" rest for servants, foreign settlers, and even cattle. Similarly, the jubilee year was conceived as a measure of restoring the landed property to the original clan, envisaging a more or less static agricultural economy, at variance with the constantly changing realities of the then increasingly dominant urban group. No less idealistic were the provisions for the poor, particularly widows and orphans. We also recall the extremely liberal demand that, upon manumitting his Hebrew slave, the master should also provide him with some necessaries for a fresh start in life.

That these and other idealistic postulates did not represent the living practice in ancient Israel we learn from the reverberating prophetic denunciations of the oppression of the poor by the rich and other social disorders. But here again we deal with even more extravagant idealistic expectations than had been expressed by the lawgivers. In the main, the Bible reflects in part the "nomadic ideals" carried down from the patriarchal age and in part the outlook of the subsequently predominant agricultural population. But the landowning aristocracy, as well as the priesthood and royal bureaucracy often residing in Jerusalem and Samaria, and the impact of foreign relations, especially wars, shaped the actual affairs of the people to a much larger extent than normative provisions or prophetic denunciations, although the latter's long-range effects far transcended in historic importance the immediate realities.

Even the far more realistic legal compilations of Mishnah, Talmud, and other rabbinic letters are still in the main ethically and psychologically oriented. This remains true for most periods of Jewish history until the emancipation era. Certain economic factors are simply taken for granted. Not even Maimonides, who tried to find rationales for many biblical rituals, considered it necessary to offer any justification for such a fundamental economic fact as private versus public ownership. There only was common agreement that good fortune is bestowed upon man by God's inscrutable will, while poverty is to be borne with patience and submission to fate. Asceticism never became a major trend in Jewish socio-religious life, although certain groups and individuals practiced it as a matter of supererogation. Similarly, the postulates of communal ownership raised by the Rechabites in the days of Jeremiah and the Essenes toward the end of the Second Temple period were only part of their rejection of alleged departures from the purity of the old law. But they remained fringe movements.

At the same time the majority's "normative" Judaism subjected private ownership to severe limitations because of ethical requirements. From the restatement by Maimonides of talmudic law, as modified by the subsequent rabbinic literature, the following categories of property clearly emerge: "(1) Public property belonging to no one and accessible to everybody for free use, e.g., deserts; (2) public property belonging to a corporate group, but open to general use, e.g., highways; (3) potentially private property belonging to no one, but available for free appropriation, namely all relinquished and some lost objects; (4) private grounds belonging to the ownerless estate of a deceased proselyte, equally open to free appropriation; (5) private grounds not yet taken over by a Jew from a gentile, open to appropriation against compensation; (6) private grounds in a walled city, open to everybody's use but not to appropriation." To these must be added the "sacred property" *(hekdesh)* of the Temple of Jerusalem, which however did not apply to the later synagogues; objects placed outside ordinary use or sale by ritualistic law; as well as the theoretical claim of every Jew in the world to the possession of four ells of land in Palestine. Based on the assumption that forcible deprivation of land never eliminates the rights of the real owner, the latter legal fiction was of practical significance only in connection with certain technical restrictions on the formal transfer of property.

With all their emphasis on private ownership the rabbis recognized its limitations necessary for the common good. To begin with, they did not acknowledge the riparian rights of owners, but considered four ells along all shores as belonging to the community at large. They also accepted the right of expropriation for purposes of roadbuilding, the erection of city walls, and other necessary public works. A city also had a right to banish certain odiferous trades, such as that of tanning, outside its walls. Even individuals trying to sell land had to respect the neighbors' right of preemption at the price offered by strangers. In general, referring to an old tradition going back to the agricultural economics of Palestine and Babylonia, Jewish leaders placed land outside the range of ordinary commodities. During the very era of semicapitalistic prosperity under Islam, they still believed in the stability of landownership as against the fluctuations in the value of any other property. Going beyond the advice of talmudic sages that prudent men should invest one-third of their funds in land, one-third in commerce, and keep one-third in ready cash, Maimonides, perhaps inspired by the severe business losses sustained by his own family on account of his brother David's shipwreck on a voyage to India, counseled his readers not to sell a field and purchase a house, or to sell a house and acquire a movable object. They should rather generously "aim to acquire wealth by converting the transitory into the permanent." The rabbis also greatly stressed the responsibility of relatives for one another, not only in such dire emergencies as the redemption of captives but also generally taught that "a relative may prove to be extremely wicked, but he nevertheless ought to be treated with due compassion."

Other ethical and psychological criteria were employed in the rabbinic approximation of the doctrine of the just price, later extensively debated by the medieval Christian scholastics. No one questioned the community's right to supervise weights and measures. Any deficiency, if purely accidental, called for restitution, but if it was premeditated it was to be punished severely. Maimonides waxed rhetorical on this subject: "The punishment for [incorrect] measures is more drastic than the sanction on incest, because the latter is an offense against God, while the former affects a fellow man. He who denies the law concerning measures is like one who denies the Exodus from Egypt which was the beginning of this commandment" (Yad, Genevah 7, 1–3, 12; 8, 1, 20 with reference to BB 89b). The community also had the right as well as the duty to set maximum prices whenever conditions demanded it. Of course, under the general rabbinic doctrine of *dina de-malkhuta dina* ("the law of the kingdom is law") all market regulations by the state, including the maximum prices set by it, were to be respected by the Jews too, except when they specifically conflicted with the divinely revealed Torah. Conversely, in many areas (for instance in Majorca in 1344) the government specifically forbade the local market supervisors to interfere in any business dealings in the Jewish quarter. In any case, with their inveterate conservatism the rabbis were reluctant to accept the law of supply and demand as the determining factor in controlling prices.

A convenient psychological expedient was found in the theory of "misrepresentation." To prevent overcharges by sellers and, to a lesser extent, the taking of excessive advantage of an existing "buyers' market," the ancient sages had already established the principle that if the price paid for an object exceeded or was below its market value by one-sixth, the sale could be nullified by the injured party. This rabbinic doctrine of "misrepresentation," which seems to have inspired some related teachings of the Church Fathers and, through them, the Code of Justinian, could prove to be a serious obstacle under the freer economy of medieval Islam or modern Europe. An escape clause was opened by the rabbis, however, through their emphasis on psychology. They taught that if a seller openly declared to the purchaser that he had overcharged him by so and so much and the purchaser accepted the deal, there was no redress. Also by removing such important areas as land, slaves, and commercial deeds — the latter particularly important in transferring properties from one individual to another — from the operation of this principle, the economic realities could reassert themselves without formally altering the law. The same exception facilitated barter trade. A man could trade, for example, a needle for a coat of mail if, for some psychological reason, he preferred the needle. This was particularly true in the case of jewelry where emotional preferences might well have outweighed purely market considerations.

Among the transactions also not subject to the law of "misrepresentation" was free labor. Although the economic importance of hired workers was much greater than that of slaves, there was no comprehensive labor legislation in rabbinic law. Generally, the leaders preferred the employment of Jewish workers as a matter of ethnoreligious policy. Typical of the rabbinic attitude was Maimonides' contention that "he who increases the number of his slaves from day to day increases sin and iniquity in the world, whereas the man who employs poor Jews in his household increases merits and religious deeds" (Yad, Mattenot 'Aniyim 10, 17). This doctrine implied a general right to work for Jewish laborers, just as it conversely stressed everybody's duty to work in order to make a living. "Skin a carcass on the streets [the lowest type of labor], rather than be dependent on other people" was an old rabbinic watchword. Because of the primarily psychological interpretations, an employer could overtly arrange with a free laborer to do work which he could not impose upon a slave, since this was but a voluntary agreement on both sides. Similarly, the ancient protective regulation in the Bible that the payment of a daily worker's wages must not be delayed overnight could be modified by mutual agreement if a labor contract extended over a longer period. On his part, the employee was obliged to do an honest piece of work and not waste any time. Following ancient precedents, however, the rabbis allowed agricultural workers to partake of some of the grapes or grain on which they were working, though not of the fruit from orchards or vegetables from truck gardens. There also were many specific regulations concerning different categories of labor, such as shepherds. Each category had its own regulations, largely derived from age-old customs prevailing in particular localities.

The most difficult problem confronting the Jewish leaders was that of moneylending on interest. From biblical times there existed the outright prohibition, "Unto thy brother thou shalt not lend upon interest" (Deuteronomy 23:21). Once again the approach of the ancient and medieval interpreters to that passage was based on ethics and psychology rather than economics. We are told in the same verse that "unto a foreigner [or stranger] thou mayest lend upon interest," but it did not occur to any of these interpreters to look for an economic rationale for this distinction. Under the conditions of ancient Palestine, lending money to a fellow Israelite usually meant extending credit to a needy farmer or craftsman for whom the return of the original amount plus the prevailing high interest was an extreme hardship. At the same time the foreigner, that is, the Phoenician-Canaanite merchant, as a rule borrowed money in order to invest it in his business for profit. Such a productive form of credit fully justified the original lender to participate in some form or other in the profits derived by the borrower. Instead, the interpretation was always purely moralistic, namely a demand that lending to a fellow Jew had to be purely charitable, while extending credit to a non-Jew could be a businesslike proposition. Without going to the extreme of St. Ambrose who considered lending to a stranger a legitimate hostile act against an enemy *(ubi ius belli ibi ius usurae)*, nor sharing the equally extreme view of some Jewish jurists who considered the biblical phrase, "unto a foreigner," a commandment ("thou shalt," rather than "thou mayest," lend on interest to a stranger), most rabbis followed the talmudic rule that for segregationist reasons all but well-informed scholars should abstain from moneylending to gentiles altogether. Yet they admitted that many Jews could not make a living any other way. Remarkably, not even the medieval Jewish Aristotelian philosophers quoted, as did their Christian counterparts, Aristotle's doctrine of the essential sterility of money. Whatever the theoretical justification of this point of view was, it ran counter to the daily experience of most Jewish sages that money could, in fact, earn greater increments than did land or any other movable property.

In their extremist ethico-psychological bent of mind the rabbis even outlawed such external forms of "usury" as nonmonetary gains. They taught, for example, that, unless the borrower used to do it before securing the loan, he was not entitled to greet the lender first or even to teach him the Torah. Echoing talmudic teachings Maimonides insisted that "it is forbidden for a man to appear before, or even to pass by, his debtor at a time when he knows that the latter cannot pay. He may frighten him or shame him, even if he does not ask for repayment" (Yad, Malveh ve-Loveh 1, 1–3). Needless to say, only a few pietistic moneylenders could live up to these high expectations. On the other hand, economic realities, particularly in countries like medieval England, France, northern Italy, and Germany, where banking became the very economic foundation of many Jewish communities, forced the Jews to make some theoretical concessions. In his apologetic tract, *Milhemet Mitzvah* of 1245, Meir ben Simon of Narbonne argued that "divine law prohibited usury, not interest. . . . Not only the peasant must borrow money, but also the lords, and even the great king of France. . . . The king would have lost many fortified places, if his faithful agent, a Jew of our city, had not secured for him money at a high price" (cited from a Ms. by Adolph Neubauer in *Archives des missions scientifiques*, 3d ser., 16, 556 f.). Addressing his own coreligionists, a German rabbi, Shalom ben Isaac Sekel, insisted that "the reason why the Torah holds a higher place in Germany than in other countries is that the Jews here charge interest to gentiles and need not engage in a [time-consuming] occupation. On this score they have time to study the Torah. He who does not study uses his profits to support the students of the Torah" (cited by Israel Isserlein's disciple, Joseph ben Moses of Hoech-stadt, in his halakhic collection, *Leket Yosher*, ed. by J. Freimann (1903–04), I, 118 f.).

Like their Muslim and Christian colleagues, the rabbis had to legitimize many practices aimed at evading the prohibition of usury. The ingenuity of business-men and jurists invented a variety of legal instruments which, formally not reflecting borrowings, nevertheless secured sizable profits for the capitalist advancing cash to a fellow Jew. Called in Europe the *contractus trinus, contractus mohatrae*, the purchase of rents, and the like, these instruments were also employed by Jewish lenders with telling effect. It was also easy to circumvent the law by the purchase of bonds. Since deeds were generally exempted from the prohibition of usury and could be discounted below their nominal value, there was much room for a lender by using an intermediary to extend a profitable loan to a third party. Agents, too, were entitled to charge a commission for securing credit for any borrower. Most importantly, the various forms of the *commenda* contract, which enabled a lender to appear as a silent partner in the enterprise, opened the gate very widely for "legitimate" profits by the "investor." The permission of that type of *iska* became quite universal and served as the major instrument for credit transactions among Jews.

These examples of the rabbis' economic teachings, which can readily be multiplied, must suffice here. They give an inkling of the great power of halakhic exegesis which made it possible for scholars to read into the established texts of Bible and Talmud provisions, as well as limitations, to suit the changing needs of Jewish society. In this way the people's intellectual leaders were able to preserve a measure of continuity within a bewildering array of diverse customs and usages. At the same time ample room was left for individual opinions, which often sharply differed. Some interpretations were derived from the simple oper-ation of juristic techniques which had an autonomous vitality of their own. However, in many cases the communal leaders, rabbinic and lay, often per-sonally immersed in a variety of economic enterprises and thus acquiring much practical experience, consciously made interpretive alterations to reflect genuine social needs. Since the entire system of Jewish law operated through inductive reasoning on the basis of cases rather than the deduction from juristic principles, as advanced by Roman jurists and their medieval disciples, the sages of various countries and generations were able to maintain a certain unity of purpose and outlook among the different segments of the Jewish dispersion. They thus lent the Jewish economic rationales the same kind of unity within diversity that permeated the entire Jewish socioreligious outlook on life.

THE EARLY MODERN PERIOD

The variety of place, social condition, and economic development puts any review of the economic aspects of Jewish life since the end of the 15th century beyond the reach of a simple unified framework. For this variety to be seen in a meaningful way, for an analysis of the leading features of the subject, there must be some preliminary, if crude, divisions of the subject. Yet even a simple temporal division of the development of almost 500 years is not free from difficulty. The pace and pattern of Western economic development differed markedly from country to country and from region to region, and as a matter of course the economic situation and activities of the Jews in those countries and regions differed widely also. The striking event, the momentous date, that might symbolize a qualitative change in Western economic structure is not to be found. If some basis is to be found for separating the early modern economic history of the Jews from the later modern developments, it must be sought in other criteria: the basic structure of the economy, its leading characteristics, and the goals of the society.

If we accept these criteria, it is not difficult to divide the whole period into two phases. During the first, economic development and economic policy were clearly and rigidly subordinated to non-economic considerations of the society, and there was relatively little room for autonomous activity prompted by considerations of economic rationality as determined by the individuals concerned. In the second phase economic interests were articulated more openly and clearly, and the idea of freedom of economic activity was accepted as leading to results generally beneficial to the community as a whole. The transitional period between the two phases saw fundamental changes occurring throughout society: the legal and social framework had to be adjusted to the new demands, as symbolized by the substitution of voluntary contract for traditional, customary relationships or for relationships hitherto determined and regulated by the usage of special privileges and governmental orders; equality before the law was established as a principle that overrode the predominant institutionally ingrained system of legal and social inequality.

This transformation took place slowly and unevenly. Decades and even centuries apart in the various regions of Europe, the process nevertheless was continued and was accompanied by major differences in the legal status, pattern of employment, and other characteristics of the various Jewish communities at each point in time. Thus, the study of the economic aspects of Jewish life over the last 500 years is basically the study of the participation of the Jews in the process of economic change and of the impact of the changing conditions upon the economic and social structure of the Jews. Even within the first period, which for reasons of convenience and convention will be called the early modern one, a distinction must be made between the conditions of the Jews living in the economically advanced regions and those prevailing in the economically less developed regions of Europe. Examples of the advanced regions would be the city-states and major commercial centers of Italy and the Low Countries; examples of less developed regions would be the countries of Central and Eastern Europe.

The discussion here of the early modern period will be confined almost exclusively to Europe, although Jews of course lived within the boundaries of the Ottoman Empire, in the Middle East, and other areas. The review is limited to Europe because most Jews lived there. Although the variety and heterogeneity of the European situation make generalization hazardous, much of what was done in one part of the continent to the Jews was more or less emulated in other parts, because of the cultural affinities of Christian Europe.

SEPHARDIM AND ASHKENAZIM

The Jewish communities in Europe at the end of the 15th century were not homogeneous in the cultural sense. The two mainstreams or dominant groups were the Sephardim, originating from the Spanish-Portuguese Jews, and the Ashkenazim, originating from the French and German Jews. These two branches grew apart especially after the time of the Crusades, each one developing a distinct vernacular language and sets of customs that underscored their differences. By the end of the 15th and beginning of the 16th centuries when the Sephardi Jews were finally expelled from the Iberian Peninsula (the date of 1492 is only of symbolic significance, since the expulsion of the Jews from the various provinces was a chain of events that lasted for decades), the two major "tribes" of European Jewry came into a much closer contact, which resulted not in integration of the two, but in tolerable coexistence and peripheral cross-cultural interchange. The intellectual impact of the Sephardim was noticeable primarily in one area, namely that of religious mysticism; in other areas the Ashkenazim excelled the Sephardim in creatively developing what could be termed Jewish culture.

In the area of economic and social activity, the difference between the Sephardim and Ashkenazim was profound. The Sephardim were on the average much more affluent, much more skilled, and better educated (at least in the secular sense) than the Ashkenazim. In comparison the Ashkenazim were not only less prosperous but less culturally influenced by the gentile environment and less successful in any attempts at finding an intellectual symbiosis between their own and the surrounding culture. Therefore, the elements of the resource endowment of the Sephardi Jews made them the more attractive group of the two for settlement and employment in any European country. The Sephardi Jews were able to bring into the new areas of their settlement highly developed skills and craftsmanship in the areas of luxury consumption and were therefore highly valued by the influential consumers of such products and services, by the nobility, gentry, and patricians – the ruling classes of the contemporary societies. From available direct and circumstantial evidence it becomes clear that some of the Sephardi Jews were able to transfer portions of their capital out of Spain and Portugal, and thus their settlement in an area was accompanied by a capital import. It is interesting to note that in most cases, as far as the Christian countries are concerned, the Sephardi Jews were attracted to and sought opportunities in the more economically advanced regions, areas with both developed trade and crafts and with a legal framework that did not hinder the economic activities of a developed money economy. These were areas actively engaged in foreign commerce in which the knowledge of commodity and money markets possessed by Sephardi Jewish merchants could be profitably utilized. An additional asset of some Sephardi Jews was their knowledge of and family and former business connections in the Iberian peninsula and the overseas empires of Spain and Portugal. The Jewish participation in trade with Spain, Portugal, and their colonies never ceased, contrary to the myth of a world-wide Jewish boycott of the Iberian peninsula.

THE ECONOMIC ENVIRONMENT

Thus it could be roughly assumed that the "territory" of the Sephardim, at least during the 16th and 17th centuries, was the city-states and commercial centers of Europe, while the "territory" of the Ashkenazim was the interior, the land-mass or hinterland of Central and Eastern Europe.

The economy of city-states like Genoa, Venice, and Dubrovnik, or of commercial centers like Antwerp, Amsterdam, and Hamburg, was based upon international and interregional trade and the exploitation of politically dependent territories where trade was carried on or which were administered by corporate bodies either in the form of trading companies or governmental agencies acting on behalf of organized mercantile interests. The main problem for the Jews, as for any group of outsiders, and even more so because of some peculiar restrictions or prejudices, was to gain entry into the organized institutions of economic activity, whether registered partnerships, trading companies, or later the commodity and money exchanges. It was difficult, if not impossible, for the Jews as newcomers to operate outside the institutional framework except in areas where their specialized skills or professions (such as medicine or science) would be recognized as exceptionally useful for the polity or economy. Thus, each outsider, including the Jews as individuals, had to fit into the pre-existing economic structure and social fabric, upon neither of which he could expect to make any significant impact. Thus the process by which the Jews were economically integrated in the city-states and commercial centers was primarily the sum total of adjustments by individuals in these occupations and activities. Much depended on individual skill or wealth, with very limited room left for the collectivity of the Jews, the autonomous and organized Jewish community, to influence significantly the pattern of economic activity of its members.

The economic environment of the majority of the Ashkenazi Jews in the areas of Central and Eastern Europe differed from that in the city-states and in the major commercial areas. In the latter the Jews were restricted in terms of numbers, place of habitat, and areas of gainful employment, and formed almost exclusively an urban element concentrated in the major cities and confined largely to trade, some specialized skills, and money and lending operations. The situation of the Jews in Central and Eastern Europe, by contrast, can be described as characterized by both greater opportunities and more severe constraints. The peculiar combination is a paradox of underdevelopment and discrimination, both operating simultaneously.

There is an inherent conflict in societies with a high propensity to have rigid institutional arrangements in their economic sphere, even if within the institutions there may be provision and conditions permitting the exercise of individual initiative. This is the conflict between such a propensity for institutional stability and the need to innovate, for it is only through innovation that the economy can grow. Within such societies it is particularly difficult for newcomers, who have to be integrated and accepted, to innovate. Outsiders are often forced to follow a circuitous road and assume greater risks in order to achieve their objectives. An interesting case in point is presented by the penetration of the Jews into the international sugar trade. Apparently finding it initially difficult to enter via trade activity, Jews of Amsterdam entered the sugar plantation business in Brazil, Surinam, and the West Indies. The result was beneficial for many parties: for Amsterdam, a widening of its foreign trade; for the Jews, entrance into sugar production and sugar trade; for Europe, presumably a decrease in the price of sugar as a result of a rapid increase in supply.

In the predominantly agrarian economies of this period, a very large sector of the population was on a subsistence level and for all practical purposes outside the exchange and money economy. The money economy included the court, the nobility, gentry, and the urban classes, but only to a very limited extent the majority of the rural population, the peasants or serfs. While the areas of traditional or routine economic activity were circumscribed and regulated to an extent that made it virtually impossible for the Jews to enter the established institutions, there was a relatively wide spectrum of activities that were not institutionalized or controlled and that could be roughly described as the broadening of the market, of the money economy. This presented a range of opportunities for individuals who possessed or were forced to have a lesser-than-average risk aversion and accordingly the returns could be higher than average.

The Jews suffered from discriminatory legislation and very seldom did their legal or social status as individuals depend upon their individual skills or the size of their personal wealth. There was no institutional arrangement by which a Jew could be integrated into his economic class or professional group. In a sense, he was the eternal outsider regardless of the economic function he performed, operating under conditions of discrimination and extreme uncertainty, dependent upon the arbitrary decisions of the rulers, and paying a high price (in the form of high taxes, bribes, ransom, etc.) for his right to be employed. Thus with the environmental conditions differing between the more advanced and less advanced countries, the ranges of opportunities and the areas of economic activity of the Jews differed, which in turn influenced the patterns of utilization of their resource endowment and their social structure.

JEWISH MIGRATION

One of the chief characteristics of Jewish economic activities in Europe during the early modern period was the relative (for this period) mobility of both capital and labor of the Jews. Even if we could consider exclusively voluntary mobility, the two other outstanding groups, the Italians and the Dutch, are in quite a different class when compared with the Jews. Thus, the migration phenomenon can be considered as one of the most significant dynamic elements of the economic and social history of the Jews. The geographic pattern of Jewish migration from the end of the 15th century could be summarized as the eastward movement from Western to Central and Eastern Europe; this continued as the main vector until the second half of the 19th century. The eastward movement overshadowed in its intensity the "return" of the Jews to the countries of Western Europe from which they were exiled in the earlier centuries, and to which they gradually returned between the 17th and 19th centuries.

The process of migration did not take the form of an even, continuous flow but proceeded through spurts and movements differing in intensity, with interruptions, reversals, and resumptions that defied regularity. It is also difficult to ascertain, apart from the general vector of the migration movement and the main routes, the average distances and time periods of the earlier phases of the migration. For the Sephardi Jews two general directions can be established: one from the Iberian peninsula to the areas adjacent to the Mediterranean toward Italy, the Balkans, and Turkey; the other toward southern France, the Netherlands, Hamburg, and England. For the Ashkenazim the direction of migration was from Western Germany over Austria toward Bohemia and Hungary, with another branch through Bohemia leading toward Poland, Lithuania, Belorussia, and the Ukraine, while eastern and northern Germany were populated primarily by Austrian and Bohemian Jews and to a lesser extent by the Western German Jews. Many aspects of Jewish migration still await thorough investigation, research, and analysis. Nevertheless, certain generalizations can be made on the basis of available evidence:

(1) By and large the eastward migration was in fact a movement of labor and capital from more highly developed to less economically developed countries and regions, from areas of greater availability of skilled labor and capital to areas of greater scarcity of these factors of production; (2) The mobility of labor and capital and thereby the migration process was facilitated not only by religious identity but also by the cultural affinity of common customs and language, by the availability of established and organized Jewish communities not far from the end destination of the migration route, and also by the relatively high level of liquidity of capital on the part of capital owners; (3) The significance of the migration process for the economy of the Jews was due to a large extent to the fact that through migration and mobility a more remunerative distribution of human and capital resources could be achieved over a large territory, while both cultural and economic intercourse could be maintained thanks to the continuing ties between the older and newer communities; (4) Some of the benefits of the process of mobility accruing to the Jewish communities were congruent with the benefits of the economies of countries that absorbed the Jewish migrants, namely the import of skilled labor and capital resources to meet a strong demand; (5) The migration process of the Jews in the eastward direction, although caused to a very large extent by economic considerations, even by the differential of economic well-being or differences in the rates of return to skills, had significant effects in other areas as well. It became a part of the "strategy for

survival" either in cases of mass-expulsions and exiles or under conditions of a clear worsening of the legal status short of expulsions. Moreover, the absence of effective internal barriers supported the prevailing notion of a single, general Jewish community in Central and Eastern Europe. Leading schools drew students from far afield; famous scholars and rabbis were not bound to a particular locale; mystics and messianic claimants attracted multitudes from all over the continent.

The first ebb on a larger scale in the eastward migration took place around the middle of the 17th century during the times of the Chmielnicki massacres in the Ukraine, Swedish and Muscovite invasions of Poland, and the subsequent worsening of the economic situation there. The flow of refugees from Eastern Europe reached Western Germany and even the Netherlands. From the middle of the 18th century, there was a small but continuous flow of Central and Eastern European Jews trying to settle in Western Europe and North America. But this early reversal of the direction of migration flow had a minimal effect upon the economic life of the communities that they left as well as the ones that they joined. It only indicated that change was possible if not imminent. Unlike the eastward mobility of movement, this countermovement showed that capital and labor will not necessarily flow in the same direction.

PATTERNS OF EMPLOYMENT

Any systematic insight into the economic activities of the Jewish population in Europe during this period requires an examination of the patterns of employment. If the chief economic characteristic of Jewish migration was the movement from more developed to less developed countries, we would expect the Jews to be employed primarily not in areas of an abundant labor supply but in the economic sectors with a scarcity of labor and capital, namely trade and highly skilled crafts. Only when the employment in such areas had reached a level of saturation or was encountering barriers would one expect the migrants to turn to less renumerative employment, yielding a lower return to the labor and capital spent. One of the main characteristics of the employment pattern of the Jews was that the great majority was employed in sectors of the economy that were directly connected with the market. Very few operated outside the exchange and money economy, while most derived their incomes from the production and sales of goods and services. It is true that the markets differed, but it is important to bear in mind that the market psychology affected the activities of the greatest majority. It is therefore appropriate to begin the review of the patterns of employment with the type of employment and activity most intimately connected with the organized markets and also yielding the highest returns. The "big business" of that period was carried on by a small group of enterprising individuals who either combined or fulfilled separately the functions of wholesale merchants, bankers, and industrial entrepreneurs. Such individuals in the economically advanced countries acted mostly in their private capacity, in the economically backward countries mostly in conjunction with government actions as a special category associated with the term Court Jews.

It is impossible to measure directly the volume of international trade carried on by Jewish wholesale merchants in the 16th–18th centuries. Obviously the volume depended upon the share of Jewish trade in the countries they inhabited and in turn upon such countries' share in the total volume of international trade. Such data are not as yet available, but it should be clear that, for example, a 10% share in the Dutch trade would probably be more than a 50% share in Poland's international trade, because of the relative sizes of the trade volume of the two countries. Direct and indirect evidence indicates that the Jews were involved in the trade of precious metals, the colonial trade, and trade of products possessing a high value per unit. Only later, with the improvement of shipping technology and cheapening of transportation costs, did Jews enter the trade of grain and other bulk products, thus expanding the trade with the agrarian economies of Central and Eastern Europe.

As bankers and bill-brokers in the economically developed countries, their operations did not differ from those of the profession. The two advantages that they might have possessed over some of their competitors was their ability to transfer money rapidly from one locality to another, as they had either family or business connections with members of other Jewish communities, and the extension of credits by using the savings deposited with them by members of the community. Jewish bankers' preference for short-term over long-term credit could perhaps be explained by the desire for a quicker turnover of their capital and the unwillingness to accept land or real estate as security for loans outstanding. The industrial entrepreneurship of the Jews in the developed areas was due to the availability of technical skills and business expertise in a number of craft and industry branches that the Jews had brought with them in migrating from one country to another.

In the less developed countries the so-called Court Jews played an interesting role, the gradual transformation of which reflected the economic development of such countries as well as the contribution such individuals made to the development process. The shortage of money and the low credit standing of most European rulers and their governments were notorious. Accordingly, the initial role of the Court Jews, as the title implies, was to serve the rulers in a double capacity, as lenders of money and as suppliers of precious metals, precious stones, and other luxury items for the consumption of the court or the mint.

The form of payment and security given were often tax farming, toll-collection, and other privileges that provided for the principal and interest of the transaction. Thus the Court Jews not only provided credit for the rulers but also performed functions in the revenue collection of the states. Two major factors contributed to the transformation of the nature of the service of the Court Jews. The first were the wars of the 17th and 18th centuries, which called not only for greater monetary outlays and thus expanding demand for credits, but also for the organizational talent to supply the numerous armies in the field with weapons, ammunition, clothing, food, and fodder. The need to contract and pay for, and to deliver large bulks of necessary supplies at great distances, called for new and substantial organizational talents. The Court Jews performed well when requested to carry out the above tasks, and in the process of doing so gained new knowledge in large-scale operations requiring greater efficiency in mobilizing economic resources of unprecedented magnitude in relatively backward economies. In so doing the Court Jews were assisting the political interests of the rulers or of the state.

The other factor contributing to the transformation of their service was the entrance of the Jews into the ranks of industrial entrepreneurs. The setting-up of mining and manufacturing industries in the economically backward countries was not a market response to a demand for such products. It was in most cases either a direct result of government action or an indirectly induced development as a result of a conscious government policy. Government policies in those countries pursued two goals. First, to develop armament industries to strengthen those countries militarily and politically in their struggles for hegemony or restoration of a power balance in Europe. Secondly, to develop industry branches that produced import-substitutes, which meant primarily of imported products used by the wealthy upper classes of society. Crudely speaking, the military needs on the one hand and the maintenance of a positive balance of payments on the other were mainly responsible for the state initiative and support given to early mining and manufacturing industries. Given the government financial or tax support for the industrial establishments, the critical factors were skilled labor and entrepreneurial and managerial talents. In providing skills the contribution of the Jews was probably inferior to the possibilities of importing skills from the advanced countries, so the primary area of their contribution, by no means exclusively Jewish, was that of entrepreneurial and managerial talent. Their previous experience in large-scale banking, military contracting, etc., provided the necessary background. The involvement in previous services for the state provided them with the knowledge and political connections necessary for obtaining licenses, priviliges, and often the labor force for the budding industrial enterprises. Thus the former Court Jew became an industrial entrepreneur, continuing along the path of social innovation, creating new types of economic organization, and helping to break old patterns and traditional systems. The economic significance for the Jewish community of this group of wholesale merchants, bankers, and industrial entrepreneurs consisted not only in their role in the accumulation of capital, but also and primarily in their collective role in creating employment opportunities for other Jews. The relatively large-scale operations of this entrepreneurial class gave rise to a demand for services that could be performed by other members of the community. For example, in such enterprises as supply-contracting, a system of subcontracting was established that provided income for a relatively large number of smaller-scale merchants, and even the administration of large landed estates provided employment for many inn-keepers, alcohol distillers, and other self-employed members of the Jewish community.

The second area of employment, which was represented by a massive participation of the members of the Jewish community, was that of smaller-scale and retail trade and of commercial intermediaries operating with limited capital resources, in many cases not their own. In the economically more advanced centers the economic activities of this employment group were rather specialized, with heavy concentration in limited areas of the retail trade and specialized services as commercial and financial intermediaries. Here too their activities were limited by the existing institutional structure of the commercial centers. In order to compete with the more established firms or individuals the Jewish merchants tried to deviate from the standards of goods being marketed and provided a greater variety in terms of quality for a broader range of prices. The economic effect of such — for that period — unorthodox behavior was a broadening of the market and an increase in the number of consumers by offering the broader price range. In the predominantly agricultural economies of that period, the Jewish merchants had to overcome both the power of the urban guilds and the customary location of actual markets in the cities. Therefore a major area of the trade of the Jewish merchants consisted in reaching the social circle beyond the orbit of the exchange economy, the peasants. The merchants sought out the areas of a marketable surplus of agricultural products. By increasing the size of shipments from the outlying areas it was possible to decrease the costs of transportation that previously had made it unprofitable to bring these products to market.

A number of varied and interesting phenomena attended this Jewish mercantile activity. First, through their penetration of the rural areas Jewish merchants and peddlers supplied both the manor and the peasant huts with manufactured goods that were in demand, and simultaneously collected the marketable surplus of grains, flax, wool, livestock. This two-way trade enabled

Watercolor and ink drawing of Florentine Jewish peddlers, c. 18th century.

the Jews to compete relatively successfully with the local merchants who conducted their trade at fixed points, primarily in the cities, and were relatively protected by their status as city dwellers and merchants. Secondly, the penetration of Jewish peddlers and merchants into the countryside enabled them to organize early, primitive forms of a putting-out system, making use of and helping in the further development of cottage industries in the rural areas, and thus organizing and supporting a form of production in competition with the urban crafts controlled and protected by the city guilds. Thirdly, the employment of Jews in inn-keeping, alcohol distilling, and livestock production in the rural areas helped further to inject into the agricultural sector the elements of an exchange and money economy. The result of the activity of the Jewish small merchants in the rural areas was to encourage the production of an agricultural surplus, to stimulate the consumption of non-agricultural goods, and to foster the alienation of some part of the former agricultural labor force from the land and to channel it into the cottage industries and into transportation services, thus helping to create a non-agricultural labor force in the rural areas that depended upon wages rather than upon returns from land.

The second largest employment group within the Jewish community was that of the artisans. Given the limited size of the market and the degree of organization of the craft guilds, the Jewish artisans faced a constant struggle for the right to compete. Since they were refused admittance to the craft guilds, they suffered from the constraints imposed on nonguild members and at best could count on a compromise that would allow them to continue their activity at the price of compensatory payments to the guilds. The alternative was to be restricted to the very narrow market for craft production provided by the Jewish community. Faced with this choice the Jewish artisans accepted the conditions of higher costs of production, including the payment of compensation to the guilds, until such time as the burden of discrimination could be lessened or alternative arrangements could create new opportunities. The range of Jewish crafts was very wide, beginning with highly specialized gold and silversmiths and jewelers, ranging to masons, carpenters, and blacksmiths, but with a heavy concentration in the clothing crafts like tailoring, cap-making, furriery, and shoe-making. This particular concentration indicates a reliance upon a mass market. Through this orientation toward an expanding market the survival of Jewish artisans was guaranteed and new arrangements for production and marketing were developed. The new arrangements took the form of what amounts to a putting-out system organized by Jewish merchants who provided the artisans with raw materials and occasionally with advance payments for their work.

"The Knife Sharpener" by I. Ryback, 1917.

Thus, the artisans were converted almost into wage laborers, but the arrangement freed them from the necessity of having their own or borrowed capital tied up in stocks of raw material or finished goods and also from involvement in the process of distribution, these functions being performed by the merchants. From the end of the 16th century the artisans started to organize Jewish craft guilds. Although there is still much debate about the actual effectiveness of these Jewish guild activities, there is no doubt that the fact of their establishment was a response to a deeply-felt need for collective action and for articulating their interests at least within the Jewish communities. Under such arrangements Jewish artisans were better able to survive at least until the time when modern industry posed new threats to the positions of small crafts and the putting-out system.

A description of the various employment categories within the Jewish milieu would be incomplete if it did not note that a certain part of the economically active population was employed within the Jewish community itself. This general area of employment can be divided into two groups: the occupations that served the Jewish community exclusively, and those providing services for which an assured demand existed within the Jewish community but of which outsiders also could avail themselves. Among the first category were rabbis, schoolteachers, ritual slaughterers, scroll scribes, employees of the ritual bath house, and keepers of synagogues and cemeteries. The demand for the services of this group was determined largely by religious laws and customs and therefore was not very flexible. Among the other category were butchers, candle-makers, book-dealers, and prayer-shawl weavers. The demand for their employment could have been a joint demand since they were capable of providing services for non-Jews as well; nevertheless the Jewish community had to sustain the costs of maintaining the bulk of their services when outside demand proved insufficient. The percentage of all these intra-community services in the total of gainful employment varied for the particular communities according to their size; but there was less variation if the Jewish population of each of the countries was viewed as a unit. While smaller communities could have shared in some of the services that each one separately could not afford, the combined percentage of the intra-communities' employment, when standardized for size, was not much different from that of the larger communities. As a rule of thumb it would probably be correct to assume that at least 10% of total employment was devoted to the internal community services.

These various categories of employment constituted a wide spectrum within the Jewish communities and absorbed much of the energy of its members; in terms of the percentage of gainful employment or actual volume of labor input within the year they were probably greater than the average for the population at large. Apart from them, however, there existed a numerous group of un-employed or unemployable members of the community. It would be fair to assume that the primary responsibility for the support and maintenance of the unemployed or unemployable rested with the extended family, as the basic social unit within the community. Whenever the family was unable to provide such support, the community accepted such people as public charges. The three major ways in which the community met its responsibilities was through private charity, institutionalized voluntary associations organized for the purpose of providing assistance through institutions — like hospitals, homes for incurables or the aged, and loan-societies — and through direct community support out of the taxation levied upon the tax-paying members. In accord with traditional beliefs, private charity was not only considered a responsibility but also an opportunity for the more prosperous members of the community. The activities of voluntary associations concerned with this type of welfare and social services prevented a full bureaucratization of the functions, which would otherwise have been taken over entirely by the community authorities, and left much room for individual initiative and energy. Needless to say, neither private charity nor the work of the voluntary associations sufficed to meet the problem. Since the number of unemployed and unemployable also depended upon general economic conditions, in times of relative prosperity the economy would tend to absorb the unemployed and the community would be in a better condition to support the unemployable, while the reverse was true during periods of eco-nomic decline. Thus the role of community taxation increased at times when the tax burden already appeared to be most heavy. Nevertheless, the communities accepted this "welfare responsibility" either out of a sense of moral obligation or in order to mitigate the social friction and conflicts that a refusal would have entailed. It is difficult to estimate the share of unemployed or paupers within the Jewish communities for this period, but depending upon the economic and legal conditions of the Jews it would be no exaggeration to estimate their share as between 15 and 25%, with a tendency to rise since the second half of the 17th century.

It is likewise difficult to document the employment distribution within the Jewish communities for countries as a whole, although we have data for separate local communities either for irregular intervals or for single years scattered all over the map of Europe. We can roughly reconstruct the employment distri-bution for the largest Jewish community in Europe — Poland-Lithuania — at the middle of the 18th century. The employment distribution differed markedly among the Jews settled in the larger cities, among those inhabiting the small towns, and among those scattered in the rural areas. In addition, the peculiarity of the settlement pattern of the Jews in Poland-Lithuania during this period was the large proportion of Jews living in rural areas, about one-third of the total Jewish population. While in the rural areas leaseholding, innkeeping, alcohol distilling, and ancillary agriculture was the prevailing pattern, the mass of Jewish artisans inhabited the larger cities and smaller towns. The social structure which emerges from the approximate data reflects the following employment distribution of the Polish Jews by the middle of the 18th century: wholesale merchants, financiers, etc. – about 2–3%; small traders, including leaseholders and innkeepers – less than 40%; artisans and other urban wage earners – more than 33%; employed in intra-community services – about 10%; unemployed and paupers – at least 15%. The most obvious conclusions that could be drawn from this employment distribution is that the vast majority of the Jews earned their livelihood from physical labor and that a substantial proportion of the population was either already impoverished or at the poverty threshold, to use a modern term.

RESOURCE ENDOWMENT AND SOURCES OF INCOME

The consideration of the employment distribution within the Jewish community sheds some light upon the problem of the sources of Jewish income and upon one particularly interesting aspect, that of resource endowment and returns to the factors of production, labor, and capital. For a very long time the prevailing view among historians of the period was that capital was the more important component of the resource endowment of the Jewish community and that returns to capital were also quantitatively the more significant component of the income earned by the Jews. Needless to say, this view was more congruent with popular images than with documental calculations. Both progress in historical research and increased sophistication of economic analysis have led to serious questioning of the view. There is no doubt that a substantial part of the capital with which the Jews operated was borrowed from non-Jews, as evidenced by the bankruptcy of the Jewish communities in Poland during the 18th century and their large indebtedness to the nobility and clergy. It is also increasingly clear that the return to skills in the pre-industrial period was relatively higher than was initially assumed. If first the labor income derived from the goods produced by Jewish artisans and craftsmen is calculated and then the labor component of the earnings in retail trade is added, the result arrived at would be a very substantial share of the total income earned. The vast majority of the Jews during this period earned the bulk of their income from labor services. The profit rate of owners of capital could be maintained only by using capital in new areas of trade and industry, thus counteracting the secular tendency of the profit rate to decline while capital was becoming relatively more abundant. The capital earnings of the members of the Jewish community were in part used through a process of income redistribution to maintain intra-community services and to aid the poor members of the community.

The income position and income level of the Jewish community depended upon prevailing economic conditions and changes. If the Jewish community is considered as being involved in an exchange of goods and services with the community at large, the economic well-being of the Jewish community would depend not only upon its employment composition and resource endowment, but also upon the "terms of trade" of its production of goods and services with the products for which it traded with the community at large. If, for simplicity's sake, it is assumed that the Jews were producing manufactured goods and consuming food and raw materials, their prosperity or lack of it would depend to some extent upon the terms of trade between manufactured goods and raw materials. In fact, the income of the Jews depended upon the economic situation of the various countries and particularly upon conditions in the agrarian sector, which provided the bulk of the consumers of the products and services produced and marketed by the Jews. Since the goods sold by the Jews were more sensitive to the income position of consumers and since prices tended to vary with regard to relatively small changes in the demand or supply of such goods, their income probably fluctuated even more than that of the primary product producers. At the same time the volume of consumption of the Jews was less liable to fluctuate, thus tending to underscore even more the vulnerability of their net income position.

The secular trend of the economic well-being of the Jewish community in Europe varied from country to country, making it difficult to establish a general trend that would fit all countries during identical periods. The most general trend in the economic conditions of the Jews, and one that helps to explain the historical direction of the migration process, is the continuous improvement of their economic status and income level in Eastern Europe until the middle of the 18th century. About the same time, actually after the recovery following the Thirty Years War in Germany (1618–48), a slow process of improvement of the economic conditions favorable for the Jews started in Central and Western Europe. While the 18th century reinforced the two diametrically opposed tendencies, the reversal of the migration pattern became discernible. The dependence of the Jews upon the economic conditions of the country and the particular society is self-explanatory. What is less clear, however, is the existence of significant differences in the attitude of different social groups toward the Jews behind the facade of a generalized "attitude."

SOCIETY AT LARGE:
ATTITUDES AND RELATIONS

The pattern of economic and especially social relations between the Jews and the social groups within the community at large remained almost unchanged throughout most of the early modern period. These relations were initially established to a very large extent upon the basis of the expected or actual relative utility of the Jews to the interests of the particular social groups. The similarities and differences of economic interests of the social groups and their relative political strength played a decisive role in shaping the constraints upon the economic activity of the Jews. In considering the social groups the following might be differentiated: the crown and the nobility; the gentry; the merchants, with differentiation between the more advanced and backward countries; the craftsmen; and the peasants. From the outset it should be noted that the Jews had no economic counterpart to some of the social groups (crown and nobility, gentry, peasants) and thus no problem of economic competition could enter into the relationship. In the cases of the craftsmen and merchants, however, the problem of direct competition created almost an *a priori* presumption of an antagonistic relationship.

For the crown, the Jews were either a source of revenue or a vehicle of economic development in the areas of foreign trade, money and credit, and later manufacturing industry. Given the degree of dependence of the Jews upon the crown, they were considered both as a pliable instrument of government policies and an important source of money income, advantages that fully compensated for the distaste or religious resentment generally felt toward the Jews. In the countries where the upper nobility shared in the power of the government, the economic convenience and money incomes from the Jews derived by the nobles employing them on the large private estates or in the discharge of the nobility's public offices rivaled the gains derived by the crown. The attitudes of the gentry toward the Jews were somewhat more ambiguous than that of the nobility. The Jews served the gentry as middlemen in the sale of their agricultural surplus and as the suppliers of manufactured goods on terms more favorable than other merchants would customarily offer. In addition they often served as a source of credit for the money-hungry, debt-ridden gentry. Like the nobility, the gentry preferred in many cases to have the Jews act as a buffer between them and the peasantry, so that for the opportunity of employment and income the Jews assumed the role of the gentry's agent in the economic exploitation of the peasantry and in effect became the scapegoat of the righteous wrath of the peasants. The presence of the Jews as a threat of competition to the urban dwellers was useful to the gentry in resisting the merchants' demands for economic and political privileges, which the gentry were loathe to give up or to share. The gentry, therefore, appeared as a defender of the Jews and of their activities as traders and craftsmen. The ambiguity in their position arose mainly in connection with their role as debtors quite unwilling to live up to their obligations.

With respect to the merchants, a distinction has to be made between the advanced and the economically backward countries. In the economically advanced ones during this period the merchants had already given up many of their special privileges in exchange for the legal protection of the business contract. The existing institutions and organizational forms of trade allowed a certain degree of competition; and the merchants as a group did not feel terribly threatened by an influx of newcomers, as long as the newcomers subscribed to the generally accepted rules of business conduct, were subject to the common jurisdiction, and were contributing to the expansion of trade. Therefore, even if the Jewish merchants were not socially accepted, they were tolerated as performing the same social function as the merchants in general. In contrast, the merchants in the economically backward countries were hostile to most newcomers and especially to the Jews for a number of reasons: the occupation of merchants was circumscribed by sets of special privileges and regulated by the guild organizations in the areas of entry, business behavior of the guild members, and the nature of the markets; the merchants in those countries subscribed very strongly to the erroneous notion that there is at each point in time a given volume of business, and the admission of more people into the profession will only reduce the share everyone already enjoys; the fear of competition, which might lead to a decrease of the profit rate, made the merchants hostile to newcomers in general and particularly to the Jews who were outside their jurisdiction; and many of the merchants in the less developed countries were themselves ethnically of foreign stock and by keeping the conspicuous Jews out they tried to mollify the popular impression that trade was almost exclusively in the hands of foreigners. Thus the merchants in such countries did their best wherever they could to limit the occupations of the Jews, trying to eliminate competition from the most lucrative areas of trade and from the conventional channels of trade.

The social group that felt subjectively most threatened by competition from the Jews were the artisans and craftsmen, who relied even more than the merchants upon benefits derived from old privileges and the guild organization. They tried to augment their meager incomes by following monopolistic practices, by regulating entry into guilds, setting a long period for apprenticeship, prescribing the production process in detail, and trying to control the market. The artisan guilds in urban areas were relatively powerful, closed corporate bodies, quite effective in controlling urban crafts. As a social group the artisans had a much narrower outlook than the merchants, were much more under the influence of the Church, and resentful and suspicious of outsiders. During this period the Jewish artisans did not succeed in being incorporated into the general guilds and had to operate outside the Christian guild organization. Attempts to set up guilds of Jewish artisans were numerous and always argued for on the basis of the need for organization for successful competition or income maintenance. Needless to say, the artisans, the plebeian masses of the cities, quite often linked their struggle against competition from Jewish craftsmen and traders to the social struggle against the gentry and urban patricians. Thus anti-Jewish sentiment often accompanied particular forms of the class struggle of the urban plebeians.

The attitudes of the peasantry to the Jews did not matter in terms of the policies toward the Jews, except in cases of peasant wars and uprisings. Nor could they prevent the Jews from exercising their economic functions whenever they were acting on behalf of the crown, gentry, and nobility. Nevertheless they affected some of the economic activities of the Jewish traders and artisans and were of importance in the social sphere, since the peasants constituted the vast majority of the population. There is no doubt that in the situations in which the Jews acted as economic agents for the landowners they were strongly resented by the peasants. But even in the many instances when the Jews helped to bring the peasants into the money economy the attitude was not one of unqualified gratitude. This was due to the fact that the peasants' entrance into and participation in the money economy was accompanied by rising demands for incomes on the part of both the landowners and the state at the expense of the peasants. In a sense, with peasant incomes rising, the rents and taxes tended to rise accordingly. It would probably not be incorrect to conclude that in spite of tangible benefits provided for the peasants by some economic activities of the Jews, the peasants did not differentiate among the various roles played by the Jews in the rural economy. They were certainly either unable or unwilling to distinguish between different categories of Jews, a trait which they shared with other social groups. The Jew was the stranger who, in the eyes of the peasants (as well as of the artisans), was suspected of undermining the traditional order. That old order was one that the peasants did not like, but they were too conservative to substitute another for it because of all the accompanying uncertainties. The Jews, in turn, especially the ones settled in the rural areas, were perhaps only a notch above the peasants economically, but they were separated from the peasants by a cultural gulf that could not be bridged. Thus suspicion on the one side was reciprocated by contempt from the other.

THE ROLE OF THE JEWISH COMMUNITY ORGANIZATION

To the extent that the relations between some groups of the general community and various social groups within the Jewish community appeared antagonistic, and to the extent that discrimination against the Jews was the prevailing characteristic of the legal framework and policies of many European states, there existed a strong tendency within the Jewish community to defend itself against discriminatory attitudes. In addition, there manifestly existed a desire to free themselves of the fetters of restrictions and controls imposed by the state, guilds, and other existing corporate bodies. But the latter attitude did not lead necessarily to a laissez-faire attitude even in areas of autonomous choice. To demand freedom of trade or to exercise one's skills freely in crafts and manufacturing did not encompass the Jewish community's demand for abolition of regulations of economic activity of its members. The adoption of such an attitude would clearly clash with existing economic realities and with the basic tenet of governmental policy toward the Jews, which was accepted, willingly or unwillingly, by the Jewish communities. The point of departure of governmental policies was the principle, explicitly stated or implicitly assumed, of collective responsibility of the community for the acts of its members. In order for the Jewish community to discharge this responsibility at least a modicum of autonomy had to be granted in areas of taxation and civil law.

Seen in historical perspective, the measures of self-regulation and control by the autonomous authorities of the Jewish community over the economic activities of their members were perhaps only minor alterations in the general framework of the economic life of the Jews, which was determined largely by the conditions of the economy and major policies of the state. Nevertheless, the details and alterations seem to have been important since they apparently influenced the well-being of many and helped minimize some effects of discrimination. In general the spirit in which particular adjustments and arrangements were made was one of pragmatic realism. Broadly it coincided with the abolition of the restriction upon Jews charging interest to their coreligionists, a move that officially sanctioned a usage originating much earlier than the beginning of the 17th century. The basic criteria for community control appear to be in the same spirit: maximum economic effectiveness for the community, the collectivity as the sum of its members; conformity with traditional standards of justice and welfare; minimal interference with individual initiative; and continuity of religious traditions and maintenance of the existing authority structure, social order, and economic stratification.

Among the most outstanding examples of community activity as a self-regulatory agency influencing the economic life of its members, the following may be mentioned: (1) The right to accept new settlers enabled communities, at least to some extent, to regulate and direct the flow of migration. By granting or refusing the "right of entry" into the community (which was tantamount to the right of habitat and employment in a certain locality), the communal authorities were able to exercise a degree of control upon the supply of labor and the extent of competition for employment and business opportunities; (2) The community had the right of enforcing the principle of *ḥazakah* − of seniority or preferential option granted in the bidding or negotiation of a new contract to the previous partner over his competitors. This was a rule that benefited the previous or current party over any new entrant and effectively limited competition among Jewish businessmen; (3) There was a right and obligation to guarantee the solvency of the members of the community in business transactions whenever such guarantees were required or requested. In practice such guarantees helped members of the community avail themselves of business opportunities and strengthen their credit position, but in some cases the community, by indicating the limits of credit, was both protecting itself and preventing its members from engaging in high-risk operations; (4) There was a right to distribute the tax-burden of the community among its members both for the purposes of poll tax payments and for its intra-community needs.

The paradox of the situation is that most of the cited examples appear to be in conflict with the idea of liberalization of economic activity by individuals. It is, however, congruent with the conviction that for a minority to survive as a distinct group it has to place the interests of group survival above the short-run interests of the individual members. It is also plausible that when the state was practicing interference with the regulation of economic life and a policy of economic discrimination an autonomous group cannot afford a laissez-faire practice and still maintain its identity and internal cohesion. In fact, when during a later period the state started to withdraw from the positions of control and regulation, the Jewish communities also had to give up most of their regulatory functions under the pressure of the individual members in order to survive as mostly voluntary associations. But during the period under consideration the Jewish community organization was still very strong in enforcing its control over an economically heterogenous and socially stratified population.

SOCIAL STRATIFICATION WITHIN THE JEWISH COMMUNITY

Since the Jewish community was differentiated with respect to economic functions, it would be well to inquire into the pattern of social stratification among the Jews during this period. The society at large was hierarchically or-ganized, and the social conditions of its members were largely predetermined either by birth (by hereditary status) or by the role and functions assigned to them by prevailing custom or by the state. We would not, however, really expect to find any perfect identity between the stratification of the society at large and the Jewish community for the simple reason that the Jews were excluded from land ownership and were therefore lacking the equivalent of the nobility, gentry, and serf-peasantry. Within the Jewish community we find the equivalent of three large groups which had their counterparts in the society at large, namely: the equivalent of the urban patricians, the equivalent of the small producers (craftsmen) and middlemen (merchants), and the wage earners and paupers.

The first group, in terms of wealth, was represented by rich merchants and entrepreneurs engaged in international and interregional trade, in ownership of industrial establishments, in banking and moneylending, as court factors, tax-farmers, etc. In terms of social prestige this group also included famous rabbinical scholars and book-publishers, although the last two categories were far inferior in terms of wealth. The second group, representing the majority of the Jewish population, included all the owners of some capital, in the form of tools or stocks of goods, to which their own or family labor was applied and who employed a small number of hired help. They were the ones who, like the vast majority of the first group, came into direct contact with the market and were exposed to all the irregularities of the early, imperfect markets of the time. Although social mobility from this group into the upper stratum was not prevented by any legal means, the dichotomy between the two groups was noticeable both in the economic and the social spheres, and the grievances voiced by this group against the upper stratum are a clear witness to the cleavage existing between them. The third group included wage earners engaged in crafts, trade, transportation, services (including domestics), and a large number of unemployables for whom the community had to provide a livelihood. While social mobility from the third group into the second was a possibility, the "plebs" of the community constituted a distinct group, inferior not only in terms of income, but also in education and skills and separated by many social and cultural barriers from the ones who were economically independent.

While the intergroup mobility was limited by economic factors and perhaps also by some cultural factors, the intragroup mobility was much more free and frequent; and in this respect the Jewish community was ahead of its times in comparison with the society at large. There were also special reasons why the tensions among the various groups and social classes were dampened and less explosive than in the society at large. Two reasons were especially significant: first, the generally oppressive attitudes of the society at large, which apart from exceptional cases and special situations was hardly in a mood to differentiate among the various categories and groups within the Jewish community; secondly, the institutionalized system of welfare within the Jewish community acted as a form of income redistribution and provided for the most basic or elementary needs of its indigent members. But even this mitigation of the internal tensions could not eliminate the intensity of the discord and the deep resentment that existed among the various social groups within the community, contrary to the superficial impressions of casual outside observers who were convinced that the Jewish community represented an example of internal harmony and solidarity. The internal conflicts were at times so intense that external, governmental authorities were drawn into the conflicts by the requests to take sides and intervene either to strengthen the forces of authority within the community or to curb the arbitrariness of the decisions and limit the authority of the ruling bodies. The various intellectual and religious movements within the Jewish community also exhibited strong social overtones and in some cases revealed the strength of subterranean resentments and open protest on the part of the lower classes of the community.

The real power in the community was located in the hands of the upper social group, and the wealthy occupied the offices of both consequence and social prestige. Although Jewish communities strongly resented the appointment of officers by government authorities, which guaranteed office-holding for the wealthiest, as an interference in community affairs, the system of electing officers (and such were often personally responsible for the fiscal obligations of the community) no less favored the election of the rich, the ones who could afford the burden of office. Wealth became almost a prerequisite for office and could be augmented by holding office, since offices provided access to information and opportunities that could be turned to business advantage by their holders. In part, some of the power of the wealthy elite was exercised because of the economic dependence of members of the community directly employed or indirectly influenced by the elite. The relatively large-scale business operations by the members of the elite provided employment opportunities for agents, salesmen, domestics, etc., which assured the elite of the support of the dependents in community affairs. The symbol of the autonomy of the Jewish communities was their right to elect their spiritual leaders, the rabbis. The communities viewed any attempt by governmental authority to appoint rabbis as an assault on their right of religious autonomy. Nonetheless, the power of the spiritual leaders was more important in maintaining the continuity of tradition and is to be seen more in their role as mitigators in internal conflicts than in the internal policies or the routine economic activities of the community. It was left to the business elite to regulate and supervise the economic activities of the community. In the cases when a conflict arose between the spiritual leaders and the upper stratum in the community, the real power, that of the elite, usually asserted itself. In the communities in which the power of office was shared by the upper stratum with representatives of the middle group, the important decisions were usually left to the "patrician" families. An important result of the existing social stratification during this period was the degree of stability provided by community leadership recruited basically from one social group. In a period when all other societies were hierarchically organized, the Jewish community could hardly afford to be organized according to any other principle.

9

THE TRANSITION PERIOD

The transition between the "old" conditions and the "new" was neither smooth nor short. It spanned two distinct periods, which differed markedly from one another with respect to the general framework of economic activity, the prevailing ideologies, and the social groups that made the important decisions. The transition reflected the change in social and economic development, in this sense exhibiting both its revolutionary aspects in respect of some institutions and individuals and its evolutionary aspects of piecemeal transformation of other institutions, habits and activities. The major characteristics of the transition in the economic sphere included acceleration in the accumulation of tangible assets (capital) as well as the possibility of transferring increasing amounts of capital from one area of economic activity to another and the willingness to do so. This phenomenon was accompanied by the development of technology, which provided labor-saving mechanical devices for the production of goods, and in turn became a strong force in creating the demand for new capital and for new skills.

Concurrent with these economic changes were new developments in generally held beliefs and opinions. Among the many, some must be singled out for their significance. Especially important was the rise of secularism at the expense of traditional religious and theological views. The turn toward secularism put man in the center of the universe and assumed that he was able and willing to subordinate the forces of nature to serve him. This led both to the development of a more generalized utilitarian approach and, with the weakening of earlier dogmatic attitudes, to the development and penetration of scientific thought, thus providing the basis for innovations and inventions in the field of technology. The spread of the idea of egalitarianism was another important element in the change of social thought. While not a characteristic feature of the period, by putting man in the abstract in the center of the universe, egalitarianism challenged the basic premises of a hierarchical society in which the accidents of birth largely determine the social position of individuals. Though egalitarianism was not yet successful during the period of transition in securing the political and social participation of a broad spectrum of the populace, it at least achieved the legitimization of merit and achievement rather than birth as the leading criteria for joining the social elite. The change of criteria was of utmost importance, while the implementation of the principle could proceed only slowly if the social fabric was not to be torn by revolution. If ideas of secularism and egalitarianism are to be intellectually tenable and socially effective, equality before the law is perhaps the first necessary step. Thus the establishment of a new legality based not upon divine law or the will of the sovereign, but upon the consensus of the governed led to new forms of individual freedoms and to social responsibilities or disciplines being shared by all citizens or inhabitants of the particular countries. That social discipline required the resolution of conflicts within a legal framework was obvious, and for the framework to be effective it had to approach universality and offer equitable treatment to all.

The transition period in Western Europe dates from about the middle of the 18th century until after the Napoleonic Wars, and in Eastern Europe runs from the Napoleonic Wars until the third quarter of the 19th century. The distinction and the lack of overlap in time is important to the extent that the Western European experience could have been considered as a model of the future economic and social development of Eastern Europe. However, if a comparison were made of the situation in Western Europe with that of Eastern Europe during a particular point in time, more striking contrasts than similarities would be found. While the economies of Western Europe were caught up in the process of economic growth, the economies of Eastern Europe during the same period were in a state of relative stagnation, in which the process of economic development either did not get off the ground or was arrested by the prevailing political regime. While in the West the end of the 18th and the beginning of the 19th centuries witnessed new economic opportunities for its indigenous population and for immigrants, the Jews included, the wholesale bankruptcy of the Jewish community organizations of Poland in the second half of the 18th century and the economic plight of the majority of the Polish and Russian Jews around the turn of the 19th century were examples of the different situations of the Jewish communities in various countries during the same points in time.

How did the Jews fare under the conditions which were defined as the transition period? There is no doubt that the initial benefits were considerable since they signified the changed status of the Jews. Even in the absence of equal civil rights or true emancipation they meant an increased sense of personal security, a decrease in arbitrariness, and a greater recourse to the prevailing law of the land. It is possible to describe, rather than measure, the economic effects of these transitional changes upon the activities of the Jews in two distinct areas, labor and capital.

The loosening of restrictions affecting places of habitat or work made it possible for labor to move more freely in search of markets with higher earnings.

Thanks to the relaxation of restrictions upon entering particular professions, Jews could avail themselves of training opportunities or enter educational institutions with hopes for upward social mobility and higher incomes. The rising demand for new types of employment, spurred by the accelerated pace of economic development, provided possibilities for absorption of at least a part of the relatively large groups of unemployed members of the Jewish communities in the labor market. The greater degree of personal safety and security of their assets had a number of effects upon Jewish owners of capital. There was a reduction of the size of reserves previously kept as personal insurance against various emergencies. The size of such reserves for Jewish merchants was variously estimated as up to a third of their wealth. By reducing the reserve it was possible to devote a larger part of total wealth to productive use. The improvement of the legal position of the Jews increased the amount of credit that could be extended to them without excessive risks on the part of the lenders. This development in turn probably led to a decrease in the rates of interest at which Jews could borrow. Added security and new opportunities enabled the Jewish owners of capital to use it in a number of areas (real estate, industry) hitherto closed to them, thus increasing both the returns and effectiveness of capital.

The removal of some discriminatory regulations (such as double taxation), which previously increased the costs for Jews of carrying on economic activities and affected the size of their income, had the effect of increasing their disposable income and could have led to simultaneous growth in, or to a redistribution of the shares of, consumption and savings. In some cases an increase of savings (or investment) could be expected, in other cases an increase of consumption or an increase in family size could follow. With regard to the last, it is clear that even partial removal of some discriminatory rules applied to the Jews, like restrictions on settlement, on marriage, and the like, resulted in an increase in the birth rate and population growth.

The transition period can be characterized as the beginnings of consideration of the "Jewish problem" as a matter of social and national policies for the states and societies in Europe, in contradistinction to earlier preoccupation with fiscal interests, Church concerns, or narrowly defined group competition. The growing concern of the state with the economic activity of the Jews was exhibited in various attempts by governments to influence such activity. Some attempts could be classified as representing a policy of "productivization" of Jews and attempts to change the social composition of the Jewish population. Interesting examples of such policies, perhaps in part also inspired by physiocratic thought, were the attempts to settle Jews on the land by "enlightened absolutist" regimes as those of Joseph II in Austria and Alexander I in Russia. It is immaterial here that such attempts were completely unsuccessful, either because the schemes were insufficiently prepared and financed or because they were sabotaged by the bureaucracy that was to administer them. The disappointments of tens of thousands of Jews and the sufferings of thousands who participated in the failing experiments are also not at issue. The important feature was the clearer realization that in part, at least, government policies were responsible for the peculiarities of Jewish economic activities or social structure and that state policies — as a part of the social and legal framework of Jewish activity — had to be brought in line with or adjusted to the economic changes that were taking place. Therefore, while during the transition period, government-sponsored agricultural colonization in southern Russia resulted in settling on land only a few thousand Jewish families and failed abysmally in Austria, it nevertheless raised by implication the problem of legal tenancy and ownership of land for Jews. This in turn resulted in the subsequent development of a small but socially diverse farming element in the Jewish communities of Eastern Europe during the 19th century.

Whatever the impact of the changing economic and social conditions upon the economic activities of the Jews, during the transition period the Jewish communities had to face an imminent, fundamental change. For the Jewish communities the problem was how to continue as a distinct group in the general society, not under conditions of forced separation but under those of free choice by their members. For the first time within the general period under consideration, it became possible for larger numbers of Jews to break away culturally and socially from the Jewish community, even while maintaining their religious beliefs, and to be accepted by the community at large. Social acceptance was offered to a small but influential minority of the Jews as remuneration for cultural assimilation. The price to pay was basically severance of their relations with the rest of the Jewish community and the abandonment of the active desire to perpetuate this community. Under the circumstances, the offer of social acceptance was a tempting one since it involved social advancement by the criteria of the community at large. That not every social group would accept its Jewish counterpart even at the price of cultural assimilation was obvious, but during the transition period personal or narrow group interests were strong and the fight for universal civil rights still very much ahead. The situation presented a challenge to the Jewish communal authority and called for its surrender of its traditional power of exclusive representation of the Jews and of its power of taxation. The weakening of the authority of the Jewish community organization could also be traced to the growing unwillingness of the more affluent groups in the community to subject themselves to income redistribution in favor of the poor. Poor-relief was "scaled down" from a duty concept to one of discretionary charity, and paupers were "encouraged" to find employment.

10
THE MODERN PERIOD

The main features of the development of the economy of the Jews during the modern period are patterns of migration, penetration into areas of industry, maintenance of a strong position in the area of services, and very limited involvement in agriculture. Decades ago economic historians were engaged in a debate about the role of the Jews in the development of capitalism, some trying to define the historically objective role of the Jews as active agents of capitalist development. Now with historical hindsight the discussion would probably be conducted and conclusions reached within a different framework. The implicit notion that capital was abundant in the Jewish sector of the economy would now be refuted and therefore the logic of portraying the Jews as "objectively acting" on behalf of a capitalist order would be rejected, although it would probably be accepted that an order of economic liberalism is one that provides greater opportunities for any minority, the Jews included, than an alternative economic system based upon a different ideology and set of political principles. An impersonal market and a high degree of division of labor may create alienation and other social ills, but by not requiring that the commodities produced have any labels other than the price tag the free market works against discrimination. A competitive market may injure high-cost producers or cause unemployment, but its principles were compatible with the ideas of social and cultural pluralism. The relatively favorable response of Jews and other minorities to the liberalization of the economic order was based primarily on an expected reduction in discrimination. However, while a liberal economic order provided the Jews with opportunities, it could not provide them with a right to work, to compete on equal terms, to the same extent that such a "right" was traditionally enjoyed by the various classes of the majority population. In addition, the phase of economic liberalism as a chief characteristic of the capitalist system was neither a permanent feature nor a very long lasting one, nor even one universally followed in all countries experiencing the capitalist type of economic growth.

In most countries of Eastern Europe the capitalist stage of development coincided with a rise of nationalism, which at various points exhibited a discriminatory attitude toward the Jews in general or toward some social groups within the Jewish community, in attempts to promote the interests of the ethnic majority. Tariff policies against foreign goods were accompanied not infrequently by discriminatory taxation imposed upon "foreigners" within the country, meaning national minorities. In the multi-national states of Eastern Europe there were ample opportunities for labeling various minorities as "foreign," "alien," and so on. Under such conditions it could hardly be expected that the Jewish masses, who were adversely affected by discriminatory policies, would consider the capitalist economic system as more desirable or attractive than an alternative promising them the "right to work."

It is against the background of insufficient employment opportunities and the presence of discrimination that the process of migration has to be viewed.

JEWISH MIGRATIONS

The pattern of Jewish migration, of spatial mobility of labor, during the modern period differed in many respects from previous migration patterns. The general direction was a western one, from Eastern Europe to the West, and from Europe overseas. As a matter of fact, the migration from Western Europe overseas was more than made up for by an influx of Jews from the East. This general direction of the migration was significant as a movement from less rapidly developing countries to more rapidly developing ones. In terms of its time dimension the inter-country migration was intensified during the 19th century and reached its peak during the decade prior to World War I. But apart from the inter-country migration of very considerable significance was the intra-country migration from the less urbanized areas to the more urbanized areas, a development that increased the degree of concentration of the Jewish population in large urban and metropolitan areas, with their developed industry, trade, and other social or cultural characteristics. Both the domestic and international migration and the pattern of settlement of the Jews contributed to urban concentration and had an impact upon the social and economic structure of the Jewish population. While it is tempting to assign the role of prime mover in Jewish migrations to purely economic causes, it would be erroneous to omit political elements such as discriminatory legislation, violent anti-Semitism, pogroms, and revolutions. Political upheavals and governmental policies influenced the pace of the migration process, but could not stop it for any appreciable length of time (the case of the Soviet Union being an exception).

What were the characteristic features and effects of the migration process as a whole and of its various forms? The migration process started as soon as the Jewish population could rise above the level of poverty and isolation to which it had deteriorated in Eastern Europe by the end of the 18th and first half of the

19th centuries and regain its age-old habits of mobility. In terms of numbers, the migration stream from Europe during the 100 years preceding World War II accounted for approximately 4,000,000 individuals, of which over 70% went to the United States, about 10% each to South America and Palestine, and the rest to Canada, South Africa, Australia, and other countries. Thus, in view of the fact that the North American continent absorbed three-quarters of the total international (or overseas) migration, the characteristics of this migration may be assumed as the most typical.

The available data indicate that the migration was a family one (of whole families, even if separated by a one- or two-year period) rather than of single individuals; that it was a migration for settlement and not for work, saving, and return; and that it was a migration involving a relatively very high percentage of skilled workers. With respect to the last characteristic, we can rely only on the data, but not do much exploration beyond; the explanation of this phenomenon can only be surmised. It is logical to assume that the process of overseas migration required payment of transportation costs, in other words some amount of savings, and thus could not involve paupers. Therefore, it is logical to assume that the migrants were either members of the industrial labor force, or entrants into the labor force who already had acquired skills, or individuals who acquired particular skills in anticipation of their migration, having made an investment over and above their transportation costs or borrowed in anticipation of future returns. It was in large measure due to the industrial skills and some working habits of the migrants that their future relative success can be explained.

Three further points need to be emphasized in connection with the migration problem. First, given the nature of the family ties within the Jewish community, the financing of migration took place within the extended family of the immigrants and was later also subsidized by the earnings of the immigrants, often virtually out of their first savings. Secondly, prior to the end of the 19th century there were already in operation well-organized voluntary associations that assisted in the migration process. In their absence the economic and psychological costs of migration would have been considerably higher. Thirdly, by organizing voluntary associations of mutual assistance, in part copying the models from Eastern Europe, the immigrants were able to help the new arrivals more effectively. Some relatively small part, probably not more than about 3% of the total of the migration movement, was financed and assisted by funds donated or collected on behalf of the migration, especially in the presence of an ideological or programatic background. The two most outstanding examples were Palestine and the agricultural settlements in Argentina.

The primary effect of both the intra-regional and international migration of the Jews was to decrease the competition for employment opportunities where such were scarce and provide a higher return for the migrants where their labor and skills were in greater demand. Thus while the income of the migrants increased in comparison with their previous income level, the income level of those who remained behind did not fall. However, it must be admitted that the movement of millions of people within a few generations deprived the established Jewish communities of a young, enterprising, and skilled element. This movement had a number of demographic, economic, and cultural repercussions on the European Jewish communities. It is difficult to pinpoint such effects, but it certainly affected the age structure of the European communities by removing some of the middle groups (age groups 20–40 in particular). It also perhaps affected adversely the growth rate of the Jewish population in Europe, although it would be difficult to predict what that rate would have been under worse economic conditions in the absence of migration. In terms of its impact upon the social structure, it probably increased the economic polarization within the Jewish communities since neither the rich nor the very poor contributed to the migration stream. In another sense the migration movement contributed to a greater stability within the Jewish communities since it absorbed much of the unruly and non-traditionally inclined element of the community. Last but not least, the migration movement contributed to an activated exchange among Jewish communities, with a money transfer to Eastern Europe that not only subsidized further migration but supported relatives and community institutions, and that was in part compensated by an export of cultural and spiritual services from Europe to the areas of new settlement.

PENETRATION INTO INDUSTRIAL EMPLOYMENT

Some assessment must be made of the conditions that enabled Jews to penetrate into industrial employment and maintain their position in the areas of services under conditions of modern industrialization. What adjustment was required on their part to attain their goals? Here we are concerned with entrepreneurial activities in the industrial sector as well as the transformation of handicraft employment into small-scale and larger scale industrial employment. This entrepreneurial activity is not being considered here in terms of "Jewish contributions" to the development of this or that country, or the amassing of wealth by individuals of Jewish descent. It is beyond the purview of this account to dwell upon the Rothschilds in England and France, on the German-Jewish bankers, or on mining-magnates in Africa or South America. In addition, a distinction should be made between large-scale and small-scale entrepreneurs. While a few Jews entered industrial entrepreneurship via high finance, the banking system, etc., the multitude consisted of small-scale industrial entre-

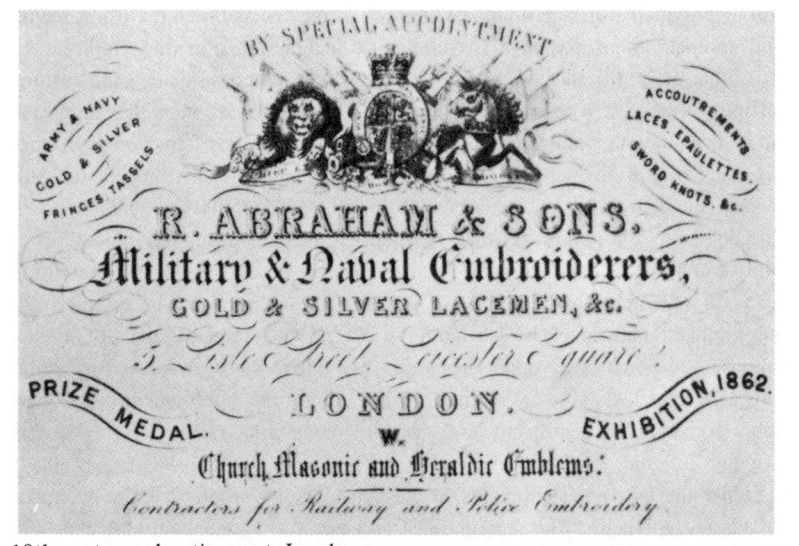

19th-century advertisement, London.

preneurs who were recruited mostly from the ranks of craftsmen and merchants, previously engaged in the putting-out system. They were subordinate to and dependent upon the large-scale industrial establishments because they could hardly compete with large-scale industrial firms in the production of goods and had therefore either to become suppliers to the large firms of some specialized goods or producers of market goods that were outside the assortment manufactured by large-scale industry. Given the scarcity of capital in the social milieu from which the small-scale producers or entrepreneurs were recruited, their proximity to industrial centers and markets was absolutely crucial. Small-scale industrial firms did not possess the capital to carry large stocks, and quick turnover was their only mode of survival. A great deal of flexibility in product-mix and in assuring sources of demand was required to keep the enterprises in operation. They also required a labor force skilled but not overly specialized and with relatively few employment alternatives to accept a less-than-regular employment. This was a typical solution for economic branches that operated with a basically backward technology at low levels of productivity, low wages, and long hours of work, in what were fringes of the consumer goods industries. It was due to the declining role of handicraft production, which was suffering from industrial competition, that this type of industrial employment was acceptable to Jewish industrial job-seekers.

Jewish entrepreneurs did, however, play an important role in providing gainful employment for large numbers of Jews. It may be assumed that for a Jewish entrepreneur there existed a "psychological income" in providing employment for other Jews, whether he did so for reasons of greater familiarity and cultural affinity or because it was considered a "good deed" in cases when discrimination in favor of Jewish employees increased his operational costs. Those costs in turn depended upon the nature of the labor supply and the distribution of skills within the Jewish labor force and within the total population. If the costs of hiring Jewish labor were less than or equal to those of hiring other members of the labor force, it can be assumed that there were no costs in the discrimination in favor of employing Jews. As we will see from a number of examples, the employment pattern of Jewish labor by Jewish entrepreneurs did not in fact impose additional costs upon the employers. There were, however, two other obstacles that had to be overcome in order to have the employment of a Jewish labor force reach a significant level. The first constraint was the assumed or real strength of the religious taboo against work on the Sabbath, regardless of whether the taboo was expressed in the behavior of workers or in the attitudes of the entrepreneurs. The second constraint was the assumed animosity of non-Jewish workers and foremen toward Jewish co-workers. There is no doubt that such constraints upon the entrepreneurs were real, especially in the later part of the 19th century in Eastern Europe.

The cases of a few industries in Europe and one in the U.S. are instructive since they provide a broad spectrum of employment opportunities created by Jewish entrepreneurs for Jewish workers. One is the textile industry in Russian Poland in which Jewish spinners, weavers, and other textile workers were predominantly employed in the smaller scale enterprises, while the larger scale factories refrained from employing them. Second is the case of the forestry trade, in which few Jewish workers and laborers could compete successfully with the low paid peasants seeking off-season employment in lumbering. Therefore, thousands of Jews were employed in this industry by Jewish firms as overseers in the forests, saw-mills, and transportation of the products, much of the output being destined for export or railroad construction. Thus, the demand for trained personnel with a degree of familiarity with the operation and quality standards in forestry and with some clerical skills attracted many Jewish workers and employees. While such a combination of skills was rare in the general labor force, and the wages and salaries accepted by the Jewish workers were generally low, there was hardly any cost of discriminating in favor of Jewish employment in the forestry trade. In the third case, the sugar and oil industries may be subsumed under one type of employment. Neither in sugar-beet growing nor in the processes of sugar refining were Jews represented. The same is true for the oil industry located outside the Jewish Pale of Settlement. The Jews could compete neither with the peasants and local oil-workers nor with the highly skilled specialists in sugar and oil refining. The areas of employment for Jews provided for them by Jewish entrepreneurs were those of distribution and trade. Thus, thousands of Jews were employed as clerical personnel, salesmen, and sales agents in the trade-networks of both the sugar and oil industries. The outstanding case of industrial employment provided by Jewish entrepreneurs for Jewish workers in the U.S. is the garment industry. The levels of skill brought over by the Jewish immigrants, the relatively low wage schedule of the garment industry and the relatively small scale of the operations of the firms led to a high concentration of Jewish workers, with the industry as a whole serving as a massive source of employment.

The above examples illustrate some of the patterns of the penetration by Jews into areas of industrial employment. They are indicative of the manner in which masses of former artisans and pauperized elements of the Jewish community could join the ranks of industrial workers and employees. As in other societies, child labor and long-term apprenticeship were the chief means of skill-acquisition for the poor. Although the capital-goods industries were virtually closed for both Jewish entrepreneurs and workers alike, industrial employment concentrated in consumer goods industries signified the adjustment to modern, industrial society and injected a new dynamism both in the social relations within the Jewish communities and with the community at large.

MAINTENANCE OF POSITIONS IN THE SERVICE SECTOR OF THE ECONOMY

The service sector includes employment in trade, transportation and communication, public and private services and the so-called free professions. For the huge segment of the Jewish population previously employed in it, largely in trade and particularly commodity trade, the problem of economic survival within this sector became absolutely essential. During the early period of industrialization when massive investments are made in the build-up of physical industrial capital — primarily in construction and equipment and in some of the services of the social overhead type such as railroad and road-building — the majority of the services are not recipients of capital. It is only when the basic capital in industry is created, and both the producers' goods and consumers' goods branches are producing at relatively high levels of productivity, that the demand for services increases on the part of a population whose general level of income has risen very substantially. The fact that Jews were heavily concentrated in the service sector in countries whose pace of development was slow, whose market growth was sluggish, and whose levels of personal income were among the lowest in Europe, did not augur well for service employees. It was, therefore, not so much a matter of historical foresight but a lack of viable alternatives that kept large masses of Jews within this sector during the early stages of industrialization. It was the gradual process of commercialization of agriculture that provided outlets for the commodity trade and thus for service employment for the Jews who were living in rural areas or small towns. Urbanization provided other opportunities for employment in trade and also in other services; but paradoxically the process of urbanization and the development of service opportunities in the large cities significantly undercut or substituted the service functions previously performed in small towns. The process of urbanization was accompanied by the development of a more dense transportation network, one creating direct links between the big cities and the hinterland, which decreased transportation and travel costs and made the big city and rural areas accessible to one another. The result was that many of the services concentrated in the small towns could no longer be performed at the prices offered in the big cities where economies of scale were more likely; and the decline of small towns under the conditions of a competitive market followed. The problem for Jewish service employment was whether the opportunities available to Jews in the big cities were sufficient to compensate or substitute for the disappearance of such opportunities in the small towns and also allow for the rate of Jewish population increase. The answer for Eastern Europe appears to be a negative one, for Western Europe a positive one. In the U.S.A. we find a secular trend of employment growth in the service sector for the Jews. In Eastern Europe the crisis of the small towns remained a continuous problem especially exacerbating for the Jews when coupled with discriminatory policies of limiting access or prohibiting the influx of Jewish service employees in such branches as the civil service, central government or municipal services, and public transportation. In countries that did not follow openly discriminatory policies, the solution of the service employment problem for the Jews became very much dependent upon both the general pace of economic development and the urbanization process.

The diversity of service employment makes it very difficult to estimate the degree of substitution of one type of employment for another or the mobility of individuals from one category to another within this sector. The required educational background differed substantially; and substitution or transfers were possible probably at the lower levels of skills, in which literacy could be considered the predominant, if not universally sufficient, prerequisite. Internal mobility within the service sector was much less frequent at higher levels of specialization and especially when the specific training presupposed a higher level of schooling. The explanation of the continuity of a high proportion of

Jewish employment in the area of services would be incomplete if two other factors were overlooked. The first was the opening up of opportunities in the so-called free professions; the second was the continued demand for special services generated within and performed expressly for the Jewish communities. The first phenomenon, entry into the free professions, was a result of the reduced effectiveness of discriminatory policies toward Jews in the area of secondary and higher education relative to the areas of the public services. Educational opportunities that provided employment possibilities in the free professions became attractive avenues of social and economic advancement for the Jewish middle class, previously employed primarily in commodity trade. Therefore, with employment in the public sector and in the civil service very much restricted and curtailed for eligible Jewish candidates, the typical employment pattern was in the private service sector, including health services, educational services, and legal services. In addition, the private service sector provided employment opportunities for a certain number of educated individuals as salaried employees, such as bookkeepers, legal clerks, and pharmacists's assistants.

The demand for services by and for the Jewish communities continued during this period, although the process of secularization tended to shift the demand from the purely religious areas to those of education, health, and social services. Attempts to maintain a general cultural and not only an exclusively religious identity helped to sustain the demand for educational services. Meanwhile, the pattern of settlement in urban and metropolitan areas created a demand for the development of a communication network by which some of the cultural needs could be met and thus supported the activities of the press, theater, literary activities, and the like. Given the fact that public services in the area of health for the total population were highly inadequate and that the Jewish population received even less than a proportionate share of those, the demand for health and social services provided within and by the Jewish community was very strong. This stimulus was instrumental in the provision of such services either on a private basis or as a part of the welfare activites carried on by the community authorities for needy members.

EMPLOYMENT IN THE AGRICULTURAL SECTOR

Farming played a very subordinate role in the employment structure of the Jewish population during this period and its share in total employment was relatively small. It is not difficult to provide an explanation for this phenomenon. During the 19th century and later agriculture in Europe was a declining industry, releasing rather than attracting labor. In addition, previous discriminatory policies prevented land ownership, and restricted land tenure for Jews to the extent that farming as a skill did not develop within the Jewish milieu. Although the lifting of some of the most severe restrictions rendered farming a plausible alternative to the precarious positions of small town traders or artisans, a number of circumstances mitigated against a mass influx of Jews into farming. Land was becoming relatively expensive in Eastern Europe, and the returns to both capital and labor in agriculture were relatively small. Settlement on large land tracts and the establishment of colonies required sizeable capital outlays and a degree of organizational effort beyond the available resources and authority of the organized Jewish communities. The pattern of individual settlement in a dispersed manner was discouraged on the one hand by religious and traditional attitudes, since it typically involved a high degree of cultural isolation, and on the other hand by an often hostile rural environment, suspicious of any aliens settling in its midst. Within the Jewish milieu or as part of Jewish folklore, the stigma of boorishness or coarseness was associated with Jewish farmers, characteristics of a low prestige status, not so much in economic terms as in general cultural ones.

In spite of all the disincentives, the 19th century witnessed the employment in agriculture of less than 5% of the economically active Jewish population. It is interesting to note that it is impossible to establish any meaningful correlation between the size of the Jewish farm population in particular countries and the levels of economic development of such countries, nor is the size of the Jewish population related to the incidence of farming among the Jews in the European countries. Thus, primarily local conditions and opportunities within the countries appear to have been important in determining the regions of greater involvement of Jews in agriculture; the inter-country comparisons do not explain much, if anything.

Outside of Europe, however, two types of development have to be considered: one, countries of rapidly developing agriculture in which the employment of Jews in this sector of the economy was not significant, the United States and Canada being prime examples; and second, countries in which the employment share of agriculture was higher than in most of Europe, the specific cases being Palestine and Argentina. With respect to the first group, two factors might explain the relatively low share of agriculture in the employment distribution. The first and foremost was the greater attractiveness of employment opportunities for immigrants in the industrial and service sectors, coupled with the preference for urban settlement, which provided additional security to the immigrants as members of their own ethnic communities. The second was the timing of the large migration streams which took place after the closing of the so-called "agricultural frontier." In the case of Palestine and Argentina we are dealing with an induced process in which some non-economic variables were of utmost importance. In the case of Palestine the ideological aspect, the Zionist idea, motivated a relatively high percentage of the immigrants to settle on land, beginning with the last decades of the 19th century; farming became as much a way of life as a profession. In Argentina a substantial segment of the immigration was sponsored by adherents of agricultural colonization schemes who induced agricultural employment by paying the transportation costs and providing land for agricultural group settlement in the name of ideas of productivization of unskilled and unemployed members of the Jewish community. However, the long-term trend both in Palestine, later the State of Israel, and in Argentina was the relative decrease of farm employment under the impact of industrialization and urbanization.

INCOME

Given the employment structure of the Jewish population during the modern period, what could be said about the level and distribution of income within this population?

At the beginning of the period and in a number of countries during much of it, the average income of the Jews was below that of the population at large, including the peasants. However, the level of income increased during this period both as a result of the total increase of incomes in Europe in general and because of the impact of migration, which given its direction from economically less prosperous areas to economically more prosperous ones, had a net impact of increasing the average income level of the Jewish population. In addition, because of its composition as an increasingly urbanized population and one concentrated in the industrial and service sectors of the economy, its income most probably increased at a higher rate than the average income of the total population of the countries of their habitat during the 100 years preceding World War II. As a rule of thumb it would probably not be incorrect to assume that the average income level of the Jewish population by the end of the period reached a level that was higher than the average for farmers and industrial workers, although probably not above the level of the skilled stratum of industrial workers and salaried employees. Another way of saying this is that Jewish income was at about the average level of the urban population. The level of Jewish income fluctuated around the general upward trend. The fluctuations were pronounced first because of the relatively large proportion of self-employed, a social group whose income is less stable than that of salaried workers and employees, secondly, because of the impact of exogenous factors such as wars and major upheavals during which the property of the Jews was much more vulnerable than that of other population groups (e.g., the forced mass exile of Russian Jews from the war zones in World War I and the wave of pogroms in the Ukraine 1918—21, during which property was either destroyed, expropriated or simply taken away by force from its rightful owners). Thirdly, during the downturns of the business-cycle Jews as a minority group usually suffered more than the average member of the society at large. But notwithstanding such fluctuations the general trend of Jewish income-growth on a global scale was an upward one.

How was this income distributed, and what were the basic determinants of its distribution? Both tendencies to increase and to decrease the income inequality were at work, and it would be very difficult to measure the separate effects with any degree of precision. Following intuitive judgment it would be sensible to assume that in the countries in which the impact of discrimination against Jews was the strongest, income inequality within the Jewish community was probably more pronounced than in the countries that followed a more liberal policy toward the Jews. That income inequality within the Jewish community led to tensions, internal struggle, and organized activities of one social group against the other is obvious. That the divergency of interests led to the development of different ideologies and that these intensified the divisive tendencies in the community is no surprise, being a reflection within the Jewish milieu of what was taking place within the population at large. It is also true that the internal struggles within the Jewish communities during the last decades of the 19th century and beginning of the 20th century made a considerable contribution toward reforming the community authorities, toward their democratization and modernization. They thereby became much more responsive to the needs of their members. But whatever generalizations are attempted in order to bring under a common denominator the economic and social trends prevailing during the modern period, the significant differences of the developmental patterns of the Jewish communities can be better understood only upon a closer examination of at least the major Jewish communities. The ones selected for further scrutiny are the Western European, the Eastern European, the U.S., and the Palestine Jewish communities.

WESTERN EUROPE

The economic development of Western European Jewish communities during the modern period can be generally characterized by their successful attempts to join the middle class. Their problems roughly paralleled the problems of the middle class in Europe, in the sense that they enjoyed apparent well-being and security under normal conditions and discovered the precariousness of their position in times of crisis. Western Europe, following the example of England, experienced the industrial revolution around the middle of the 19th century and was busily involved in adjusting its institutional structure to fit the new economic order. Since the institutional adjustment was more complicated, while vestiges of the older order had to be destroyed, eliminated or transformed, and the state played a much more decisive role in the process of economic transformation on the European continent than in England, one finds there a greater degree of politization of economic issues than in England. The politization of economic issues provided a specific impetus for the activities of the middle class and had a profound impact upon the activities and attitudes of the Western European Jews.

At a time when new economic opportunities were being created in Western Europe, the Jewish population of those countries was relatively sparse and the Jews constituted a negligible percentage of the total population. Therefore, we find within the Jewish communities very little of the fierce competition for relatively scarce economic opportunities which characterized the situation of the Eastern European Jews. The process of urbanization and concentration of the Jewish population in Western and Central Europe started relatively early, but proceeded gradually, largely undisturbed by outside political factors. Migration, both internal and overseas, by the less prosperous members of the Jewish communities helped to achieve the aims of both the migrants as well as those who stayed behind, and resulted in strengthening of the drive to penetrate into the middle class. The gradualism of the process of economic growth, coupled with the availability of economic opportunities in the new centers of industry and commerce, helped to develop among the Western European Jews a preference for independent economic activity. In other words, the Jews accepted middle class values and acted accordingly. Economic integration of the Jews in Western European society meant self-employment in trade, finance, industry and free professions and not in manual labor. This process was facilitated by their utilization of the opportunities provided by the educational system and the marked decrease in discriminatory attitudes and policies.

The groundwork for the development of more liberal attitudes toward the Jews and for the readiness on the part of the Jews to take advantage of the new economic and social opportunities was prepared by the ideas of the Enlightenment period and by the impact of the Enlightenment upon the Jewish milieu. Originally the new opportunities for social acceptance were offered to the upper strata of Jewish communities for the price of language assimilation and severance of their ties with the Jewish community. The upper strata of the Jews found the conditions acceptable and acted accordingly. When the opportunities to join the middle class became available to a larger number of Western European Jews and after they joined the political struggle of the middle class for broader suffrage, the problem of emancipation and of their civil rights was raised by the members of the Jewish middle class. Emancipation and civil rights for Jews meant a further integration of the Jews with the society, not within the concept of a Christian state but within a modern, secularized state. In the latter case language assimilation of the Jews was considered an insufficient prerequisite. The existence of Jewish Orthodoxy both as a symbol and major characteristic of their culture was considered a serious obstacle to real integration. Thus we find both the changing patterns of employment among the Jews and the desire for cultural assimilation at the roots of the religious Reform movement which spread from Germany. As a result we observe that the gradual adjustment of religious rituals to modern conditions and some relaxation of the Orthodox law, which previously supported the exclusiveness and guarded the separation of the Jews from their environment, gained in appeal to the majority of the Western European Jews. An interesting by-product of the changes in the social position and cultural attitudes was the growing gulf between the Western European and Eastern European Jews. The cultural ties were becoming looser and the sense of a common destiny weaker.

The penetration of the Jews into the middle class was a slow process which marked the second half of the 19th century. Its success over the period was unmistaken, but not necessarily continuous and certainly not without problems. It was challenged first by a wave of nationalism at the end of the century, when it became clear that the new social order in Europe could not guarantee the universal fulfillment of the rising expectations in the short run. The new wave of nationalism exhibited anti-Semitic aspects which gained currency among members of the European middle class. The Dreyfus affair and other manifestations of anti-Semitism had a profound impact upon some members of the Western European Jewish communities and forced them to rethink and revise their notions of social and cultural integration. Although the majority continued to behave according to previously established patterns, a minority turned to solutions of either cultural pluralism or Jewish nationalism as the more satisfactory for the long run. A greater need was also felt for the maintenance of Jewish cultural (including religious) continuity and for closer ties with other Jewish communities. The net result was a somewhat decreased atomization of the Western European Jewish communities and their activities as well as the development of new cultural and economic institutions which strengthened the sense of Jewish identity and were instrumental in the moments of crises that lay ahead.

EASTERN EUROPE

To explain the economic activities of the Jewish communities in Eastern Europe during the third quarter of the 19th century and until World War II in purely economic terms, in terms of the market opportunities, demand for products and labor supply would be not only a difficult task but would provide incomplete and sometimes misleading answers. Since we know so much more about the economic conditions of this period, we are keenly aware of the interaction of the economic and extra-economic factors, be they political, legal, or psychological. The outstanding characteristic of the other factors was the existence of a measure of discrimination against the Jews that was much more intense in this part of the world than elsewhere. Thus, in spite of the progress of a modern market economy, in spite of the process of industrialization that took place there, there was a strong residue of discrimination that limited the benefits of economic progress for the Jews and affected their economic activities. One rather striking example is to be found in the exile of Jews from the rural areas of Russia in the 1880s. The process of urbanization that took place as a result of industrial development is a familiar phenomenon and one that affected Jews in the rural areas. But there is a qualitative difference between a process that creates new opportunities in urban areas and draws labor away from the rural areas, and a mass exile that uproots tens of thousands and forcibly transplants them in a new economic and social environment with no visible means for their economic survival and with no economic alternatives since the demand for their labor or service is absent. Apart from such major catastrophes, the conditions of discrimination included a whole chain of minor calamities which created an atmosphere of uncertainty and determined the behavior of large masses of the Jewish population in Eastern Europe. Thus, the development of a capitalist society in Eastern Europe, while creating new economic opportunities was, as far as the Jews were concerned, accompanied by unsettling features that were constantly threatening to destroy the benefits bestowed by the economic progress.

It is thus proper to emphasize that the economic and social conditions of the majority of the Jews in Eastern Europe were influenced by a number of external constraints, one of which was the Pale of Settlement in Russia. The existence of the Pale of Settlement limited the mobility of most of the Jews and virtually excluded them from some of the more important regions and dynamic centers of industry, trade, and public life and often forced them to accept opportunities that could be described as second best. The existence of legal and economic discrimination made the process of social mobility much more difficult and expensive for the Jews. The limitations on entering areas of employment, professions, public service, and education decreased their chances of fully contributing to the process of economic development and benefiting from it.

While the advancement of the industrialization process destroyed some traditional areas of Jewish economic activity and created new ones, the process itself was erratic and did not allow for the formation of long-term expectations or less costly adjustments. Thus, while on the whole the Jewish population benefited from the process, growing in size and slowly improving in income position, the accompanying hardships were burdensome and unsettling. Given the relatively slow pace of economic progress of the regions of concentrated Jewish population in Eastern Europe (western part of the Russian empire, north-eastern part of the Hapsburg Empire, and Rumania), coupled with the existence of discriminatory policies, these regions were primarily involved in the emigration of Jews to Western Europe and America. But although emigration had the function of a safety valve, it could not counteract the impact of the industrialization process, which, while injecting a new dynamism in the economic and social sphere, affected the life of the Jewish communities by creating new areas of internal conflicts and was threatening to destroy the traditional values built up through centuries of relative cultural isolation. To the extent that they represented breaks with previous traditions and emphasized the existence of new opportunities, the very processes of industrialization and urbanization raised the level of expectations of the Jewish masses and made them more aware of their relationship to the outer world. This led to the development of new patterns of thought, increased sensitivity to the conditions of discrimination, and a more intensive search for new solutions to the specific problems of the Jews. The awareness of common specific problems was demonstrated not only in the economic but also in the cultural sphere. In spite of some tangible returns to the cultural assimilation of groups of Jews, until the end of the period a cultural homogeneity of the Jewish population in Eastern Europe was preserved. This culture embraced the basic elements of traditional moral and religious values with an addition of modern elements developed during the period following the Enlightenment in Eastern Europe. While the symbiosis of the elements of the traditional culture with those of a secular, modern and nationally oriented one was by no means harmonious, the tensions had a culturally stimulating effect. The period became one of very intensive cultural activity and creativity by the Eastern European Jews, marked by the revival and modernization of Hebrew literature and development of modern Jewish literature in Yiddish. For the first time in the history of the Jews cultural activities, apart from rudimentary religious training and bare literacy, penetrated and affected the Jewish lower classes, who had previously been excluded from most of their cultural heritage.

The period between World War I and World War II witnessed a number of new developments in Eastern Europe that were of major significance for the

Jewish population. The most important events were the revolution in Russia and the establishment of new national states in the region on the ruins of the two large empires that had long dominated the political scene in Eastern Europe prior to World War I. The positive effect of the political changes was the granting of citizenship and civil rights to the Jews in the new states. On the negative side were the growth of nationalism of the dominant ethnic groups and continuation of de facto discrimination against the Jews in most countries. Coupled with the difficult economic conditions in those countries, which were even more aggravated by government interference in the economic sphere, the precarious power balance in Europe, and the impact of the economic depression of the late 1920s and 1930s, thus worsened rather than improved the economic conditions of the Jewish population.

In the Soviet Union, after an initial gain resulting from the granting of civil rights and abolition of the Pale of Settlement by the democratic government of 1917, the period of the civil war inflicted heavy population losses upon the Jews, particularly in the Ukraine. The three outstanding features of Soviet policy toward the Jews were: the isolation of Soviet Jews from the Jewish communities abroad; the slow but consistent policy of destruction of their cultural autonomy, institutions, and organized forms of communal life, leaving cultural assimilation as the solution to their problems as individuals; and the destruction of the small town, the former locus of economic activity of the majority of Russian Jews as a result of the forced industrialization drive and the mobilization of human resources to build up the industrial base of the country. This policy led to a mass migration from the western parts of the Soviet Union (Belorussia and the Ukraine) to the metropolitan areas and new centers of industrial activity. Since education became one of the major vehicles of social advancement and was made available in the first instance to the urban population, a large proportion of the Jewish population took advantage of the opportunities and a marked shift in the employment pattern as well as in the professional composition took place. The Jews entered en masse into industrial employment and various service branches, all of which were nationalized and under the centralized control of the government. Although the social and economic advancement of the Jews in the Soviet Union should not be disputed, it raised two grave issues; one of cultural assimilation and the loss of group identity of the Jews, of their existence as a distinct cultural or religious entity; and the second, of their dependence as a group or as individuals upon the decisions lodged in the hands of the supreme policy makers of the country. The gravity of both issues arose, however, in a later period, following World War II.

THE UNITED STATES

The chief characteristic of the development of the Jewish community in the United States during the late 19th and early 20th centuries was its rapid numerical growth in comparison with other Jewish communities. The growth occurred primarily as a result of the immigration of the Jews, rather than because of the birth rate of the Jewish population per se. The attraction of the U.S. for Jewish immigrants could be explained both in terms of a wage-level relatively higher than in Europe, as well as an open immigration policy and the lack of specific anti-Jewish discrimination. However, the pace of immigration cannot be explained only in terms of increasing attraction, and the impetus to immigration of the Jews can be traced to events in the European countries of their origin, and the influence of the turns of the business cycle in the United States on the size of the immigration stream can be demonstrated. During the modern period there were two streams of Jewish immigration, one of Western European Jews and the other involving almost entirely Eastern European ones. Each of these streams, although different in terms of its occupational or professional endowment, was faced by similar problems of economic integration and general acculturation with the environment.

While the German Jews arrived with the experience of language assimilation and weakened sense of cultural traditions, and with the articulated desire to join the middle class, the Eastern European Jews arrived with industrial skills and the expressed willingness to be employed in any sector of the economy where opportunities were available, but without the experience of previous cultural assimilation. There was, therefore, among Jewish immigrants from Eastern Europe a strong preference for settling in compact masses for reasons of economic and psychological security. At the time of the first waves of mass immigration from Eastern Europe the Western European Jews (mostly immigrants from Germany) had already acquired in the U.S. a basically middle class or quasi-middle-class status, and their pattern of employment reflected a high percentage of self-employment and concentration in the area of services. The mass influx of Eastern European Jews changed for at least two generations the social composition of the Jewish community in the United States. It became a predominantly industrial and labor oriented community concentrated in major cities. The symbiosis of the two elements, the German and the East European, was ridden by conflicts and prejudices, by distinctions in wealth and status, the latter being derived from the degree of "americanization" or the duration of residence in the U.S. The German Jews, often in the role of employers of the recent immigrants, especially in the garment industry, tried to maintain the social distance between themselves and the immigrants arriving from the culturally most backward areas of Europe. Faced with the model of success presented by the German Jews the Eastern European immigrants could not avoid aspiring to positions of social and economic advancement. And while they accepted their status as manual workers and laborers as inevitable and drew from it a number of conclusions, expressed by their political orientation, trade union activities, etc., they actively sought an improvement in the economic position and status for their offspring. Thus, while the process of acculturation of the immigrants took time, the gradual social advancement of some was counterbalanced by the successive waves of immigration swelling the ranks of the Jewish industrial working population. It was not until after World War I and the harsh restrictions against Eastern European immigration that the process of penetration into the service sector and self-employment category became much more visible.

The rapid growth of the economy, the decline of agriculture and changes in its industrial structure, accompanied by a sustained, relatively high level of income made it possible for the service sector to develop. Aided by the availability of educational opportunities, the almost exclusively urban Jewish population found outlets for its employment in the service sector and the percentage of employment as unskilled labor, domestic service, or low paid industrial employment declined. It would be wrong to assume that the shift in employment and the resulting improvement in the income position of the Jews in the United States before World War II took place in the total absence of discrimination. There was in fact a whole range of discriminatory attitudes operating against the Jews, as against many other ethnic groups representing relatively recent immigration. There was, however, a major difference between the U.S. and Europe in that discrimination was a de facto attitude rather than a de jure, statutory, or legal arrangement, that it was a private matter rather than one of public policy. Like other groups of European origin, the Jews were relatively successful in minimizing the effects of discrimination, first by improving their economic position and second by using political power derived from their numbers and concentration in some major urban centers of the country. In addition, discrimination was met by the Jews with an almost atavistic reflex of communal activity. The Jewish community developed a time-honored self-defense mechanism against discrimination in the form of institutions designed to meet specific needs of individuals or groups within the community. In the absence of organized communal authorities, recognized either by the outside world or by the Jews themselves or representing their collective interests, the role of voluntary associations and institutions was even more significant for the discharge of group responsibilities and for the maintenance of whatever cohesion was possible within the Jewish community.

The numerical growth and economic advancement of the United States' Jewish community resulted in a change in the relationships among Jewish communities in the world, the U.S. Jewish community becoming an important source of economic assistance for the others. In a certain sense the bonds between American and European Jews, or the American and the Palestinian Jewish communities, provided a community of interest and purpose for the various groups of American Jewry, giving expression to their Jewish identity. At a time when the process of language assimilation in the U.S. was in progress, when the commonality of cultural concerns was diminishing, the "foreign aid" of American Jews provided them with much needed psychological satisfaction and helped to maintain their identity. This process turned out to be of particular importance for the subsequent developments, during and after World War II.

PALESTINE

While the first systematic attempts of organized mass colonization in Palestine go back to the 1870s and 1880s, a marked acceleration of the immigration stream occurred at the beginning of the 20th century, primarily as a result of the growth of a modern nationalist movement making immigration and settlement in Palestine the cornerstone of its ideology. The more organized manner of immigration and settlement, in part directed by a long-term national vision, led to the establishment of a social infra-structure within and for the Jewish population in Palestine, and to the establishment of modern social, economic, and educational institutions in an otherwise primitive and backward country. The introduction of modern institutions was accompanied by a striking attempt to modernize agriculture, a successful undertaking that integrated the need for economic modernization with the ideological factor of the need to recover the land, producing a sizeable agricultural sector within the Jewish community in Palestine. The fact that the agricultural sector embraced a variety of organizational forms of production, that alongside private agriculture a cooperative and even a communal network of farms was created, was of considerable importance for the further development of the economy. The ideas of cooperation were also applied to other sectors of the economy, in industry, construction and the services. Such enterprises had to reconcile private and social criteria in their decision making and had to accept procedures for social control, arrangements that provided a particular atmosphere for economic activity within the Jewish community.

The continuous numerical growth of the Jewish population, resulting from successive immigration waves and natural population increase and the emotional intensity of the issues connected with its development and its role among Jewish communities in the world, often obscured the interesting pattern of economic and social development of the Jewish community in Palestine. An important feature of the Jewish population in Palestine was its relatively homogeneous cultural background since the majority of immigrants came from Europe, Eastern Europe providing the lion's share. It possessed or created a full array of industrial, agricultural, and service skills at various levels, coupled with a level of education that was compatible with, if not in excess of the level of skills. The economic activities of the Jewish population, apart from restrictions on immigration, were conducted under conditions of virtual absence of discriminatory policies, particularly during the inter-war period. This in turn created a basically stable economic structure; the employment distribution did not change drastically over time. There was relatively less income inequality than within other Jewish communities. The level of income of the Jewish population in Palestine provided for the consumption needs of the population, with investment funds either imported by private investors from abroad, borrowed abroad, or provided as a form on nonreturnable transfers (gifts) from other Jewish communities to the Jewish community in Palestine.

While the above characteristics appear to portray the main features of economic and social conditions of the Jewish community in Palestine until World War II, they obviously do not convey the dynamics of the process of economic development per se. A more detailed treatment of this subject would have to include the economic relationships with the majority of the population, the Arabs; the extent of self-sufficiency achieved within the Jewish community; and the economic relations with the foreign markets to which some of the products of Jewish labor, land, and capital were exported and from which income was derived.

EPILOGUE

The interwar period that ended with the catastrophe of World War II, an event in the history of the Jews whose dimensions and consequences our present generation is still unable to perceive let alone define, was marked by the following characteristics: (1) the forced separation and isolation of one of the largest Jewish communities, namely that in the Soviet Union, from the rest of world Jewry; (2) the growth of the Jewish population in the United States and its relative economic strength in comparison with Jewish communities elsewhere created a new element in the balance and relationship between Jewish communities and indicated a future trend; (3) the economic situation of the European Jews, and especially of the East European communities, which worsened since economic and political uncertainty had become the norm even before the rise of Fascism and Nazism; (4) the rise of Nazism which created a direct danger to Jewish life and property in Central Europe, and the spread of discriminatory policies modeled upon the early legislation of Nazi Germany which became a real threat to a large part of European Jewry; given the limited opportunities for migration, the European Jewish population did not possess any real alternatives; (5) the growth of the Jewish community in Palestine which became an important cultural factor in the life of other Jewish communities, but its small relative size and the severe limitations imposed by the British upon Jewish immigration kept it from having a larger impact and from contributing toward a solution of European Jews' distress.

Therefore, prior to World War II, the Jewish communities found themselves at a crossroad, with the direction of their future fate and development depending upon exogenous, primarily political forces. The tragic results of World War II have left most of Europe virtually without Jews. There are now two major communities, that of the United States and that of the State of Israel, to shape the future of the Jews as a national entity. The third community, that of the Soviet Union, is a potential reservoir of future activity but for the time being largely an object of discriminatory policies. This situation of the Jewish communities, recovering from the physical disaster and psychological shock of World War II, made the economic relationship between the American Jewish community and the State of Israel one of the cornerstones of a policy of survival. The economics of the Jews, apart from the parochial interests of economists and economic historians, was geared toward the survival of the group during most of its recorded history.

Part Two

AGRICULTURE

1

Agriculture

In the Middle Ages. The transition of the Jews in the Diaspora to an urban population mainly constituted of merchants and artisans began from about the end of the eighth century. Yet Jews continued to regard agriculture as the ideal and most important Jewish occupation, the basis of the way of life and social ethics emerging from the Bible and permeating the whole of talmudic literature. In 13th-century Germany the Jewish moralist Eleazar ben Judah of Worms, in describing the primary, divinely ordained state of society, relates that God "created the world so that all shall live in pleasantness, that all shall be equal, that one shall not lord it over the other, that all shall cultivate the land . . ." However, "when warriors multiplied, and every man relied on his might, when they left off cultivating the land and turned to robbery, He brought down on them the Flood" (*Hokhmat ha-Nefesh*, 22b). The utopian agricultural society is here described as being destroyed by knightly feudal behavior which brought divine retribution on the world. Ideals of this kind continued to persist and have inspired the return to the soil in Zionism and related attempts at Jewish colonization in modern times.

The place of agriculture in Jewish economic and social life steadily diminished from the fourth century. Increasingly severe edicts were issued by Christian emperors prohibiting Jews from keeping slaves, first applying to Christian slaves only and then to all slaves. These restrictions obviated any large-scale Jewish agricultural undertakings by depriving them of workers. The Church also developed the conception that Jews should be denied any positions of authority or honor. This attitude later automatically excluded Jews from the feudal structure based on land ownership and the social structure which it combined. In these conditions, Jews were only fit for the lowest rank of serfs, but the religious and moral aspects of such a position made this impossible for all practical purposes.

Under Islamic administrations, both Jewish and Christian farmers bore the additional burden of a special land tax, the *Kharaj*, and suffered from a policy by which the produce delivered in land taxes was excessively undervalued. In Iraq, where there was a large concentration of Jews engaged in agriculture, they suffered from the general neglect of irrigation in the first two generations of Muslim rule. On the other hand, urban life and trading as an occupation were respected in Islamic society; they were a powerful attraction in the Caliphate, in particular to the Jew who wanted to escape oppressive discrimination in the villages. From the second half of the ninth century, the cultural milieux of the great Muslim cities like Baghdad drew increasing numbers of the population. The expansion of the Caliphate and the diversification of its economy provided growing opportunities for Jews in urban occupations. Additionally, the requirements of organized religion formed a further incentive to urbanization for the majority of Jews.

Thus from the end of the eighth century agriculture became a marginal Jewish occupation in both Christian and Muslim lands. However, Jews continued as farmers wherever legal and social conditions permitted. Large groups of Jewish farmers are known in North Africa in the ninth century. They are mentioned in connection with irrigation, gardening, viticulture, and the commercial production of cheese (which is known to have been stamped with the word *berakhah*, "blessing"). Livestock breeding was apparently an unimportant branch in Jewish agriculture. In Egypt in the 12th century Jews entrusted cattle or sheep to non-Jews to be raised for meat. Similarly, they frequently handed over fields, vineyards, orchards, and gardens to Gentile sharecroppers, although Jewish *bustāni* (gardeners) are mentioned in documents of the Cairo *Genizah*. They perhaps worked in "the orchard of the synagogue of the Palestinians" in Old Cairo (Fostat). While cheese making and beekeeping by Jews have a large place in the *Genizah* records, they are overshadowed by the production of wine. Naturally "pressers" of grapes are mentioned, although these probably worked only on a seasonal basis. Another agricultural specialist frequently mentioned in the *Genizah* from the 11th to the 13th centuries was the *sukkari*, the manufacturer and seller of sugar, which was produced mostly from cane but sometimes from raisins or dates. In western North Africa (the Maghreb) Jews owned cultivated land in the villages and city outskirts. Some of the tales of Rabbi Nissim ben Jacob of Kairouan (first half of the 11th century) have a rural or semirural setting and are probably located in North Africa.

After the Muslim conquest of Spain in 711, Jews there gradually entered the agrarian sphere taking advantage of changes such as the apportionment of land, liquidation sales, or the expropriation of rebels. Andalusia attracted a stream of immigrants from North Africa, including numerous Jews who were often skilled farmers. These possibly constituted the majority of Jewish landowners and peasants mentioned there in tenth-century records. Problems concerning cornfields and orchards are dealt with at length in the Spanish rabbinical responsa of the period, which also mention technical innovations, for instance pumping

methods. The Jewish *karram* (winegrower) had to see to every aspect of viticulture, from amelioration of the soil to grape pressing. After the Spanish territories passed to Christian rule, Jews continued to engage in agriculture. In Leon
and Castile, Aragon and Catalonia, Jews are often recorded as settlers and devel-
opers of newly occupied areas, frequently in collaboration with the monasteries.
Jews owned large tracts of land, in particular near the towns, since many members of the Jewish upper strata participated in the parcellation and recolon-
ization of lands captured from the Muslims during the Christian Reconquest
from the 12th century on. Some Jewish smallholders cultivated their own plots:
fields and pastures, orchards and gardens are mentioned. Jews also employed
hired labor. Some dealt in livestock and agricultural products, or engaged in
crafts based on agricultural materials, such as hides and fibers. It is not known
whether the raw material for the important Spanish-Jewish silk industry was
produced locally or bought from Sicilian Jews.

In Italy, Jewish economic activity was not subjected to legal restrictions until
the 16th century, but the majority of Jews there lived in the cities. However
their (probably uninterrupted) presence in rural areas, particularly in central and
southern Italy, is evidenced. Jews were among the first to cultivate the mulberry
in Italy, and the flourishing silk industry was largely controlled by Jews. In
Sicily Jews owned and cultivated vineyards and olive groves. Some excelled in
cultivating the date palm; Frederick II gave certain Jews the stewardship of his
private grove. Beside these farmers there were Jewish fishermen. Sicilian Jews
also owned land or herds which were looked after by non-Jews on a share-
cropping basis. Many Jews in Sicily in the 13th and 14th centuries were engaged
in commerce or crafts based on agriculture.

In southern France, especially in Provence, conditions were similar to those in
Spain and Italy. Great Jewish *allodia* are mentioned in the early Middle Ages;
some near Narbonne are recalled in a legendary context. In the greater part of
medieval France and Germany, however, the Jews who engaged in agriculture
were the exception rather than the rule. In the time of Charlemagne (eighth–
ninth centuries), some Jews still farmed large tracts of land. In suitable regions
Jews are found specializing in viticulture, fruit growing, and dairy farming. These
capital intensive and semiurban branches of agriculture could be combined with
commercial activities. In addition, while vineyards or orchards required expert
supervision, they did not demand continual labor, so that even scholars like
Rashi and Jacob Tam could grow grapes for a living while devoting time to
study.

In the Balkans and Greece, Benjamin of Tudela (mid-12th century) found a
Jewish community of 200 (families?) in Crissa, engaged in agriculture, and
another near Mount Parnassus. Further east, Jewish farmers are already found in

the tenth century. On the northern shores of the Black Sea they introduced advanced techniques of plowing and perhaps also new irrigation methods, and rice growing. Rice was in fact widely grown in the Volga region under the Khazars, but was discontinued after their downfall.

In Eastern Europe, Jews turned to the countryside more frequently from the 14th century. When expelled from many of the cities, they settled on the estates of the nobility and in villages. The transition was also due to their increasing connection with the growing and sale of wine. In Lithuania, Jewish settlement in the towns was early combined with agricultural activity. Thus Grand Duke Witold granted the Jews of Grodno in 1389 the right to "use the sown pasture land which they hold now or may acquire in the future, paying to our treasury the same as the gentile citizens." With the development of the *arenda* ("leasehold"; see p. 125) system and trade in agricultural products, the Jews in Poland-Lithuania became increasingly involved in agriculture as leaseholders of agricultural assets, for instance of distilleries or mills, or as administrators of the rural estates; they also dealt in everything pertaining to agriculture and supplied the needs of both peasants and landlords. The Jewish leaseholder *(arendar)* of agricultural assets on a large scale gradually developed into a kind of capitalist farmer, entering agriculture by providing capital and business management. The large number of small-scale *arendars* also became increasingly involved in village life and affairs. Not only the many Jews living near or in the villages, but also those in the small Jewish townships that became characteristic of Polish and Lithuanian Jewry owned vegetable gardens and orchards near their houses. Their livelihood and way of life was closely bound up with peasant life and activities. However, the number of Jews who may be classified as belonging to the agricultural sector at any given time in the period remains a moot point. These connections to a certain degree enabled the renewal of Jewish agriculture in modern times. It is safe to generalize that the greater part of Eastern European Jewry was conditioned by semirural environment until well into the 19th century.

In the early Middle Ages Jewish international trade mainly consisted of commerce in agricultural products from the Far and Middle East destined for luxury consumption in Western Europe. Jewish merchants traded in spices at least from the sixth century, and also in dyestuffs. Conducted on a large scale, this trade was naturally based on the contacts established by Jews in the Orient with local producers and merchants. Information from the end of the tenth century shows extensive activity in this sphere by Jewish merchants from Egypt, Tunisia, and Syria. During the 11th and 12th centuries trading in agricultural products was carried on by Jews in all the Mediterranean countries, either as individual enterprises or, when on a larger scale, frequently in partnerships, which sometimes also included Muslim merchants. The trade included sugar exported from Egypt, and dried fruits, especially from Syria, as well as condiments, dyes, oil, cheese, and wines throughout the area.

The small Jewish merchants at that time included peddlers who acted as intermediaries between the rural producers and the city. In the Near East as well as in the more backward European countries they traded their goods for agricultural products which they sold at the urban markets. Jews living in the Aegean islands of Byzantium sometimes leased the state revenues from the trade in grain and wines. Attempts to oust Jews from dealing in wines, grain, and other foodstuffs were made in France and Germany in the eighth and ninth centuries, for instance by the Synod of Frankfort in 794. Bishop Agobard complained that the Jews of Lyons in his day dealt in wines and meat. Jews owned vineyards and dealt in wines in France up to the 12th century. In England, the *Statutum de judeismo* of 1275, after forbidding the Jews to engage in moneylending, authorized them to practice trades and crafts. A large number of wealthy Jews therefore turned to trade in grain and wool. While the Jewish merchants of Bristol, Canterbury, Exeter, and Hereford mainly dealt in grain, those of Lincoln, Norwich, and Oxford were wool merchants. In the states of Christian Spain, the Jewish trade in agricultural products was widely developed, and in some places ordinances regulating this trade were issued by the local communities. In Portugal in the 14th century the authorities restricted the activities of Jewish peddlers and traders who bought honey, oil, and wax from the mountain villages and sold these commodities in the cities.

Even when moneylending became the paramount Jewish economic activity in Western Europe the Jews in the West continued to deal in agricultural products, in particular in wines, wool, and grain, frequently in combination with their loan activities. This is attested in the responsa literature of the period. In the 15th century many Jews in the southeastern parts of the German Empire acted as middlemen in buying the products of the villages and landed estates *(Gut)* and selling them to the towns. Buying up, and especially horse-trading, became the specialties of Jews in Bavaria and Franconia, in which they continued to engage well into modern times. The Jewish peddler later found in the United States was continuing a traditional Jewish occupation in Germany and Eastern Europe. However, the anti-Jewish enactments passed by the Church frequently succeeded in preventing Jews from trading in agricultural products. The bull issued by Pope Paul IV in 1555 included a provision prohibiting Jews from dealing in grain. In Venice the *ricondotta* of 1777 prohibited Jews from trading in grain and foodstuffs. With the economic development of Western Europe after the great geographic discoveries of the 15th and 16th centuries, Poland-Lithuania became the chief supplier of agricultural products, cattle, and forest produce to the West.

Up to the time of the partitions of Poland at the end of the 18th century Jews took a considerable part in the extraction and sale of the agricultural produce on which the *arenda* system was based, and thus became associated with the export trade to the West, using both the river and land routes.

In the late 17th and during the 18th centuries the role of Court Jews as victuallers to the armies of the Hapsburg Empire and princes of Germany was largely facilitated by their contacts with Jews in Poland-Lithuania who provided the necessary supplies. The financial success of Jews in this field often became the basis for the accumulation of large capital. Trade in cattle, and especially oxen, was one of the most important branches of the export trade in which Jews took part from the 16th century. It entailed the driving of cattle from Eastern Europe to the West, then the best way of transporting meat. The major part of the herd was bought in Moldavia; the cattle were fattened for a time in the Ukraine, and with the additions bought there were driven to Silesia, West Germany, and France. Jewish dealers sold part of their cattle at the large fairs in Brzeg on the Oder. After the partitions of Poland and up to the present century, the traditional Jewish trade in agricultural products continued, despite attempts by the Russian authorities to expel the Jews from the villages. In the *shtetls* of the Pale of Settlement in Belorussia, Volhynia, and the Ukraine the small-scale Jewish trader would buy goods from the peasants on market days, or through itinerant peddlers and dealers, and sell the village products in bulk to the larger Jewish merchants, who then exported them to Germany. In consequence, trade in essential agricultural products used in industry, such as bristles, flax, and hemp, was almost a Jewish monopoly in this area during the period. Identical in structure was the grain trade in Galicia and Poland in the 19th century, in which the *Dorfgaenger* or *Dorfgeher* were engaged. The Jewish traders traveled from village to village, visiting markets and fairs in the small towns where they bought grain and also cattle, despite official attempts to prohibit them from doing so.

The grain trade of Poland became almost exclusively a Jewish preserve during the 19th century. Many Jewish firms dealt in grain, and Jews also acted as the agents for German and French firms, some also in Jewish ownership. There were 36,907 Jews occupied in the grain trade in Poland in 1897, i.e., 6.9% of the Jewish merchants living in this area. Of the 124 grain merchants in business in Warsaw in 1867, 214 were Jews. In 1873, five Jews became members of the constituent committee of the Corn Exchange in Warsaw. Jewish grain dealers were also prominent during the establishment of the state grain stores in Prussia, Silesia, and Galicia in the 18th century. Jewish contractors undertook to provide approximately 74% of the grain during the shortage in Galicia in 1785–86. Several communities in East Prussia and Latvia, such as those of Koenigsberg and Riga, owe their origin and development to the expansion of Jewish interests in the grain trade. In the 18th century the bulk of the grain exported by the land route from Poland to Silesia was concentrated in Jewish hands. In Lithuania, Jews who exported grain to Silesia bought colonial goods in Breslau, which they supplied to the Lithuanian towns. A large part of the wine export trade of Hungary, which in the 18th and 19th centuries went largely to Poland, Ukraine, and Czechoslovakia, was in Jewish hands. The wine merchants sometimes organized armed caravans to defend the transports from marauders. Between the two world wars a large number of Jews in Poland and the Baltic States continued to engage in the trade in agricultural products, from peddling to large-scale export business, although attempts were made on a governmental level to oust the Jews from this economic sector and, through the creation of state-subsidized agricultural cooperatives, to all but eliminate Jews from trading with the local agriculturists. Thus from the end of the Middle Ages Jews played an important role – and, in many regions, a pioneering one – in the development of trade between manor and village on the one hand and the city on the other, an essential factor in the rise of modern economy.

In Modern Europe. In the modern period, Jews in Europe developed direct contact with agriculture in various ways. Jewish businessmen in Western Europe entered the agricultural sphere as part of their share in the development of capitalist economy. Many of the merchants owning plantations in the West Indies, especially of sugar cane, were Jews. In continental Europe from the late 18th century Jewish merchant bankers frequently branched out into mining and industry, and also into forestry and capitalist farming. This type of activity, chiefly financial and commercial at least in origin, for example sugar beet growing, was developed by a significant number of Jews in southern Germany in the first half of the 19th century and in Russia in the second half of the century. The number of such pioneer businessmen who were actively involved in farm management by the end of the 19th century cannot be ascertained. Apparently at least in Galicia, Slovakia, and Rumania, the class of Jewish capitalist owners or tenants of agricultural lands or assets had become quite large by 1900, and was directly concerned with farming.

It was in Eastern Europe that the movement to settle numbers of Jews on the land took place. From the middle of the 19th century the rapid growth of population and deteriorating economic conditions in Russia forced many of the Jews there out of their traditional occupations. A large minority turned to agriculture, chiefly the suburban type of dairy and truck farming. By doing so, the small-scale Jewish farmer could remain in the same locality, avoid the difficulties of obtaining larger areas of land, and concentrate on intensive cultivation of commercial crops.

Already from the 18th century the population increase and economic impoverishment, combined with new ideologies which envisioned a more "natural" mode of existence for the Jews, began to press for changes in Jewish social life. The theoreticians proposed alterations in the Jewish occupational structure with the aim of achieving a more balanced Jewish social stratification. This, they considered, would make Jews less open to the attacks of anti-Semites who condemned Jews for their pursuit of "non-productive" economic activities. Various schemes were proposed on both governmental and private initiative for the "productivization" of the Jewish masses and included plans for Jewish agricultural settlement. These were either confined to the country concerned, or combined programs for emigration and colonization with broader social and political issues. Among these the most notable are the Zionist movement and the projects of Baron Hirsch, as well as the Birobidzhan scheme.

Jewish researchers estimate that the number of Jewish agriculturalists of all types in Eastern Europe reached a maximum of between 400,000 and 500,000 in the early 1930s, i.e., forming up to 6% of the total Jewish population there. They varied both in the form of agricultural organization and the type of farming undertaken. They included the Jewish shepherds in the Carpathian mountains, beekeepers, owners of milch cows, or vegetable growers in the small Galician and Bessarabian towns, and the mixed farming colonists in the Ukraine. Although the Jewish output was insignificant in the total agricultural sector, Jews took an important part and even predominated in certain branches. In northern Poland, Jewish farmers predominated in vegetable growing, including hotbed crops, notably cucumbers. In certain districts in Poland and Bessarabia, tobacco was practically a Jewish speciality.

The recent development of a Jewish agricultural sector has undergone many vicissitudes both in direction and scope, through ideological and political changes, both within Jewish society and in the attitudes of the environing societies and states. These are revealed in the history of the Zionist movement in Erez Israel and of the settlements in Crimea and Birobidzhan. The greatest interruptions were caused by the Russian Revolution of 1917 and the British Mandate in Palestine.

The Ukraine. Although proposals for Jewish agricultural colonization were aired in Austria and Prussia at the end of the 18th century, the first substantial attempts to carry out such a scheme were initiated by the czarist government in 1804. They were commenced in the districts of Kherson and Yekaterinoslav as part of renewed efforts by the government to colonize the steppe and at the same time to assimilate the Jews, to remove them from the villages and townships of the Ukraine Pale of Settlement, and to make them less "parasitical." A total of 38 villages, each with 100 to 300 family farms, were founded in these areas. Some were given Hebrew names, such as Nahar-Tov and Sedeh Menuḥah. According to Russian official data, these 38 villages included almost 7,000 farms with 42,000 inhabitants in 1913. The average area of the holding was 11.8 *desyatines* (about 32 acres).

The Jewish settlements in the Ukraine suffered severely after World War I during the revolution and the civil war, but most were reconstructed with aid from Jewish organizations such as ORT and ICA. In 1924 additional villages, now with Yiddish names such as Blumenfeld and Frayland, were founded, partly by younger members of the old settlements. In 1927 there were 35,000 Jews living in 48 villages in the Ukraine, farming a total of about 250,000 acres.

At first confined to grain production, the colonies in the Ukraine later diversified their output by introducing livestock and fodder, vegetables, and fruits. After the war the production of irrigated crops, notably grapes, was much increased, and cooperative dairies were set up. Loans and instructors supplied by ICA and ORT assisted these developments, which resulted in well established prosperous communities of a pronounced Jewish and rural character. In the late 1920s the Soviet government allocated additional land for Jewish settlements. Around the existing core there developed three administrative districts with a majority of Jewish farmers: Kalinindorf, Nay-Zlatopol, and Stalindorf. The Ukraine thus harbored the largest concentration of Jewish agriculturalists in Europe, who had their own schools, a newspaper *(Der Stalindorfer Emes)*, and a Yiddish theater. The new villages, numbering over 50, were based on mechanized cooperative farming, with more livestock and acreage per family than previously. Machinery and instruction were supplied partly by the government and partly by ICA. Two further sections of Jewish settlement developed in the Ukraine in the 1920s, in the vicinity of Odessa and in the district of Pervomaysk. After economic changes villages and agricultural suburbs comprising several thousands of Jewish families grew up in these two districts. The movement of Jews to the soil in the southern Ukraine received a renewed impetus in 1928–30 with the Soviet drive for collectivization.

Belorussia. The czarist regulations of 1835 provided a legal basis for Jewish colonies within the Pale of Settlement. These western Russian provinces, which then included Lithuania and Volhynia, provided many of the settlers of the Ukraine and also saw the growth of a similar Jewish agricultural sector themselves. However the climate and soil in the west were much less favorable. Settlement was more scattered and land tenure less uniform. At the beginning of the 20th century there were 258 Jewish settlements in the western provinces, with almost 6,000 farms and 36,000 inhabitants. These villages each had a maximum of 40 family units, farming an average of 18 acres. On government land a unit might comprise 30 acres, but on land privately leased or purchased they ranged from 5 to 13 acres. This led to intensification (an average of two cows per unit was high for these regions) and the search for supplementary employment. Tillage remained according to local technique on a three-year rotation. Technical and living standards improved from the beginning of the 20th century, due to the aid furnished by ORT and ICA. In these conditions, the settlers in the area who overcame the initial hardships never reached prosperity, but developed a specific Jewish rural way of life in which they took pride.

After the war most of these villages remained in the USSR. All had suffered severely from the years of fighting in World War I and the revolution of 1917. In the early 1920s thousands of Belorussians, including Jews, were driven by hunger to become farmers. The Jews tended to prefer suburban lots, but collectives received higher land quotas. In the collective, it was also easier to maintain Jewish cohesion and cling to some vestiges of Jewish religious life. Thus, about 40% of the 2,300 families who settled on the land before 1925 were members of collective groups. The movement, encouraged by allocation of public land, continued until 1929. There was then a total of 9,100 Jewish farmer families in Belorussia, with 58,500 members and 170,000 acres. Most of these specialized in dairy farming, preferring fodder crops to grains, and many kept orchards and gardens. The introduction of tractors facilitated the replacement of draft horses by dairy cattle. In the Mogilev and Bobruisk districts the majority of Jewish agriculturalists were individual farmers living on the fringes of the small towns, receiving aid from ORT. Collectives predominated in the Minsk district; they received government assistance and later became kolkhozes. Many of the Jewish kolkhozes eventually merged with non-Jewish ones and lost their Jewish identity.

Poland. The dissolution of the state toward the end of the 18th century, combined with efforts to reform Polish society and political life, invested the attempts to turn Jews to agriculture with an importance and attention far beyond their real scope. Even so, there were considerable achievements, for which the initiative came from various sources, including the upper circles of Jewish society, enlightened members of the Polish gentry, and Russian governmental circles. They succeeded in bringing the movement for settling Jews on the land to public attention, and in developing Jewish village life. By the middle of the 19th century there were about 30,000 Jews living from agriculture in the central districts of Poland. Ten Jewish villages were considered models for the surrounding areas.

After World War I, Poland inherited the Lithuanian and Volhynian areas of

Jewish agricultural settlers in the Crimea, 1920s.

Belorussia, where there were 1,400 Jewish farms. About half were in the northern section, where only one-third of the farms had less than 15 acres; in the more fertile south the majority were small-scale units. Especially in the early 1920s, additional Jewish families turned to farming in northern Poland, settling in areas adjacent to established units as well as in new locations. The new settlers were all tenants, and in this respect were worse off economically than their forerunners. They concentrated in the small towns and city suburbs rather than in the villages, specializing in truck farming, notably of cucumbers; from the suburbs of Vilna and other cities they marketed hotbed vegetables as far as Warsaw. Near Grodno, Jews specialized in tobacco growing. In the mid-1930s there were close to 2,900 Jewish farm units in 142 locations in northeastern Poland, with approximately 60,000 acres. In Volhynia, 940 units in 20-odd locations farmed an additional 11,000 acres.

In Galicia, entirely different conditions had prevailed under Austrian rule. Here the Jewish agricultural sector comprised three classes: large landlords; tenants and agents; farm hands and smallholders. According to Austrian data of 1902, out of 2,430 large land- and forest-owners, 438 Jews owned a total of over 750,000 acres. Generally these were absentee owners: merchants, bankers, and industrialists, but some were actively concerned with farm management, and a few made a name for themselves as proficient farmers. Below the two upper classes, a stratum of Jewish subagents and even farm hands had developed. However, the majority of East Galician Jewish agriculturists were village shopkeepers, who also each owned a small plot. On part he grew vegetables and fodder; the rest he let to his non-Jewish neighbor. With the development of rural cooperative stores, however, many such shopkeepers were forced toward the end of the 19th century to turn to these plots as their chief source of livelihood. The agricultural society of Jewish landlords, as well as Baron Hirsch's foundation, supported the movement to agriculture and encouraged marketing and dairy cooperatives. The 1921 census records 48,000 Jewish earners as at least partially subsisting on agriculture.

Developments in the interwar period, particularly after 1929, caused a renewed movement of Galician Jews to agriculture. In 1932 ICA opened a central agency in Lvov, and at the same time grass-roots initiative culminated in the foundation of YILAG ("Yidishe Landvirtshaftlikhe Gezelshaft": Jewish Agricultural Society). The credit facilities, education, and instruction provided by these two organizations encouraged modernization and cooperation. YILAG published the monthly *Der Yidisher Landvirt* from 1933 to 1939. In 1933 there were already eight Jewish farming cooperatives and 12 cooperative dairies in Galicia, with a total membership of 1,400. The dairies processed 4½ million liters of milk annually. Dairy farming was quite profitable in the hill regions, where natural pasture enabled a family to keep up to five milch cows if the problems of marketing could be solved. The cooperatives therefore developed transportation as well as processing facilities, and branched out into retailing. Eventually six shops (four in Lvov alone) for dairy and poultry products under the name "Ḥemah" ("butter" in Hebrew) became very popular with the Jewish urban customer.

After World War II, Jewish survivors of the Holocaust, of whom some had been farmers before the war, settled in villages in the districts formerly in Germany. ORT renewed its activity in Poland and undertook the vocational guidance of the new farmers. Various educational projects were started. However, the whole movement was short-lived, and most participants soon left the soil (and the country).

Rumania. The various sections of Rumania differ greatly in their geography and history. In Bukovina, Austrian rule created social and political conditions similar to those of Galicia, with an accordingly similar structure of the Jewish agricultural sector. Of the small-scale farmers, who numbered 2,000 families before 1914, many owned their holdings, which averaged five to 25 acres. However, only approximately 500 families survived on the land after World War I, and these were completely impoverished. In the 1930s their reconstruction was planned and financed by ICA, based on dairy or sugar-beet farming. In Bessarabia early settlements had been part of the czarist projects, especially from 1850. Additional villages and scattered farms brought the number of Jewish farmers up to perhaps 5,500 families in the late 1920s. Of special interest in this region were the tobacco growers, who worked diminutive plots with effort and skill. Although well known for the high yield of their land and the quality of the leaves they produced, the Jewish tobacco growers could still barely subsist because of high rents and fluctuating prices. Before 1914, over 90% of the tobacco growers in Bessarabia had been Jews; they continued to predominate in the inter-war period. There were also many Jewish winegrowers in Bessarabia working under similar conditions, and with like success. Mixed farming, with much maize, was also represented in the Jewish sector. In the Carpathian Maramures, part of which belonged to Rumania and part to Czechoslovakia in the inter-war period, numerous extremely poor Jews, perhaps numbering up to 60,000, gained a subsistence from cattle and sheep, with some supplementary orchards and beehives. Dairies were set up there by ICA in the 1930s.

The process of the return of Jews in Europe to the countryside and villages from the towns is in part due to an intensification of the historical and economic trends which began in the later Middle Ages. However, the driving forces both from within Jewry itself and outside it have been mainly ideological and political.

The United States. As indicated in colonial records, there were individual Jewish landowners and farmers early in the 18th century. The first attempt to establish a Jewish farm community, however, dates back to the 1820s, when Mordecai Manuel Noah received permission to found his model community of Ararat in the Niagara River region of New York. During the same period, Moses Elias Levy settled Jews on a Florida tract, and by 1837, 13 families launched the Sholem farm colony in Wawarsing, New York. Within five years the last were forced to disperse, partly because of depressed economic conditions. There were other isolated instances of Jewish farmers, including some in California, throughout the century.

By 1881, however, with the beginning of massive Jewish immigration from Eastern Europe, group settlement received a major impetus. Many of the newcomers were imbued with the agrarian idealism of the *Am Olam*, stressing the nobility of farm labor as the most honest of occupations; a few had experience as agriculturalists in Russia. At the same time, the relatively small American Jewish community hoped to develop among the immigrants a healthy yeoman class, away from the cities; it became increasingly sensitive also to anti-immigration sentiment stemming not only from nativist elements, but also from the new urban working class. In a rural setting, philanthropy would combine with self help to absorb the newcomers. Such settlement efforts were aided by the Alliance Israélite Universelle, and a number of new American organizations: at first the Hebrew Emigrant Aid Society (1882–83), then the Baron de Hirsch

Fund (1891–   ) and its subsidiary, the Jewish Agricultural Society (1900–   ). A score of colonies were established in areas ranging from the swampy bayous of Louisiana to the dry prairies of Kansas and the Dakotas, and as far northwest as Oregon; within a few years all failed for such reasons as poor site selection, floods, droughts, factionalism, insect blight, and always inadequate experience and financing. In the East, however, the settlements ringing Vineland, N.J. (1882), and the all-Jewish town of Woodbine, N.J. (1891), survived into the 20th century. Their staples were vegetables, especially sweet potatoes and small fruits.

Early in the 20th century, both Vineland and Woodbine unfurled the banner of "Chickenville," joined later by Jewish farm communities in Toms River and Farmingdale, N.J. Thereby, the poultry industry was able to absorb Jewish immigrants in the 1930s, and beyond World War II, with new centers in the Lakewood, N.J. area, Colchester, Manchester, and Danielson, Conn., and Petaluma, Calif. (north of San Francisco). New York's Jewish farmers, especially throughout Sullivan and Ulster counties, have been well represented since the turn of the century in the poultry industry, dairying, vegetables, and resort facilities. In Connecticut, Jewish farmers specialized in dairying also, as well as

Silos at Baron de Hirsch Agricultural School in Woodbine, New Jersey.

tobacco and potatoes; others pioneered in the famed potato industry of Aroostook County, Maine.

Some notable contributions stand out: in the area of education, the Baron de Hirsch Agricultural School (Woodbine, N.J.) and the National Farm School (Doylestown, Pa.), both pioneering institutions. Also, Jewish farmers founded cooperatives for joint marketing, especially of poultry and eggs, purchase of feed and fertilizer, insurance, and comprehensive community service programs.

At the end of World War II, there were about 20,000 Jewish farm families with perhaps fewer than half that number by the late 1960s – mainly because of trends which have led to a decline of American agriculture generally down to only five per cent of the total population. Jews continue to be represented in all branches of American agriculture, whether citrus in Florida or vegetables in California's Imperial Valley.

Canada. Canada's vast and underpopulated expanses of fertile land were hardly known to the Jews in czarist Russia and other countries who were seeking asylum. Thus, despite Canada's favorable attitude to immigration, only a small segment of the Jewish emigrants from Europe went to Canada. The first attempt to establish Jewish agricultural settlement in Canada was made in 1884 when a small group tried to farm 560 acres near Moosomin, Saskatchewan. Their experiment ended in failure after five years of struggle. A few years later, the Young Men's Hebrew Benevolent Society of Montreal approached Baron de Hirsch to assist Jewish immigrants in Canada, as he did the immigrants in the U.S.A., and soon afterward the Jewish Colonization Association (ICA) established a special Canadian committee for the promotion of agricultural settlement among the Jewish immigrants. The Canadian government also responded to a request to assist Jewish immigrants and placed free land at their disposal, especially in the western regions. A total of 17 Jewish farming settlements was soon established, mainly with the ICA's assistance, mostly in Saskatchewan. Among the best known are Oxbow and Wapella (1888), Hirsch (1892), Lipton (1901), Edinbridge and Sonnenfeld (1906), and Rumsey (1908).

By 1920 the population in those settlements reached 3,500, while their annual produce totaled over $1,000,000. It has been estimated that Jewish farmers in Canada produced enough wheat in the 1930s to feed the entire population of Canada. Some 200,000 acres were allocated for grain and the farmers' assets were valued at $7,000,000. The Jewish settlers, new arrivals from the Ukraine, Rumania, or Lithuania, had almost no training in agriculture, nor any knowledge of the environment, so that their achievement was considerable. Despite the extremely difficult climatic conditions in the prairies, which are covered with snow for eight or nine months of the year, the small and isolated communities maintained strong Jewish cultural activity, often using their last means to bring over itinerant Hebrew teachers for the homesteads. Sometimes a teacher would stay with one family for a whole winter. The younger generation went to study at the colleges of the prairie cities of Winnipeg, Regina, Saskatoon, Edmonton, and Calgary. In time, they became doctors, lawyers, agronomists, and businessmen and settled in town. When the government imposed immigration quotas, the settlements began to suffer manpower shortages and the aging parents, no longer able to carry the burden of isolation, loneliness, and hard work, gradually joined their children in the cities. Some farmsteads fell into decay and were sold; others are still owned by the descendants of the original settlers. Only individual Jewish families have remained on farms, especially those in the proximity of the cities.

Latin America. Jewish agriculture in Latin America was concentrated in three separate regions during various periods. The first region, the plantation area, was located in the northeast of the continent and in the Caribbean Islands. From the beginning of the 16th century – only a few years after the discovery of Brazil – New Christians were engaged in exploiting the resources of the Brazil tree and exporting its products to Europe. The same group most probably brought the cultivation of sugar from Madeira to Brazil. From that time on, Marranos played a leading role in the development of the sugar cane and sugar refinery industries at Engenhos. In the middle of the 17th century, after the Dutch rule ended and the Portuguese took over, Jews engaged in the cultivation of sugar cane (and

Colonists and gauchos at Mauricio, Argentina.

possibly other branches of agriculture) in the Caribbean Islands, especially in the areas of Guiana that remained under Dutch rule. In Surinam, the memory of this period of Jewish agricultural settlement has been preserved in the name of a village, Joden Savanne.

In the wake of mass immigration by Russian Jews toward the end of the 19th century, new and large agricultural settlements were established in the grain and beef areas of southeastern Latin America. The widespread development of agriculture in the Argentian *pampas* and the large-scale immigration campaign that the government conducted in Europe brought the settlement project of Baron de Hirsch to Argentina. Even though the Hirsch project did not fulfill the expectations of its founder, i.e., to concentrate hundreds of thousands of Jewish settlers in a compact and autonomous area, the total area of the project's agricultural land amounted during its peak period (1925) to 617,468 hectares (1,525,146 acres). The total Jewish agricultural population in the five provinces reached 33,135, of whom 20,382 were farmers and their families and the rest were hired laborers and artisans, etc., in 1925.

In 1903 the Jewish Colonization Association (ICA) began to develop additional agricultural settlements in Rio Grande do Sul, southern Brazil. One hundred thousand hectares (247,000 acres) were acquired and two settlements were established that encompassed several agricultural centers. This Brazilian project was never consolidated. Attempts at agricultural settlement in Uruguay on government-owned land in 1914 and on private land in 1938–39 were also unsuccessful.

The persecution of the Jews in Germany during the 1930s and the limitations imposed upon immigration by the governments of Argentina and Brazil led to additional experiments in Jewish agricultural settlement in other geographical areas, mainly in the Andes. Of all these attempts only one, the settlement of Sosua, which was established with the support of the American Jewish Joint Distribution Committee in the Dominican Republic, partially succeeded.

Israel. The continuity of Jewish agriculture in Erez Israel had almost faded out by the late nineteenth century, when the Zionist revival changed the picture entirely. The Mikveh Israel agricultural school was founded by the Alliance in 1870, and the first colonies were settled by Jews from the Old *Yishuv*; but the real turning point came with the First Aliyah. Zionist ideology assigned to "redemption" of the land of Israel and to the "return" to working the land a focal role, from all aspects – economic, political, social, and cultural. Concurrently, the extreme hardships of settlement and the unpreparedness of most settlers compelled the Zionist Organization to give investments in agricultural development a high priority. Thus, purchase and improvement of land, long-term

Cultivator in a cotton field in the northern Negev, 1972.

and short-term agricultural credit, and research and education for farmers became central activities for Jewish national institutions in Ereẓ Israel; due to their pioneering and self-denying lifestyle and to their ideological fervor, agricultural settlers contributed an unproportionately high share of the social élite and political leadership of the *Yishuv*.

Israeli agriculture has a record of outstanding achievements in two directions. One is that of cooperative and collective organizational patterns, of which the *kibbutz* and *moshav* are the best known. The second is that of creating a modern, capital-intensive agricultural sector, pioneering in science and technology, which can afford its members a competitive standard of living while contributing its fair share to the national product. Both aspects have also played their role in Israel's technical aid to developing countries.

In 1970, agriculture accounted for 10.8% of the Jewish population in Israel and for 8.5% of the Jewish labor force. It supplied all domestic demand for vegetables and fruit, milk, eggs and poultry; about 70% of the fish, 40% of the meat, and above 25% of the grain and legumes consumed; and about 18% of the commodity exports of Israel, with citrus accounting for 70% of agricultural exports.

2
Arenda

Arenda is a Polish term designating the lease of fixed assets or of prerogatives, such as land, mills, inns, breweries, distilleries, or of special rights, such as the collection of customs duties and taxes. The term was adopted with the same meaning in Hebrew and Yiddish from the 16th century (with the lessee, in particular the small-scale lessee, being called the *arenda*). The *arenda* system was widespread in the economy of Poland-Lithuania from the late Middle Ages.

I. "Great arenda." This term refers to the lease of public revenues and monopolies. The first leases to be held by Jews were of royal revenues and functions: the mint, salt mines, customs, and tax farming. Large-scale operations of this type were conducted by the Jews Lewko (14th century) and Volchko (15th century). The number of Jewish lessees of central and regional customs duties and of salt mines increased in the 15th century, especially in the eastern districts. Often the same persons leased both the customs and the mines. In western Poland the nobility, possessing more capital, prevented Jews from leasing royal revenues, this being a highly lucrative activity. As the power of the nobility increased during the 16th and 17th centuries, they tried to obtain a monopoly on leasing the royal prerogatives. In 1538 the Polish Sejm ("diet") prohibited the lease of royal revenues to Jews. From fear of retaliation by the nobility, the Jewish autonomous body, the Council of Four Lands, in 1580 forbade Jews to lease the great *arenda*. However, none of these enactments succeeded in eliminating Jewish enterprise completely from this sphere. Even where the nobility monopolized the lease of the royal prerogatives, there remained a broad field for Jewish enterprise and capital in the lease of revenues and functions from towns and private townships. These revenues were taxes on products and services, especially flour milling, potash and pitch, fish ponds, and alcoholic beverages (both production and sale); but sometimes the lease of whole estates was involved. All these types of lease were linked with the agricultural *arenda* (see below). Until the middle of the 16th century, Jews were among the chief lessees of the customs in the stations in Lithuania and Belorussia. Some moved there from Poland for this purpose. In 1569 the Lithuanian Sejm accorded the nobility the monopoly on leases in Lithuania, which also included Belorussia and the Ukraine. The economic consequences of this prohibition would have been disastrous for Lithuanian Jewry, which felt strong enough to defy it openly. The Va'ad Medinat Lita ("Lithuanian Council") therefore twice passed a resolution supporting the lease of customs and taxes by Jews, stating: "We have openly seen the great danger deriving from the operation of customs in Gentile hands; for the customs to be in Jewish hands is a pivot on which everything (in commerce) turns, since thereby Jews may exert control." In Lithuania, Jews openly held concessions for the great *arenda*, with the exception of the mint, until late in the 17th century.

In the 16th and 17th centuries the Jews in Red Russia also occupied a not insignificant place in the lease of customs, salt mines, taxes from drinks, etc. The lessees of these large economic undertakings often contracted them out to sub-lessees, mainly to Jews, as well. That Jews actually operated customs stations is attested by customs registers of 1580, written in mixed Hebrew and Yiddish, even where and when the prohibition of Jewish customs leasing formally remained in force. Jewish expertise and financial ability in this field were in demand. Jews are later found as silent partners of the nominal Christian lessees, often Armenians.

II. **"Agricultural arenda."** This term refers to the lease of landed estates or of specific branches (in agriculture, forestry, and processing), in which Jews gradually became predominant in eastern Poland during the 16th and 17th centuries. There were several reasons for this development. The increasing exports of agricultural products to Western Europe and the development of processing industries (especially of alcoholic beverages) led to the progressive commercialization of the landed estates, but the majority of the nobility had little interest in the actual administration of their vast (and remote) *latifundia*, as well as insufficient capital and commercial skills. Thus they turned to the capital, enterprise, and expertise of Jewish lessees. These, on the other hand, showed growing interest in this activity as a result of increasing competition and discrimination against Jews in the towns. Many a lease originated in a loan to the estate owner, who mortgaged the general or certain specific revenues from his land as security.

In Lithuania and Red Russia in this period Jews leased from the magnates not only single estates but also whole demesnes and towns. In 1598 Israel of Zloczów leased the land owned by the Zloczów gentry, together with all the taxes, the monopoly on the taverns, and the corvée, for 4,500 zloty yearly. Jewish lessees played a central role in the colonization of the Ukraine. The Jewish lessee frequently became the economic adviser and factotum of the Polish magnate. The Jewish sublessee could also exert considerable economic leverage and social influence from his position in the tavern, but his financial situation was not necessarily good.

Because of the importance of agricultural *arenda* in Jewish economic life, problems concerning this institution were often the subject of resolutions of the Councils of the Lands. One of the most far-reaching *takkanot* ("regulations") introduced by the Council was that of *hazakah* to prevent undercutting among Jews in this field. This regulation interdicted a Jew from attempting by any means to acquire a lease already held by another Jew for three years. Other *takkanot* dealt with problems of Sabbath observance or halakhic points arising in the course of management of estates with Christian owners. In southeastern Poland, Jewish lessees found themselves between the hammer and the anvil, under pressure from the extortionate nobility for whom they were agents, and hated by the peasantry. The attitude of the Jews themselves toward the peasants was often much more humane than that of the Polish landlords. A council of rabbis and communal leaders of Volhynia, a central district of the agricultural *arenda*, urged Jewish lessees in 1602 to forego the work due from peasants on the Sabbath: "If the villagers are obliged to do the work on weekdays [i.e., Monday through Saturday] . . . let them forego the Sabbath and [Jewish] holidays altogether. Living in exile and under the Egyptian yoke, our forefathers chose the Sabbath day for resting . . . Therefore also where Gentiles are under their hand [the Jews] are obliged to keep the Law . . . Let them not be ungrateful to the Giver of bounty, the very bounty given; let the name of the Lord be glorified through them." However, the Jews were frequently maligned. They were accused falsely of interfering in the affairs of Greek Orthodox (Pravoslav) churches in villages leased by them. All the Jews living in the south-eastern parts of Poland were attacked and thousands massacred in the Cossack and peasant uprisings in the 17th century.

The last years of the Polish "republic of the nobility" (1648–c. 1772) were a period of economic and cultural decline accompanied by growing Catholic reaction to the Reformation. The central administrative authority progressively weakened and the nobility felt itself free to act unfettered by law. The conditions, character, and role of Jewish leaseholding changed for the worse in this situation. At that time in certain districts village Jews formed a third of the total Jewish population. The 1764 census shows that around 2% of the Jews in Poland were lessees (generally tavern keepers) in towns; in rural areas, while only a few were large-scale lessees on the magnates' estates, the number of Jewish lessees of taverns and inns had increased. In the district of Lublin at this date, 89% of the village Jews engaged in leaseholding operations were inn or tavern keepers. An insignificant number of larger-scale lessees held more than one inn or tavern. The rest, nearly 11%, leased mills and dairy processes. Petty lessees often combined trade with a craft, such as hatters, tailors and pitch burners. Solomon Maimon, in the late 18th century, depicts in his autobiography the poverty of the Jewish innkeeper who plied his trade in a smoky hut with peasants sitting on the floor and drinking vodka, while the Jewish teacher taught the half-naked children of the proprietor. The Polish poet Ignacy Krasicki describes an inn as a barn where the Jewish innkeeper had not even a bundle of straw to serve as a bed for his guests. Arbitrary arrests and humiliation were part of the lot of the Jews in these occupations. In the 18th century the petty squires and the general public demanded the expulsion of the Jews from the villages, especially the lessees of the taverns. During the period of the Partitions of Poland, the limitation which had been imposed on the lease of revenues and real property by Jews remained in force until the formal political emancipation of the Jews in each partition district.

The weight and importance of leaseholding in the occupational structure of Eastern European Jewry decreased in the 19th century with urbanization and industrialization and the process of Jewish migration to the cities and industrial and commercial centers. Formerly, the system of agricultural *arenda* had brought Jews to the villages and incorporated them in village life. It provided a broad area of settlement and sources of livelihood enabling the growth of the Jewish population in Poland-Lithuania. Even during its decline, and despite the tarnishing of its image from the 18th century, the *arenda* system for a considerable time played an important role in both Jewish and Polish economic and social life.

3

Trade in Livestock

The laws of ritual slaughter made it necessary for Jews to buy cattle for their own consumption. In Muslim countries the gentile population bought meat from Jewish butchers. In Christian countries many charters granted to the Jews contained articles regulating the slaughter of livestock by Jews as well as the right to sell meat to non-Jews. This was necessary because the surplus, ritually unclean, parts of animals had to be sold to the Christian populace, to the great resentment of the guild of Christian butchers. Churchmen also were indignant that Jews sold to Christians meat that they considered unfit to eat according to the law. Protests by butchers against the irregular sale of meat by Jews were common occurrences in most medieval cities, often resulting in limitations in Jewish trade which had been beneficial both to Jews and to most Christians. Trade in livestock became much more intensive following the expulsions of the 15th and 16th centuries, which had resulted in a considerable section of Central European Jewry adopting a rural mode of life. Henceforth their main occupations were as peddlers, traders, brokers in agricultural products, and livestock traders. Many villages were composed largely of traders in cattle, goats, and horses. For example, in Eichstetten, Baden, four-fifths of the 68 Jewish families were livestock traders in the 19th century. In Poland-Lithuania Jews traded in cattle on a larger scale. Herds of cattle, often numbering thousands of heads, were driven for sale to the west. In the *arenda* (see p. 125) system the Jewish lesee would obtain both ritually clean and unclean animals. The problems arising from the maintenance and sale of the latter are dealt with in much of the halakhic literature of the 17th and 18th centuries.

Jewish participation in the livestock trade was a mainstay of the activity of military contractors. Supplies from Poland-Lithuania helped boost this trade among German and Austrian Jews. Herds of draft oxen, cattle for meat, and horses for the cavalry were supplied by Samuel Oppenheimer and Samson Wertheimer of Vienna and many other Court Jews. In Poland the Nakhmanovich family specialized in supplying large quantities of horses to the armies. The thousands of beasts necessary were amassed through a system of contractors and subcontractors, reaching down to the petty rural livestock trader. Isaac, son of

Daniel Itzig, became bankrupt in 1795 when he did not receive payment from Cerfberr for delivering 8,835 out of 10,000 horses contracted for. The livestock trade was a predominantly Jewish occupation in Bohemia-Moravia, Hungary, and Eastern Europe. The familiar presence of the Jewish livestock trader made him a common figure in local folksong; a Westphalian example goes:

> Jew Itzig bought a cow
> and a calf as well;
> Itzig Jew didn't notice,
> the calf was *mo'beres.*

The use of a Hebrew word (*mo'beres-me'ubberet*, "pregnant") is typical, for the professional livestock traders' language in most of Europe was full of Hebrew and Yiddish phrases. The special vocabulary of non-Jewish livestock traders in Holland after World War II consisted of about 90% corrupted Hebrew and Yiddish words. Jewish horse traders developed a secret trade dialect which non-Jewish horse traders first tried to understand and then eventually adopted for their own mercantile purposes.

In Switzerland, from which the Jews had been expelled in the 15th and 16th centuries and finally in 1622, Jewish livestock traders were nevertheless present throughout the country. Pacific Switzerland attracted the Jewish horse traders supplying the armies of neighboring states. The various cantons were forced to accept and encourage their presence, or to suffer stagnation in the livestock trade. Attempts were made to differentiate between the needed livestock buyers and unwanted traders and peddlers. The few Jewish communities that existed in Switzerland in the 18th and early 19th centuries subsisted primarily from livestock trading. In Endingen, of 144 heads of families, 48 were engaged in livestock trading and 5 were butchers. In relatively isolated Endigen and Lengnau a special horse-traders' language persisted into the 20th century without passing through a process of de-Hebraization and Germanization.

When in 1689 the Nuremberg council wanted to prohibit all trade between Jews and Christians, the Christian butchers protested and the council was forced to make an exception for the livestock trade. As against 1,590 transactions in cattle conducted by Jews between 1784 and 1800 in Winterborn (in the Palatinate), only 82 were conducted by Christians. This predominance in rural markets had its anti-Jewish ramifications. Jewish livestock traders were frequently accused of trickery, primarily of usury and exploitation, for the animals were generally bought and sold on credit. Accusations against Jewish livestock traders were particularly common in Alsace-Lorraine, Bavaria, Hesse, and Eastern Europe. Through channeling the resentment of the farmers in backward

Milking goats at a Jewish Colonization Association colony in Bessarabia, c. 1925.

rural Hesse against Jewish livestock traders, Otto Boeckel was elected to the Reichstag. This type of anti-Semitic agitation was later adopted by the Nazis, particularly by the party's agricultural experts. Immediately after the Nazi seizure of power concerted steps were taken to break the Jews' dominant position in livestock markets, both on the local, regional, and national levels. Traditional markets were boycotted and special *judenfreie* ones were established, where farmers were urged to bring their livestock. Eventually, heavy pressure, both public and legal, had to be exerted in order to induce the farmers to sever their ties with Jewish traders. The campaign was intensified in the middle and late 1930s. On Jan. 26, 1937, only pure-blooded Germans were permitted to deal in livestock, and on Nov. 12, 1938, after the *Kristallnacht*, Jews were totally forbidden to attend markets and fairs.

Goats and cattle were raised on a small scale by many Jewish households; in the *shtetl* the owner of a few cows or goats supplied kosher milk and dairy products. Tales of such men were common in folklore and literature, the most famous being Tevye the milkman by Shalom Aleichem.

Wine and Liquor

As a result of both the historio-economic and the religious factors, during the Middle Ages viticulture was one of the branches of agriculture in which Jews had traditional interest and technical proficiency. The rabbinical responsa and *takkanot* provide ample instances of the endeavors made by Jews to obtain supplies of suitably pure wine and the arrangements made for doing so. This was perhaps one of the main reasons that the Jews continued to engage in viticulture longer than in other types of agriculture in this period, though from the 11th century the sources mention that Jews in Western Europe also drank mead. In several areas, Jewish winegrowers or vintners also sold wine to Christians. In the region of Troyes, the teacher of Rashi (b. 1050) used to sell "from his barrel to the gentile" (Rashi, Resp., no. 159). The Jews of Speyer and Worms were licensed by the emperor in 1090 "to sell their wine to Christians" (Aronius, Regesten, nos. 170–1).

The antagonisms created by the sale of a product to which Jews and Christians attached divergent sacral usages and regulations are reflected in complaints such as that "on the insolence of the Jews" by Archbishop Agobard of Lyons, who wrote (c. 825): "As to wine which even they themselves consider unclean and use only for sale to Christians – if it should happen that some of it is spilt on the earth, even in a dirty place, they hasten to collect it and return it for keeping in jars." The problem is even more strongly presented by Pope Innocent III in his letter of January 1208: "At the vintage season the Jew, shod in linen boots, treads the wine; and having extracted the purer wine in accordance with the Jewish rite they retain some for their own pleasure, and the rest, the part which is abominable to them, they leave to the faithful Christians; and with this, now and again, the sacrament of the blood of Christ is performed." The description may apply either to Jewish vintners and vineyard owners or to Jews who made arrangements with Christian owners to permit the Jews to extract pure wine in accordance with Jewish law.

In the Muslim countries the Jewish wine trade assumed considerable proportions, as indicated by examples from 12th-century Egypt. It is reported in 1136 that "four partners [all Jews] joined in the production of wine with the enor-

132

mous sum of 1,510 dinars"; upon liquidating the partnership and paying their taxes, all expressed their satisfaction (S. D. Goitein, *A Mediterranean Society* 1 (1967), 364). In about 1150 a Jewish estate included 1,937 jars of wine, worth about 200–300 dinars (*ibid.,* 264). The amounts cited indicate that such thriving business had Muslim customers besides Jews and Christians. In England, in the 12th and 13th centuries, Jews imported wine, and "were exempt from paying any custom or toll or any due on wine, in just the same way as the king himself, whose chattels they were" (Roth, England, 102–3; cf. also 115, note). In Central Europe, Jewish drinking habits were already gradually changing in the 13th century, as shown by the man who asked R. Meir b. Baruch of Rothenburg for his opinion "about beer [i.e., whether this might be used for *Kiddush*], for in his locality there is sometimes a lack of wine." R. Meir answered: "There is no wine in Westphalia, but in all [other] principalities there is abundant wine; and there is wine in your city throughout the year. It seems to me that you personally drink mostly wine; and if at the end of the year there is some dearth of wine you will find it in your neighborhood. . . . Certainly you know that it is proper to recite *Kiddush* over wine" (Meir b. Baruch of Rothenburg, *Responsa*, ed. by Y. Z. Kahana, vol. 1, nos. 72, 80).

While by the 15th century Jews must have practically ceased to own vineyards and practice viticulture, trade in wine and other alcoholic beverages was becoming a major Jewish occupation in the German and west Slavic lands. This was part of the general trend of increasing commerce between town and country in this period in which Jews took an active part, not least because they were expelled from the larger cities. The competition of the Jewish vintner was an object of complaints by the guilds, as in Regensburg in 1516. In part, this commerce was combined with credit extension, as explained by Jews in Regensburg in 1518, who lent money to the boatmen carrying wine to the city and were sometimes repaid in kind.

In both Muslim and Christian Spain, the sale and consumption of wine in the Middle Ages were subject to taxation by the autonomous Jewish communal administration. The unbroken records give evidence of the significant scale on which Spanish Jewry engaged in business. Copious wine drinking by the upper Jewish social strata is also frequently mentioned in Jewish poetry in Spain. After 1391 exiles from Spain carried their wine trade to Islamic countries, and occasionally aroused opposition from their hosts. These traditions and trends were in part continued, in part considerably modified, in the course of the 16th and 17th centuries.

From the 16th to the 19th centuries the production and sale of alcoholic beverages was a major industry in Poland-Lithuania and Russia. It also occupied an important place in the economy of Bohemia, Silesia, Hungary, and Bess-

Painted ceramic jug for alcoholic beverages representing a Jewish *arenda* tavern keeper, with mocking inscription. Poland, 17th century.

arabia. As essentially connected with agriculture, it was carried out in rural estates and formed one of the main sources of revenue for their proprietors. The Jews entered this industry under the *arenda* system in the rural economy in which by the 16th century they played an essential role. The Jewish tavern keeper became part of the regular socioeconomic pattern of life in the town and village. The association of the Jew with this activity contributed another negative feature to the popularly created image of the Jew while also affecting Jewish living habits and standards. The alcoholic beverage industry afforded to the Jews a variety of occupations and a source of livelihood enabling them to raise their living standards.

In almost all the rural estates in Poland, the owners held the monopoly over the production and sale of alcoholic beverages, and the heavy drinking habits of the peasants in these countries made it a highly lucrative prerogative. The participation of Jews took the form of leasing in one of the following ways: The lease of breweries, distilleries, and taverns which was part of the wider *arenda* system in Poland and in Ukrainian and Belorussian territories; often, the lease of breweries and distilleries, together with taverns, formed a separate concession; the basic leasehold concession of the single tavern, which was rented either directly from the noble estate owner or from a larger-scale Jewish leaseholder. All leases were granted for a limited term, often for three years, sometimes for one year only. Jewish communal regulations *(takkanot)* effectively limited competition between Jews in bidding for the leases at least to the end of the 17th century. Tavern keepers were the largest group of Jews occupied in the industry. They frequently belonged to the poorer class of Jew who had contact with the peasants.

The industry also accounted for an appreciable number of brewers and distillers who worked for the brewery or distillery leaseholders as employees. They were sometimes also employed by taverners. In the middle of the 17th century, this group represented about 30% of the Jews engaged in the production and sale of alcoholic beverages on Polish territory. On the crown estates, the income from the production and sale of alcoholic beverages amounted to 0.3% of the total revenues in 1564, and to about 40% in 1789, an immense increase directly connected with the participation of the Jews in this industry.

Jews also played a similar role in the towns. The location privileges accorded to townships in Eastern Europe usually granted the municipality the right to lease production and sale of alcoholic beverages in the town to an individual local resident. Jews also often competed with other townsmen for this concession, and were generally more ready to supply credit than their Christian competitors. In 1600 the magistrate of Kazimierz complained: "The Jews are not permitted to keep taverns, and yet they deal openly in the sale of vodka, wine, and mead; they hire musicians to tempt in people." Jewish sources confirm the nature of the competition that took place in the cities. The communal regulations for the district of Volhynia of about 1602 enjoin that:

In order to prevent the entry ... [to Jewish houses] of gentiles, who came to buy on Saturdays and Festivals, they [the Jewish taverners] should all of them be compelled to take down the sign that they hang up over the entrance to the house on weekdays to let it be known that there is beer and mead inside for sale. That sign shall they take down before the beginning of Sabbath until its end (see H. H. Ben-Sasson, in: *Zion*, 21 (1956), 199).

In Belaya Tserkov in about 1648, 17 taverns were owned by Jews, although the Jewish population consisted of only 100 families. In towns in Poland and Lithuania where the monopoly was held by the city, it was also leased to Jews. The municipal prerogative was usurped by the manorial owners of the towns during the 17th century, and the concessions for production and sale of alcoholic beverages were leased to Jews on an increasing scale. In the old crown cities, Jews also often leased the tavern from the city authority.

In the second half of the 16th and the first half of the 17th centuries, a considerable number of Jewish distillers, brewers, and taverners were thus occupied on the estates of the magnates situated in the Belorussian and Ukrainian territories under Poland. Ruin came in 1648–51, following the Chmielnicki uprising. After the truce was concluded between Poland and Russia in 1667, Jewish taverners could again settle in the Ukraine in the region on the right bank of the River Dnieper; the lands on the left bank passed to Russia, from which Jews were excluded. Jewish taverners were not therefore found in the latter area until the end of the 18th and beginning of the 19th centuries. The proportion of Jews gainfully engaged in the production and sale of alcoholic beverages amounted in 1765 to 15% of the Jewish residents in the towns, and at the period of the partitions of Poland-Lithuania (1772–95) to about 85% of Jewish residents in rural areas. In 1791 it was estimated that if the Jews were to be debarred from leasing taverns, about 50,000 people would have to replace them in this occupation, and this was used as an argument against the Russian authorities when they wished to exclude the Jews, in territories then annexed to Russia, from this source of livelihood.

In the period before 1648, Jewish participation in the liquor trade as taverners gave rise to social tensions, which are reflected in contemporary Jewish works and communal regulations, while furnishing a source for anti-Jewish accusations and conflicts between the peasants and Jewish taverners. Anti-Semites ascribed the drunkenness prevalent among the peasants, and their permanent state of indebtedness, to the wily Jewish taverner, who also extended credit to them. During the 17th and 18th centuries there were uprisings against Jewish leaseholders on numerous estates in Poland, and the complaints of the peasants on the crown estates were often taken up by the courts. After 1648, as opportunities for employment narrowed with the progressive deterioration in Poland of the economy and culture, the hostility intensified and conditions became more difficult for the Jews, in particular for the keeper of the single tavern. He was at the mercy of the despotic noble who ruled the village.

Toward the end of the 18th century, in particular after the Haidamack massacres of 1768, spokesmen of Polish mercantilist and physiocratic theories represented the presence of Jews in the villages and taverns as highly detrimental to Polish economy and society. With few exceptions, the opinion prevailed that the Jewish leaseholders were responsible for the deterioration of the towns and the misery of the countryside. To gain control of these concessions was of greatest importance to the impoverished Polish towns, as the production and sale of alcoholic beverages was a principal branch of the urban economy and its principal source of revenue. Elimination of Jews from this occupation became, therefore, one of the main slogans of the All-Polish middle-class movement between 1788 and 1892. The Polish Sejm ("diet") had passed a bill in 1776 establishing the prior right of the citizen to the lease of the production and sale of alcoholic beverages in smaller towns. However, few candidates with the necessary capital could be found, and these soon had to give it up. As a result, in these towns also the lease passed to Jews. In 1783 an order was issued in Belorussia debarring Jews from traffic in alcoholic beverages in the towns, and the income from taverns was given to the municipalities; but this was canceled in 1785.

Following the partitions of Poland-Lithuania, the Jews in the taverns and villages became the scapegoats of the Russian and Polish ruling classes for the poverty and wretchedness of the peasants. These classes were closely bound by social interests and class consciousness, although divided by national and religious enmities. In the large tracts now occupied by Russia the peasants were of the Greek Orthodox faith, and although despised socially, were now the concern of the Russian authorities. The allegation against the Jew as "the scourge of the village," intoxicating the ignorant peasant because of his vile disposition, became a spurious slogan for social reform for both the rulers of Russia and their Polish opponents. Elimination of Jewish taverners started before the partitions of Poland, and continued with the approval of the Russian governors.

The other states which had gained Polish territory also took up this policy, although with less concentration. The Patent of Tolerance issued by the Austrian emperor Joseph II in 1782 ordered all the owners of estates to discharge Jewish leaseholders from their domains within two years. This decision was, however, not carried out. About 1805 the Prussian authorities prepared a ban against leasing taverns to Jews, but owing to the occupation of the country by Napoleon, it was never put into effect. In 1804 Russian legislation prohibited Jews from living in the villages. In the period of Napoleon's ascendancy, the Russian authorities refrained from taking action, and in 1812 the orders were suspended. However, after 1830, the stereotype of Jewish guilt for the drunkenness of the peasants was widely propagated in the Polish press. Steps were taken for supervision of the Jews in the name of benefiting the peasant. In Bessarabia the participation of Jews in the production and sale of alcoholic beverages was limited in 1818. Legislation passed in Russia in 1835 prohibited the Jews from selling alcoholic beverages on credit to the peasants, and canceled all the peasants' debts to Jewish taverners. A law of 1866 permitted Jews to lease breweries and distilleries only in towns and villages inhabited by Jews. These measures had little effect. In Belorussia between 1883 and 1888, 31.6% of the distilleries in the province of Vitebsk and 76.3% in that of Grodno were Jewish-owned. Full rights to produce and trade in alcoholic beverages in Russia had been permitted to Jews belonging to the category of "merchants of the first class," but after 1882 restrictions were also applied against them.

The part played by Jews in the liquor industry continued to concern the Russian government well into the 20th century, even though assuming other forms. The emancipation of the peasants, cancellation of the compulsory quota of consumption, and abrogation of the monopoly of the estate owners changed the economic character and social aspects of the problem. In independent Poland between the two world wars, various economic and legal measures were taken to drive the Jews from this branch, including regulations for hygiene and manipulation of the state monopoly on the sale of vodka. The development of capitalist industry and trade in the second half of the 19th century and freer access to Jews to take up crafts, enabled many Jews in Eastern Europe to enter other branches of the economy. Even so, the image of the Jew invoked by anti-Semites in Eastern Europe still made frequent use of the hated Jewish taverner.

The feelings of loathing with which the Jew regarded his place behind the tavern counter is powerfully expressed by the poet Ḥ. N. Bialik. The taverner and his family saw themselves placed at the:

> meeting between the gates of purity and defilement . . .
> There, in a human swine cave, in the sacrilege of a tavern,
> in streams of impious libation, . . .
> over a yellow-leaved volume,
> my father's head appeared, the skull of a tortured martyr . . .
> . . . in smoke clouds, his face sick with sorrow, eyes shedding blood . . .
> the faces were monstrous . . . the words a filthy stream . . .
> To a child's ear alone . . .
> serenely quietly flowed, the murmur of Torah . . . the words of the living God
> He [the taverner] would sit . . . among stretched-out revelers,
> . . . mounting the scaffold each day, thrown to the lions each day . . .
> (trans. by Robert Friend, in S. Y. Penueli and A. Ukhmani (eds.), *Anthology of Modern Hebrew Poetry*, 1 (1966), 47–48.)

North America. In addition to the prohibition against partaking of non-Jewish wine, its ceremonial use for various occasions, such as *Kiddush* and on all festive occasions, as well as the need for all wine and liquors to be *kasher* for Passover, observances both practiced even by those who were not particular with regard to non-Jewish wine for ordinary use, resulted in a specific Jewish trade in wine (and for Passover in other liquors) for specific Jewish consumption in all countries. The needs of the Jewish population were met by local manufacturers especially where wine could not be imported from Ereẓ Israel.

U.S. Jews tended to make their wine personally or in small shops. The 19th amendment to the U.S. Constitution and the Volstead Act, which prohibited the manufacture and sale of intoxicating beverages, made an exception in favor of such beverages when needed for religious purposes. Abuses of this privilege by some Jews to supply the illegal liquor market disturbed U.S. Jewry. They led to the issuance of a controversial responsum by the talmudic scholar Louis Ginzberg, *Teshuvah al Devar Yeinot* etc., permitting grape juice to be used for religious purposes instead of wine. Following the end of Prohibition in 1933, the business of several Jewish wine manufacturers reached national proportions, supplying the non-Jewish as well as the Jewish market. In the U.S. few Jews were tavern keepers. However, they were prominent among distillers and retailers. Such families as Bernheim, Lilienthal, and Publicker were important distillers, and the general prominence of Jews as retail merchants included the selling of bottled liquor.

Some Jewish firms grew to considerable proportions in Europe as well as the U.S. Many expanded their activity to include general trade in wine and liquors and this may be the origin of the extensive representation of Jews in the English public house trade, for example, the firm of Levy and Franks.

Sedgewick's, owned by the Bronfman family of Canada, became one of the largest distilleries in the world.

Israel. In Erez Israel a few small wine-presses were owned by Jews, mainly in the Old City of Jerusalem and in the other ancient cities inhabited by Jews, before the beginning of modern Jewish settlement in the second half of the 19th century. These were simple household winepresses, catering chiefly to local consumption. The raw material was supplied by Arab vineyards in the surrounding hill regions. The first vines of European variety were planted at the Mikveh Israel agricultural school founded in 1870. The school also built the first European-style wine cellar, which is still in use. With the beginning of modern Jewish settlement, the first vineyards were planted at Rishon le-Zion and later in other moshavot. Baron Edmond de Rothschild, who sponsored early Jewish pioneer settlement in Erez Israel, had high hopes that viticulture would develop as one of the main economic bases for the Jewish villages. He invited specialists from abroad, who selected high-grade varieties in order to produce quality wines. After the harvest of the first crops, he built large wine cellars at Rishon le-Zion (1889) for Judea, and at Zikhron Ya'akov (1892) for Samaria. These cellars were equipped with refrigerators to retard fermentation and thereby improve quality.

The Baron paid high prices for the grapes in order to assure the settlers a decent standard of living. Economic prosperity resulted in a rapid development of viticulture, and, at the end of the century, vineyards covered about half of the total Jewish land under cultivation. In the course of time, millions of francs were paid to maintain high wine prices, and many settlers concentrated on making wine as their sole occupation. A large overstock of wine accumulated, and wine surpluses continued to increase until a crisis was reached. It was decided to uproot one-third of the vineyards in order to reduce the size of the crop and maintain prices. The winegrowers were compensated by the Baron, and, instead of vineyards, planted almond trees, olives, and the first citrus groves. In 1890–91, the vineyards in Samaria and Galilee were attacked by phylloxera, which ruined the Rosh Pinnah plantations. The infected vines had to be uprooted and replaced by pest-resistant plants brought from India.

In 1906 the management of the wine cellars at Rishon le-Zion and Zikhron Ya'akov was handed over to the farmers, who founded the Carmel Wine Growers Cooperative. At the same time, several private wine cellars, such as Ha-Tikvah and Nahalat Zevi were established. Their wine was sold both locally and abroad. During World War I, the local wine found a greatly increased market among the German, British, and Australian troops passing through the country. After the war, however, the Erez Israel wine industry lost its principal markets: Russia, because of the Revolution; the United States, because of Prohibition; and Egypt and the Middle East, because of Arab nationalism. The industry had to undergo a period of adaptation. The acreage under grapes was reduced, chiefly in Judea, where vineyards were replaced by citrus groves. On the other hand, additional areas were planted, mainly in the Zikhron Ya'akov area. During World War II, new plantations were developed on a smaller scale, and with the establishment of the State of Israel (1948), the wine-growing areas covered about 2,500 acres (10,000 dunams). At that time there were 14 wine cellars in Israel.

Large new areas were planted in the Negev, the Jerusalem area, Adullam, and Galilee – some of which had never previously been considered suitable for wine growing. With successive waves of immigrants, drinking habits have changed. During the earlier period 70%–75% of the wine consumed was sweet, but later, two-thirds of the total consumption was dry wine. The Israel Wine Institute, established in cooperation with the industry and the government, undertakes research for the improvement of wine production in Israel. Preference is given to wine plantations in the hilly regions. Varieties of better quality are selected, and new varieties are introduced. Israel wine is exported to many countries of the world. It is widely in demand among Jews for ritual purposes but efforts have been made to broaden the market.

Part Three
INDUSTRY

1

Construction

Jewish activity in this industry was restricted in the Diaspora and was narrowed down to the construction and repair of synagogues and houses for the community. Apparently Jews worked in the building crafts, such as carpentry, masonry, and bricklaying, throughout the Middle Ages and early modern times. The trade was organized on traditional lines, with established terms and conditions such as provisions for the meals of the masters. Where moneylending became the main Jewish occupation, the number of Jewish artisans in the

Illustration from a 15th-century *Haggadah* showing Jews building.

building trade declined along with those in other crafts. In Christian countries Jews were excluded from guild membership, but were still occasionally found in building occupations. In countries where Jewish artisans were more common, as in Spain, Portugal, and Italy, this representation was correspondingly larger. It can thus not be generally assumed that all houses, or even synagogues, in the Jewish communities were built by Jewish contractors and workers. On the other hand the scanty mention of this profession in the sources is no conclusive evidence of its complete decline. Such mention is of great geographical variety. An account of building operations carried out in 1040 at the synagogue of the Erez Israel community in Fostat (Old Cairo), Egypt, describes a Jewish master mason with his helpers, a carpenter and his "boy," and their working conditions. Jewish masons, layers of floor tiles, workers in clay, stucco workers, and their "boys," as well as their working terms, in Egypt are mentioned in Jewish sources. In Hebron, it is recorded that the whole community took part in pulling down a synagogue and erecting a new one. In the summer of 1045 seven masons in succession worked on a building. The 13th-century *Sefer Ḥasidim* castigates a Jewish householder, whose house was built by Jewish and Christian workmen, for not releasing his Jewish employees on Sabbath eve. A contemporary Czech chronicle mentions a Jew, Podivi, who built the town of Podivin. In 1451 a Jew who won acclaim for building the royal palace in Palermo was made a master of the local Jewish carpenters' guild.

However, it was in Eastern Europe, from the 19th century on, that significant numbers of Jews first engaged in building. Visitors to backward Rumania in the mid-19th century noted that the building trades, carpentry, masonry, plumbing, etc., were all exclusively represented by Jews, who built synagogues as well. Whereas no Jews engaged in the building profession in Poland before the 18th century, there were, in Congress Poland, excluding Warsaw, in 1856, 1,973 Jewish masons, 2,591 glaziers, 1,259 plumbers, and 1,289 locksmiths. In the eastern regions Jews were even more numerous in these trades, particularly for work on high buildings, steeples, and roofs, where Christian workmen were reluctant to go. Synagogues, which from the 18th century had often been embellished and decorated by wandering Jewish artisans, were now also built by them. With the rise of the Court Jews, and the increasing numbers of Jewish army purveyors and bankers, numerous large-scale construction projects — palaces, fortresses, roads, and railroads — were organized and financed by Jews. In Poland in 1931, 23.745 Jews were engaged in the building and construction industry, about 10% of the total number, which approximated the proportion of Jews in the general population. Of these, 4,585 were glaziers (80% of the total in this occupation) and 8,034 house painters and decorators (30%); 17.7% of independent employers in these trades were Jews, representing a much lower

"The Glazier"
by I. Ryback, 1917.

proportion than in others, such as clothing, textiles, and foodstuffs. Within the Russian Pale of Settlement the proportion of Jews in the industry was even higher: 28.5% in Vitebsk government (province) in 1897, and 30.4% in Mogilev government (province), although these were employed mainly on repairs and building maintenance. This trend was manifested in countries to which these Jews emigrated. Thus, in Germany, the proportion was high, the majority being glaziers, painters, and decorators in small family firms. The Haberland family (Solomon Georg (1861–1933) and Kurt), a prominent exception, built parts of Berlin before World War I, and rebuilt cities in East Prussia after the war. Julius Berger founded the internationally known firm bearing his name which constructed tunnels and bridges.

The Jewish mass emigration from Eastern Europe coincided with the New York building boom around the beginning of the 20th century, and large numbers of Jews entered the trade. Harry Fischel encouraged Jews to enter the building trades by enabling the keeping of the Sabbath and offering half-pay for those who did not work on that day. Many left the trade again, however, either because of a chance to better themselves or because of discrimination. The unions, in particular, in effect barred Jews from the better-paid types of construction work and forced them to become house painters, plumbers, or decorators, and to concentrate on repairs and remodeling. In 1890 there were nearly 900 Jewish house painters and carpenters on the Lower East Side, and associations of Jewish immigrants in these trades were to be found in many U.S. cities. As a result of the general upward mobility of the American Jewish population, however, few young Jews entered these occupations by mid-20th century.

Similarly, in the East End of London, many Jews from Eastern Europe took up these trades around the beginning of the 20th century. Although many Jews in Britain were prominent in the development of housing schemes after World War II, they were mainly occupied in acquiring sites and developing new housing estates and modern blocks of offices. The actual construction was carried out by non-Jewish firms, but there was one large construction company, one of the foremost of its kind, "Bovis" founded by Sir Samuel Joseph.

Their managerial and financial abilities and experience also led Jews to enter the mass-construction industry in America through real estate brokerage, and Jews were especially prominent in the New York, Chicago, and Miami building booms of the 1920s. In New York City, the major part of the Bronx and the Borough Park and Bensonhurst neighborhoods of Brooklyn were build by Jewish contractors and Jewish realtors, who have played a prominent role in reshaping the face of 20th-century America's cities and their environs (e.g., William Zeckendorf, Benjamin Swig, Percy and Harold Uris, William Levitt, and Samuel Lefrak.)

In the 19th and 20th centuries Jews developed real estate on an increasing scale. The large numbers of Jews who took up engineering and architecture had a place in the planning and supervision of construction projects. In Erez Israel building became an important Jewish enterprise. The building concern Solel Boneh has developed into a big construction and industrial combine. It and Rassco built agricultural villages and housing estates designed for middle-class settlement. Both these firms as well as a number of private ones have built roads, bridges, and public buildings in Asian and African countries.

Construction workers in Tel Aviv, 1971.

2
Crafts

The Jewish occupational structure was gradually eroded with the destruction of the ancient Jewish social pattern and with the change in social attitudes through the relentless pressure from the Christian church, from the fourth century on. With the burgeoning of city life in the lands of Islam and the gradual exclusion from and relinquishment by Jews of agriculture under both Muslim and Christian rule, a process which had been accomplished more or less by the eighth century, crafts became almost the only economic sphere where Jews still worked with their hands. The respect paid to crafts in the period immediately preceding this profound change in Jewish life waned in the atmosphere of the medieval cities, where the merchant and trade had a more honored status.

Two entirely different patterns in the practice of crafts and their place in Jewish life and society are discernible throughout the Middle Ages. One characterizes the communities in countries around the Mediterranean, including in the south those in the continents of Asia and Africa, and in the north extending more or less to an imaginary demarcation line from the Pyrenees to the northern end of the Balkans. The other, in the Christian countries of Europe, was more or less north of the Pyrenees-Balkans line.

In the ancient places of Jewish settlement, crafts continued to be a major occupation of a large part of the Jewish population. The Karaite Benjamin Nahāwendī described in the ninth century those who "come to another's house, do his work and make what he needs for him to pay — like the tailor and the launderer, the worker in iron, in copper, tin, and lead, the dyer and the weaver as well as every other artisan." There was thus a wide range of itinerant Jewish craftsmen in Persia and its vicinity. In the same century a hostile Muslim denigrated the Jews because among them are found "only dyers, tanners, bloodletters, butchers, and cobblers." This limitation in Jewish society must have been a figment of his imagination, but in any case he must have found many Jews in these occupations in Egypt and its surroundings in his time. The responsa of the *geonim* contain ample evidence of Jewish crafts and craftsmen throughout the Muslim Empire in the 10th and 11th centuries.

In the 11th and 12th centuries extensive Jewish activity in crafts is attested.

S. D. Goitein has shown (*A Mediterranean Society*, 1 (1967), 362–7) how widespread and ramified were partnerships in crafts. He states (p. 87) that these partnerships "range in date between 1016 and 1240 . . . . Concerned are gold- and silversmithing and other metal work . . ., dyeing (purple . . . indigo . . . silk), . . . the manufacture of glass vessels, . . . weaving, . . . silk work, . . . the making of wine, . . . and cheese, sugar factories, . . . and a pharmacy." The amounts of money and quantities of materials involved in these partnerships and in other craft enterprises (*ibid.*, 80–89) indicate a wide range in scale of the work. Sometimes the equipment of such a workshop is mentioned: "An inventory of the workshop of a silk-weaver, dated 1157, contained 32 items, . . . He possessed four looms, three combs connected with silk-weaving, three cylinders of wood on which the woven materials were rolled, two irons, one for the pressing of robes and another for the pressing of fabrics worn as turbans, wicker-work baskets full of warps, various quantities of bleached and other linen (which was woven together with silk), a small pot with weaver's reeds, copper threads covered with silver, and other items not preserved. The instruments taken away from a silk-weaver in Dahshū (the village famous for its pyramids) counted 26 items, of which nine were different from those just mentioned" (*ibid.*, 86). Most workshops were smaller.

The 12th-century traveler, Benjamin of Tudela, began to find Jewish craftsmen on his travels only on reaching Greece. At Thebes he found "about two thousand Jews. They are the good masters for preparing silk and purple clothes in the land of the Greeks, and among them are great sages in Mishnah and Talmud." He also found the Jews of Salonika, numbering about 500, among them scholars, "and they busy themselves in silk work." At Constantinople he was told that Jews are hated mainly on account of the tanners. Benjamin's information not only expressed the usual superiority of merchants toward craftsmen in a medieval city, but also gave evidence of differing attitudes – an inimical one, toward "base" professions, like tannery, and a more friendly one toward "better" professions like silk manufacture and dyeing, among Jews.

Throughout the later Middle Ages and up to modern times the same structure of Jewish society persisted in Islamic countries, in which a broad layer of various Jewish craftsmen was a distinct feature. Several crafts – like silk work and dyeing, in some countries also silver and gold work (e.g., in Yemen) – were considered a Jewish speciality.

Not only Sicily under Norman and Hohenstaufen rule relied on Jews for silk work and dyeing, but in Italy there were many Jewish craftsmen, in particular in the south. It would seem that Thomas Aquinas was referring to them in his letter *Ad ducissam Brabantiae* (March 7, 1274), advising Christian rulers that "they would do better to compel the Jews to work for their living as is done in parts of

Italy." The same situation was found by Obadiah of Bertinoro. Writing in 1488, he describes the community of Palermo, which "contains about 850 Jewish families. . . . They are poverty-stricken artisans, such as coppersmiths and ironsmiths, porters and peasants . . . despised by the Christians because they are all tattered and dirty . . . They are compelled to go into the service of the king whenever any new labor project arises; they have to drag ships to the shore, to construct dykes, and so on. They are also employed in administering corporal punishment and in carrying out the sentence of death" (ed. A. Yaari, in *Iggerot Erez Yisrael* (1943), 104). He found a similar situation at Messina, where he counted "about four hundred Jewish family heads . . . better off than those of Palermo, all of them craftsmen, though a few are merchants" (*ibid.*, 108). As in the 12th century, so in the 15th century, the Jewish onlooker from the north expresses shock at and a sense of superiority toward this artisan Jewish society.

In the kingdoms of Christian Spain, craftsmen made up a large and important sector in Jewish occupations and society. The family name Escapat, Scapat, derives originally from an Aramaic term for a shoemaker. In many communities artisans were the majority or formed at least half of the income earners. In Segovia, in the late 14th century, out of 55 Jewish earners "23 were artisans – weavers, shoemakers, tailors, furriers, blacksmiths, saddlers, potters, and dyers" (Baer, *History of the Jews in Christian Spain*, 1 (1961), 198). "There was a street known as Shoemakers' Lane in the *judería* of Toledo in the 14th century" (*ibid.*, 197). "Conspicuous in Aragon are Jewish bookbinders, scientists who devise scientific instruments, and gold- and silversmiths" (*ibid.*, 426). Baer assumes that in the 14th century "at least half of the Jews of Barcelona . . . were artisans: weavers, dyers, tailors, shoemakers, engravers, blacksmiths, silversmiths (including some highly esteemed craftsmen who made Christian religious objects), bookbinders (who bound the registers of the royal chancery), workers in coral, and porters" (*ibid.*, 2 (1966), 37). The same holds more or less true for Saragossa (*ibid.*, 55–56). The anti-Jewish laws of 1412 stated that "Jewish artisans (blacksmiths, tailors, shoemakers, etc.) might not serve Christian customers" (*ibid.*, 168).

There is every reason to assume that the main outlines of Jewish society in the kingdoms of Christian Spain were a continuation of its structure in the kingdoms of Muslim Spain. The importance of artisans was evident in Jewish social and even cultural life there. The artisans were the mainstay of the opposition led by the mystic trend to the rule of the rationalist patrician stratum in Spanish communities. Artisan guilds were behind many of the demands for democratization of community leadership and for equal distribution of taxes in communities like Saragossa and Barcelona in the 13th and 14th centuries. Shocked by the catastrophe of the persecutions of 1391, the moralist Solomon ibn Laḥmish Alami demanded in 1415 of the Spanish Jew: "Teach yourself a craft, to earn your living by your work . . . for it is to the honor of men to live off their work and toil, not as the proud ones thought in their foolishness" (*Iggeret Musar*, ed. A. M. Habermann (1946), 29).

"The artisans had always been the most faithful element in Spanish Jewry. During the mass conversions of 1391–1415, many devout artisans remained steadfast" (Baer, *op. cit.*, 2 (1966), 354). No wonder that King Alfonso V stated in 1417 that community leadership had passed to "the artisans and the little people" and Solomon Bonafed complained about this time that in Spanish Jewry "the tailors render judgment, and the saddlers sit in courts" (quoted by Baer, *ibid.*, 248).

The workshop of the Jewish artisan in Spain was not always a small one. Mention is made of workshops on a large scale for the manufacture of clothes in Saragossa and Huesca (Baer, *ibid.*, 1 (1961), 425). About the beginning of the 14th century there came before the rabbinical authority Asher b. Jehiel (the *Rosh*) the case of a dyer or saddler "who has an annual expense in the form of gifts to the judges and officials, to keep them from trumping up charges against him – the usual contribution that craftsmen are required to make out of their handiwork" (quoted by Baer, *ibid.*, 201). At the other end of artisan society there would be the case of that "worthless scamp among the artisans [who] will marry a woman here today and then become enamored of another and go and marry her elsewhere and return brazenly to his home town" (responsum quoted by Baer, *ibid.*, 424).

After the expulsion from Spain the exiled artisans merged into the artisan class of the communities in North Africa and the Ottoman Empire. It would seem that many other exiles took up crafts in their new straitened circumstances; some would even see it as a moral obligation. The Safed community in its days of glory in the 16th century was based on a broad stratum of craftsmen practicing on a large and small scale. Stories about Isaac Luria (the Ari) tell much about the social relationships and place of artisans in this community. One of the exiles who went to Jerusalem advised his correspondents: "Let anyone who wants to, come. For they can live out their lives earning through crafts. These are the worthwhile crafts here – gold- and silversmithery, tailoring, carpentry, shoemaking, weaving and smithery . . . I who know no craft except for my learning derive my needs from Torah study" (A. Yaari (ed.), *Iggerot Erez Yisrael* (1943), 181).

North of the Pyrenees and in the Balkans crafts played a very small role as a Jewish occupation, from the inception of Jewish settlement there. At the beginning of the 11th century mention is made of a Jew in northern France who owned a furnace and made his living by working it with Christian hired men and

Jewish wood turner, Marrakesh, Morocco.

letting it out for baking to other people (S. Eidelberg (ed.), *Teshuvot Rabbenu Gershom* (1956), 61–63, no. 8).

Neither the documents of privileges granted to Jews in these countries up to the 15th century nor their own writings reveal much concern with crafts or the presence of craftsmen. Certainly the Christian guilds prevented the growth of a Jewish artisan class in the cities of Western and Central Europe up to the 15th century. Since moneylending brought various articles in pawn into Jewish houses, to be able to return them undamaged or to sell them profitably the Jew had to learn to repair them and keep them in good condition. Hence a part-time, unspecialized kind of "pottering" artisanship always existed in those countries and times where Jews were engaged in moneylending. Jews attempted to maintain their own butchers for the sake of *kashrut*, although Christian butchers' guilds always tried, often with success, to thwart this aim. It is reasonable to assume that there were always at least part-time tailors among Jews everywhere, to avoid using the forbidden admixture of wool and flax *(sha'atnez).*

From these beginnings there developed from the 15th century a resumption of crafts among communities in Southern and Central Europe (Bohemia, Moravia, and Austria) and especially in Poland-Lithuania.

Rabbinical responsa tell of women — widows or spinsters — who worked in shawl-making and thread-making for gentile customers. Jewish craftsmen are mentioned in Poland in 1460. In 1485 the municipal council of Cracow permitted "poor Jewesses to sell every day shawls and scarves made by their own hands and craft." Jews increasingly penetrated crafts in the towns of Poland in the 16th century as the constant complaints of guilds and municipal councils abundantly show. The same development is reflected even more strongly in the various royal decisions and agreements between municipalities and Jews, or Christian guilds and their Jewish counterparts, all of which combine to give a picture of consistent, even if much hampered, penetration of Jews into various crafts.

In the grand duchy of Lithuania, the Jews of Grodno already had permission in 1389 in their charter of privileges "to exercise different crafts." In time, crafts became a well-developed sector of the Jewish economic structure. When needy displaced refugee children from Germany arrived in Lithuania in the wake of the destruction of the Thirty Years' War, the Council of Lithuania gave the compassionate instruction: "It has been resolved and decided to accept 57 boys into our country to be under our protection, to divide them among the communities to feed them, to clothe and shoe them. Boys to whom God has granted wisdom that their study will be successful shall be induced to study Torah at school; boys whose abilities are not sufficient for the study of the Torah shall be induced to take service or to learn the work of some craft" (S. Dubnow (ed.), *Pinkas ha-Medinah* (1925), 73, no. 351). This indicates both that there was opportunity for learning a craft, and the disregard in which it was held by the leaders of Jewish society. Accordingly crafts are associated with intellectual incapability; it would be a sin, it seems, to send an able boy to be apprenticed to an artisan. The council also dealt with supervision of Jewish tailors to ensure that they should not transgress Jewish law in their work (*ibid.*, 178, no. 728). The increase in craftsmen is reflected in the hostile decision of the Council of Lithuania in 1761 forbidding craftsmen in all large communities from taking part in the assemblies of the community (*ibid.*, 268, no. 983). Indeed, in the bitter divisions in the Vilna community in the second half of the 18th century craftsmen played an important role in the opposition groups and activities.

Despite a general disparagement of crafts, printing was considered an honorable profession. The Cracow community is found in 1595 trying to defend the printers of Cracow and Lublin against competition from Italian printers.

In the rapidly developing southeast of Poland a Jewish craftsman named Kalman, mentioned as a proficient tanner and furrier in Przemysl, was important enough to be granted a special privilege by King Stephan Báthory in 1578. In the same town – which was certainly not exceptional in economic structure – the king defended in 1638 "the Jewish craftsmen who do their work for Jews only" against restrictions by the municipal authorities. The Jews, however, penetrated the Christian market there. In 1645 the same king ratified an agreement between the municipal authorities and the Jews, paragraphs 5–14 of which show Jewish craftsmen as serious competitors to the Christian craftsmen in the branches of tanning, furriery, tailoring, barbering, goldsmithery, painting, cobbling, saddlery, baking, candle-making, hat-making, and sword-making; some of their products were intended by the Jewish craftsmen for the Jewish market only – or so their Christian competitors demanded. Some were entered on the Christian market with the reluctant agreement of the guilds. By the end of the 17th century the citizens of Przemysl prepared a complaint which generalized that "every Jew is either a merchant or a craftsman." They state that the Jews had "totally ruined the goldsmiths', the tailors', the butchers', and the bakers' guilds." The method of competition used by the Jews is described. They employ mobility and initiative. "They [i.e., the Jews] have totally eradicated the barber-bloodletters' guild for there are several Jewish barbers who go with their physicians to the manor houses to the patients there, letting blood, putting on suction cups; the same they do in town. There were not a few Christian soap-makers; now there remains only one, and at that, very poor. But there are several Jews who make soap, carrying it down river and selling it in town too." In this town, as in others, Jewish guilds developed, and from the last quarter of the 17th century various ordinances and regulations are extant of the Przemysl Jewish tailors' guild – which called itself grandiloquently "the holy society of the dressers of the naked ones" (חברא קדישא דמלבישי ערומים) – showing relations between masters and apprentices, and between masters and hired workers, and demonstrating the strict supervision by the community and rabbi over the observance of *sha'atnez* laws by the tailors.

The situation in the west of Poland-Lithuania, i.e., Great Poland, is seen clearly in various ordinances of the Poznan community. In 1535 a council of community elders – usually very conservative and patrician in its attitude – admonished the Jews in their jurisdiction "to remember for their good the clothes makers of Swerzeniec community, a reminder of help and mercy, to look upon some among them with care and particular supervision – for we have seen that crafts are diminishing daily and many of our people have deserted craftsmanship, hence it is fitting to strengthen the hands of the artisans, not to let them fall, for this is a great benefit and an important rule for the entire society" (D. Avron (ed.), *Pinkas ha-Kesherim shel Kehillat Poznan* (1966), 55–66, no. 273). The same council devised in 1747 a set of model ordinances for guilds in the community and for regulating their relations with other community institutions (*ibid.*, 398–403).

By the end of the 18th century the Poznan community had a well-developed artisan class. In 1797 there were in the town 923 Jewish and 676 Christian tailors; 22 Jewish goldsmiths and 19 Christian; 51 Jewish hatters, 24 Christian; 52 Jewish buttonmakers, 6 Christian; 238 Jewish ironsmiths, 6 Christian; 51

Polish shoemaker, 1920s.

Jewish bakers, 607 Christian. In total there were 1,592 Jewish craftsmen, about one-third of the 4,921 craftsmen in Poznan in this year.

In Bohemia-Moravia also, as well as in southern Germany, Jews increasingly engaged in crafts. A community like that of Prague had long-standing and well-developed Jewish guilds by this period based on a ramified craft structure and professional life and organization.

Some circles of these craftsmen developed a specific ethos and pride in their own calling. As early as the 17th century there were tailors in Poland-Lithuania who asked to be buried with the boards of their tailoring tables, being certain of the honesty and righteousness of their life's work.

Modern Times. In the aspirations for emancipation of the Jews and spread of Enlightenment – and as a corollary of the program for "productivization" of the Jews – occupation in crafts became an issue of the ideological and political strivings for change and betterment in legal status and social standing. Christian W. von Dohm regarded the encouragement to enter crafts as part of his proposals for "betterment of the Jews." Emperor Joseph II included encouragement of crafts among Jews in his legislation for them.

Yet, the practical changes in crafts did not eventuate from this ideology or legal enactments, but from the actual economic and social situation among the masses of Jews in Poland-Lithuania and later on in the Pale of Settlement in czarist Russia. In the 18th century many Jewish craftsmen in the private towns of the Polish nobility began to bring their products to fairs and market days in the main royal towns. The general tendency, in which craftsmen were now working for the open market instead of producing to order, encouraged this development. The Jewish craftsman — being outside the guild structure — was unattached and ready to prepare stock and sell it in free competition. He thus became anathema to the Christian craftsmen and the guilds.

In the early 19th century Jews in the impoverished and overcrowded *shtetl* in the Pale of Settlement tended either to continue in the old crafts — mainly tailoring, textiles, and cobbling — or to enter new professions where not much training or outlay was needed, such as leather work, and carting. Many of those craftsmen peddled their work in villages around the townlets. Through the 19th century a specific Jewish crafts structure developed in Eastern Europe, as reflected in the following table for the end of the century:

Crafts Structure in the Pale of Settlement, 1898

Crafts	Masters	Hired Workers	Apprentices	Total	
Garment	108,527	80,402	61,923	250,852	This table shows the small
	(43.3%)	(32%)	(24.7%)		scale of the Jewish crafts-
Food	43,665	9,675	4,547	57,887	man in Russia, and the
	(75.5%)	(16.7%)	(7.8%)		large proportion of those
Woodwork	25,653	14,119	9,816	49,588	engaged in garment and
	(51.7%)	(28.5%)	(19.8%)		textile manufacture; the
Metalwork	25,499	12,892	10,530	48,921	situation is reflected in the
	(52.1%)	(26.4%)	(21.5%)		character of Jewish emi-
Construction	19,791	7,094	4,705	31,590	gration.
	(62.7%)	(22.4%)	(14.9%)		
Textiles	10,589	4,582	3,257	18,428	
	(57.4%)	(24.9%)	(17.7%)		
Leather	6,123	3,343	1,964	12,040	
	(50.9%)	(32.8%)	(16.3%)		
Paper and Print	5,998	3,343	2,354	11,695	
	(51.3%)	(28.6%)	(20.1%)		
Chemicals	2,764	594	259	3,617	
	(76.4%)	(16.4%)	(7.2%)		
Other Crafts	10,787	3,874	1,707	16,368	
	(65.9%)	(23.7%)	(10.4%)		
Total	259,396	140,528	101,062	500,986	
	(51.8%)	(28%)	(20.2%)	(100%)	

This situation made for hardship and competition among Jewish crafts in the Pale of Settlement. It also gave rise to a specific way of life, and even folklore among the masses of Jewish workers. By the end of the 19th century, Eastern Europe had a strong element of class-conscious Jewish craftsmen who through their poverty and hardship formed an embryonic Jewish proletariat. Much of the force of the Jewish revolutionary movement and sentiment, the bitterness and impulsion to social activity, came from this stratum of Jewish society.

In the same period of the 19th and early 20th centuries, Jewish crafts in the old centers, for instance Prague and in Bavaria, disintegrated under the impact of flourishing capitalism and the crossing over of Jews in Central and Western Europe to the more profitable and "respectable" professions of the middle class. Emancipation in these countries brought about not productivization but practically the end of Jewish participation in crafts.

Jewish emigration in the second half of the 19th century, and in a large measure up to the 1930s, was predicated on and characterized by this craftsmen element.

Among the Jewish immigrants to the United States before World War I, over one-third were craftsmen, mostly tailors, whereas among non-Jews only 20% of the immigrants had a skilled profession. Of 106,236 Jewish immigrants to the United States in 1903–04 there were 16,426 tailors, 4,078 carpenters, 2,763 cobblers, 1,970 glaziers and painters, 1,400 butchers, 1,173 bakers, and 14,830 in miscellaneous crafts. In Paris in 1910 Jewish immigrants from Eastern Europe included 16,060 craftsmen of whom 11,460 (71.4%) were in garment manufacture − 7,000 tailors, 2,000 hatters, 1,900 furriers, 1,200 cobblers − 2,700 (16.8%) iron workers, 1,000 (6.2%) woodworkers, 600 (3.7%) leather workers, and 300 (1.9%) in other crafts. The same structure held good for Eastern European Jewish immigrants in England as well as other countries.

Thus the sweatshop of New York, London, and other centers of Jewish immigration and the preponderance of Jews in tailoring and ready-made clothes businesses in countries of large immigration from Eastern Europe derived from the structure of the Jewish crafts world which had taken shape during the 19th and early 20th centuries in Eastern Europe.

This situation underwent many changes, mostly destructive, between the two world wars. In Soviet Russia the general trend against the practice of the independent craftsman and the industrialization of the country diminished the role of crafts among Jews. In the countries built on the ruins of the empires of czarist Russia and Austria-Hungary − like Poland, or Lithuania − the old enmity of the Christian craftsmen rapidly reasserted itself in modern guise. Jews were pushed out or barred from crafts either explicitly or more frequently by seemingly innocuous demands by the trade unions or authorities. Entry to the trade, for instance, was made conditional upon proper apprenticeship with proper masters (and Christian masters only were usually recognized as such); stringent demands for modern equipment and modern conditions of work were usually formulated in a way that hampered the Jewish craftsman in particular. The response of Jewish crafts to this challenge was pioneered by cooperatives and loan banks; a stimulus was given to schooling and the establishment of educational systems; vocational training was provided by the ORT organization.

In modern Erez Israel crafts were part of that constantly growing private sector of the Jewish economy which has received less attention in historical surveys than the public and Histadrut sectors. In the economy of the State of Israel their role is largely determined by the trends inherent in modern economic growth: industrialization of many branches on the one hand, and the growing need for service, maintenance and repairs (in which small firms have many advantages) on the other hand.

By the end of World War II, a large segment of Jewish craftsmen had disappeared as a result of the Holocaust. The specific technical requirements and social structure of the State of Israel and its growing prosperity, with the predominance of the middle-class, liberal and administrative professions governing the structure and ethos of Jewish economy and society in the countries of the West (Western Europe, the United States, Great Britain and the Commonwealth, South Africa, South America), have created a situation where in many places Jewish occupation in crafts is at vanishing point, and in others they play an increasingly minor role. The large concentrations of Jewish tailors and tailoring in New York, London, and elsewhere have almost disappeared in the lower echelons of the craft in particular. A 1957 survey conducted by the U.S. Bureau of the Census found that 9% of employed male Jews were working in crafts. A similar breakdown in Canada put the percentage at 14%.

On the other hand, the large scale immigration of Jews from Near Eastern countries to Israel and the entry of survivors of the Holocaust to Israel and some western countries brought a certain temporary revival of Jewish crafts there.

It now seems that despite efforts at modernization and the near disappearance of many of the old inimical forces, Jewish occupation in crafts and the role of craftsmen as an important factor in Jewish society are disappearing, as in other societies, through the influence of modern industrial techniques and organization.

3

Diamond Trade and Industry

Jews have been prominent in the trade and in working of precious stones, of which diamonds and pearls provided the bulk, from the Middle Ages to the modern era. They took an active part in opening up the diamond markets of India and Brazil, the resources of South Africa, the London diamond market, and the diamond industries of the Low Countries. Because the diamond trade routes corresponded with the links between Jewish centers in the Diaspora – in the Ottoman Empire, the Netherlands, in some of the cities of northwest Germany, and in Poland-Lithuania in the 16th to 18th centuries – the trade was particularly suited to Jewish enterprise. Additionally, as diamonds were still a relatively rare and new commodity in Europe up to the 16th century, this was a branch free of medieval trade and guild restrictions. Up to the 18th century the overwhelming majority of uncut diamonds came from India. Commerce and crafts pursued by Jews along the Indian Ocean trade routes, in Egypt, the Maghreb, and along the shores of southern Europe, included trade and workmanship in precious stones, pearls, and jewelry. The Fatimid caliphs were supplied with gems by the brothers Abu Sa'd al-Tustarī and Abu Naṣr al-Tustarī, influential bankers and diamond merchants in the 11th century at Cairo. As moneylenders, Jews in Western and Central Europe had much to do with the assessment, repair, and sale of precious stones and jewelry which they received in pawn.

With the rise of Amsterdam as a major center of the European diamond trade and industry in the 16th century, Dutch Jews, mostly members of the Portuguese Sephardi community who had been prominent in Portugal's diamond trade, played an important part in both. By the middle of the 17th century the preponderance of Jews in the newly developed trade was so marked that the resettlement of the Jews in England brought about a major shift in its structure. The Sephardi presence in London, combined with the growing ascendancy of England in the Eastern trade, resulted in the diversion of the greater part of Europe's diamond imports to England. A few years after the arrival of the first Jewish immigrants, the British East India Company, which had a monopoly of England's Indian trade, permitted independent merchants to import uncut diamonds under a system of individual licenses issued by India House. Until the end of the 18th century most Indian stones used by the European diamond industry were imported through London. The records of the East India Company show that the majority of the importers were Jewish and that they dominated the trade throughout most of this time. The diamond merchants exported silver and coral to India, the proceeds of which were invested in diamonds. The coral was first brought to London from Leghorn, mostly by Jewish merchants of that city who often had a direct share in the Indian diamond trade through Jewish agents in London. The Indian end of the trade was managed by agents of English firms — mainly English Jews who went out to India for this purpose. Around 1750 there were about ten Jewish diamond agents at Madras.

In London the diamonds were usually sold to merchants who sent them to Amsterdam for cutting. Amsterdam remained throughout the 18th century the chief seat of the diamond industry, while Antwerp, which was later to overshadow it, was of secondary importance, dealing mainly in stones of inferior quality. From Amsterdam the finished diamonds were distributed throughout Europe. From its inception, the diamond trade and industry of Amsterdam was largely in Jewish hands. Portuguese Jewish diamond polishers are recorded in 1615; they later employed their poorer Ashkenazi brethren who gradually established their own businesses. Diamond cutting and polishing was a profitable profession, but suffered from the vicissitudes of an unstable market as well as an occupational disease — tuberculosis. The main demand for diamonds came from the courts of Europe, and jewel purvey was both a stepping-stone to and a major part of the post of Court Jew. An important stage in the transfer of precious stones from London to Amsterdam, and thence to the courts of Germany, was Hamburg, where a sizable community of Sephardi Jews monopolized the diamond trade in the 17th and 18th centuries. One of the earliest Court Jews, Lippold, was a supplier of gems and other luxury articles, as were almost all the Court Jews of the era. Aaron Isaac of Sweden, the Oppenheimers of Vienna and Wuerttemberg, and the Ephraim family all owed their success, at least initially, to their dealings in gems. Glueckel of Hameln, a shrewd dealer in precious stones, gives a detailed picture in her autobiography both of the international commerce in precious stones and gold as well as of small-scale trading by German Jews in this sphere. After 1700 Ashkenazi Jews began to play an increasingly important role in the London center of the diamond trade. By the 1720s the investments of the Ashkenazi Franks family in the Indian diamond trade were approximately equal to those of the biggest Sephardi enterprise — that of the brothers Franco — and 60 years later the Ashkenazi merchant Israel Levin Salomons (Prager) attained a dominant position for a time.

The discovery of diamonds in Brazil around 1730 ended India's monopoly as a producer of uncut diamonds and for a time weakened the hold which London and its Jewish diamond merchants had on the import trade, though Brazilian stones were soon reaching London illegally in considerable quantities. In the long run this development diminished neither the prominence of Jews in the diamond trade and industry nor London's position as the chief international market for uncut diamonds. Jews continued to be dominant in the diamond-cutting industry of Amsterdam, and later of Antwerp, where in the late 19th century they constituted about one-fifth of the workers but three-quarters of the brokers and an even higher proportion of the factory owners. The diamond glut of the 1890s terminated a boom in the course of which the number of diamond workers had tripled through immigration of Jews from Eastern Europe. A period of reorganization followed, in which national and international diamond workers' unions in Belgium and Holland were organized under the leadership of Henry Polak. The diamond workers union spearheaded in 1893 a general strike in Belgium for a minimum wage.

The rise of Fascism in Europe created a crisis for Jews engaged in the diamond industry and trades. During World War II diamond-cutting centers were established in Erez Israel (see below), Cuba, Brazil, Mexico, and the United States by Jewish refugees. The Nazi occupation authorities in Belgium and Holland made Jewish diamond merchants and industrialists their particular victims. Jews have still not reattained their former dominance in the field in Amsterdam, although they have succeeded in doing so in Antwerp.

Jewish enterprise had a large share in the development of the South African diamond mines, which became the chief source of diamond supply after 1870, including the formation of De Beers Consolidated Mines Ltd. (1888), which in the 1960s controlled the production and marketing of the greater part of all uncut diamonds. German Jews were among the earliest pioneers of the South African diamond rush. Among the prospectors were many from London's East End, one of whom, Barney Barnato, was a formidable rival and later partner of Cecil Rhodes. Alfred Beit was the architect of the De Beers syndicate which S. B. Joel first headed. Ernest and Harry Oppenheimer followed in his footsteps.

A diamond industry was founded in Palestine before World War II by immigrants from the Low Countries, who brought with them the necessary technical skills and commercial connections.

During World War II Palestine replaced Belgium and the Netherlands as the gem diamond center of the free world. Palestine received its supplies of rough diamonds from the De Beers central selling organization ("The Syndicate") and sold its polished products mainly to the U.S. At its peak during this period, the industry employed some four thousand polishers, mainly in Netanyah. The value of the diamond exports reached some $16,000,000 a year.

Diamond brokers sampling polished diamonds at the Diamond Exchange, Ramat Gan, 1969.

The revival of the centers in Belgium and the Netherlands after the war, the diversion of raw material by the Syndicate to these countries, and the Israel War of Independence drastically contracted the diamond-cutting industry in Israel. By 1949 it was almost at a standstill. However, the industry revived in 1950 and, in the early 1960s, became the second largest diamond gem center in the world, after Belgium. Its share of the world trade in polished diamonds is between a quarter and a third, and it maintains the same proportion in the numbers of polishers employed.

The secure and steady supply of rough diamonds was a constant concern of the industry. The De Beers Syndicate directly controls the distribution of over 80% of the world output of rough diamonds. Between 1950 and 1959 its direct sales to Israel were frozen at approximately $7,000,000 a year. The industry had therefore to obtain its supplies from other sources, the proportion of which in the total import rose from 24% in 1950 to 84% in 1959. At the end of this period the special high premium of the indirect supplies was so severe that it endangered the prospects for further development.

Israel agencies (among them *Pittu'aḥ* (Development), a company whose shares are owned by the Israel Government) were encouraged to exploit firsthand sources of supply in western Africa. Negotiations were conducted with the Syndicate with a view to assuring the industry in Israel an adequate share of the diamonds under the Syndicate's control. As a result, from 1961, the proportion of the supply from the Syndicate rose and gradually constituted more than half of the imports.

The industry consists of some 400 enterprises, about half of which employ less than 15 workers. Only 45 enterprises employ more than 50 workers and only three have more than 100 workers. Over half of the enterprises, and of the workers, are located in and around Tel Aviv (where the Diamond Exchange is also located), over a quarter in Netanyah, and the rest in Jerusalem and the development areas.

Dyeing

As the Jews had been masters of the techniques of the craft from ancient times, in some districts, especially in the Mediterranean region, the preparation of dyes and dyeing of cloth was considered mainly a Jewish occupation. Such occupations were generally despised and their practice by Jews was seen as part of the general humiliation of the Jewish people. However, some sources indicate that dyeing was a highly respectable profession. The apparent contradiction points to a difference in social and economic standing between the artisan engaged in the craft and the merchant who dealt in the ingredients (though this distinction was not always explicit in the sources). In the Middle Ages, Jewish trade in dyestuffs expanded extensively. Jewish merchants imported reseda from eastern India, via Egypt and Tunisia, to Italy and Spain, and exported saffron from Tunisia to Southern Europe. Those trading in indigo between Egypt and Europe were known as *al-nili* (nil–indigo). Contemporary letters illustrate the range of the undertakings: a Jewish merchant of Kairouan wrote to his friend in Egypt that in Sicily only indigo of the best quality could be sold; another merchant, head of the Babylonian congregation of Fostat (Old Cairo), wrote to an associate in Tyre in the eleventh century, "The price of indigo has risen over the last fortnight because it was in great demand among the people of Syria and the West . . ." Documents also point to the high prices of these commodities: 270 pounds of indigo cost from 100 to 300 quarter dinars.

Jews also developed the manufacture of dyes, especially in Greece and Italy, where they were most active in the south, and in Sicily; important dyeing centers existed in Brindisi, Benevento, Salerno, Agrigento, Trani, and Cosenza. In these localities, the dyehouse was sometimes the center of the Jewish quarter, along with the synagogue. Benjamin of Tudela found Jews engaged in dyeing in several localities in Erez Israel, notably in Jerusalem, Jezreel, Lydda, Bethlehem, and Bet Nubi. In Jerusalem, their shops were situated in a special building which they had obtained from King Baldwin II. In 1231, Emperor Frederick II created a crown monopoly of the silk and dyeing industries and Jewish firms in Trani were appointed to administer it. When the monopoly came to an end with the death of the emperor in 1250, the Jews continued to engage in this industry,

Dyeing plants at Tel Beth-Mirsim dating from the end of the Israelite period, 589 B.C.E. The groove around the rim of the stone vat caught the dye, which ran back into the vat through the connecting hole.

which also spread to the north of Italy. In Montpellier, France, Jews were prominent in the manufacture of dyes, while in Spain they had engaged in the craft from the Muslim period, especially in Seville and Saragossa. After the Christian reconquest, the Jews continued in this occupation, in particular in Saragossa where they owned special workshops. Among the responsa of Solomon b. Abraham Adret (late 13th cent.) are clear allusions to the existence of dyers' guilds. During the 16th century, the occupation expanded after Safed had become the Jewish center of the wool weaving industry.

During this period, dyeing was highly developed in a number of Jewish communities in the Ottoman Empire, especially in Salonika and Constantinople. During the 17th century, the Salonika dye industry declined, along with weaving, mainly as a result of competition from Venice and Ancona. Jews of Brest-Litovsk are often mentioned as experts in manufacture in Poland and Lithuania. Responsa literature contains numerous accounts of the craft of dyeing, the tools employed, and the various methods used in the preparation of dyes. There are descriptions of a dyeing shop where the work was carried out; of a dye-pit; and of barrels in which wool was dyed.

In the Near East, the Jews continued to practice this profession during the 19th century. The surname Zebag ("dyer"), still widespread among oriental Jews, is evidence of the fact. In Damascus in the middle of the 19th century, 70 of the 5,000 Jews were dyers. Jews also played an important part in the development of dye ingredients in the Americas. Planting of indigo was introduced in Georgia during the 17th century and Moses Lindo from London invested large sums in the cultivation of indigo in South Carolina in 1756. The development of modern chemistry and the chemical industry, in which Jewish scientists and entrepreneurs played a considerable role, brought to a close the traditional methods in the manufacture of dyes and dyeing.

Goldsmiths and Silversmiths

The two closely related professions of refining, casting, beating, and filigreeing silver and gold have occupied Jewish craftsmen uninterruptedly from biblical times to the present. The highly skilled nature of the work, the relatively constant value of the two precious metals and the universal demand for artifacts made of them, their ready transportability, and not least, their use throughout the ages in Jewish ritual and ceremonial objects, all help account for the fact that Jewish goldsmiths and silversmiths can be found in almost every period of Jewish history wherever Jewish communities existed. However, because their creations were so often melted down or plundered for their metallic worth, no identifiable work of any Jewish craftsman has survived from before late medieval times, except for the artifacts and cult objects that have been excavated.

Like the practice of crafts in general by Jews in the Middle Ages, the intricate craft of the goldsmith and silversmith continued to be a widespread Jewish occupation south of the Pyrenees and in the Mediterranean lands, while there was little activity among Jews in this profession north of this demarcation line. The specific combination of skills and financial acumen needed for the goldsmith's trade is evidenced in the information that has been preserved about the plying of this craft by Jews in Muslim countries. The records of the *Genizah* of Cairo show that goldsmithing was a common, lucrative, and highly specialized profession of Jews in Egypt and the surrounding area as far as Aden in the 11th and 12th centuries. In Iraq, Persia, Yemen, and the Maghreb many of the goldsmiths were Jews. That this was a widespread Jewish occupation in Muslim countries may be explained by the contempt in which artisans were held by the Arabs. In pre-Islamic Arabia there was a tribe of Jewish goldsmiths, the Zuaynuga, who were defeated and forced to accept Islam by Muhammad. The preponderance of Jews in goldsmithing and silversmithing, particularly in the manufacture of jewelry, continued well into the modern period. In Baghdad, in 1844, 250 of 1,607 Jewish families employed in industry and trade were goldsmiths by profession. In Yemen in particular, the Jewish artisans attained a high standard of skill and artistry. Jews there even believed that the few Muslim goldsmiths were descendants of Jews who had been forcibly converted. The mass

Silversmith from Yemen in Israel, 1960.

immigration to Israel after 1948 of the Jews of Yemen and other Arab countries helped to develop a local jewelry industry.

Jewish goldsmiths are among the first Jews mentioned in Muslim Spain, and are repeatedly referred to there in the following centuries. In Christian Spain Jewish goldsmiths were to be found in practically every sizable town; they were employed by the royal households and occupied their own row of shops in large cities like Tudela and Pamplona. The Augustinian eremites of Barcelona in 1399 commissioned a Jewish artisan to make them a silver reliquary. Jews manufactured Christian religious artifacts in violation of Jewish law and the antipope Benedict XIII in 1415 had to forbid Spanish Jews to produce such objects as goblets and crucifixes. Jewish silversmithing was expressly permitted in the 15th century: in Aragon in 1401 and in Castile in 1419. The expulsion from Spain in 1492 left many Marranos in the Iberian peninsula and Balearic Islands who now engaged freely in silversmithing and goldsmithing. Numbers of the exiles from Spain and Portugal entered these crafts in the Ottoman Empire. This was recognizable particularly in Walachia where Jews sometimes even headed the silversmith guilds. In Erez Israel, in particular in Safed, goldsmithing was considered one of the profitable crafts for Jews in the 16th century. In Italy the refugees from Spain met local well-established Jews in the craft. An apostate of Ferrara, Ercole dei Fideli (before baptism, Solomon de Sessa), was celebrated in this renaissance environment for the ornamental daggers and other works he produced (1465–1519). The gold- and silversmith Abraham b. Moses Zoref ("goldsmith") is mentioned in Venice in the early 18th century. Jewish goldsmiths are found in Rome in 1726. In Bohemia-Moravia gold- and silversmithing developed as a flourishing craft among Jews from the 16th century. Emperor Rudolf II appointed Isaac Goldscheider ("gold refiner") elder of Bohemian Jewry in 1560. He was followed in the craft by his son Jacob. The profession became widespread there, as attested by the frequent appearance of the name Zoref on Prague tombstones until 1740. In the 18th century Jewish goldsmithing was combined with the Jewish trade in precious stones and metals centered in Amsterdam and Hamburg. The craft continued to develop. There were eight goldsmiths among the Jews who returned to Prague in 1749. Several families practiced the craft for successive generations. The program of "enlightenment" and "productivization" of the Jews, animating the legislation of Emperor Joseph II, encouraged practice of the craft among Jews; a separate Jewish guild came into existence in 1805 and continued until the abolition of the guilds in 1859. There were 29 Jewish apprentices recorded in Prague in 1804 and in 1830 there were 55 goldsmiths. In Germany, Jews did not begin to enter the craft until the middle of the 19th century when, however, the general developments in Jewish society were tending to deflect them from occupation in crafts. Silesia was an exception, for Jewish goldsmiths and silversmiths were working there in the second half of the 18th century. In Poland-Lithuania Jews entered this craft as they entered others, as a result of the weakness of the guilds and the activities of Jews in the private towns of the nobility. In 1664 Hirsch Jelenowicz was officially called "goldsmith to His Majesty" in Poland. With the mass emigration of Jews from Eastern Europe to Western Europe and the Americas, Jewish goldsmiths — now combining the profession with watchmaking — joined the few Sephardi goldsmiths who had arrived there earlier. The most noted of early Jewish goldsmiths in the United States was Myer Myers (1723–1795). Between 1725 and 1837, 50 Jewish goldsmiths are recorded in England. Thus in modern times Jewish goldsmiths in Northern and Central Europe severed the old connection with moneylending and pawnbroking and the trade became allied with formal banking, on the one hand, and with the making of delicate instruments and the watch trade, on the other. Jewish art, in particular, the ornamentation of Torah scrolls, *mezuzot*, and similar cult objects, was influenced by the Christian artisans who did the work for Jews, especially in Northern, Central, and Eastern Europe in the early Middle Ages. Family names like Goldschmidt, Goldsmith, Goldsmid, Zoref or Soref, and Orefice (Italian) generally indicate that at some stage in its history the family derived its livelihood from goldsmithing.

6

Leather Industry and Trade

In the East. Throughout the early Middle Ages, in countries under Muslim rule, tanning and leather craft remained in Jewish hands because of the low status of the profession. In 985 Muhammad ibn-Aḥmed al Magdisi reported that most tanners in Palestine and Syria were Jews. From the 12th to the 15th centuries the Dung Gate of the Old City of Jerusalem was called the Tanners' Gate because of its proximity to the Pool of Siloam, whose waters were considered unfit to drink but excellent for tanning purposes. Jews as tanners are mentioned frequently in Byzantium: in the biography of an archbishop who flourished around 1150, they are compared to "hungry, leather-gnawing dogs." Benjamin of Tudela considered that the Greeks of late 12th-century Constantinople hated the Jews because the Jewish tanners spilled their sewage water into the streets outside their houses and contaminated the Jewish quarter. The classical scholar Maximus Planudes mentions Jewish tanners in Constantinople in 1296; they lived in a separate quarter and were organized into a guild. Shortly after 1300 Jewish tanners who were Venetian subjects signed an agreement with the subjects of the empire, endorsed by the authorities, permitting them to lease ground for building houses and to pursue their trade in the city. To avoid competition, tasks were divided: the newcomers were to do the scraping, while the veterans did the tanning itself. In 1319 Emperor Andronicus II prohibited his subjects from engaging in tanning and ordered them to pursue other trades. The Venetian subjects seized the opportunity to break the earlier agreement and capture the whole trade. An imperial squad seized and destroyed their hides, and they were evicted from their houses. After protracted negotiations between the imperial and Venetian authorities, the Venetian claim for damages was refused. This was one instance of a conflict arising from the Byzantine policy of ousting Venice from the commerce in hides, furs, and leather from Crimea to Constantinople.

On his journey to Ereẓ Israel in 1488, Obadiah of Bertinoro found Jewish tanners in Rhodes. He thought it worthy of note that their clothes were clean and their manners good.

In the 16th and 17th centuries, the production of leather and the export of hides and leather was one of the most important Jewish economic enterprises.

Merchants from Salonika bought hides from the Balkans and resold them after finishing. To put a stop to this competition the merchants of Monastir (now Bitolj) forbade the sale of hides out of town. In the rabbinical responsa, trade in hides and mainly Cordoban leather is often mentioned. The responsa of Samuel b. Moses de Medina (1506–1589) record a hide and leather merchant with his own shop in Pleven (Plevna, Bulgaria) as well as the export of hides from Adrianople (Edirne, Turkey) to Ancona and Ragusa (Dubrovnik, Yugoslavia). According to Joseph b. David Lev (c. 1502–1588) and Joseph Moses Mitrani (1569–1639), who dealt with exports to Venice, these transactions were usually conducted in partnership. Solomon b. Aaron Hason (d. before 1733) frequently dealt with the large-scale export of Cordoban leather to France via Venice; in one case there were 21 bales exported by five partners.

Jews of Fez at the beginning of the 18th century dried, salted, and exported hides to Spain, Portugal, and Gibraltar; after payment of a special tax (*fayid*), the royal seal was affixed. In Algiers in 1899 there were 45 Jewish tanners and 730 shoemakers.

In Europe. In Muslim Spain there were many Jewish tanners. The famous Cordoba leather was exported to North Africa and Europe. In the Jewish quarter of Seville there were two tanners' squares. Three saddlers from Saragossa were Obadiah of Bertinoro's shipmates (1486–88). A tanners' street (Teneria) existed in the Jewish quarter of Saragossa around 1336 and tanners were mentioned in Castile in 1443.

At the beginning of the 14th century, there were Jewish tanners in the Kingdom of Naples. Under the rule of Frederick II Hohenstaufen, trade in skins and in leather goods was one of their basic economic activities in Sicily. Jewish tanners are mentioned in several Sicilian localities in the first half of the 15th century.

Jewish tanners are mentioned in Paris in 1258 and in Montpellier in 1293. There is also mention of one tannery in Troyes in 1189 and two in 1233. Jews in Central and Eastern Europe frequently engaged in tanning and other crafts connected with leather, from the Middle Ages onward. This was largely because the Christian attitude toward the trade was identical with the feeling prevalent in talmudic times. The family names which occur so frequently among European Jews, such as Gerber, Garber, Lederer, and Ledermann (German), Korzownik, Skurnik, Ganbarz, and Garbowski (Polish), and Kozelu (Czech), bear witness to their occupations.

In Bohemia and Moravia, buying hides from the local noblemen was one of the main tasks of the Jews, as stipulated in the charters on which their protection was based; purchasing the skins of small animals from peasants and from butchers was an important side line. Jews also imported and exported hides. At the end of the 16th century, Marcus Meisel was granted the monopoly of the leather trade in Prague. In 1629 the gentile tanners of Tachov included a clause in their charter forbidding any of their number to finish hides for Jews because the Jewish leather trade was undercutting the tanners. When the Jews were expelled from Litomerice in 1541, one man had to be allowed to remain because he alone was capable of supplying hides and tanning bark to the tanners. In Prague in 1729 there were 70 Jewish hide and leather merchants. The Jews who settled in Kremsier (Kromeriz) in 1670 after their expulsion from Vienna were permitted to deal in "various crude and finished leather." Leather and hide merchants frequented the large fairs, mainly the one at Breslau (Wroclaw), which was a center for the import of hides from Eastern Europe.

Jews were also active in tanning itself; since it was one of the trades outside guild control it was open to Jews, and after the Thirty Years' War tanneries became one of the most important Jewish economic outlets. When the Moravian guilds protested against the renewal of Jewish privileges in 1659, one of their arguments was the claim that the methods of tanning employed by the Jews were unsatisfactory. Jews were permitted to settle as tanners in localities otherwise forbidden to them. Most of the tanneries were the property of the local nobleman and were leased to the Jewish *randar* (see Arenda), who was sometimes not a tanner himself but the employer of one. However, some Jews had their own tanneries. In Polna the community as such leased the tannery from the municipality (1681) and in Kolin the community bought the tannery (1724). The council of Moravian Jewry issued several ordinances concerning the leather industry: it forbade the attempt to gain a monopoly on buying hides and other merchandise from a local nobleman, yet in another ordinance it forbade anyone to buy in a locality where someone else had a monopoloy by the terms of his contract with the local nobleman. It was considered the duty of the *Landrabbiner* to protect Moravian Jews from the competition of buyers from other districts. The council did not hold tanners (nor butchers) in high esteem: in 1709 it ruled that they could be members of the council only if they also held public office in their home community.

Early in the 17th century the Hapsburg rulers, true to their mercantilist policies, were interested in encouraging tanning. A survey that they carried out in Moravia in 1719 revealed that there were two tanneries owned by Jews and 79 leased by Jews from local noblemen; six of them employed one gentile laborer each; the lease of 13 of these tanneries was connected with the lease of a distillery; only ten tanneries in Moravia were run by gentiles. In Bohemia in 1724 there were 80 Jewish tanners and furriers (grouped together under one heading) and 26 tanneries were leased to Jews; 252 Jews were occupied in the leather industry; 146 were hide and leather merchants, and 106 were engaged in tanning. In the 18th century tanning and trading in leather were often connected. One specialty of the Jewish leather trade in Moravia was the kid trousers which, finished and colored in various ways, were an important feature of the peasants' national costume. The tanners were the first craftsmen in the Hapsburg Empire who were permitted to hire open salesrooms *(Verkaufsgewoelbe)* in Vienna (1781). This offered several Jews the opportunity to settle there.

These tanneries continued to flourish in the 19th century, and when new chemical methods were introduced many of them became important factories, as in Golcuv Jenikov and Kosova Hora (Amschelberg). Jews also founded new factories where no tanneries had existed before: e.g., in Pilsen where the first factory producing Moroccan-style leather was established in 1829 and in Brno where a factory producing French-style leather was founded in 1846. Over 20 of the leather factories in Bohemia in 1863 were run by Jews, and a large part of their export trade was with the United States. Leather production remained a Jewish craft for many years. After chromium tanning was introduced (1884) Jewish factories led the move to modernization. Between the two world wars Jewish firms played an important role in the production and export of leather goods.

Germany. In 1331 Jewish tanners were permitted, in return for a fee, to join the guild in Esslingen am Neckar. In 1406 there were Jewish saddle-makers in Frankfort, but Jewish tanners in general were not numerous. As late as the 17th century Jews were forbidden to engage in this craft in Hesse-Kassel. The Christian and Jewish tanners frequently clashed over the buying of hides and sale of the leather. In some districts, as in Hesse-Darmstadt, the trade was forbidden to Jews, and in all districts the tanners guild had an option on the hides for 24 hours after slaughtering. In 1718 the Berlin merchants' guild included hides and furs in a suggested list of merchandise in which Jews should be permitted to trade. In 1736 Samuel Slomka was granted the concession to establish a leather factory in Tilsit (Sovetsk) to produce, besides ordinary leather, Russian-style leather. At the turn of the 17th century, Jewish merchants supplied tanners in Berlin with hides and processed the leather according to the putting-out system. The Prussian *General-Reglement* of 1750 limited Jewish trade in hides and leather to fairs.

Frederick II founded, at his own expense, a factory for English-style leather, run by a Scottish expert, but it failed to prosper. After various unsuccessful endeavors to improve it, the firm was handed over to Daniel Itzig (1761). Army regiments were commanded to place their orders there. Daniel's son, Elias, continued to manage the factory until it closed down in 1818. Daniel Itzig himself founded another factory for chamois leather. The ordinances permitting Jews to import leather frequently stipulated that this should be in exchange for exporting locally manufactured textiles.

At the end of the 19th century, Jews were important in the leather industry of Germany. Between the world wars the trust founded by Adler and Oppenheimer, until 1918 in Strasbourg, developed into one of the largest industries of its kind in the world (S. Kaznelson (ed.), *Die Juden im deutschen Kulturbereich* (1962), 792–3). However, Jewish participation in actual tanning decreased: in 1907 there were only 334 Jewish tanners in Germany compared with 49,000 gentile ones. Many Jews were engaged in the production of leather goods such as purses, wallets, valises, etc. as entrepreneurs, managers, and workers, since conditions were similar to those in tailoring: it was a light industry, easily adaptable to piece work and to home and family enterprises. Many of the leather firms in Germany, particularly in Offenbach, were owned by Jews, and immigrant East European Jews supplied the labor.

Poland, Lithuania, and Russia. In 1460 Jewish tanners are mentioned as having lived "for a long time" in a Lemberg (Lvov) suburb. In Przemysl Jewish tanners are mentioned in the 16th century. There was a Jewish tanners' guild in Leszno (Lissa) in the 18th century. With the industrial development of the 1790s, Jewish entrepreneurs, among them Samuel Zbitkover, established tanneries: e.g., in Praga (suburb of Warsaw) which employed 15 laborers, in Cracow, Wegrow, and Lutomiersk. The Jewish community of Opoczno ran a tannery. Tanning and the leather trades became an outstanding Jewish occupation toward the end of the 19th century, employing tens of thousands of Jews. In some localities, such as Lukow, Kozienice, Siedlce, Radom, Bialystok, and Kielce, a large proportion of the Jewish inhabitants worked in the leather trade, which lost its main market in the 1917 Revolution. In 1894, 400 Jewish tanning workers in Krynki founded the Po'alei Zedek, one of the first trade unions in Russia (by 1898 they had 800 members). To fight the workers' demands the tannery owners founded the Agudat Ahim in 1906. In the eastern regions of the Pale of Settlement, 64.6% of all leather workers were Jews. In czarist Russia 287 out of 530 tanneries were owned by Jews (162 of them in Russian Poland). The largest was in Shavli (Siauliai). Other important centers were in Vilna, Smorgon, Mogilev, Minsk, and Dvinsk (Daugaupils, Latvia). Jewish participation in the leather trade in independent Poland remained considerable: in 1927 41% of all tanners were and in 1931 15,705 Jews were employed in the leather industries (45% of all leather workers). While among the gentiles, leather workers formed 0.9% of all industrial laborers, among Jews the percentage was 2.9; 31.8% of the independent employers of the larger and technologically developed factories were

Jewish tanners of Strykow, Lodz province, Poland.

Jews, but only 4.8% of the laborers in these factories were Jews. The percentage of Jews employed in the leather industries (45%) was even higher than that of the needleworkers (44.1%; R. Mahler, *Yehudei Polin Bein Shetei Milḥamot Olam* (1968), 73–98, passim). Their trade unions (Leder-farayn) were strong; in Warsaw there were two after 1922, one dominated by the Bund and one by the Communists (B. Hayyim, in *Pinkes Varshe*, 1 (1955), 387–96).

Israel. The leather industry received its impetus from immigrants from Central Europe in the middle 1930s; in 1937, 850 workers were employed in 61 firms. Production of boots for the British army increased from 80,000 pairs in 1942 to 400,000 in 1944; an additional 700,000 were produced by artisans and workshops. Production, which increased after the establishment of the State of Israel, was encouraged by the population increase and by the rise in the standard of living. In 1969 it totaled 1.5% of the total industrial production; exports totaled $3,500,000 (1.5% of all industrial exports). According to a 1965 industrial census 7,440 workers were employed in 2,580 firms: only 111 employed more than 10 workers; most work was done in family-style workshops.

7

Metals and Mining

A study of the part played by Jews in the mining and metal industries proves that there has been too great a tendency to minimize their participation in the promotion and development of these branches. It is true that the objective restrictions which kept the Jews off the land and prevented their ownership of it, especially in medieval society, contributed in no small measure to limiting their opportunities of exploiting natural resources in general and various metals in particular. Yet despite all this the Jews succeeded, at different times and in various countries, in penetrating several branches connected with the mining of metals, their contribution to the advance of the industry being at times of great significance.

Very little information on the exploitation of the earth's resources has come down to us from the mishnaic and talmudic periods. Until the end of the fourth century there were copper mines at Punon, at the south of the Dead Sea. The literature of these periods frequently mentions coal and copper refiners; it may be assumed that the "refiner" mentioned in the Mishnah (Ketubbot 7:10) is merely a copper smelter. As mentioned, the separation of Jews from the land in the Middle Ages had implications for the mining industry. In those times mining was frequently connected with agricultural labor, and thus in Germany, for instance, there were farmers who were engaged in extracting iron ore in their free time. It is therefore evident that since the Jews were cut off from agriculture their opportunities for extracting metals were limited. Added to this, in Christian Europe minerals were considered crown property, so that private ownership of mines was impossible. Yet in spite of all these restrictions Jews were to be found in various branches of the mining industry, as lessees and managers, traders in metals, and even miners. As for precious metals, there can be no doubt that their employment as minters of coins, especially in absolutist Europe at the time when Court Jews flourished, brought them into direct contact with gold and silver mining (see Mintmasters and Moneyers p. 250). A similar state of affairs prevailed with regard to the extraction of precious stones (see Diamond Trade and Industry p. 158), since the Jews were prominent in the international trade in luxury goods and in purveying them to royal courts, at least from the days of the Carolingian kingdom up to the time of the absolutist states in modern Europe. In such countries as Spain and Poland, where Jews played an outstanding part as colonizers, they were prominent as lessees of salt mines.

There were also Jews in different countries throughout the Middle Ages who were engaged in extracting both heavy and light metals of various kinds. In England, for instance, Jews had worked in tin mining in Cornwall in 1198. Joachim Gaunse appeared in 1581 and suggested to the English government new methods for processing copper. When it became known that he was a Jew from Prague he was arrested by the authorities and his fate is unknown. In Sicily, there was a long tradition of Jewish activity in the mines from the times of the emperor Tiberius, who sent 4,000 Jewish youths as slaves to the mines. Jews were commonly engaged there not only in the manufacture of metalware but also in mining silver and iron. In spite of the opposition of the local authorities, a royal decree of 1327 ordered Sicilian officials to support Jewish mine prospectors and miners. At the beginning of the 15th century two Jews of Alghero received special authorization to exploit the resources of the region, on condition that half the output be handed over to the crown. Attempts by Jews to extract metals in Germany are also known: in 1625 Duke Frederick Ulrich of Brunswick asked the theologians of the University of Helmstedt if he might be allowed to hand over the lead trade to two Jews and authorize them to move freely through his state for that purpose. After the members of the faculty had agreed, these Jews mined lead from the Harz Mountains.

In modern times the part played by Jews in the mining and metal industries of Germany reached considerable dimensions. After Aron Hirsch (1783–1842) had established a firm for buying and selling copper in 1805 Halberstadt became the cradle of the modern German nonferrous metal trade. In 1820 he became a partner in founding copper enterprises in Werne and Ilsenburg. When his son Joseph (1809–1871) joined the business its name was changed to Aron Hirsch and Son. In 1863 they acquired the copper works of Heegermuehle, near Eberswalde. A branch was established in New York in 1894 and the firm began to take an interest in the metal enterprises of France, Belgium, and England and the mines of Australia, America, and Eastern Asia. At the close of the 19th century Aaron Siegmund Hirsch initiated the establishment of the zinc enterprises of Vladivostok. The firm of Hirsch Kupfer- und Messingwerke A. G. was founded in 1906; World War I and the economic crisis of 1929–32 caused it to be liquidated in 1932. Dr. Emil Hirsch (1870–1938) then founded a new enterprise in Berlin, the Erze und Metalle Hirsch A.G., with a branch in Amsterdam, but the firm was liquidated when the Nazis came to power. Philipp Abraham Cohen, a descendant of the Hanover banking family, transferred the family business to Frankfort in 1821. In Hanover they had been connected with the mining enterprises in the Harz

Mountains. Philipp Abraham Cohen's son-in-law established the metal-trading firm of Henry R. Merton and Co. in London. In the meantime the Frankfort firm extended its scope and traded in American copper and tin from the Dutch Indies. This enterprise was also involved in the nickel and aluminum trades, and until 1873, when the Deutsche Gold und Silber-Scheideanstalt was established, in the silver trade too. In 1881 the branches in England and Frankfort established the Metallgesellschaft, Frankfort on the Main, which became the leading German firm in the metal trade. Among other enterprises, they established the Usine de Désargentation (de-silverizing plant) in Hoboken, near Antwerp. In 1896, together with the firms of Hirsch and Beer, and Sondheimer and Co., they undertook zinc and lead mining. The Metallurgische Gesellschaft (Lurgi) was established in 1897; together with the Metallgesellschaft, it founded the Berg und Metallbank A. G. in 1906. Once the firm had successfully overcome the post-World War I crisis, branches were established in Amsterdam, Basle, Brussels, Copenhagen, Madrid, Milan, Prague, Stockholm, and Vienna. It was liquidated as a Jewish firm when Hitler came to power.

The Jews of Russia, too, had considerable achievements to their credit in the mining of certain metals and in associated industries. In 1807 there were 253 Jewish copper and tin workers in Minsk, Kiev, and Yekaterinoslav, that is, 6.8% of the Jewish craftsmen in these towns. ICA statistics of 1897 reveal that there were then 15,669 Jewish smiths and 11,801 Jewish craftsmen in the various branches of the metal industry. The Jews were also well represented in the development of the industry: in Moscow four metal factories were established by Jews between 1869 and 1878, and a further two factories in the Moscow area between 1878 and 1880. Of the 96 large iron and tin plants in Odessa in 1910, 88 belonged to Jews. The laws of 1882 and 1887 excluded the Jews from the mines, but in spite of this they played a considerable role in the gold mines. Descendants of exiles and Jewish settlers in Siberia were among the pioneers of gold mining there. The director of the largest gold-mining enterprise in Russia in 1913, Lena Goldfields Co., was Baron Alfred Guenzburg.

In the U.S. there were several prominent Jewish firms engaged in copper extraction. In 1813 Harmon Hendricks established in Belleville, New Jersey, the Soho Copper Rolling Mills, later known as the Belleville Copper Mills. His descendants were prominent in the metal trade. In 1891 Meyer Guggenheim (1828–1905), formerly a peddler and dry-goods merchant, acquired copper mines and then established an enterprise in Aguas Calientes, Mexico. Together with his sons he founded the mining company of M. Guggenheim's Sons. In 1901 they merged with the American Smelting and Refining Co. and the Guggenheim sons directed the enterprise.

Coal, which had been practically unknown in medieval Europe, was introduced into various branches of industry in England at the beginning of the 17th century because of the rise in the price of firewood. The Industrial Revolution increased the importance of coal, which came into use in the other countries of Europe during the 18th and the beginning of the 19th centuries. In Eastern and Central Europe the Jews were pioneers in developing coal mines. In Poland, prospecting by Solomon Isaac of Bytom led to the establishment of two large coal mining enterprises in 1790: the Krol mine near Chorzow and the Królowa Ludwika mine near Zabrze, which were worked for about 50 years. Between 1874 and 1879 many Jews studied at the mining school of Tarnowskie Gory; they were later employed as miners and engineers in Upper Silesia. Jews participated in the wholesale coal and iron trade until World War II. The large coal concern of Katowice was a development of the important coal firm of Emmanuel Friedlander and Co. Their activity in the coal mines led them to develop an interest in other minerals, and thus brought them into various branches of the metal industry. In 1805 there were three copper foundries in Podolia employing 42 Jewish workers; in Warsaw a Jewish iron factory, which employed 200 Jewish workers, was established in 1848. Until 1938, when the cartel organizations introduced their policy of ousting all factories not connected with international concerns, the iron foundry of Cracow belonged to Jews. In the wholesale iron trade, the old-established Warsaw firms of Priwess, and Freilach and Carmel were prominent; both prospered between the two world wars. According to the census of 1931, 1,462 Jews were employed in the mines (including 853 miners); 33,318 Jews were employed in metal foundries and in the metal and machinery industries (9,185 manual workers), and 4,209 Jews in the minerals industry (1,440 manual workers). The great majority of the Jews employed in the metal branch (73.9%) were craftsmen.

The Jews of Germany, too, were active in the coal industry in that country: many of them entered it via the coal trade or real estate business. In various parts of Czechoslovakia the Jews were the first to extract coal. The first person to exploit the coal mines of Ostrava-Karvina (Moravia), in 1840, was David Gutmann of Lipnik nad Becvu. After obtaining the support of the Rothschild family, who owned iron works in Vitkovice, they established joint iron and mining enterprises there.

In South Africa Jews were among the pioneers in the exploitation of South Africa's mineral resources. They were early in the field when industrial development started during the second half of the 19th century, and they remained prominent in the opening up of the country's coal, diamond, gold, and base metal mines. Jews like Barney Barnato, the Joel brothers, Lionel Phillips, the Beit brothers, and the Albu brothers were among the prospectors, explorers, diggers, and financiers who flocked to the diamond fields at Kimberley in the

1870s. Sammy Marks began coal mining on a large scale in the Transvaal and laid the foundations of the steelworks at Vereeniging. When the industrial focus moved to Johannesburg with the discovery of gold there in 1886, the Kimberley Jews played a foremost role in the creation of the great mining groups which developed the Witwatersrand. Here Sir Ernest Oppenheimer created the powerful Anglo-American Corporation, headed the De Beers group, and stabilized the diamond market through the Diamond Corporation. Oppenheimer also pioneered the copper industry in Northern Rhodesia (now Zambia) and after World War II led the development of the new goldfields in the Orange Free State and in the Eastern Transvaal. During this period A. S. Hersov and S. G. Menell created the Anglo-Vaal mining and industrial group. Jewish financiers also promoted the exploitation of platinum, manganese, and asbestos deposits.

From the above it is clear that the notion that Jews succeeded in forming part of the metal industry in the Diaspora only in secondary branches, close to the consumer, ignores the specific part they played in developing the primary branches. Even if this part was not quantitatively significant, there is no doubt that it was qualitatively important. It would appear that in those times and countries in which Jews were able to enter these branches of industry they engaged in them with great success.

Jewish Craftsmen in Metal Trades. The agent of the king of France in Constantinople during the first half of the 16th century tells of the numerous Marranos who revealed to the Turks the secrets of manufacturing cannons, guns, warships, and war machines. Obadiah of Bertinoro found many Jewish copper and ironsmiths in Palermo in 1487. When an expulsion decree was issued against the Jews of Sicily, in the wake of the expulsion from Spain, the local authorities complained that tremendous loss would result "because almost all the craftsmen" in Sicily were Jews; their expulsion would deprive the Christians of "workers who manufacture metal utensils, arms, and ironware." A similar complaint was heard in Portugal as a result of the expulsion order of 1496.

Many Jewish craftsmen and artisans were engaged in the metal industry in Christian Spain. In 1365 three Jewish smithies are mentioned in Toledo, and there were also Jewish workshops in Avila, Valladolid, Valdeolivas near Cuenca, and Talavera de la Reina; a Jewish tinsmith, Solomon (Culeman) b. Abraham Toledano of Avila, is mentioned in a document of 1375; at the close of the 14th century Jewish smiths were called upon to repair the copper fountain of Burgos. Before 1391 many Jewish smiths, engravers, and goldsmiths lived in Barcelona. From a Saragossa register of 1401 we learn that there were many Jewish engravers and artisans in copper and iron. The local engraver's synagogue was used for the meetings of the community administration.

Jewish metalworkers continued to pursue their crafts along traditional medieval lines in various Muslim lands, where manual occupations were often despised and therefore pursued by religious minorities, particularly Jews. The report of the French consul on the condition of the Jews in Morocco at the close of the 18th century speaks of Jewish armorers there. The traveler Benjamin II relates that Jews were employed in the iron industry in Libya in the middle of the 19th century. Visiting Yemen in the late 1850s R. Jacob Saphir found many Jewish smiths.

Israel. The main limitation to industrial development in Israel, the scarcity of raw materials and energy sources, is particularly severe with respect to heavy industry. On the other hand, the needs of a rapidly growing modern economy as well as considerations of military security have weighed heavily in favor of encouraging metal industries. Thus, this branch took part in industrial growth, particularly during World War II, when British Army demands were met by private Jewish initiative, and during the 1960s, when the Israel government allocated resources to rapid industrial expansion. Still, Israel metal industries are most successful at the finishing stages, in which skills and knowledge account for most of the value added. As to the exploitation of mineral resources in Israel, it is limited mainly to providing materials for certain chemical industries; chief among them is the extraction of Dead Sea minerals and the Negev phosphates on the one hand, and quarrying for cement and building stones on the other hand.

Artisan working in copper, Marrakesh, Morocco.

8

Petroleum and Oil Products

In modern times Jews took part in the development of the oil industry, some in pioneering the extraction of oil and trade in its products in their respective countries, and some in financing the industry abroad.

Oil prospecting and the development of the oilfields of eastern Galicia from the middle of the nineteenth century was due to a large measure to the initiative of Jews. In Borislav the first attempts to find petroleum were made by a Jew, Schreiner, before the middle of the 19th century. Ozocerite, which became a substitute for the expensive beeswax in the manufacture of candles, was then discovered there. Ozocerite candles were soon extensively marketed in the region. The great demand for ozocerite led many Jews in Drogobych to acquire plots of land in Borislav to extract it. Thousands of Jews streamed from surrounding townlets and villages to work there, in primitive conditions. The work was performed in two shifts of 12 hours each; women and children also were employed on the easier tasks. Abraham Schreiner, son of the discoverer of petroleum in Galicia, attempted to separate the petroleum from the earth admixture. After many failures, he succeeded in establishing the first petroleum refinery in Borislav in 1854. Many railway companies then ordered petroleum from him for lighting their carriages and stations. Thus he became the world's first "petroleum king" until the destruction of his refinery in a fire in 1886.

In the 1880s the enterprise, capital, and modern methods of corporations drove out the Jewish entrepreneurs with their inadequate means and primitive methods. As a result, 5,000 Jewish workers in Borislav addressed themselves to the second Zionist Congress in Basle in 1898, described their plight, and requested assistance for *aliyah* to Erez Israel. Some Jews were still active in the oilfields of Galicia between the two world wars.

As the oil wells in czarist Russia were situated outside the Pale of Settlement Jews were at first unable to participate in the industry. Later on Jewish chemists succeeded in entering the petroleum trade and subsequently also the industry. By 1910, 15% of oil extraction was carried out by Jews, as well as 44% of the manufacture of kerosene, 32% of the manufacture of lubrication oils, and 49.6% of the trade in oil products on the Baku exchange.

During the second half of the 19th century Jews were engaged in the transportation of petroleum. The Jewish petroleum company Dembo & Kagan, whose owners were A. Dembo of Kovno and Kh. Kagan of Brest-Litovsk, laid the first oil pipeline in Russia in 1870. They set up a petroleum refinery in a suburb of Baku and established relations with shipping companies of the Caspian region which transported the oil by sea, whence it was expedited by rail throughout Russia. Because of the monopolistic position of the Nobel Company in the Caucasus, Dembo & Kagan could only operate for five years, after which it was compelled to confine itself to the marketing of oil.

The brothers Saveli and Mikhail Polyak and the engineer Arkadi Beylin, in partnership with the Rothschild Bank, founded the Mazut Company of Baku, later amalgamated with the Shell Company. The Rothschild house also financed the Batum Oil Association, founded after the construction of the Trans-Caucasian railroad and owned mainly by Jews. The Pereire family of Paris invested considerable sums in the oil fields of the Caucasus. A. M. Feigel, one of the initiators of the petroleum trade in Baku, organized, with, A. Beylin, a syndicate of oil companies to compete with the American Standard Oil. The Dembat brothers succeeded in publicizing mazut as a cheap fuel oil for ships and locomotives. They were the first Jews to be permitted by the Russian government, in appreciation of their activities, to acquire oil wells. With Baron Horace Guenzburg, they established the Volga-Caspian Petroleum Company.

In Czechoslovakia Jews were active in oil refining, and in general branches of the trade and industry. The Kralupy refinery on the river Vltava was established by Jindřich Eisenschimel and Ludvik Heller. The refinery owned by David Fanto was prominent in the industry by 1924. The Vacuum Oil Company was headed by Charles Wachtel and Bedřich Stránsky, who transferred their affairs to New York in 1939.

In England, Marcus Samuel, Viscount Bearstead, played a central role, sometimes in cooperation with the house of Rothschild, in developing the trade and transportation of petroleum and oil on a large international scale from 1897. In 1907 he founded the Shell Royal Dutch Company together with Royal Dutch, which launched England as an oil power. He was one of the first to initiate the haulage of petroleum through the Suez Canal. During World War I, he played a role of prime importance in the supply of oil to the British Navy. Sir Robert Waley Cohen was active in the Shell Company from 1901, and in 1905 was appointed director of the Asiatic Petroleum Company. From 1907 he served as director of the Anglo-Saxon Petroleum Company. During World War I he served as adviser on oil affairs to the Army Council.

In France, in addition to the investments of the house of Rothschild of Paris and the Pereire family, Alexandre Deutsch founded the Société de Pétrole, and his sons Emile (1847–1924) and Henri (1846–1918) Deutsch de la Meurthe succeeded him. Henri published a work on petroleum and its use and headed the petroleum industry exhibit at the Paris International Exhibition in 1889.

The role of Jews in the petroleum industry in the U.S. was negligible. The petroleum industry in the U.S. was in the hands of a small number of Protestant families which did not as a rule hire Jews. The Arab boycott after 1948 strengthened this tendency not to employ Jews so as to avoid friction with the Arab oil states. An exception was the Blaustein family, founder of the American Oil Company.

In Israel. The main oil field is at Ḥeleẓ, some 35 mi. (55 km.) south of Tel Aviv and 7 mi. (11 km.) east of the coast. Drilling was started in 1947 by Petroleum Development of Palestine (a subsidiary of the Anglo-Iranian Oil Co.) but was terminated early in 1948, due to the outbreak of hostilities, at a depth of 3,600 ft. (1,105 m.) It was resumed in 1955 by Lapidoth Israel Oil Prospecting Co., which struck oil at 5,000 ft. (1,500 m.) in lower cretaceous sands. Thirty-seven wells have been drilled in the field since, and 22 were in operation in 1970. Oil was struck at the Kokhav field, a northern extension of Ḥeleẓ, in September 1962. Eleven out of 24 wells are productive and, up to January 1968, produced 2,700,000 barrels; in 1970, 16 wells were in operation.

Gas fields were found at Zohar, Kidod, and Kanna'im, near Arad, approximately at the border between the Judean Desert and the Negev. The first offshore well was drilled in 1970 by Belco at Barbur, 10 mi. (16 km.) west of Ashkelon, in 260 ft. (80 m.) of water. Offshore exploration is also carried out by Lapidoth, Naphtha, Israel National, Mayflower, and others.

Railroads

Jewish financiers played a considerable role in the construction of railroads in France and in Central and Eastern Europe from the 1830s until the beginning of the 20th century. These Jewish financiers were the only investors – besides the British – among the private bankers dominant in Europe until the second half of the 19th century (see also Banking p. 209) who were prepared to risk their capital in the pioneer stage of railroad construction. In the second half of the 19th century, when large banking joint-stock firms sprang up and expanded, private banks were increasingly pressed into the background, and the share of private Jewish capital in railroad investment diminished accordingly. In the majority of European countries this tendency became linked to nationalization of the railroads when financial crises occurred in private railroad companies. The nationalization of Prussian railroads was organized on the financial side by Bismarck's adviser Gerson von Bleichroeder. In the 19th-century era of "railroad fever" former Court Jews who had become private bankers with considerable funds took part in furthering the industrial revolution through their investments in railroad construction.

The Rothschilds were urged by Nathan Mayer Rothschild soon after the opening of the first successful railroad in England (1825) to invest money on the continent in railroad construction. Salomon Rothschild of Vienna sent Professor F. X. Riepel from the Vienna Institute of Technology to England to study the new means of transportation with Rothschild's secretary Leopold von Wertheimstein. Subsequently they proposed the construction (1829) of a first line to run straight through the Hapsburg Empire, connecting Vienna with Galicia and Trieste. The July Revolution postponed the execution of Rothschild's plans. It was only in 1836, after overcoming many obstacles (especially the rivalry of the Viennese banking houses of Arnstein and Eskeles) that he began construction of the northern line from Vienna to Bochnia, in Galicia. The railroad was only completed in 1858. The house of Rothschild sold the shares on the stock market mainly to small investors.

James Rothschild of Paris was encouraged to construct the local line between Paris and St. Germain (opened in 1837) by Emile Pereire. Emile Pereire and his brother Isaac viewed the railroad as the salvation of the future, producing work for the masses, connecting nations, and conducive to world welfare and peace. The two brothers could later boast that through their efforts more than 6,000 miles (10,000 km.) of railroads had come into existence. In the 1840s they were the rivals of the Rothschilds in this field.

After the success of the Paris–St. Germain line, James Rothschild and the Fould brothers (apostate Jews) were eager to receive the concession for the Paris-Versailles line. The government eventually approved two plans, so that Rothschild constructed his line on the left bank of the River Seine and the Foulds on the right bank. In 1839 the railroad was opened, and in 1840 the two companies merged. This did not diminish the rivalry between them and the Pereire brothers. James Rothschild also succeeded in obtaining the concession for the construction of a northern line connecting Paris with England and the industries of northern France. The financial means of the Rothschilds were thereby severely strained, but the line was at last opened in 1846.

Nathan Mayer Rothschild and his sons helped finance the state-constructed railroad network in Belgium in the years 1834 to 1843. The Antwerp-Ghent line was built by the first private railway company in Belgium formed by Leopold Koenigswarter. The Rothschilds were the chief financiers of the world-spanning railroad politics of Leopold I. They also raised funds for building railroads in Italy, Spain, and Brazil.

The Pereire brothers were second only to the Rothschilds in the first stage of railroad network development on the continent until 1869. The first half of their organizational activity was spent on a substantial part of the French railroad network. While the Rothschilds constructed the "northern" line in the 1840s, the Pereires were responsible for the "southern" one. The 1848 revolution plunged the railroads into a severe crisis (the "southern" line, managed by Isaac Pereire, was also financially ruined). The Pereire brothers wished to overcome this crisis by diverting to plans for a "railroad bank," a bank that would solve all the current financial difficulties of the French economy. The Crédit Mobilier (1852) was intended not only to finance railroad construction but also heavy industry. Pereire introduced a new type of railroad security, the 500-franc capital bond (*obligation*), paying 15 francs annual interest and issued at whatever the market would bring, generally between 300 and 400 francs. With interest guaranteed by the state these bonds were ideally suited to the investor of moderate means. They quickly replaced other types of railroad borrowing and greatly facilitated railroad finance.

In the first years of its establishment the Crédit Mobilier financed (through advance payments and increased circulation of bonds) the "southern" line, the "grand central," the French "eastern" line, and many others in their first years.

Through its contribution the railroad network expanded from 2,000 miles (3,600 km.) in 1852 to 11,000 miles (18,000 km.) in 1870. The Pereire brothers did not neglect to finance railroad construction and industrial ventures abroad. They contributed to the predominance of French finance in the development of foreign railroads in the post-1850 decade: in Austria, where there was fierce competition between the Pereires and the Rothschilds, the Pereires founded the important Austrian State-Railroad Company, in conjunction with Sina, Arnstein, and Eskeles, while the Rothschilds were successful in buying the Lombard-Venetian and the Central Italian Railway (1856). In Spain there was lively rivalry between the Rothschilds, Pereires, and Jules Isaac Mirès; and in Hungary they built the "Franz-Joseph" line (1857). The Crédit Mobilier also financed Swiss railroads.

The importance of railroads was grasped in Russia only after its defeat in the Crimean War. The Grande Société des Chemins de fer Russes (1857) had, besides the Pereires, other Jewish bankers as founders: Alexander Stieglitz of St. Petersburg, S. A. Fraenkel of Warsaw, and the Mendelssohns of Berlin. An important figure in Russian railroad construction in the 1860s and 1870s was Samuel Poliakoff. He built railroads of supreme importance for the Russian grain export trade, and also wrote on the political aspect of railroad construction. He and other Jewish entrepreneurs succeeded in attracting foreign capital without which their plans would have been unattainable. Railroad construction by Jewish bankers in Russia created employment for numbers of Jews, who filled technical and administrative posts. The advent of the railroad brought many changes in Jewish economic and social life, described, for instance, in the poem *Shenei Yosef ben Shim'on* of J. L. Gordon.

Bethel Henry Strousberg started by working for English firms, and when he had accumulated enough capital, founded railway companies in Prussia and later in Hungary. He also acquired locomotive factories and rolling mills for rails, and subsequently coal mines. A careless venture into Rumanian railroad construction ruined his enterprise. His bankruptcy influenced public opinion in favor of nationalization of railroad lines in Germany. It also revealed malpractices and bribery, which were given a prominent place in anti-Semitic propaganda.

Jewish bankers were large-scale investors in railroad construction outside Europe. Baron Maurice de Hirsch bought, in 1869, the concession for railroad building in Turkey from the bankrupt International Land Credit Company. His connection by marriage with the Jewish banking enterprise Bischoffsheim and Goldschmidt aided him initially. In 1869 he began the first stage of extending the Austro-Hungarian lines southward. However, before beginning construction on the Oriental Railroad, he took steps to secure financial backing, and chose a new type of 3% government loan. "Turkish lottery bonds," which attracted small investors in France and Germany, were offered on the general market. Hirsch concluded his project in 1888.

At first Jewish financiers, mainly of German origin, acted as intermediaries between foreign finance and the United States. When the Civil War broke out in 1861, railway bonds, mainly distributed by Jewish bankers in Europe, served as a means of payment for munitions bought in Europe. The Speyer, Stern, and Seligman New York banking houses all dealt in railway shares. A leading personality in late 19th- and early 20th-century American financing was Jacob H. Schiff. In 1875 he became a member of the banking firm of Kuhn, Loeb & Company (a firm long engaged in railroad financing) which he eventually dominated. In 1897 he reorganized the Union Pacific Railroad, which was described at the time as being "battered, bankrupt and decrepit." According to financial authorities the Harriman-Schiff railway combination became the most powerful and most successful that America had ever known. Schiff was one of the first supporters and associates of James Hill, who, by building the Great Northern Railway, virtually became the founder of a vast empire in the northwest. His firm aided other railroads by financial operations until the end of World War I. Schlesinger-Trier in Berlin, together with other Jewish banks, imported the shares of the Canadian Pacific railroad and offered them on the Berlin stock market.

A position similar to that of Schiff in financing railway companies in the United States was held by Sir Ernest Cassel in England. He had a share in developing Swedish, American, and Mexican railway companies. The Vickers and Central London Railway Company was connected with his name.

10

Ships and Sailing

As long as the Mediterranean remained open to the European West (up to the ninth century), Jewish traders were prominent in maritime contacts between the Mediterranean coast and the southern shores of the sea. Gregory of Tours (sixth century) tells of a ship manned by Jews plying the coast of Provence and Liguria. Norman ships sighted in Carolingian times were thought to be either Jewish, African, or British. During the Muslim domination of the Mediterranean there is evidence in contracts, responsa, and descriptions of partnerships of Jews "in ships," i.e., in cargoes; Jewish ownership of "a third of a ship" is mentioned. Maimonides distinguishes between various legal forms of this financing of maritime trade. In the main, such Jewish merchants conducted their manifold and widespread trade in ships owned by gentiles. There were, however, notable exceptions: Benjamin of Tudela observed that the Jews in Tyre were shipowners. In southern France, particularly in Marseilles, Jewish shipowners, who were barely differentiated from their Christian competitors, were active from the Byzantine era until well into the Middle Ages. Evidence of some Jewish shipping activities may be found in Aragon, Barcelona, Portugal, and the Balearic Islands in the late Middle Ages. Most Mediterranean ports contained Jewish merchants, brokers, and insurers, engaged in various aspects of shipping.

Jewish scholars may have helped spread the knowledge of early nautical aids like the compass, quadrant (predecessor of the sextant), astrolabe, and astronomical tables from the Arab East to the Christian West. Levi b. Gershom (1288–1344) devised an improved quadrant which continued in use for four centuries and was known as "Jacob's staff"; his invention was itself a refinement of the "Quadrans Judaicus" of Judah b. Machir. The famous "Alfonsine Tables" were translated into Spanish and amended by two Jewish physicians at the court of Aragon in the late 13th century. Majorca was known for its nautical instruments, produced by Jewish craftsmen, and for its Jewish mapmakers, the most renowned of whom were Abraham Cresques (d. 1387) and his son Judah, who completed his father's lifework, a map of the world. Apostatizing after the massacres of 1391, Judah Cresques entered the service of Prince Henry the Navigator and became director of his nautical academy at Sagres. Abraham

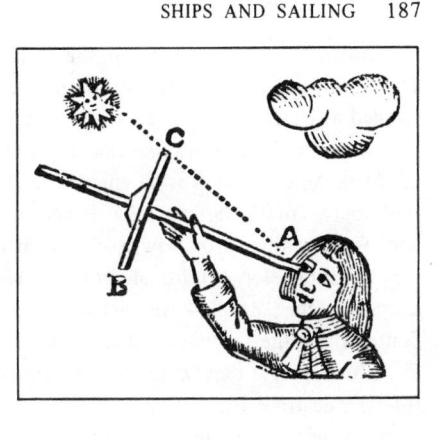

The "Jacob's staff," a mariners' instrument invented by Levi ben Gershom in the 14th century.

Zacuto constructed the first metal astrolabe, compiled astronomical tables, and was consulted by Columbus, Vasco de Gama, and other leading navigators of the Age of Discovery. Some Jews participated in the great European voyages of discovery. Jewish merchants on the Barbary Coast and other Muslim Mediterranean coasts sometimes engaged in privateering and piracy.

The Marrano Diaspora in the Mediterranean world, Northern Europe (Amsterdam, Hamburg, London), and the New World was active in international maritime commerce, mainly as entrepreneurs, merchants, brokers, and insurers. In Altona and later in Copenhagen Portuguese Jews participated in the shipbuilding industry, developed the trade with Greenland, and pioneered in whaling; the authorities of Glueckstadt attracted Portuguese Jews by offering them the right to engage in shipbuilding, from which they were excluded in all Hanseatic cities. In England a Marrano, Simon Fernandez, was chief pilot of Sir Walter Raleigh. In his "Humble Address on behalf of the Jewish Nation petitioning Oliver Cromwell to readmit the Jews to England" Manasseh Ben Israel emphasized the services the Jews could render to English shipping. Members of the Shomberg family achieved distinction in the royal navy and merchant marines. Joseph d'Aguilar Samuda (1813–1885), a pioneer in the building of iron steamships, helped found the Institute of Naval Architects. Gustav Wilhelm Wolff, joint founder of the Harland and Wolff shipyards of Belfast, one of the world's largest, joined the Church of England at an advanced age. Sephardi Jews played an important role in colonial trade. The Furtado and Gradis families (who pioneered the Canada trade) were prominent among the shipping merchants of Bordeaux. Marrano shipowners and shipbuilders were active in Leghorn. In Antwerp the Mendes-Nasi family were prominent shippers in the spice trade and even had their own ships built.

Jews sailed the Indian Ocean, mainly in non-Jewish ships, playing a not inconsiderable role in shipping in the 11th–12th centuries and once more in the 16th–18th centuries. They were also active in shipping in Constantinople and worked as boatmen or porters in the ports of Constantinople (where the Jewish boatmen were known as *kaikjes*) and Salonika. In the British and Dutch colonies of North America, Jews were engaged in the oceanic colonial trade as well as in trade between the various colonies and in fishing enterprises. Michael and Bernard Gratz, shippers of New York, outfitted privateers in the War of Independence. Captain John Ordronalux (1778–1841) was a highly successful privateer captain in the 1812–14 war between the United States and Great Britain. In South Africa the De Pass brothers were the largest shipowners for many years in the 19th century; they were connected mainly with developing the whaling and fishing industries.

In modern times, Jewish participation in shipbuilding – as in other heavy industries – was not common. However, there were exceptions. When Alexander Moses of Koenigsberg began building a ship in 1781, the German builders protested; Frederick II allowed him to finish this one but not to build another. Albert Ballin raised the standard of the Hamburg-Amerika Line and brought it international repute by introducing modern passenger services and winter pleasure cruises. Jens and Lucie Borchardt (1878–1969) developed tugboat shipping in Hamburg harbor; after the Nazi rise to power they continued their activity in Great Britain. In 1870 W. Kuntsmann (1844–1934) of Stettin founded the largest shipping firm on the eastern coast of Prussia. In Russia Jews helped develop the internal river traffic: David S. Margolin organized a firm which owned 62 river steamboats on the Dnieper and in the 1880s G. Polyak built a fleet of petroleum tankers that plied from the Caspian Sea up the Volga. Austrian Lloyd was organized by Italian Jews from Trieste, as was the Navigazione Generale Italiana. Jacob Hecht formed the Rhenania Rheinschiffahrts group in 1908 and the Neptun company in 1920 for river shipping.

11

Sugar Trade and Industry

In the Middle Ages sugar was a luxury article, and sugar for European consumption was produced in Syria, Palestine, Crete, Egypt, Sicily, and southern Spain. The Cairo *Genizah* records reveal that making and selling sugar from sugarcane was one of the most common occupations of Jews in the Middle Ages; Sukkari was a common family appellation from the beginning of the 11th until the end of the 13th centuries in Egypt and in North Africa. Sugar refineries were often in Jewish hands. Jews are mentioned as exporters of sugar from Crete in the 15th century. When sugar began to be used for everyday consumption (15th century), Marranos played a leading role in introducing sugarcane cultivation to the Atlantic islands of Madeira, the Azores, the Cape Verde Islands, and São Tomé and Príncipe in the Gulf of Guinea, and in the 16th century to the Caribbean Islands. They also brought the cultivation of sugarcane from Madeira to America, and the first great proprietor of plantations and sugar mills, Duarte Coelho Pereira, allowed numerous Jewish experts on sugar processing to come to Brazil. Among them was one of the first important Jewish proprietors of sugar mills, Diogo Fernandes.

In Europe Marranos who were active in international commerce, such as the merchant family of Ximenes, played an important role in the import of sugar to Lisbon and thence to northwestern Europe, especially Antwerp. During the 16th and the beginning of the 17th centuries there were many Jews among the merchants of Antwerp, the Portuguese colony, which was central to the sugar trade in the port and played a vital part in the development of Antwerp as the central European sugar market, where many refineries were established. They made Brazil, where several Portuguese Jews had established sugar plantations and mills, the most important area of sugar production in the world. From around the 1620s Amsterdam took the place of Antwerp in the sugar trade and many Marranos left Brazil and Portugal to settle in Amsterdam. Some Jews (e.g., Abraham and Isaac Pereire and David de Aguilar) owned refineries in Amsterdam. In 1639 ten of the 166 *"engenhos"* in Dutch Brazil belonged to declared Jews, while others belonged to Marranos who kept their Jewishness secret. The Jews of Brazil were not important as proprietors of mills but rather as financial agents, brokers, and export merchants. When Brazil came again under Portuguese rule in the second half of the 17th century many Jews emigrated to Surinam, Barbados, Curaçao, and Jamaica, where they acquired large sugarcane plantations and became the leading entrepreneurs in the sugar trade. Benjamin d'Acosta introduced sugarcane to Martinique in 1655, bringing with him 900 Jews (who were expelled in 1683). Sugar production was introduced into South Africa in the 1840s by Aaron de Pass of Natal. From the beginning of the 17th century Hamburg played a growing role in the European sugar trade – to a considerable extent thanks to the activities of the Marranos who had settled there. Early in the 18th century Portuguese Jews lost their leading position in the sugar trade, in Hamburg because of the growth of competition, and in Brazil because of persecutions of the Marranos and the general decline of the trade in that country. In the first half of the 18th century, London gradually ousted Amsterdam as the center of the sugar trade; at the same time the role of the Jews became less important.

Jews also played a leading role in the development of the sugar-beet industry in Poland, Russia, the Ukraine, Hungary, and Bohemia. In Eastern Europe Jews were the traditional buyers of agricultural produce from the estates and often leased the local refinery and mill from the landowners. Requests by Polish Jews to erect sugar refineries were turned down by the authorities in 1816, 1827, 1834, and 1837. Finally, Hermann Epstein built his first refinery in 1838 and by 1852 his was the largest and most modern in Poland. He was joined by L. Kronenberg and other leading Polish Jewish industrialists and financiers. In the Ukraine Israel Brodsky first helped finance Count Bobrinski, pioneer of Russian sugar-beet, and later he and his sons established numerous refineries. Other Jews entered this field (such as M. Halperin and M. Sachs) until by 1872 one-quarter of the total sugar production in Russia was in Jewish hands. In 1914, 86 refineries in Russia (32% of the total) were owned by Jews; 42.7% of the administrators of the joint-stock sugar companies were Jewish, and two-thirds of the sugar trade was in Jewish hands. The percentage of Jewish workers, managers, technicians, and scientists employed in the field was correspondingly high. Between the two world wars, Jews in Poland were squeezed out of the sugar trade through the anti-Semitic economic policy. In Hungary a pioneering role in the development of the sugar-beet industry was played by Ignac Deutsch; his grandson Sándor de Hatvany Deutsch (1852–1913) enlarged the firm and represented Hungary at international sugar conferences.

12
Tailoring

The Hebrew word for "tailor," *ḥayyat*, first appears in mishnaic and midrashic literature. Tailors are mentioned frequently in the Talmud, and Jewish tailors were to be found in Muslim countries at this period, but rarely in significant numbers. Almost every Jewish community had its own tailor whose presence was necessitated by the obligatory ritual commandments such as *sha'atnez*. The Church was also interested in enforcing the wearing of special Jewish garments. Moneylending entailed some knowledge of tailoring since it was necessary to keep pawned clothes in good repair. Although both Church pressure and moneylending were absent in Islamic countries, tailoring on a small- and medium-scale became an important element in Jewish society. In Yemen entire Jewish villages subsisted on weaving and tailoring until 1948. The main obstacles to Jewish tailors in medieval Europe were raised by the guilds, who continuously tried to restrict their activity to producing their own distinctive clothing for Jewish clients alone. However, in Christian Spain, where there were many Jewish tailors as the Christian guilds were comparatively weak, the rulers often intervened on their behalf when their livelihood was threatened by the encroachment of local guilds and authorities. In 1489 Ferdinand and Isabella of Spain annulled an ordinance enacted in Burgos which prohibited Jewish tailors and other craftsmen from plying their trade outside the Jewish quarter. The connection between tailoring and the trade in secondhand goods and old clothes, which had to be repaired and resold, was most clearly in evidence in Italy, especially in Rome, where a Jewish tailors' guild existed from the 15th century and between one-quarter and one-half of the Jewish community was engaged in various branches of the clothing trade in the 16th century. Bernardino Ramazzini (1633–1714), an early authority on occupational diseases, noted that many Jews suffered from weak eyesight, legs, and lungs, caused by repairing old clothes in poorly lit and badly ventilated rooms. Many Italian cities tried to prohibit Jews from refurbishing old clothes because this often provided a springboard for the prohibited manufacture and sale of new garments. The nexus of tailoring and trading in old clothes remained important in Italian Jewry until the 20th century.

Jewish tailoring in central Europe, as elsewhere, was conditioned by *sha'atnez* laws and the tie with the repair and sale of used clothing, but it grew in scope wherever conditions became more favorable. In Prague a continuous struggle was waged between the Christian and the Jewish guilds because the Jewish tailors were accused of illegally selling new clothes. The banner of the Jewish tailors' guild, a colorful patchwork of cloth, bore a pair of scissors embroidered in gold. These conflicts were operative in the expulsion of the Prague community (1745), but the move affected the Christian tailors since the expelled Jews now produced wares for the countryside and nobody came to Prague to buy new clothes. Among the 1,418 Jewish families who returned to Prague were 91 tailors and tailoresses, eight trouser sewers, seven linen menders, and 37 button makers, as well as dozens of artisans and merchants dealing in a variety of haberdashery and clothing articles. The number of Jewish tailors in Moravia increased from between one and three in each community at the beginning of the 18th century to between four and 12 at its end.

In Poland-Lithuania tailoring was one of the first crafts plied extensively in the 16th and 17th centuries and the earliest in which independent guilds were formed by Jews. Their ranks were reinforced by the embroiderers and cap makers, almost exclusively Jewish crafts. Jewish tailors were soon locked in fierce and often bloody competition with their Christian competitors, particularly in Lublin. Riots were often provoked by artisans who accused Jews of selling ready-to-wear clothing or of selling to Christians. In Warsaw in 1795 there were 74 Jewish tailors supplying custom-made garments and 53 tailors and 36 sellers of ready-to-wear clothing. The number of tailors in other cities was also large: Vilna had 88 in 1765 and Lublin 90 in 1759. In Poznan province they were particularly numerous: in the late 18th century 48 of the 50 tailors in Krotoszyn were Jews, as were 32 of 51 in Leszno (Lissa), 31 of 46 in Ostrow Wielkopolski, and 56 of 57 in Rogozno. In the Pale of Settlement tailoring both at home and as an itinerant craft in the villages became the mainstay of a growing section of the impoverished population of the shtetl. The life-syle, songs, and folklore of the *amkho sher un ayren* ("the simple people of the scissors and ironing board") became in Yiddish literature the expression of the joys and sufferings of Jewish workers. This way of life was carried overseas in the mass emigrations to France, England, and the U.S. In Poland in 1931, 504,570 Jews constituted 44.1% of all those active in the clothing industry; these were fairly evenly divided into employed manual and white-collar workers and home workers. About 52% of the independent employers in the clothing industry were Jews, though most Jewish firms were small or medium sized. Polish anti-Semitic policy in the 1930s compelled them to adopt new forms of work and organization.

In Germany — except for the production of clothes for Jewish needs and the

Polish tailor, 1920s

repair of clothing held in pawn – Jews entered the general field of tailoring as sellers: 41 Christian tailors were employed by Jews in Frankfort on the Main in 1611. During the 17th century protests were heard throughout the country that Jewish peddlers were selling new clothes, above all at the Leipzig fairs and other such markets. With the growth of cities in the 19th century Jews gradually established stores for haberdashery and the like, then moved into large-scale wholesale clothing manufacture. Between one-third and one-half of the manufacturing firms in the German clothing industry were owned by Jews, and the same proportion of wholesale houses; their share in this trade was highest in Berlin. The production of hats and caps was almost entirely Jewish owned. Various Jewish clothing stores were set up in different places, forming the basis of the later department stores. In 1644, in Vienna, Christian tailors complained that Jewish tailors were making ready-to-wear garments and employing Christian tailors, but in fact Jewish tailors did not become significant until the 19th century. The sale of used European clothing to the Balkans and the Near East, which was centered on Vienna, was managed by Jews. The production of hats, caps, and umbrellas was almost exclusively Jewish, as was that of underclothes, which had been freed of guild restrictions by Maria Theresa.

Though Jews in France (Avignon, Bordeaux, and Alsace) had long been engaged in buying, repairing, and selling old clothes, this activity declined after the French Revolution. The mass emigration of Jews from Eastern Europe after the pogroms of 1881–83 and 1903–05 and between the world wars brought to Paris thousands of impoverished Jews who, driven by both experience and necessity, turned en masse to certain sectors of the clothing industry, particularly hat-

and cap-making. Since they worked for low pay in "sweatshops" and doing piecework at home, Jews were in the forefront of the unionization of Parisian clothing workers. When 55 Jewish hat makers wanted to found a union in 1892, they had to wait until some of them were naturalized for none of these workers was French. This union remained entirely Jewish (289 members) until 1936, when the proportion of Jews became 53.6% of the 1,445 members. In the hosiery union their percentage − 90.9 (200 out of 220) before 1936 − declined to 39.6 (720 out of 1,820). The handbag-makers' union was 80% Jewish (160 out of 200) before 1936 and remained so afterward as well (2,400 out of 3,000). After World War I Polish Jews gained a prominent share of the knitware and hosiery industries. However, the role of Jews in the French clothing industries, particularly in production in small family firms, declined after World War II. Jews did not penetrate the field of haute couture in Paris.

In England Jews were first connected with the clothing trade to a sub-stantial degree as secondhand clothes dealers in the 18th century. At the end of the 18th century there were 1,000–1,500 Jewish dealers in old clothes and even in 1850 between 500 and 600 were still active. They either sold complete garments, or, where these were too worn, cut them up into smaller articles, such as waistcoats. That Jews in this period were particularly concerned with cheap clothing is confirmed by their activity as buyers at the East India Company's auctions of imported cloth, where they seem to have dominated the market in cheap or damaged cloth. Their activity as navy agents (supplying ships with stores at a time when the governments left such matters to contractors) naturally made them suppliers of "slop clothing" for sailors' dress − a connection with the supply of uniforms which persisted to contemporary times. Jews were also prominent in the hat trade, both as sellers and makers.

As the community grew, efforts were made by the communal authorities to cut down the number of hawkers and to apprentice Jewish youth to trades, particularly tailoring, hat-making, and shoe-making. Thus by 1850 London (perhaps the first large city to do so) had developed an indigenous Jewish artisan class, as well as middle-class clothing entrepreneurs, contractors, and middlemen. By enabling the working classes to buy new clothing in the same styles − al-though not of the same quality − as those worn by the rich, they began a social revolution. Two firms especially, Hyam, which employed 6,000 people and had a payroll of £200,000 a year, and E. Moses & Son, famous for its advertising techniques, pioneered the new development. These and similar firms supplied outfits for emigrants to the colonies. To supply the needs of these firms small tailoring workshops proliferated, encouraged by the import of the Singer sewing machine in the 1850s and 1860s. The waves of immigrants from Eastern Europe from the 1880s increased the number and concentration of Jews in tailoring.

The 1901 census figures of Russian-Polish immigrants show that about 40 out of every 100 men (and 50 out of every 100 women) who were gainfully employed worked in tailoring and 12 or 13 in the boot, shoe, and slipper trades.

Cap-making in London and Manchester was almost exclusively a Jewish immigrant trade. In Manchester, too, waterproofing had been developed by earlier Jewish immigrants, first in workshops and then in factories, but waterproofing was superseded by the technologically superior rainproof garment. The immigrant tailors had no effect on the bespoke trade; in London, they supplied ready-made garments for merchants and wholesale clothiers and they virtually introduced the ladies' jacket and mantle-making industry to Britain. The principle was subdivision of labor, whereby each operative's task was graded to his skill (or lack of it). Working long hours in small, badly ventilated workshops, the immigrant employees strove to become masters in their turn. This pattern delayed in London and Manchester the introduction of a factory system such as had operated from about 1860 in Leeds, where at the beginning of the 20th century Montague Burton adapted bespoke tailoring to factory production and opened a chain of shops for retail distribution. In this he anticipated the Jewish role in the clothing trade of the 20th century with its tendency toward the organization of mass production and of distribution. The Marks & Spencer chain of stores may be cited as an outstanding example. Jews were also active in large-scale distribution in the textile trade, as clothing retailers, and as manufacturers of a wide range of women's ready-made garments. It is noteworthy, however, that Jewish women and girls who before 1939 worked as dressmakers

Clothing manufacture at Burtons' factory in Leeds, England.

or in tailoring, in the mid-20th century preferred office work. For two centuries, Anglo-Jewry has been connected with the clothing industry. Only the roles have changed: from hawker to retailer, from operative to manufacturer, and from merchant to wholesaler.

United States. Before 1880 Jews from Germany had already become the leading manufacturers of ready-made clothing. German Jewish immigrants had often been connected with the secondhand clothing business in Europe, and many moved into the same occupation upon arriving in America. After the Civil War the market for ready-made clothing expanded among the increasing number of urban dwellers, and the mechanical cutting knife of the 1870s permitted more rapid production of the basic portion of the garment. Ready-made clothing was distributed through secondhand garment merchants, many of whom were German Jews. Some of these men soon began to manufacture ready-made clothing as well as to distribute it. However, it would be erroneous to make too close a connection between the movement of Eastern European Jews into the clothing industry after 1880 and the presence of German Jewish employers in this area. In Chicago, Bohemian immigrants were the first workers in the ready-made clothing industry. The entry of Eastern European Jews into the clothing industry was primarily the result of their need for work immediately after their arrival in America − a condition shared by all immigrant groups − and the availability of the clothing industry because of its rapid growth in the late 19th century and its particular manufacturing methods.

Unlike many American industries, the garment trades were not mechanized. Manufacturers quickly discovered that clothing could be finished through a series of simple processes that could be learned easily even by inexperienced workers. As the demand for ready-made clothing grew, the East European Jew who arrived in America found the clothing industry to be a source of immediate work, especially since many immigrant Jews often had had some experience in tailoring. Italians, Poles, Lithuanians, and Bohemians who entered the United States from 1894 to 1914 also entered the clothing industry and competed with the Jewish worker. The lack of expensive equipment allowed the clothing industry in most cities to fragment into numerous small shops, most of which finished the goods supplied by the manufacturers. These shops appeared throughout the ghetto areas as they followed the labor supply, and within them developed the "sweatshop" conditions that marked this industry for many decades. These small, overcrowded, poorly-maintained shops were operated by a contractor who secured the unfinished garment from the manufacturer and completed the work. The contractors competed with each other for work from the manufacturers, and they in turn tried to make a profit by subdividing the

Advertisements from Providence, Rhode Island, c. 1857.

finishing of the clothing and lowering the cost per piece to a minimum. This produced continuous pressure on the piece rates, and long hours of hectic labor in the "season," followed by stretches of unemployment. There was constant friction between the worker and the contractor over the piece rate and the amount of work required to earn the rate. Contractors often sought out the newly arrived immigrants in the expectation that they would accept lower wages. In addition, many contractors gave out part of the finishing work to be done in the homes of the workers. This encouraged the conversion of over-crowded tenement apartments into extensions of the shop, resulting in child labor and continuous work by entire families for minimal piece rates.

Although the older trade unions in the clothing industry opposed these developments, they represented only small groups of skilled workers, and it was not until the formation of unions such as the International Ladies' Garment Workers' Union in 1900 and the Amalgamated Clothing Workers' Union in 1914 that the efforts to organize the immigrant workers achieved any permanent success. These labor organizations, which had a strongly Jewish leadership, were divided on political grounds as moderate trade unionists, Socialists, and Communists contended for control. The dominant tendency was for a mildly Socialistic rhetoric to be combined with trade unionist bargaining procedures. The garment unions also became social and educational institutions, and this contributed significantly to the Americanization of the immigrant membership. As immigrant Jews from Eastern Europe accumulated some experience in America, and a small amount of capital, they attempted to become employers within the garment industry. By World War I East European Jews dominated the ranks of the employers, particularly among the contractors and jobbers where capital requirements were minimal. This persisted until the 1970s, but the character of the work force did not remain ethnically stable. Jewish workers still comprised a significant portion of the employees, but few young persons from Jewish families entered these trades. Thus the proportion of Jewish workers declined steadily as older workers left the industry. Italian workers had become a major group in the needle trades by World War I, but their percentage of the work force also declined as Black and Puerto Rican workers were increasingly employed in New York City and some of the other metropolitan centers. In addition, as the ladies' garment industry decentralized in search of cheaper labor its ethnic character became more diverse. Thus despite the continued participation of Jews in the garment trades, by 1970 the crucial role of the clothing industry in the lives of American Jews was past.

Israel. Tailoring and allied industries have developed rapidly in Israel, particularly because of (1) the fast increase in local demand as a result of the increase in population and purchasing power; (2) restrictions on imports, especially in the 1950s and early 1960s, which opened up the market for local manufacturers; and (3) large-scale government aid in financing investments, guaranteeing prices, etc.

Since the market demanded more than it was in the power of this industry to offer, it was in its early stages characteristically a sellers' market. The manufacturers did not endeavor, therefore, to promote new models in order to attract buyers, but were content to copy foreign models. The quality, too, was not always up to the required standard.

In the early 1960s a number of developments occurred, mainly in the policy of the government, which encouraged a change in the manufacturers' outlook and in their general attitude, as regards both fashion and quality. The main change in governmental policy took place in 1962, and allowed for the gradual import of competitive goods from abroad, as well as encouraging more extensive exports. The competition for the local market and the need to export provided an impetus for improving quality, and increasing fashion consciousness and internal efficiency. In relatively few years Israel succeeded in achieving a position in the world fashion industry with a considerable number of products: swimsuits and beachwear, knits, women's underclothes (brassieres, panty hose, panties, etc.), men's neckties, sports clothes, raincoats for men and women, leather coats, etc.

Most Israel fashions are the work of Israel fashion designers, and Israel has succeeded in penetrating the world fashion centers of France, Italy, and the American continent.

13
Textiles

The prominence of Jews in the manufacture of textiles in the Mediterranean Basin in the Middle Ages was connected with the widespread commerce in textiles, particularly silk and the more expensive fabrics, in general, and with Jewish commercial activity in this sphere in particular. Cheaper types of cloth were also an important article of trade; thus, in the sources of the period, wherever a Jewish merchant is mentioned plying his trade he was most commonly dealing in textiles. In medieval Egypt the silk trade "fulfilled a function similar to that of stocks and bonds in our own society. In other words, it represented a healthy range of speculation, while providing at the same time a high degree of security" (S. D. Goitein, *A Mediterranean Society* 1(1967), 223).

In Muslim Spain, where many Jews engaged in the silk industry, there "were two brothers, merchants, the manufacturers of silk, Jacob ibn Jau and . . . Joseph . . . they became .successful in the silk business, making clothing of high quality as was not duplicated in all of Spain" (Ibn Daud, Sefer ha-Qabbalah, ed. G. D. Cohen, 68–69). To King Roger of Sicily was attributed the introduction of the silk industry into his lands by means of captured Jewish craftsmen from the Balkans (1147). Benjamin of Tudela describes the Jews of Thebes as "the good craftsmen in making silk and purple clothes in the land of the Greeks"; at Salonika he also noted that "they deal in the craft of silk," while among the Jews of Constantinople he found "craftsmen in silk." The occupation of dyeing (see p. 162) then widespread among Jews and often mentioned by him was connected with textiles. In Spain woolen cloth, produced from the famed local merino sheep, was produced by Jewish weavers, particularly in Majorca and the eastern cities of Barcelona, Valencia, and Saragossa. The weaver's guild in Calatayud had its own synagogue. Moneylending in Western and Central Europe brought Jews into contact with valuable textiles given in pawn which they had to maintain in good state, and also often to sell.

In the Ottoman Empire. Many of the exiles from Spain and Portugal (1492, 1497) continued their former occupations in the textile trade or crafts in their new places of settlement in the Ottoman Empire, or turned to them when they arrived in the Balkans and came into contact with the old tradition of Jewish occupation in this field. Salonika had been established as a center of the textile industry before the arrival of the refugees, many of whom joined in manufacture of the produce of the Balkan hinterland. Thus in the 16th century thousands of Jews engaged there in all stages of the production of cloth (known as *"abba"*). A textile workshop could be found in almost every Jewish home, where the head of the household worked with his wife and children. Jews also distributed and sold the local cloth. Textile workshops were bequeathed to synagogues and charitable institutions. At Ḥanukkah it was customary to donate pieces of cloth to poor yeshivah students. The scope and problems of the industry and trade in textiles in Salonika are seen by the many communal regulations and rabbinical injunctions issued against price slashing, the sale of wool to foreigners, and the purchase of raw wool with cash (which only the wealthy could afford to do). Locally made garments only could be put up for sale, and every Jew over 20 years old had to wear clothes locally produced. From 1586 the tax on Salonika Jewry levied by the Ottoman authorities was payable by a quota of cloth (1,200 standard pieces of cloth), which was presented to the janissaries.

The most flourishing period for the Jewish textile industry in Salonika was between 1500 and 1580, but afterward there was a gradual decline. A financial crisis in 1584, and others that succeeded it, forced many Jewish artisans to leave for other textile centers (Verria, Rhodes, Smyrna). The Ottoman authorities afforded the industry no protection against the superior, foreign-made, European textiles, which swamped the market. Hence the Salonika Jews began to specialize in carpets and other local wares.

At the peak period of activity in the Safed textile center in Ereẓ Israel (1530–60), the majority of earners among the approximately 15,000 Jews there were employed in the manufacture of high-quality woolen cloth, produced from raw, short-fibered wool sent from the Balkans to Safed via Sidon. All stages of production were carried out in Safed; the fulling mills (known as *batan*) utilized the many local springs; one is still standing. Tales of the leading Safed mystics show that many owned such textile mills. Both the trade and the community itself began to decline rapidly after 1560, for the same reasons as had operated against Salonika and because of transport hazards at sea.

Eastern Europe. Their occupation in *arenda* and their predominant role in the grain and forest produce export trade in Poland-Lithuania enabled Jews to take an important part in the import trade of textiles there. From the 16th century Jews traded extensively in textiles on every level of the trade and in all types and qualities of cloth. Though never occupied directly in weaving or spinning, Jews were predominant in the trade in raw wool, yarn, and textiles of all types. Three Jewish weavers are mentioned in Plotsk in the 16th century. In Mezhirech the Christian weavers attacked some Jewish rivals in 1636. The Poznan community declared the trade in raw wool produced in the region to be protected, and appointed a special wool official in the 17th century to prevent foreign merchants from buying it up. In the Poznan region Jewish merchants would advance money, or farm out herds of sheep, in order to obtain the raw wool, which they gave out to local Christian craftsmen to make up into cloth for them. This expertise in capitalist entrepreneurship was in modern times transposed by many Jews of this region to Germany after the partitions of Poland-Lithuania at the end of the 18th century. Jewish peddlers, in particular in the Pale of Settlement and parts of Austria-Hungary, bought up raw materials in the villages, and supplied them to large-scale Jewish traders, and also sold fabrics and clothes in the villages.

Under Russian rule in modern times Jews were active on various levels in the development of the Polish textile industry, and in its celebrated center at Lodz. In 1842, 39 of 82 Jews engaged in commerce in Lodz were suppliers of wool or yarn to artisans. In the early 1840s Jewish wool and yarn merchants and cotton importers began founding firms of their own. In 1864 there were more than 50 independent Jewish manufacturers in Lodz. The early 1860s witnessed a growing increase in Jewish investment and industrial ventures in textiles, with Jews leading in technological innovations and business organization methods at Lodz as well as at Bialystok. In 1867 about 11% of the factory owners in Lodz were Jewish, but these accounted for only 8.5% of the total production. However, entrepreneurs such as Israel Poznanski, Bielchowsky, Joshua Birnbaum, and others forged ahead to become the leading Lodz textile manufacturers. Jewish participation in the textile industry there reached its peak before World War I, when 45.6% of all Lodz textile factories were owned by Jews and almost 27,000 Jewish workers were engaged in various branches of the industry and trade. Of these, one-third were still using manual looms, living in indescribable poverty in the Balut suburb of Lodz. Very few were employed in factories and virtually none in specialized technical work.

In independent Poland between the two world wars, Jewish participation in the Lodz and Bialystok textile industry was hard hit by the anti-Jewish discriminatory policies of the state. Some, however, like Oscar Cohn, managed to develop their factories with foreign capital. By 1931 textile enterprises in Jewish ownership were mainly on a smaller scale, and Jews were employed in the industry in clerical posts rather than as workers. In 1931, 16% of those employed in the textile industry in Poland were Jews, and 71.4% of the independent employers.

Central Europe. Jewish traders, generally from Poland-Lithuania, played a considerable role both as buyers and sellers of fabrics and clothes on market days and at the fairs in Central Europe. At Vienna, the entrepôt of all types of textile goods, Jewish merchants from the wool-producing provinces, Hungary, and Galicia, traded there with Jews from the textile-manufacturing areas of Bohemia and Moravia, while the imperial army, and the city itself, took a large part of the products. Among the Viennese privileged manufacturers were Hermann Todesco, who developed the silk industry there (further developed by S. Trebitsch and sons), and Michael L. Biedermann, by whose single-handed efforts Vienna displaced Budapest as center of the wool trade in the Hapsburg Empire. Another privileged merchant manufacturer who was ennobled was M. Koenigswarter. In 1846, 33 of 133 textile printing firms in Vienna were Jewish-owned, 11 of 72 cotton producers were Jews, as were also 27 of 53 textile commission agents, primarily for the Balkans and the Orient. In 1855 there were 89 Jewish-owned printing and weaving enterprises, about 5% of the total. After the official abolition of all restrictions on Jewish trade (1859; 1867) the participation of Jews in the Viennese textile trade became virtually a monopoly; even after World War I, when each of the Hapsburg successor states developed and protected its own textile industries. The Hungarian wool trade was conducted almost entirely by Jews, who were thus in a position to establish textile industries. Adolf and Heinrich Kohner, originally Moravian feather merchants, established Hungary's first modern wool textile factories. Other notable textile manufacturers were Robert Szurday (originally Weiss, ennobled in 1899), Leo Buday (originally Goldberger), and Samuel Goldberger (ennobled in 1867).

Bohemia and Moravia, the most industrialized areas in the Hapsburg Empire, also produced most of its textiles, and Jews played a prominent role in this industry. From the 17th century Jews had been almost the sole dealers in raw wool, bought from the peasants together with furs, hides, livestock, and other agricultural produce. The peddler, who maintained immediate contact with the peasant, sold his wares to a Jewish merchant who had the wool washed and bleached, spun by peasants, and woven by artisans, and then sold it at the fairs. One of the earliest cloth manufacturers was Feith Ehrenstamm of Prossnitz, who supplied the imperial army with large quantities during the Napoleonic wars by organizing the production of hundreds of local weavers.

In Brno three of the first seven modern steam weaving factories were established by Jews, who had previously been supplying weavers with wool. Among the larger firms was that of L. Auspitz, inherited and expanded by Phillipp Gomperz, as well as the Loew-Baer factories, and those of the Popper brothers and Salomon Strakosch. The textile industry also followed the same pattern in Reichenberg (Liberec) where the earliest suppliers of wool there were the sons of

Jacob Bassevi of Treuenberg in the 17th century. Jews not only supplied the raw material but sold off the finished goods, primarily in Prague, where almost all the textile merchants were Jews (459 compared with 39 gentiles in 1772). Some of them established factories for cloth printing and other end processes, among them Moses and Leopold Porges, Salomon Brandeis, Simon Laemel, and many members of leading Prague Jewish families. In Czechoslovakia after World War I Jewish activity in textiles continued and developed. The nationalization of the jute industry after 1918 was organized by Emanuel Weissenstein and Richard Morawitz, who remained president of the "Juta" concern until 1939. In Trutnov, the center of the flax industry, Alexander Videky was chairman of the flax exchange for many years.

The mercantilist policies of 18th-century Prussia encouraged Court Jews and other Jewish financiers and purveyors to become entrepreneurs of various branches of the textile industry there. Levi Ulff brought Dutch artisans to Brandenburg in 1714 and founded a ribbon factory, which was soon commissioned to supply all the royal regiments. The elders of the Berlin Jewish community proposed setting up woolen cloth factories in Pomerania at their own cost (and to import 3,000 workers), in return for freeing the Jewish community from a newly imposed silver tax, but their proposal was rejected. Many Jews initiated new factories, some in new branches of textiles, such as Pinthus Levi of Rathenow, a horse and grain purveyor, who set up a canvas factory in 1763, which employed more than 1,000 workers. Isaac Bernhard, who imported silk from Italy, received state support in establishing a factory which soon employed 120 looms (his trusted bookkeeper was Moses Mendelssohn, whose residence in Berlin depended on his employment). David Friedlaender was a large-scale silk manufacturer. After the first partition of Poland (1772) Benjamin Veitel Ephraim utilized the semi-professional local labor of Jewish women and girls in the Netze district, where Jews formed 6% of the total and one-quarter of the urban population. He established schools for teaching pillow-lace manufacture, and by 1785 was employing about 700 Jewish women and girls.

At Stuttgart, center of the south German textile industry, there were in 1930 about 170 Jewish manufacturers and the same number of merchants; mainly in processing semi-raw products, semi-finished goods, and finishing, and particularly in the manufacture and trade in tricots and knitwear. Jews were also active in the nearby textile centers of Untertuerkheim, Bocholt, Westphalia, and Landeshut, Silesia, where the linen-manufacturing firm of H. Gruenfeld was well known. Jews participated in the trade and import of wool and in the finishing stages of the industry. Generally, Jewish entrepreneurs tended to concentrate in specific sectors, such as the manufacture of jute sacks, and drapery – lace ribbons, suspenders, garters, neckties, etc. – knitwear, and carpets. Between the two world wars the most important Jewish textile merchant in Germany was James Simon, multi-millionaire philanthropist. A distinguishing feature of the Jewish participation in the German textile trade was its close connection with Great Britain, from which goods were imported, methods followed, and designs imitated, by means of agents and relatives. Jewish participation in the trade in finished textile goods (about 40%) was twice as high as their participation in the industrial sector of the textile industry.

Great Britain and United States. Jews had mainly entered the textile industry and trade in Great Britain after the industrial revolution. One of the first was Nathan M. Rothschild who established himself as a cotton-goods manufacturer (especially of uniforms) in Manchester in 1797. He was followed by many Jewish buyers from Jewish and non-Jewish firms from Germany and the continent, many of whom became independent exporters of cotton goods. At Bradford, Jacob Behrens became important after 1838, and several other German Jews were active there, as well as in other textile centers. In Scotland, they were prominent in the local jute industry in the last quarter of the 19th century, and Sir Otto Jaffe was a leading figure in Northern Ireland.

In the United States few Jews entered the textile industry, an outstanding exception being the Cone family of Carolina. However, Jews became prominent in raw cotton and wool brokerage, as well as in the wholesale and retail trade in fabrics. None of the large producers of synthetic fibers was Jewish-owned.

Israel. In the late 1960s the textile industry became one of the largest industrial branches in Israel, second only to the foodstuff industry. The output in 1969 was 10% of the total industrial output, amounting to IL 925,000,000. At the same time textile products constituted about 12% of industrial exports, totaling $ 66,000,000, the second largest export branch after diamonds.

By 1937 there were already 86 spinning and weaving plants in Erez Israel, with about 1,500 employees. The necessary capital and technical knowledge were brought by Jewish professionals from Europe, an example of such enterprise being the Ata plant near Haifa. The development of the textile industry received considerable impetus in World War II which cut off the European supply, stimulating local manufacture for army needs. In 1943 the number of factories had grown to 250, employing about 5,630 workers; invested capital had grown fourfold and the output value tenfold.

After the establishment of the State of Israel, during the government's drive to step up industry, the textile industry expanded, and special emphasis was put on its establishment in development areas. By 1965, 25% of the textile workers were employed in the three large cities — Jerusalem, Tel Aviv, Haifa — while the rest were concentrated in new industrial areas, in particular in the development areas of Lachish, Ashkelon, and in the Negev and Galilee. The new plants were equipped with the latest machinery, including improved automatic weaving looms, which gave employment to hundreds of workers. While the older plants located in the central part of Israel employed about ten workers each, plants in the development areas employed an average of 50 workers each. There was a rapid growth in production, which before 1955 was mainly concerned with finishing processes. The products were then processed from the raw cotton stage. Apart from increase in quantity of production, there was an improvement in design and techniques. Export of textiles was expanded, and in 1971 exports had increased to one-fifth of the industry's output. In 1965 there were 1,007 textile factories employing 26,300 workers, including 100 plants employing more than 50 workers each. In 1970 there were 300,000 cotton-spinning machines and 50,000 wool-spinning machines, compared with 55,000 cotton spinning machines before the outbreak of World War II. The number of mechanical looms grew from 2,000 before 1948 to 6,000 in 1970, more than half of them automatic and up-to-date.

Tobacco Trade and Industries

Throughout the first two centuries after the discovery of tobacco for Europe through Christopher Columbus, Marranos took part in spreading its cultivation and in introducing it to Europe. Jews took up smoking (widespread from the 17th century) and snuff-taking (widespread from the 18th), and entered the trade in tobacco, which, starting out as a luxury article, became a mass consumer commodity.

At Amsterdam, the first important tobacco importing and processing center in the 17th century, Isak Italiaander was the largest importer, and ten of the 30 leading tobacco importers were Jews. Ashkenazi and poor Sephardi Jews were employed in processing tobacco for snuff: the profession of 14 out of 24 bridegrooms in a list of 1649–53 was tobacco dressing. In this period Jews took an active part in the tobacco trade of the Hamburg center. The first Jews to settle in Mecklenburg in the late 17th century were tobacco traders from Hamburg who leased the ducal tobacco monopoly; outstanding was Michael Hinrichsen, nicknamed "Tabakspinner." Sephardi Jews filled an important role in the *"appalto"* system of contracting for the monopoly on the tobacco trade (or other products). The monopoly concession system was also practiced in the Austrian provinces and the southern German states. In this, Sephardi Jews were often the contractors because of their previous experience. The business carried considerable risks, including fluctuating prices, varying quality, deterioration through adulteration, and the hazards of war.

Diego d'Aguilar managed to hold the tobacco monopoly in Austria in 1734–48, using Christian nobles as men of straw. In the second half of the 18th century the tobacco monopoly of Bohemia and Moravia was in the hands of members of the Dobruschka, Popper, and Hoenig families, whereby they rose to importance and amassed wealth. Jews succeeded in holding the tobacco monopoly in only a few principalities in Germany. In the 19th century Jews entered the open tobacco market. In 1933 Jews engaged in about 5% of the German tobacco trade and industry, primarily as cigar manufacturers.

In Eastern Europe snuff processing was widespread, and tobacco was a staple ware of the Jewish peddler. When in the mid-19th century cigars and cigarettes entered the mass market Leopold Kronenberg, the Jewish industrialist and financier, was one of the main entrepreneurs in Poland, owning 12 factories in 1867 and producing 25% of the total. Of 110 tobacco factories in the Pale of Settlement in 1897, 83 were owned by Jews, and over 80% of the workers were Jewish. This participation continued into the 20th century, and the Jewish tobacco workers were active in the ranks of socialism. The huge Y. Shereshevsky tobacco factory in Grodno employed, before World War I, some 1,800 workers. The nationalization in Poland of the tobacco and liquor industries in 1923–24 was a severe blow to the many Jews who gained their livelihood from them. The leading tobacco factories in Riga, Latvia, were owned by two wealthy Karaites, Asimakis and Maikapar.

On the American continent Jews traded in tobacco as early as 1658. It frequently served as legal tender and was a stock retail article of the Jewish peddler. However, Jews played a considerable part only in the snuff trade, among them the firms of Asher and Solomon, and Gomez. Judah Morris, who wrote the first Hebrew book to be printed in North America, became a snuff trader. The last quarter of the 19th century brought an influx of impoverished Jewish immigrants from Eastern Europe who entered the cigar and cigarette industry, and, after the garment industry, it had the largest concentration of Jewish workers in the United States. The first professional cigar makers were generally Jews of Dutch or German origin, who employed the immigrants in their factories or in sweatshops. The Jewish firm of Keeney Brothers, makers of "Sweet Caporals," employed approximately 2,000 Jewish workers. The Durham factory employed Jews almost exclusively. Tobacco workers, organized by Samuel Gompers, became the spearhead of the labor union movement in the United States in the 1870s and 1880s. Subsequently Jewish participation in the cigarette industry declined through the creation of large concerns, though many cigar firms remained under Jewish ownership. In New York and other major cities the tobacco retail trade occupied a high proportion of Jews. A survey by *Fortune* magazine (*Jews in America*; 1935) stated that "Jews have practically blanketed the tobacco buying business, where Jews and buyer are synonomous words, and they control three of the four leading cigar-manufacturing concerns, including Fred Hirschhorn's General Cigar, which makes every seventh cigar smoked in America." In Canada Jews played a leading role in introducing the tobacco industry; Mortimer B. Davis was known as the "tobacco king" of Canada.

In Great Britain cigar making was traditionally associated with Dutch Jews, who formed the main body of Jewish immigrants in the mid-19th century; cigar making was the most widespread occupation in London's East End in 1860. In 1850, 44% of the meerschaum pipe makers were Jewish as were 22% of the cigar manufacturers. East European Jewish immigrants introduced cigarette making into England. In 1880 Jacob Kamusch, an Austrian Jewish cigarette entrepreneur, brought 310 workers, mainly Jewish, to his Glasgow cigarette factory. Isidore Gluckstein founded his first tobacconist shop in 1872 and became the biggest retail tobacconist in England, up to 1904. Bernhard Baron was a large-scale cigarette manufacturer in America and England.

Sephardi Jews played an active role in the tobacco trade from its beginnings in the Ottoman Empire. The Recanati banking family began as Salonika tobacco merchants. Thrace and Macedonia were major tobacco-growing areas; the Alatino (Alatini) family became sole suppliers of the Italian tobacco monopoly.

Tobacco growing was first introduced in Israel in 1923/24, in order to solve problems of unemployment. New immigrants from Bulgaria and Greece took an important part in the development of the industry. All kinds of tobacco products are manufactured in Israel. In 1969 the overall production included 3,700 tons of cigarettes, 15,000 kg. of cigars, 60,600 kg. of tumbak, 40,100 kg. of snuff, and 16,600 kg. of pipe tobacco. In the same year the consumption of tobacco products amounted to nearly IL200,000,000 (about 2% of the total private consumption in Israel), including mainly locally produced products but also about $6,000,000 worth of imported products. There are 15 manufacturing plants in Israel, employing 875 workers and processing mostly locally grown tobacco of oriental aroma. Tobacco is grown mainly in the non-Jewish sector in northern Israel. In 1950 tobacco-growing areas amounted to 9,000 dunams, and tobacco-product manufacture reached 600 tons at a value of IL 200,000. By 1969 tobacco was grown on 35,000 dunams and production increased to 2,200 tons at a value of IL7,600,000.

Part Four
SERVICES

1

Banking and Bankers

The Caliphate. With the rapid development of city life and commerce in the caliphate of Baghdad from the late eighth century and the transition of the majority of Jews under caliphate rule from agriculture and a village environment to the cities, banking became one of the occupations of some upper-class Jews, especially in Baghdad and later under the Fatimids (from 968) in Egypt. This *Jahbadhiyya*, as it was called, was a form of banking based on the savings and economic activities of the whole Jewish merchant class and not only on the fortunes of the very rich: the bankers loaned to the state and its officers money deposited with them as well as from their own fortunes. The vast sums at the disposal of these Jewish bankers and their relative immunity from confiscation by the autocratic authorities both tend to confirm that these Jewish "court bankers" from the beginning of the tenth century onward were well-known to their Muslim debtors as a kind of "deposit banker" for Jewish merchants. Under the Fatimid caliph al-Mustanṣir the brothers Abu Saʿd al-Tustarī and Abu Naṣr Ḥesed b. Sahl al-Tustarī (both died in 1048) were influential in the finances of Egypt. With the rise of Saladin and the foundation of the Ayyubid dynasty in Egypt (1169), the position of the Jews deteriorated but they were able to continue their moneychanging activities at least. Toward the end of the Mamluk period (1517), Samuel, a moneychanger in Cairo, must have possessed considerable wealth, for the Arab chronicler Ibn Iyās tells that the sultan extorted from him more than 500,000 dinars. During the Muslim rule on the Iberian peninsula, Córdoba Jews were active in the financial administration in the tenth and eleventh centuries. The responsa of this period show a highly developed money economy existing before the First and Second Crusades.

Europe. Persecution, such as occurred in Alexandria in 414, or the oppressive measures promulgated in the Byzantine Empire beginning with Constantine and intensified under Justinian, may have contributed to the fact that from the fifth century Jewish merchants followed their Greek and Syrian counterparts to Gaul and not only traded in luxury goods but also loaned money. With the disappearance of the Syrians and Greeks from Europe in the seventh century, the Jewish merchants were able to extend their activities. Within the administration of the Merovingian kings (from 481) Jews possibly farmed taxes or advanced money on revenues to high officials; according to Gregory of Tours (c. 538–94), the count of Tours and his vicar were indebted to the Jew Armentarius. During the Carolingian period (from the mid-eighth century), Jews settled in the Rhineland again as they had done during the Roman Empire – some of them lending money on pledges or giving money to merchants in a kind of commenda partnership. Archbishop Anno of Cologne (d. 1075), as well as Emperor Henry IV (1056–1106), borrowed money from Jews.

After the First Crusade (1096) the Jewish merchant no longer enjoyed even minimal physical security in his necessarily long journeys. In Western and Central Europe, especially in Spain, the crystallization of the essentially Christian nature of the rising city communes combined with this insecurity to drive the Jews from commerce and prohibit them from engaging in crafts. In France, England (up to 1290), Germany, Austria, Bohemia, Moravia, and northern and central Italy, Jews had to turn to loan-banking on a larger or smaller scale in order to make a living. The canonical prohibition against taking interest by Christians, which was stressed in successive Church councils (especially the Fourth Lateran Council of 1215), and the vast opportunities for capital investment in land and sea trade open to the wealthy Christian made lending on interest for consumer and emergency needs virtually a Jewish monopoly in Western and Central Europe between the 12th and 15th centuries. By the 13th century the notion that the *Wucherer* ("usurer") was a Jew was already current, for example, in the writings of Berthold of Regensburg, Walther von der Vogelweide, and Ulrich von Lichtenstein. The word *judaizare* became identical with "taking interest." Testimony from the 12th century shows that moneylending was then becoming the main occupation of the Jews; this was the case of those of Bacharach (1146) and of Muenzenberg (1188). There is little data to suggest that Jewish banking transactions were on a large scale even in the 13th century, but there is evidence that the bishop of Basle had debts with Basle Jews and that various monasteries had Jewish creditors.

The transition from a natural economy to a money economy in the course of the "commercial revolution," and the stabilization of territorial principalities opened new possibilities for Jewish banking activity, especially in the Rhineland and in southern Germany. Jews from Siegburg, Trier, Mainz, Speyer, Strasbourg, and Basle as well as from Ulm and Nuremberg appear as sources of credit. The most important banking transaction in the first half of the 14th century went through the hands of Vivelin the Red, who transmitted 61,000 florins in gold which King Edward III of England paid to Baldwin of Trier for allying himself with him against France. Margrave Rudolf III of Baden was indebted to David

German woodcut of a Jewish moneychanger, 15th century.

the Elder, called Watch, and to Jekelin of Strasbourg and his partners. Muskin and Jacob Daniels served the archbishop of Trier in the administration of his finances; during the first half of the 14th century, Daniels was probably the most important Jewish banker of the Rhineland. He was followed in the service of the archbishop by his son-in-law Michael. At the same time Abraham von Kreuznach at Bingen had a similar position with the archbishop of Mainz. Gottschalk von Recklinghausen and his company formed another group on the lower Rhine. Such banking activity is recorded in other parts of Central Europe as far as Silesia.

Moneychanging and coinage privileges were often combined with money-lending, and Jews were frequently the sole agents arranging loans. From the first half of the 12th century moneychanging as a special form of banking is supported by documentary evidence. To spread the risk, partnerships of between two and ten persons were formed. As security, custom at first recognized mainly pledges, but from the middle of the 13th century the letter of credit came into use, though princes still preferred to pledge jewels. Often, instead of a pawn, bail was given by several persons. In western Germany hypothecation of real estate was preferred, and in this way Jews acquired in pledge houses, vineyards, farms, villages, castles, towns, and even seigneuries. Interest rates do not seem to have exceeded 36% but in the case of deferred payment they could rise to 100% or beyond. From the 12th century popes and princes exploited the financial capacity of the Jews by frequent remission of debts or forced loans. The Black Death and consequent persecutions of Jews gave rulers an opportunity forcibly to seize property and to restore pawns and letters of credit to debtors. The liquidation of Jewish debts by King Wenceslaus IV of Bohemia around the end of the 14th century is a well-known example of such royal rapacity. With these and other measures and the rise of the merchant class, who gradually took over the function of loan-bankers to the princes and even to emperors during the 15th and early 16th centuries, the Jews were deprived of imperial protection and forced to leave the towns. They retired to the small seigneuries or migrated to Eastern Europe, where a less-developed economy offered them possibilities of making a livelihood. In Bohemia, Hungary, and in Poland and Lithuania both princes and nobility made use of their financial help. As the Eastern European kingdoms developed with the colonization of the forests, Jews played an increasing part in commerce and especially in the *arenda*. In the larger towns some engaged in moneylending and banking activities.

In 12th-century France moneylending was an important Jewish business, but in the 13th century the Jews came up against the superior competition of the Lombards, a rivalry even more intense in the Netherlands. In England, where Aaron of Lincoln and Aaron of York were powerful bankers, a special Exchequer of the Jews was set up to centralize Jewish transactions. However in the 13th century the crown began to rely on the greater resources of the Cahorsins and Italian bankers and in 1290 the Jews were expelled. In Italy Jewish bankers could expand their sphere of activity under the silent protection of the popes, despite resistance on the part of the Christian burghers. From the second half of the 13th century they spread throughout central Italy and gradually expanded toward the north, migrating at first to the smaller and medium-sized towns. In Pisa and then in Florence the Da Pisa family became important loan-bankers; in Florence in 1437 Cosimo de' Medici permitted a Jewish group to establish four loan-banks; in Venice in 1366 Jews, probably of German origin, obtained the right to lend on pledges. Here as in other places in northern Italy, Jewish loan-bankers from the south came into competition with Jews migrating from Germany or southern France. Finally only few towns, such as Milan and Genoa, refused to admit Jewish loan-bankers. However, their activities were seriously challenged when the anti-Jewish preaching of the Franciscans resulted in the establishment of branches of the *Monti di Pietà* toward the middle of the 15th century.

The Iberian Peninsula after the Christian reconquest offers many examples of large-scale credit activities and tax farming by Jews. It is known that they provided money for armaments against the Moors. El Cid borrowed from Raquel and Vidas, Jews of Burgos, for his expedition against Valencia. King Alfonso VI of Castile (1072–1109) also obtained loans from Jews for his military expeditions. His successors employed Jews in the financial administration, especially as *almoxarifes* (revenue collectors), an activity combined with moneylending. Thus,

Judah Ibn Ezra was in the service of Alfonso VII, Joseph Ibn Shoshan of Alfonso VIII, and Solomon ibn Zadok (Don Çulema) and his son Çag de la Maleha were *almoxarifes* in the service of Alfonso X, while Meir ibn Shoshan served as his treasurer. When Sancho IV (1258–95) came to the throne, Abraham el-Barchilon was prominent in the financial administration, supervising the farming of the taxes. Generally, in Castile the Jews abstained from farming the direct taxes, which the Cortes opposed from 1288. The Jews therefore tended to prefer the administration of the customs and other rights belonging to the office of *almoxarife*. The court of Aragon relied on Jewish financial administrators in a similar fashion. King James I employed Benveniste de Porta as a banker, probably giving him as security for his advances the office of bailiff of Barcelona and Gerona. Judah de la Cavalleria, the most powerful Jew in the Aragonese administration, had control over all the bailiffs of the kingdom. Under Pedro III the family of Ravaya was most influential. Though during the 14th century the Jews in Aragon and Navarre were subjected to increasing pressures, Judah Ha-Levi and Abraham Aben-Josef of Estella were general farmers of the rents under Charles II and Charles III of Navarre. In Castile — in spite of the Cortes' opposition — Jews such as the Abrabanel family in Seville continued to be active as *almoxarifes*. The young Alfonso XI appointed Joseph de Écija as his *almoxarife mayor* (c. 1322); Pedro the Cruel (1350–69) made Samuel ben Meir ha-Levi Abulafia of Toledo, known as the richest Jew of his time, his chief treasurer, and Henry of Trastamara had Joseph Picho as his financial officer (*contador mayor*) despite his promise to remove all Jews from royal office (1367).

The persecutions of 1391 and the mass conversions which followed brought an important change. Some of the Conversos were able to use the act of baptism to climb to high positions in the financial administration: examples are Luis de la Cavalleria, chief treasurer under John II of Aragon, Luis Sánchez, royal bailiff of the kingdom of Aragon (c. 1490), and his brother Gabriel Sánchez, who was treasurer-general. Under Henry IV of Castile (1454–74) Diego Arias de Avila was the king's secretary and auditor of the royal accounts; in spite of Diego's unpopularity his son Pedro succeeded him. Even Isabella the Catholic depended on the financial advice of the Jew Abraham Senior, from 1476 chief tax gatherer in Castile, and Isaac Abrabanel, who after having been banker of Alfonso V of Portugal served as the queen's private financial agent and loaned her a considerable sum for the war against Granada. The Converso Luis de Santangel, chancellor and comptroller of the royal household and great-grandson of the Jew Noah Chinillo, loaned Isabella money to finance Columbus' expedition to America. Though some men like Isaac Abrabanel, who went to Naples, remained faithful to Judaism, a number of Jews of Spanish origin stayed in Portugal and, after accepting baptism, rose to financial influence there, especially in combination with the East Indian spice trade. Prominent among them were Francisco and Diogo Mendes. The latter, who took up residence in Antwerp, became one of the most important merchant bankers there, lending money to the king of Portugal, the emperor, and Henry VIII of England. The firm "Herdeiros de Francisco e Diogo Mendes" was administered for some time after Diogo's death (1543) by Francisco's widow, Doña Beatrice de Luna (Gracia Nasi) and her nephew Joǎo Miques (Joseph Nasi). They subsequently emigrated to Turkey, where the latter combined commercial and banking activity with political influence. Another to rise to high position was Alvaro Mendes from Tavira, Portugal, who in Constantinople took the name Solomon Abenaes. Jewish moneychangers and tax farmers were to be found in many places of the Ottoman Empire. After the union between Spain and Portugal (1580), a number of influential Conversos took the opportunity to invest their capital in financing the various ventures of the crown, provisioning the army in Flanders and in the East Indies, and supplying contracts for Africa. Their activities expanded especially after the financial crisis of 1626 and continued until the Portuguese revolt of 1640 which restored independent sovereignty to the country. After this all members of the *gente de naçao* (as Conversos were called) living in Spain became suspect. The last important financial venture by New Christians in Portugal was the financing of the Brazil Company established in 1649.

Jewish involvement in banking proper really begins with the activities of those Conversos who, fleeing the Inquisition in Portugal and Spain, settled in Antwerp, Hamburg, and Amsterdam, some remaining nominally Christian and some openly returning to Judaism. In Antwerp the Ximenes and Rodrigues d'Evora families were outstanding among an important group of merchant bankers who had commercial relations extending as far as the East Indies and Brazil. While they remained Catholics (like the Mendes de Brito group in Portugal), those who emigrated to Hamburg and Amsterdam formed Sephardi communities. In Hamburg they participated in the founding of the bank in 1619; 30 (by 1623, 46) local Jews were among its first shareholders, and some of them were financial agents for various North European courts, especially those of Denmark and Schleswig-Holstein. Most famous in Antwerp were Diego Teixeira de Sampaio (Abraham Senior), consul and paymaster general for the Spanish government, and his son Manuel (Isaac Hayyim Senior), who succeeded him as financial agent of Christina of Sweden. Manuel Teixeira was an outstanding member of the Hamburg exchange and participated actively in the transfer of Western European subsidies to the German or Scandinavian courts.

In Amsterdam at first only a few Jews were shareholders in the bank founded in 1609 and of the East India Company. One hundred and six Portuguese had accounts in 1620. Generally their resources were not sufficiently great to add any special weight to the formative stage of Amsterdam capitalism. Through Holland's developing overseas trade, especially with Brazil (until 1654) and then with the West Indies, as well as through the growth of the Amsterdam capital market and the transfer of subsidies and provisioning of armies through Amsterdam, Jewish financiers rose to importance in the exchange market, and were especially active in trading company shares. Outstanding were the Pinto family and Antonio (Isaac) Lopez Suasso (Baron d'Avernas le Gras); nevertheless the wealth of the Sephardi families remained far below that of their Christian counterparts.

Partly as a consequence of the marriage between Charles II of England and Catherine of Braganza (1662), and especially after William and Mary became joint sovereigns of England (1689), London, too, became a center of Sephardi banking, leading figures being Anthony (Moses) da Costa, Solomon de Medina, and Isaac Pereira. In the reign of Queen Anne (1702–14), Manasseh Lopes was a leading banker; during the 18th century Samson Gideon, Francis and Joseph Salvador, and the Goldsmid brothers, leading members of the Ashkenazi community, were outstanding. In the middle of the 18th century Jacob Henriques claimed that his father had planned the establishment of the Bank of England (1694).

Only a few Jewish financiers, such as Joseph zum goldenen Schwan at Frankfort or Michel Jud, were active in the German principalities in the 16th century. In the early 17th century the Hapsburgs employed the services of Jacob Bassevi of Treuenberg of Prague, Joseph Pincherle of Gorizia, and Moses and Jacob Marburger of Gradisca. The rise of the absolute monarchies in Central Europe brought numbers of Jews, mostly of Ashkenazi origin, into the position of negotiating loans for the various courts, giving rise to the phenomenon of Court Jews. The most famous and most active of them in financial affairs were, in the second half of the 17th and the beginning of the 18th century, Leffmann Behrends in Hanover, Behrend Lehmann in Halberstadt, Bendix Goldschmidt in Hamburg, Aaron Beer in Frankfort, and Samuel Oppenheimer and Samson Wertheimer in Vienna. Later Diego d'Aguilar, and the Arnstein and Eskeles families became prominent. In the early 18th century Joseph Suess Oppenheimer was the outstanding figure in southern Germany, especially in Wuerttemberg. Important court bankers around the end of the 18th century were Israel Jacobson in Brunswick, the Bleichroeder family in Berlin, Simon Baruch and Solomon Oppenheimer in Bonn, the Rothschilds in Frankfort, the Reutlinger, Seligmann, and Haber families in Karlsruhe, the Kaulla family in Stuttgart, and Aron Elias Seligmann, later baron of Eichthal, in Munich.

In the 15th and beginning of the 16th century the Italian loan-bankers reached their greatest eminence, including the Pisa, Volterra, Norsa, Del Banco,

Rieti, and Tivoli families. In their wealth and style of life these men belonged to the Renaissance milieu as much as the artists and men of letters. However, with the expansion of the institution of the *Monte di Pietà* and the restrictive policy of the popes of the Counterreformation, their influence declined. The Da Pisa disappeared from Florence in 1570. However there were still between 60 and 70 loan-bankers operating in Rome toward the end of the 16th century and a century later about 20 were still in existence. In the first half of the 16th century about 500 loan-bankers were active throughout Italy; toward the end of the century about 280 remained in 131 places.

19th and 20th centuries. Jewish banking in the 19th century begins with the rise of the house of Rothschild in Frankfort, a city which became the new banking center of Europe as a result of the political upheaval caused by the French Revolution and the Napoleonic Wars. The founder of the house (which became the symbol of the 19th-century type of merchant banking), Mayer Amschel Rothschild, started as a banker to the elector of Hesse-Kassel. His sons rose to prominence as the major European bankers Amschel Mayer in Frankfort, Salomon Mayer in Vienna, Karl Mayer in Naples, James Mayer in Paris, and Nathan Mayer in London. After the death of Abraham Goldsmid and Francis Baring in 1810, Nathan Rothschild became the dominant figure in the London money market. The majority of the English financial dealings with the continent went through the Rothschilds' offices. After the Congress of Vienna (1815) the Rothschilds extended their business into most European states, specializing in the liquidation of inflated paper currencies and in the foundation of floating public debts. In 1818 they made loans to European governments, beginning with Prussia and following with issues to England, Austria, Naples, Russia, and other states, partly in collaboration with Baring, Reid, Irving and Company. Between 1815 and 1828 the total capital of the Rothschilds rose from 3,332,000 to 118,400,000 francs.

Prominent merchant bankers in Germany besides the Rothschilds were Joseph Mendelssohn and Samuel Bleichroeder. Mendelssohn founded his firm in Berlin in 1795, and was joined by his brother Abraham Mendelssohn in 1804; they issued state loans for industrial development to several foreign countries, particularly Russia. Samuel Bleichroeder, Berlin correspondent of the Rothschilds, established his own business in 1803. His son Gerson Bleichroeder became a confidant of Bismarck and served as his agent for financing the war of 1866 and for the transfer of the French war indemnity in 1871. The Bleichroeder bank also made loans to foreign states. After the death of Gerson Bleichroeder in 1893 his partner Paul Schwabach continued the business. The brothers Moses, Marcus, and Gerson Warburg founded a bank in Hamburg in 1798. Its

Mayer Amschel   Amschel Mayer   Salomon Mayer

Karl Mayer   James Mayer   Nathan Mayer

The Rothschild family.

main business was concerned with the Hamburg overseas trade, especially trans-actions with England and the United States. Paul M. Warburg, a brother of Max M. Warburg, head of the Hamburg bank before World War I, established a branch office in New York. Toward the end of the 18th century J. M. Speyer, through his bank's provisioning of armies and exchange business, had a capital of 420,000 florins, the largest Jewish fortune in Frankfort at that time. In 1809 G. J. Elissen opened a banking house which took the name of J. L. Speyer-Elissen in 1818 and Lazard Speyer-Elissen in 1838. Philipp Speyer and Co., the U.S. branch, negotiated the American credit during the Civil War, participated in the development of the railroads in America, and conducted transactions in Mexico and Cuba, partly in association with the Deutsche Bank. In 1928 Speyer amalga-mated with C. Schlesinger, Trier, and Company to form Lazard Speyer-Elissen K. a. A., Frankfort and Berlin. The bank established by Solomon Oppenheim in Bonn in 1789 acquired a leading position; at the beginning of the 19th century

Solomon moved to Cologne, where his son Abraham became one of the most influential bankers in the Rhineland, financing insurance associations, railroad construction, and industrial investment.

Jewish bankers played an important part in the development of joint stock banks. Ludwig Bamberger and Hermann Markuse were among the founders of the Deutsche Bank (1870), which was active in financing German foreign trade. The Disconto-Gesellschaft, established by David Hansemann in 1851, which amalgamated with the Deutsche Bank in 1929, had several Jewish partners. Eugen Gutmann was the main founder of the Dresdener Bank, and Abraham Oppenheim was one of the founders of the Bank fuer Handel und Industrie (Darmstaedter Bank; 1853). The leading personality in the Berliner Handels-gesellschaft (established in 1856) was Carl Fuerstenberg. Richard Witting, brother of Maximilian Harden, was one of the directors of the Nationalbank fuer Deutschland; when it merged with the Darmstaedter Bank in 1921, Jacob Goldschmidt, then director of the latter, took control of the new enterprise. In 1932 the two other most important banks in Germany, the Deutsche Bank and the Dresdener Bank, were directed by Oskar Wassermann and Herbert Gutman respectively.

In England, banks were established by Sir David Salomons (London and Westminster Bank, 1832), the Stern brothers (1833), Samuel Montagu (1853), Emile Erlanger (1859), the Speyer brothers, Seligman brothers, and S. Japhet and Co., many of them immigrants from Frankfort; the Speyer bank negotiated loans on behalf of Greece, Bulgaria, and Hungary, as well as for Latin American states. David Sassoon and Company, established in Bombay in 1832, had branches throughout the Orient, handling extensive transactions. Sir Ernest Cassel, partly in association with Sir Carl Meyer, established banks in Egypt and Turkey. Industrial banks were organized by Sir Moses Montefiore and the Anglo-American Corporation, which was connected with the diamond and finance corporation of A. Dunkelsbueler, established by Sir Ernest Oppenheimer. In South Africa the General Mining and Finance Corporation was set up by Hamilton Ehrlich and Turk, and one of the most important enterprises in South African financing was the Barnato brothers' company.

In France Achille Fould, a competitor of the Rothschilds, was a supporter of Napoleon III and later his finance minister. Together with his brother Benoit he inherited the Paris firm of Fould, Oppenheimer et Cie., which had been established by his father. Meanwhile the brothers Emile and Isaac Péreire, who moved to Paris from Marseilles in 1822, financed railway construction in France and Spain. Through the Crédit Mobilier, organized in 1852, they mobilized credit for various investment projects, but ran into difficulties in 1867. Among the other important Jewish banks was the Banque de Paris et des Pays-Bas (1872), with

Henri Bamberger as one of the directors. The leading position among the private banks was held by Rothschild; from 1889 to 1901 all loans to Russia from Paris were issued through the Rothschild bank. Baron Maurice de Hirsch from Munich, son-in-law of the Brussels banker Raphael Jonathan Bischoffsheim, invested successfully in railroad construction. Other Jewish banks were those of Louis Dreyfus and Lazard Frères. In Italy, where Luigi Luzzatti's agricultural associations were largely philanthropic, Jewish bankers played a leading part in the foundation of the Banca Commerciale Italiana and the Credito Italiano.

A number of Jewish banks were established in Vienna during the 19th century, the most influential of which was Arnstein and Eskeles. This bank however was declared bankrupt in 1859. Weikersheim and Company and from 1821 Salomon Rothschild also established banks in Vienna. Jews participated in the foundation of the Niederoesterreichische Eskomptgessellschaft (1853) and the Kreditanstalt (1855), which made an essential contribution to the development of the Vienna stock exchange and extended international loan facilities, also investing in industry and railroads. Leading private banks in Hungary were of Jewish origin, such as the Ungarische Allgemeine Kreditbank (Hungarian General Credit Bank; established in 1867) with Siegmund Kornfeld as a general director, the Pester Ungarische Kommerzialbank (Hungarian Commercial Bank at Pest), established in 1841 by Moritz Ullman, and the Ungarische Hypothekenbank (Hungarian Hypothecary Credit Bank; 1869) with Nandor (Ferdinand) Beck de Madarassy as its general director. In Prague the Petschek family established a bank in 1920; in Galicia, under the Austrian regime, Brody (Nathanson, Kallir) and Lemberg had Jewish banks.

Between the end of the 18th century and the beginning of the 19th Jewish banks of some importance rose in Russia. In St. Petersburg Nicolai and Ludwig Stieglitz, immigrants from Germany, opened a bank in 1803, which under Ludwig (who with his brother was converted to Christianity in 1812) became one of the leading financial institutions in Russia. Otherwise Jewish banking activity was limited to southern Russia, especially to Berdichev and Odessa. In 1860 Yozel (Yerzel) Guenzburg, originally a tax farmer, established the St. Petersburg bank J. Y. Guenzburg, and later the discount and credit bank there, managed by his son Horace; Guenzburg also established banks in Kiev and Odessa. Lazar (Eliezer) Poliakoff opened a bank at Moscow in 1860 and participated in the foundation of the Moskowsky Zemelny Bank and other Moscow banks. Poliakoff and his two brothers also founded banks in southern Russia. Abram Zak was director of the Petersburg Discount and Credit Bank (1871–93), and Soloveitchik established the Siberian Trade Bank. At the beginning of the 20th century private banks of some importance were those of H. Wawelberg in St. Petersburg, and O. Chayes and R. Sonschein and Company in Odessa.

Toward the end of the 18th century several bankers such as Koenigsberger, Levy, and Simon Simoni emigrated from the west to Poland. Jacob Epstein, court purveyor to King Stanislas II Augustus, founded an important dynasty of bankers. The Polish revolt of 1863 caused the bankruptcy of many Jewish banks. The bank of Wilhelm Landauer in Warsaw, established in 1857, closed in that year. However, Landauer returned to Warsaw some years later and opened a joint stock company in 1913. Mieczyslaw Epstein founded the Warsaw Discount Bank in 1871. Leopold Kronenberg took part in the foundation of the Warsaw Credit Union in 1869 and the following year established the first joint stock bank in Poland, Bank Handlowy at Warsaw.

The Goeteborgs Bank in 1848 was established in Sweden through the agency of L. E. Magnes, Morris Jacobsson, Edward Magnus, and others. Theodor Mannheimer was the first managing director of Scandinaviska Kreditakteibolaget, and Louis Fraenkel managed Stockholm's Handelsbank from 1893 to 1911. The Danish merchant financiers Joseph Hambro and his son Carl Joachim Hambro settled in London in 1832 and founded Hambro's Bank there. A leading Danish banker was Isaac Glückstadt, who managed the Landsmans-Bank at Copenhagen from 1872 until his death in 1910; he was succeeded by his son Emil. A. Levy Martin was finance minister in 1870 and from 1873 till 1897 director of the Copenhagen Handelsbank. From 1913 until his death in 1923, Markus Rubin was director of the Danish Notenbank. In Holland the firm of Lissa and Kann was established in 1805. Another Dutch firm of the same era was Wertheimer and Gompertz, later known as the Bankassociatie. In 1859 the firm of Lippman, Rosenthal and Company was established as a subsidiary of the International Bank of Luxembourg. Its international activities were widespread, especially through Netherlands state loans. The bank of Elzbacher in Amsterdam later merged with the Amsterdamsche Bank. In Rotterdam Rothschild was represented by Moses Ezechiels en Zonen (liquidated in 1888). The bank of Benjamin Marx (established in 1869), later Marx and Company, was in existence until 1922. In Belgium Jacques Errera, Joseph Oppenheim, and Isaac Stern, all from Brussels, and the brothers Sulzbach and J. May from Frankfort participated in the foundation of the Banque de Bruxelles in 1871. Private banks were those of F. M. Philippson and Company, the Societé Henri Lambert and Cassel and Company. Moving from Alsace to Switzerland in 1812, Isaac Dreyfus established a bank in Basle; after 1849 the firm was known as Isaac Dreyfus Soehne. It participated in the foundation of the Basler Handelsbank as well as the Basler Bankverein. The Hitler regime spelled the end of Jewish banking in the greater part of Europe, and all Jewish banks in Germany were liquidated or transfered.

The United States. Already in early colonial times individual Jews were active in

America as money brokers, such as Asser Levy, who functioned in New York City during the second.half of the 17th century. Often such figures were helped by their extensive family or fellow-Jewish contacts overseas, as was the case with David Franks, who was instrumental in raising money for the British army during the French and Indian War with the aid of his brother Moses, a London financier. The best known Jewish financier of the times was the legendary patriot Haym Salomon, an immigrant from Poland who succeeded under extremely trying conditions in raising large amounts of desperately needed cash for the American Revolution by negotiating bills of exchange with France and the Netherlands. Yet another figure who helped finance the war for American independence was Isaac Moses, later among the founders of the Bank of New York.

It was not until the middle of the 19th century, however, with the arrival in America of a large German-Jewish immigration, that Jewish banking houses on the European model came to exist in the United States. Some of the founders of these firms, like Philip and Gustav Speyer of Speyer & Co., went to the United States as American representatives of already established European concerns; others, like August Belmont, crossed the Atlantic with a degree of previously acquired banking experience; still others, like the Lehman brothers, Meyer and Emanuel, were essentially self-made men. Among other Jewish banking houses started by immigrants from Germany that developed into financial powers during the years 1840–1880 were Kuhn, Loeb Co., Lazard Frères, J. W. Seligman Co., Goldman, Sachs & Co., and Ladenburg, Thalman & Co. All of these firms functioned essentially as investment bankers – the more established field of commercial banking offered relatively few opportunities to the German-Jewish immigrant – a capacity in which they helped to finance large numbers of American utilities and corporations whose rapid growth throughout the latter half of the 19th century created an insatiable demand for capital. To raise such funds these Jewish houses not only freely utilized their widespread European connections, particularly in France, England, and Germany, but created a chain of interlocking associations and directorates among themselves which enabled them quickly to mobilize sums many times larger than their individual holdings and to compete successfully with gentile firms several times their size. Not only was it common for the children and relatives of a given firm to marry each other, but marital alliances frequently occurred as well among different Jewish banking families, as was the case with the Loebs, the Kuhns, the Schiffs, and the Warburgs. Frequently too the children of such families married into families of large German-Jewish companies in a variety of other fields and the latter would then proceed to raise capital through the banking houses which they had joined. Socially, the result of such commercial and kinship ties was the creation of a German-Jewish banking and business aristocracy based in New

York City whose descendants continued for over a century to play a dominant role in the financial, cultural, and political life of the American Jewish community, and to a lesser extent, of the nation at large. The contribution of such Jewish banking houses to the process of capital formation in the United States in the late 19th and early 20th century was considerable by any standard. Several of them, such as Speyer & Co., August Belmont & Co., and J. & W. Seligman, raised large sums for the federal government both during and after the Civil War (the Jewish house of Erlanger Co., on the other hand, obtained sizeable loans for the Confederacy); others, such as Kuhn, Loeb, were particularly active in the westward expansion of the railroads. In the late 19th century Seligman Co. alone was capitalized at an estimated $10,000,000, while during the Russo-Japanese War of 1905 Jacob Schiff of Kuhn, Loeb was able on short notice to float a bond issue of $200,000,000 on behalf of the Japanese government.

Although the total assets of such Jewish firms were small compared to those of the American banking system as a whole, their clannishness and ability to coordinate their actions made them the focus of anti-Semitic agitation from the 1890s on, when caricatures of ruthless Jewish oligarchs at the head of an international Jewish money conspiracy began to abound in the ranks of the Populist movement. In reality, however, the fiscal policies of the German-Jewish firms tended to be highly conservative and their owners exercised their fortunes with an unusual degree of social as well as fiscal responsibility. Although a number of the great 19th-century Jewish banking houses such as Lazard Frères and Kuhn, Loeb have survived into the present, none has continued as a family or even exclusively Jewish concern and even the most prosperous of them have lost their former importance as a result of the steady trend in the American financial market toward the predominance of ever larger and more impersonal corporations. At the same time, the general field of commercial banking in the United States has remained relatively closed to Jewish participation despite heavy Jewish involvement in such related fields as stock brokerage, investment analysis, and corporate management. A study undertaken by B'nai B'rith in 1939 revealed that out of 93,000 bankers in the United States only 0.6% were Jewish, and that even in New York City Jews formed only 6% of banking executives as compared to 28% of the general population. Similar statistics for a later period are unavailable, but reports of discrimination against Jews in major banks throughout the country persist and in 1968 the American Jewish Committee publicly filed a complaint before the Human Rights Commission of New York City charging the banking system with job bias against Jews.

As shown above, Jewish activity, in particular in the late Middle Ages and in the 18th and 19th centuries, often played an important, sometimes a central, constructive role in the economy and social life of various countries – sometimes even internationally. However, banking always remained a subsidiary Jewish economic activity. Frequently, when Jews appeared to command large assets, they gave this impression because they mostly owned mobile property. The wealthy Jews always formed a small group, particularly in comparison with the wealthy nobles or Christian merchants. It was really only in the 19th century that Jewish financiers achieved remarkable wealth, largely resulting from the activities of some European courts in consequence of the upheavals brought about by the French Revolution and the Napoleonic Wars. With the growth of joint stock banks and of central banks in the middle of the 19th century the field of private banking became limited. Around the beginning of the 20th century, Jewish influence in finance and banking had reached its zenith; afterward it declined at an accelerating rate.

Israel. In nineteenth-century Erez Israel banking was principally a secondary activity of certain merchant houses, some of which were Jewish. By the end of the Ottoman period four modern joint-stock banks were active in the country, one of which was the Anglo-Palestine Company, founded by the Zionist Organization. During the period of British rule, as part of the growing Jewish economy, an adequate and diversified banking sector developed, led by the financial institutions that were national in their capital-sources and policies: the Anglo-Palestine Bank, Workers' Bank, General Mortgage Bank, Palestine Corporation, Mizrachi Bank, and the co-operative credit societies. These were joined in the 1930s by a large number of private banks, established by German and other Central European newcomers, but only some of these survived. Still, during that period much of the banking business in Erez Israel was in the hands of foreign firms, among which Barclays Bank D.C.O. enjoyed a privileged position as the government banker.

With the establishment of the State of Israel the Anglo-Palestine Bank (from 1951 Bank Leumi) became banker to the government and bank of issue; but its official functions as central bank were transferred in December 1954 to the new Bank of Israel. In 1972 the Israeli banking system comprised 21 commercial banks with 769 branches; 13 cooperative credit institutions; 20 mortgage and investment banks (mostly affiliates of the commercial banks); and 13 others. Its leaders were Bank Leumi Le-Israel, Israel Discount Bank, and Bank Hapoalim (the Workers' Bank); all three have absorbed smaller banks, set up specialized banks and investment funds, and own subsidiaries abroad. Still, medium- and long-term credit in Israel, even when channelled through the banks, is mostly mobilized and allocated by the government.

2
Brokers

The large variety of commercial intermediaries and agents to which this term refers, in both medieval and modern times, has generally included a substantial proportion of Jews. They were particularly numerous at the fairs and in ports which were centers of interregional trade, and later also in the various types of exchanges. In this kind of occupation skill and information, a wide command of languages, and international connections were the chief requirements, and even men with little initial capital of their own could make a living and often a fortune.

Jewish brokers, itinerant and resident, were frequently found in the Mediterranean commercial centers throughout the Middle Ages. In Muslim countries brokerage was often specialized to a high degree. The activity of Jewish brokers was not distinct from that of non-Jews, but benefited periodically from Christian-Muslim political tension. In Christian countries the economic value of brokers was not widely recognized in the early Middle Ages, and their activity was often curtailed. In addition, Jewish traders and brokers suffered from religious animus. Nevertheless Jewish brokers were found in major ports such as Marseilles, Pisa, Barcelona, and Venice. In Spain the position of *corredor* ("broker") was a lucrative one, licensed by the king's bailiffs. Their activity was not limited to the ports, for they were also active in the countryside, particularly on royal and noble estates where they were in charge of selling agricultural produce and buying luxury commodities. The economic and social position of the broker within the Jewish community was generally inferior to that of the merchant. Brokers were excluded from community leadership in Majorca in 1356.

A new era in the history of Jewish brokerage began in the 16th century with the waves of exiles from Spain and Portugal to the ports of Italy, northern Europe, North Africa, the Balkans, and the Ottoman Empire, which coincided with European maritime expansion. Many of the exiles turned to brokerage, utilizing connections between their far-flung places of refuge. In Amsterdam brokerage in goods from the colonies, especially tobacco and sugar, was very profitable; Jewish brokers were allowed to operate unhindered; the entire bro-

"The Lithuanian Stock Exchange," wood engraving, Paris, 1846.

kerage of Brazilian sugar was in Jewish hands. In 1612 ten of the 300 authorized brokers were Jewish, and 30 of 430 in 1645. Among the 1,000 unauthorized brokers were many Ashkenazim. Of the 442 Jews who had an annual income exceeding 800 guilders in 1743, 25 were licensed and 100 unlicensed brokers. Marrano brokers had been active in England even before the readmittance (1656). In 1668 there were ten Jewish brokers on the London exchange; in addition there were also many unlicensed ones. An attempt to suppress the activities of unauthorized brokers (and to evict the Jews) led to a parliamentary commission which in 1697 regulated the number of brokers at 100 Englishmen, 12 aliens, and 12 Jews. Attempts to raise the permitted number of Jews failed in 1723, 1730, and 1739. In Hamburg there were four professional Portuguese-Jewish brokers in the early 17th century in addition to numerous unauthorized ones, mainly Ashkenazi; by 1692 there were 20 Sephardi and 100 Christian brokers. The city council succeeded in lowering the ratio and total number of Jewish brokers in the 18th century.

A different type of Jewish brokerage developed in Poland-Lithuania. During the 16th and 17th centuries domestic commerce as well as export (timber, grain, furs, and import (cloth, wine, luxuries) were for the most part in Jewish hands, and brokers played an important role, particularly at the regular fairs. The anti-Jewish polemicist Sebastian Miczyński wrote in 1618, "A short while ago ... the Jews made, among themselves, a general agreement and regulation whereby no Jew is to deal with a Christian for their profit, neither to act as inter-mediary for any merchandise if they request it of him, nor to lead a merchant to

Christian merchants or craftsmen, but to Jews alone. And on whoever transgresses this agreement they have applied great bans, curses, and punishments." This is a hostile presentation of a real conflict within the Jewish community. Merchants, who were predominant in community leadership, struggled to preserve their vested interests against brokers.

Tension between brokers and merchants is illustrated by the Poznan community, where resident brokers dealing with foreign merchants were vigorously harassed. Between 1626 and 1696 the community records dealt with their activity almost annually, but warnings, fines, and excommunications were to no avail for their numbers increased. Their commission was fixed between ½ and 1%, a rate that could be profitable only given a high turnover. Merchants were considered as justified in paying the regular fee only, even when a higher one had been agreed upon; brokers were accused of causing the economic ills of the community, in particular of revealing trade secrets to gentiles; they were sometimes equated with informers. Toward the end of the 17th century pronouncements against brokers became milder and rarer. The community, in economic straits, had acquiesced to a situation in which ever-growing numbers of its members were brokers or prepared to deal in brokerage.

On their arrival in Western Europe and the United States immigrants from Eastern Europe found a niche in several new types of brokerage, among them many new intermediary businesses like real estate brokerage, employment agencies, commodity and security exchanges, and commission agencies. In Central Europe the position of Jewish brokers combined Eastern and Western characteristics. Jews handled a large proportion of the trade between town and country, particularly grain and livestock, but were often excluded from the exchanges in the main cities. The first Jewish merchant to enter the Danzig exchange did so in 1808, accompanied by French gendarmes, after the occupation of the city. In Leipzig, center of the fur trade, six Jews were appointed brokers for the duration of the fur fair in 1813. By 1818, 28 of 35 fair brokers were Jews, 14 of them from Brody. Jews were prominent in regional as well as central exchanges in southern and central Germany, Hungary, and Rumania. Their position deteriorated in the 20th century as a result of the rise of producers' cooperatives, which attempted to bypass the middleman, and other developments hostile to small traders.

3

Contractors

While the initial possession of financial and commercial expertise and substantial resources was a necessary prerequisite for engaging in contracting for army supply and building, mainly road construction, it provided a successful means of enrichment and also opened the way to a certain measure of social acceptance and political influence from which as members of a hated group Jews were otherwise excluded. In Christian Spain Jews were prominent as military suppliers to kings. A noted example was Judah de la Cavalleria, who supplied arms to the king of Aragon in 1276 for his wars against the Muslims in Valencia. The Ravaya brothers supplied arms to King Pedro III of Aragon (1276–1285) in his wars against the rebel nobility of Catalonia. The wealthy Muça de Portella also supplied arms to Pedro III of Aragon. Isaac Abrabanel was military supplier to Ferdinand and Isabella from 1489 to 1492, while Abraham Senior was the chief supplier of military equipment to the Spanish troops who fought in Granada. Jews also played a prominent role in the production of military equipment, metal casting, and armament manufacture. There is evidence of Jewish arms manufacture in Spain, and in 1495 large numbers of Jewish arms manufacturers entered Portugal after the king had promised them special rights, such as payment of only half the sum for entry imposed on Jewish immigrants from Spain. Portuguese chroniclers, among them Damião da Goes, recount that some members of the king's council opposed the expulsion of the Jews from Portugal on the ground that the Jews possessed many secret methods of armament manufacture which should not be allowed to pass into the hands of the Turkish infidels. The Jewish chronicler Elijah Capsali describes the exiles from Spain as having introduced firearms to the Ottoman Empire and army, this being one of the reasons why they were well received by the sultans.

Probably Jews served as military suppliers during this period in Central Europe also; there is no lack of evidence for their participation in the arms trade. A decision of the Bruenn (Brno) tribunal permitted the Jews of Uherske Hradiste to trade in arms. A number of Jewish military suppliers are found in Germany in the 16th century. Isaac Meyer was permitted to reside in Halberstadt in 1537 in order to supply the monastery with weapons. Joseph (Joselmann) ben

Gershon of Rosheim in 1548 was granted a writ of protection by the emperor which also specified his activities as a military supplier.

Portuguese Jews in Amsterdam in the 17th and 18th centuries were active as military suppliers to the armies of Holland, Morocco, and England. The internal wars in Morocco during the 17th century enabled many Dutch Jews, who acted as military suppliers to all sides involved in the conflict, to enter the arms trade.

The Court Jews were regarded by their rulers as capable of supplying the whole range of military equipment: horses, food, uniforms, and weapons. Jewish commerce in Germany and Austria consequently prospered. Although the Court Jews themselves constituted only a minute proportion of the Jewish population, they required a widespread network of subcontractors, petty merchants, etc., who were also Jewish, in order to fulfill their functions as major contractor-suppliers, especially in wartime. Large-scale provisioning was achieved through contacts with Jewish dealers in agricultural products from Eastern Europe. Anti-Semites contended that in Germany at this time "all the military suppliers were Jews, and all the Jews were military suppliers." Samuel Julius was military supplier to Frederick Augustus, elector of Saxony. The Model family were court suppliers and military contractors to the duchy of Ansbach during the 17th and 18th centuries. Joseph Suess Oppenheimer acted as military supplier first to the landgrave Ernest Augustus of Hesse-Darmstadt, and then to Charles Alexander, duke of Wuerttemberg. The Gomperz family of Cleves acted as military contractors and commercial agents to six Prussian rulers, notably Elias Gomperz who founded his firm in Emmerich in the second half of the 17th century. His contemporary Israel Aaron, who had close commercial ties with Pomerania, Mecklenburg, Amsterdam, and Hamburg, also acted as military supplier to Prussia. The Wertheimer, Mayer, and Herschel families, as well as others who were permitted to settle in Vienna during the rule of Emperor Leopold, also acted as military contractors.

The ability of the absolutist rulers to maintain organized and well-regulated armies under their control and command may be attributed to a considerable degree to both the acumen of the Jewish contractors and their connections with fellow Jews. The part played by Jews in supplying the armies of England in the 17th and 18th centuries was no less decisive. Abraham Israel (Antonio Fernandez) Carvajal was the most important military contractor during the rule of Cromwell, and one of the five London merchants to sign a contract to supply the army with wheat in 1649. William of Orange was enabled to sail to England in 1688 by an interest-free loan of two million crowns made him by Francisco Lopez Suasso of the Hague, while another Jew, Francisco de Cordova, was in charge of military supplies for the campaign in partnership with Isaac Pereira. Solomon de Medina, military supplier to the Duke of Marlborough's troops, was granted a title in 1700 for his services to William III. In Ireland the firm of Machado and Pereira provisioned the Duke of Schomberg's armies.

Jews can be found among French military suppliers as early as the 16th century. A number of Jewish families were permitted to settle in Metz in 1567 by Marshal de Vieilleville on condition that they undertook to supply his troops, but their activities were limited to small-scale local operations. The part played by some of the wealthiest French Jews in military supplies reached considerable proportions during the reign of Louis XIV. Jacob Worms was chief military contractor to Louis XIV, and in the latter half of the 18th century Herz Cerfberr rose to prominence in this field. When in 1776 it was decided to end the system of private contracting for military supplies, an exception was made in the case of Cerfberr, who remained the supplier for the army in Alsace-Lorraine. In 1785 he divided the management of his business enterprises, allocating his banking activities to his sons and sons-in-law, while concentrating his own efforts on military supplies. Moses Belin, military supplier in Metz, and Moses Eliezer Liefmann Calmer of Hanover, military supplier from 1769, were among many other Jews prominent in this field in France. Most important was the wealthy Abraham Gradis, who acted as military supplier to the French army in Canada and did much for French troops there, especially during the Seven Years' War. From 1748 to 1779 he organized, with the assistance of Raphael Mendes, Benjamin Gradis, and other Jewish shipowners, the embarkation of French warships from Europe to Canada.

Jews played a prominent part in supplying weapons and provisions to the English army in the colonies. Mathias Bush supplied the Pennsylvanian troops in the war against the French. The Franks family, with branches in London and New York, acted as contractors to the English army in the American colonies. David Franks continued to serve the English crown even after 1775, supplying provisions and uniforms to English prisoners of war. Among other Jews, the Sheftall family of Georgia were suppliers to the American army as well.

In Russia in the 19th century contracting for construction of army buildings — fortifications and barracks — and for provisions, was frequently combined with contracting for the construction of state-built roads and railroads. The modern Jewish "white collar" worker first emerged in the network of offices as clerks or works supervisors of these contractors. Several Jewish entrepreneurs rose in this way from the poverty of the Pale to opulence, such as Judah Opatow. After their initial success many of these contractors — better known under the Russian designation "Podryachiki" — combined contracting with banking, as for instance the houses of Kroenenberg and Poliakoff.

Court Jews

Medieval princes used the commercial and financial services of individual Jews (see Banking and Bankers, p. 209). However, as an institution, the Court Jew is a feature of the absolutist state, especially in Central Europe, from the end of the 16th century onward. Trying as far as possible to extend his power over the whole of his territory, the ruler set up a centralized administration as part of his court, which at the same time became the power center, presenting a lavish display of luxury. Economically, a Jew could be of great service to such a ruler. In Poland many landed estates were administered by Jews (see Arenda, p. 125) and a large part of the trade in agricultural products was in their hands (see Agriculture, p. 107). This, combined with the emergence of early Jewish capitalist commercial activity by Sephardim in the Netherlands, with their connections with Levantine trade through Jews in the Ottoman Empire, made the Jew in Central Europe particularly suited to be an agent for provisioning armies with grain, timber, and cattle, as well as a supplier of diamonds and other goods for conspicuous consumption. As tax-collecting and enlargement of the scope of taxation often lagged considerably behind the growing expenditure of court, army, and bureaucracy, this type of regime developed an almost chronic financial deficit. Here the Jews with their organizational skill and their far-reaching connections could help, through the frequent supply of commercial credit or ready cash, as also through the supply of foodstuffs, cloth, and weapons for the army, the most important instrument of the prince's power.

The institution of the Court Jew developed gradually during the 16th and 17th centuries. Early Court Jews like Michel Jud and the mintmaster Lippold were exceptions. Another phase is represented by Jews who were entrepreneurs of the mints during the *"Kipperzeit"* (a period of economic instability at the beginning of the Thirty Years' War, 1618–48, characterized by galloping inflation). The best known of this period, Jacob Bassevi von Treuenberg of Prague (1570–1634), was the outstanding minting entrepreneur. Several Jews in the Hamburg region maintained close contacts with the courts of the neighborhood, such as Samuel Herscheider with the court of the archbishop of Bremen, Nathan Spanier with the count of Bueckeburg, and Alvaro Dinis with King

Christian IV of Denmark. In the Thirty Years' War Jews were employed as army provisioners and spies by both the Swedish and imperial forces. It was only during the second half of the 17th century, with the further evolution of the mercantilist policy and baroque culture of the absolute state, that the Court Jew became a kind of requisite of the princes' courts, a member of the group of officials through whom the state or territory was governed. Court Jews were then found in most of the principalities of the Holy Roman Empire, and in some of the adjoining states, such as Poland and Denmark. In some places they lived near the court, and in others the court made use of their services in one of the great commercial centers like Frankfort or Hamburg. They were given a great variety of titles: *Hofjude, Hoffaktor, Hofprovediteur, Hoflieferant, Hofagent, Kabinettfactor, Proviantlieferant, Kommerzienrat, Kommerziendirektor,* and the higher appellations of *Oberhoffaktor, Obermilizfaktor,* or *Generalprovediteur*; many had titles from several princes. Their rights were similarly various; the chief privileges included a limited official standing, sometimes combined with a salary, direct access to the prince, exemption from the jurisdiction of the rabbinical courts (and submission to the jurisdiction of the royal court – *Hofgericht*), and freedom to travel and settle anywhere in the empire. Their highly varied activities included finance, commerce, and diplomacy, but they were responsible especially for providing the prince and his court with merchandise and money, supplying metal for the mint, provisioning the army, undertaking commercial and diplomatic missions, and investigating proposals for the promotion of trade and industry, e.g., tobacco.

Industrious and often restless, the Court Jews showed a strong drive toward success, both in business and social status, with the allied urge "to assimilate as completely as possible to his environment in speech, dress, and manners" (S. Stern, *Court Jew* (1950), 11). A decidedly dynastic attitude led them to prefer marriages with the families of other Court Jews and to attempt to secure their positions for their descendants, both contributing factors to the tendency of their families to form a particular group within Jewry. The personal relationship between the prince and the Court Jew was based not only on common interests but also on the isolation in which both lived: the prince in his omnipotence and inaccessibility and the Court Jew because of his descent and religion. Thanks to his privileged position, the Court Jew was often able to act as *shtadlan* for the Jewish groups; frequently he was the head of the community and could procure the right to establish new settlements and prepare the way for emancipation. On the other hand, his often adventurous and risky career, necessarily involved with the court intrigues, could end abruptly on the death of the prince, with the gravest consequences for the Court Jew's property, and even life.

Protestant and Catholic princes alike opened their courts to Jews. Among the earliest were Frederick William, elector of Brandenburg from 1540, and Christoph Bernhard von Galen, who was elected prince-bishop of Muenster in 1650. The latter, partly influenced by tolerant motives, was at the same time eager to include the Jews in his mercantilist-expansionist policy: in the 1650s he employed the services of the Gomperz family on the lower Rhine; Nini Levi was made *Judenbefehlshaber* in 1651, and later Abraham Isaac became Court Jew. In the bishopric of Minden Behrend Levi gained access to the court. From 1655 Israel Aaron was an army factor in Prussia; he was permitted to live in Berlin in 1663 and two years later became a salaried servant of the court. His widow Esther Schulhoff married Jost Liebmann, who then succeeded to Israel Aaron's position and supplied the court with jewels. At the same time Simon Model, whose brother-in-law Bonaventura Sachs was influential at the court of Saxony, was Court Jew to the margrave of Ansbach, and Leffmann Behrends served the court of Hanover; the latter's contribution was instrumental in the elevation of Hanover to an electorate, and he also made substantial loans to the Hapsburgs and other dynasties. Other Court Jews were his cousin Behrend Lehmann at Halberstadt, who also gave financial assistance to Elector Frederick Augustus II of Saxony, and Aaron Beer at Frankfort. Behrend Lehmann and his cousin both helped Frederick Augustus of Saxony to gain the throne of Poland, where he also employed Jewish factors. Samuel Oppenheimer and Samson Wertheimer made their careers at the imperial court in Vienna, where later they were fol-

Portrait of Samuel Oppenheimer, Court Jew and banker of Leopold I of Austria.

lowed by members of the Arnstein, Eskeles, and Pereira families. Emperor Charles VI favored employing Jews in his court; Prince Eugene of Savoy, commander of the Austrian army, depended heavily on Jewish army purveyors. During these decisive years, when Austria rose to the status of a great power through her wars with the Turks, Jewish loans probably accounted for one-third of the annual revenue. The Karlskirche in Vienna was financed by Jewish loans as was Schoenbrunn Palace built by Maria Theresa. Five generations of the Gomperz family served at the Hohenzollern courts; later, members of the Ephraim, Isaak, and Itzig families were mintmasters. Also influential were Marx Assur, who received the title of *Hoffaktor* in Saxony and Sweden, and Behrend Lehmann's brother-in-law Jonas Meyer, who took up residence in Dresden, where Lehmann's son Lehmann Behrend also lived. The Saxon court probably used the services of the largest number of Jews; around 1707 it had connections with about 20 Jewish jewelers.

As in the south, the greater number of Court Jews came from Frankfort, so in the north, Hamburg (with Altona and Wandsbeck) became a similar center. Various members of both the Sephardi and Ashkenazi communities were in the service of the Danish court, beginning with Alvaro Dinis (Samuel Jachia) at Glueckstadt; later, members of the de Lima and de Casseres families served as factors and financial or diplomatic agents. Gabriel Gomez (Samuel de Casseres) was made *Generalfaktor und Hofprovisor* by Christian IV, retaining his position on the succession of Frederick III and later being appointed *Finanzkommissarius* as well. Diego Teixeira de Sampaio (Abraham Senior) and his son Manuel (Isaac Hayyim) served Queen Christina of Sweden as financial agents and resident ministers. In the service of the crown of Portugal abroad, notwithstanding their religious status, similar positions were held by Duarte Nuñes da Costa (Jacob Curiel), his son Manuel, and his brother Jeronimo (the latter of Amsterdam), while Manuel Bocarro (Jacob Rosales) was in the service of Spain, and Daniel and Joshua Abensur in that of Poland. However, they were employed in diplomatic or consular, rather than financial functions. From 1683 Jacob Mussafia, a mintmaster, was Court Jew of Duke Christian Albert of Schleswig-Holstein-Gottorp and later of Duke Frederick IV and his prime minister Wedderkop; he was followed by his son Joseph, who was involved in a famous lawsuit following the fall of Wedderkop. Other outstanding families of Court Jews in Hamburg were the Fuersts and the Goldschmidts: Samuel Fuerst served Bernhard and Johann Asolf, dukes of Schleswig-Holstein-Sonderburg; Jeremiah Fuerst became Court Jew of Duke Christian Louis of Mecklenburg in 1679 and of Sachsen-Lauenburg; Israel Fuerst served the court of Holstein-Gottorp. Bendix Goldschmidt and the Hindrichsen family were financial associates of the Fuersts; remaining in Hamburg, Goldschmidt became an agent of Goertz and later served the Danish court as a *Kammeragent*, while the Hinrichsen family took up residence in Mecklenburg-Schwerin. Ruben Hinrichsen became the salaried *Hofagent* of Duke Leopold II; Moses Josephs (Moses Wessely) of Glueckstadt was in the service of Peter I of Russia, and at the same time had dealings with the Danish court. All the petty German courts had their Court Jews: there was Moses Benjamin Wulff, Saul Samuel, and Moses Heyman at Weissenfels; Berend Wulff and Assur Marx at Sachsen-Merseburg and Sachsen-Zeitz; Samson von Baiersdorf at Bayreuth; the Van Geldern family at Duesseldorf; Simon Baruch at Kurkoeln; and the Heine family at Bueckeburg. Noah Samuel Isaac of Sulzbach, who helped finance the marriage of the Wittelsbach prince-elector Charles Albert in 1722, was also a banker of the elector of Cologne and of the Teutonic Order.

Joseph Suess Oppenheimer, court factor of Duke Charles Alexander of Wuerttemberg, had dealings with many other rulers, including the elector of Cologne, the landgraf of Hesse, and the elector of the Palatinate, but it was in Wuerttemberg where his financial influence reached its peak. At the same time, he saw possibilities of political action which would transform the duchy into a modern absolutist state based on mercantilist principles. He failed, however, and was executed in 1738. By then the zenith of the Court Jew had already passed. Although Jews served the German courts as mint entrepreneurs well into the first half of the 19th century, in general, the French Revolution and the Napoleonic Wars, which gave rise to wide-ranging changes in patterns of finance, commerce, and international trade, put an end to the epoch of the Court Jews.

In all their varied activities, the Court Jews played a remarkable part in the development of international credit facilities especially in the Central European states and to some degree in northern Europe also, from the mid-17th to late-18th centuries. Generally they were agents who arranged transfers of credit rather than possessors of vast capital in their own right; through their far-reaching commercial relationships and their organizing skill they were able to provide funds more swiftly than most Christian bankers. Because of their specialization in the money business they were able to furnish the silver for the mints more easily and could better act as army purveyors, once more because of their ability to organize and their network of family relationships. With their entrepreneurial spirit, they contributed in part to the process of industrialization within the frame of mercantilist policies. There is no doubt that they were instrumental in the growth of the modern absolute state, and at the end of the era there emerged a group of several important Jewish private bankers, who exemplify the transition to modern methods of economy and government, primarily the Rothschilds, the Goldschmidts, the Oppenheimers, and the Seligmanns. However, it should not be forgotten that the courts had their Christian bankers, entrepreneurs, and army agents too, who also played a part in this development.

5

Department Stores

The department store was an innovation first recognizable in mid-19th-century France. Similar contemporaneous developments were consumer cooperatives in Britain, and mail-order houses, chain stores, and "five-and-ten" stores in the United States. Only in Central Europe were department stores initiated and developed by Jewish entrepreneurs, except for the outstanding cases in Britain, South Africa, and the United States noted below. Of the five German department chain stores — Schocken, Tietz, Wertheim, Karstadt, and Kaufhof — the first three were owned by Jews; although the last two were owned by non-Jews, they employed many Jews in top managerial positions. Jewish department stores were prominently situated in major cities; the N. Israel and Kadewe stores of Berlin and the Gerngross of Vienna were widely known. In addition, most medium and small towns had their own department stores, which were often Jewish-owned. The north German stores, founded in the last quarter of the 19th century for the sale of textiles, a field in which Jews were traditionally prominent, adapted to rapid industrialization and urbanization by expansion and diversification. Although department stores in Germany did not account for more than 4–5% of the total retail commerce, they aroused widespread and lasting hostility. The complaints and anxieties of small or specialized shopkeepers found support in conservative circles in general. Economic accusations of dishonest advertising and other unfair competitive practices merged with anti-Semitic attacks: the importance of the new type of Jewish shopkeeper was unpalatable to many; the very employment of Christian salesgirls was distorted — they were pictured as being placed in danger of moral corruption by lustful Jewish bosses. In the late 19th and early 20th centuries this anti-department store pressure resulted in the levy of special taxes on department stores.

Under the Weimar Republic these laws were abolished and the stores entered a period of growth and expansion. However economic instability and unemployment again made the stores a focus of popular resentment which the Nazis were quick to utilize. Before and especially after the Nazis seized power the stores were frequently sabotaged and their owners attacked in the streets. The nationwide boycott of April 1, 1933, was specifically aimed against Jewish department stores, which continued to be harassed after the boycott was called off. Julius Streicher, as *Gauleiter* of Franconia, led a vicious campaign against the Nuremberg Schocken store. The German government was eventually forced to ease the pressure for economic reasons and even to save the Tietz company from bankruptcy. On "Kristallnacht" (Nov. 9–10, 1938), the department stores, as symbols of Jewish economic oppression, were burned and looted along with the synagogues.

Jews played a major role in the development and ownership of department stores in the United States. The majority of such Jewish-owned stores originated with the 19th-century Germany-Jewish immigration to America. Many of these immigrants began théir commercial careers as itinerant peddlers or small retailers in rural areas, where they enjoyed a virtual monopoly on merchandising; from there they expanded to large general stores, which eventually developed into the modern department stores of the late 19th and 20th centuries. A typical case was the Gimbel family: after Adam Gimbel, a native of Germany, had opened a general store in the small town of Vincennes, Indiana, his seven sons established department stores first in Milwaukee, then in Philadelphia, and finally in New York, where Gimbels ultimately became one of the city's largest retail establishments. Its greatest competitor, Macy's, was not originally Jewish-owned, but was bought out in 1887 by the Straus brothers, Isidore and Nathan, who had started by renting its basement to display the produce of the small glassware firm founded by their father Lazarus. In Brooklyn the brothers went into partnership with another German immigrant, Abraham Abraham, to found Abraham & Straus. Bloomingdale's in New York grew out of a small drygoods store on Third Avenue owned by the Bloomingdale brothers. Other New York department stores, such as B. Altman, Stern, Saks, S. Klein, and Ohrbach had similar histories, the latter two founded by 20th-century immigrants. Elsewhere in the U.S. large department store empires were also frequently the creation of Jews, such as I. Magnin and Levi Straus on the West Coast, William Filene's Sons Co. in the Boston area, Kauffmann Brothers in Pennsylvania, and Neimann & Marcus in Texas. The Chicago company of Sears, Roebuck, which came under the ownership of Julius Rosenwald during the 1890s, became a vast mail order firm. Sears, Roebuck and other mail order firms, together with urban growth and the automobile, brought about the virtual extinction of countryside peddling as successfully practiced by Jewish immigrants. Jewish prominence in department store ownership continued, however. A highly successful chain of discount stores founded by a syndicate of young Jewish businessmen after the Korean War was E. J. Korvette, an acronym for "Eight Jewish Korean Veterans."

In Great Britain Simon Marks and Israel Sieff developed Marks and Spencer, famous for its high-quality, reasonably priced goods, and Sir Isaac Wolfson founded Great Universal Stores. The Cohen family of Liverpool established Lewis' chain of department stores in the north of England. In English-speaking countries public opinion was not hostile to department stores and recognized their advantages to the community. The leading Australian department store line was founded by Sidney (Simcha Baevski) Myer, founder of the Melbourne Myer Emporium. Jewish businessmen and industrialists played an important part in the development of the modern department store in South Africa, sometimes called there a "bazaar." In 1927, Sam Cohen and Michael Miller, who had been in business together for 11 years, founded the O.K. Bazaars in Johannesburg and in time made it the largest chain-store business in South Africa. In 1931, Woolworths − independent of the company of similar name abroad − was started in Cape Town by Max Sonnenberg and developed with Elie Suzman to operate in other South African cities. In 1947 they became associated with Marks and Spencer of Britain. Other department stores such as Greatermans and the Belfast Warehouse were also developed by Jewish enterprise, while the countryside pharmacies of the South African Druggists Ltd. were largely the creation of Herman Karnovsky.

In Israel the Histadrut developed a chain of small department stores called Ha-Mashbir la-Ẓarkhan. The first one opened in 1947 and by 1970 there were 14 branches throughout the country. A single large department store, Kol Bo Shalom, opened in Tel Aviv in 1965.

Artist's impression of the 19th-century Grainger Market, Newcastle, England, which still operates as Marks & Spencer's smallest branch.

6

Jewish Autonomous Finances

The public finances of the autonomous Jewish community in the Middle Ages and early modern times were conditioned by the need to support communal institutions as well as to meet sudden and often huge demands for money in order to defend communities or individuals against attacks and libels. The provision of charity by the communal purse also became urgent following massacres and expulsions. The methods of internal taxation adopted were often influenced, for better or worse, by the fact that the community was held collectively responsible for the collection and apportionment of taxes levied on Jews by the state, this being one of the main features of Jewish communal autonomy. They were also shaped to a large extent by the methods of taxation of the gentile town where the community was located.

Under the *geonim* and *negidim* in the eastern countries and in Muslim Spain, up to the end of the 11th century and even beyond, local tax levies and allocations were mostly directed by the central leadership through local appointees. The finances of the Babylonian academies and the court of the exilarch were regulated and their expenditure was covered by the levy of fixed imposts on the Jewish population, as well as by voluntary donations and income from landed property owned by these institutions.

In countries and periods in which the leadership was less centralistic, various methods of financial management were developed. *Takkanot* (regulations) ascribed to Gershom ben Judah, but in reality drawn up around the 12th century, envisage a case where "if the *kahal* (community) has established an ordinance to help the poor . . . with the agreement of the majority, the minority may not refuse to obey it" (L. Finkelstein, *Jewish Self-Government in the Middle Ages* (1924), 132); this is the first overt indication of a local system of taxation for charity within the framework of the medieval community.

In *takkanot* of Jacob ben Meir Tam of the 12th century the period of residence before having to contribute to the charity fund is laid down: "to come under the *ḥerem* (ban) to 'bring the tithe to the treasure house' [Mal. 3:10] one must be but one month in the city. Members of a community who cannot give charity may compel others who can afford to give" (op. cit., 185–6; see also 209–10).

This concept of the tithe (*ma'aser*) as a contribution to charity — whether enforced or voluntary — was to be one of the financial pillars of Ashkenazi communities. Thus certain medieval forms of internal Jewish taxes were based on and defined by ancient terminology and ideology.

In Christian Spain the communities largely covered their needs by an indirect consumption tax mainly on wine and meat, but combining this with direct taxation in the *cisa* system, subject to changes and variations of time and place.

In Poland-Lithuania, the intensive internal taxation and spending were not sufficient to cover needs, in particular as the harsh and irregular exactions of state dignitaries and the despotic nobility mounted. Eventually the Councils of the Lands as well as individual communities had to rely increasingly on loans. As their debts increased, higher interest rates were charged by Christian noblemen and churchmen, as well as by Jews. In several Polish communities of the 18th century the cost of defrayment of debts amounted to 40% of their annual budgets. In some instances these loans were of 150 years' standing. Separate collections were often made for the salaries of rabbis and preachers. The financial problems and methods of expenditure of a large community with a relatively secure and legal position are shown in the budget of Poznan Jewry for 1637–38:

	Zlotys	per-cent
Taxes, etc.	12,000	37.1
King	200	0.6
Palatin	2,000	6.2
Vice-Palatin	1,000	3.1
Vice-Palatin's Secretary	150	0.5
The General	1,000	3.1
The General's Secretary	150	0.5
Other officials	250	0.8
Bishop	200	0.6
Clergy and monks	785	2.4
Town taxes and expenses	523	1.6
Officials in Gnesen	200	0.6
Other expenses	3,800	11.8
Various expenses at the fairs	1,400	4.3
Relief	4,809	14.8
Education (Talmud Torah)	692.20	2.1
For Palestine	303.20	1.0
Poor brides	150	0.5
Others	500	1.5
Salaries for rabbis, sextons, physicians and others	1,892	5.8
Guards	258	0.8
Various	95	0.3
Total	32,358.10	100.0

(B.D. Weinryb, in PAAJR, 19 (1950), 50.)

Coin used in payment of the tax on ritual slaughter, Italy.

The much more detailed original Hebrew text of the budget (*ibid.*, no. 138, Heb. pagin. 57–60) shows very interesting items of expenditure. The highest-paid official of the community was the *shtadlan* who received 300 zlotys a year, while the rabbi was paid only 130 zlotys in salary and an allowance of 100 zlotys for living expenses. The main preacher was paid 156 zlotys while a separate collection for this purpose would bring in "approximately 107 zlotys." Six Jewish guards were paid 108 zlotys for the winter period only. Expenses for water pipes amounted to 400 zlotys. The main Christian dignitaries and the various Christian religious orders not only received fixed amounts of money but also spices and carpets on credit. To its foreseen outlay the community had to expend within the period 1637/38 to 1641/42 two payments on "tumults" and "all this in addition to various expenses amounting to thousands of zlotys given to the wojewoda [provincial governor], the general, and other dignitaries."

From about the middle of the 17th century local communities of Poland-Lithuania developed the *korobka* (basket tax), a system of indirect consumption tax frequently collected in dues for ritual slaughter. It was later broadened under Russian and Austrian rule mainly in the form of a candle tax (on candles for Sabbath and the like). Synagogues also gained an income from pew-selling. Scholars and the very poor were exempt in principle from most taxation.

With the advance of emancipation, the power of tax enforcement was gradually removed from communal jurisdiction, and all internal needs had subsequently to be financed on a voluntary basis.

The gap between the medieval *kehillah* (community) and the modern fund-raising agencies was filled by the *hevrah*, the society which assumed the function of activating voluntary giving as well as operating the social welfare and other institutions of the community. The most viable among these associations was the *ḥevra kaddisha*, the burial society, which by its monopolistic and lucrative ownership of the community's cemetery plots was sufficiently solvent not only to operate many social welfare, cultural, and educational enterprises, but also to help other associations maintain their services. As late as the 20th century, the dues of Central and South American burial societies financed communal activities. Sometimes the *ḥevra kaddisha* there assumed the functions of a *kahal* (e.g., in Buenos Aires).

In the 20th century the stupendous needs created by two world wars, the Nazi Holocaust, and the restoration of Israel prompted Jewish communities in Western countries to develop highly efficient fund-raising techniques. Thus the medieval system of compulsory financing was effectively converted into voluntary giving in modern times.

When having to act as collectors or farmers of state tax, the individual communities, Councils of the Lands, federations of communities, *Landesjudenschaften*, or government-appointed rabbis each had to develop their own methods of tax collection and apportionment according to circumstances as well as to try diplomatic means at negotiating an equitable tax load as far as possible.

State imposition was usually mechanical. Taxes were generally imposed *per capita*, or according to the estimated combined wealth of the Jews of the given unit. The communal or other appointees in the Jewish leadership usually tried to calculate a just and equitable distribution of this burden among its members. Thus to assess the means of members they appointed special officers (Heb. *shamma'im*), whose composition gave rise to class tensions in the larger and socially variegated communities. The assessment of taxes also involved problems of social justice and definitions of services and duties. In Christian Spain and Poland-Lithuania especially, the methods employed and principles involved were frequently called in question. An instructive example of application of these principles in Christian Spain is summed up by Y. F. Baer. The tax statute of the aljama [Jewish community] Huesca of the year 1340 opens with a paragraph dealing with the poll tax and exemptions from it. Among the groups exempted were members of the community whose wealth amounted to less than 50 sueldos, scholars 'who study day and night, having no other occupation,' the poor supported by charity, and servants. The communal leaders were authorized to exempt certain needy members from payment of this tax, provided the total sum involved in these exemptions would not exceed a certain specified figure. Then there followed a complex system of taxes of varying rates, levied upon both property and business transactions. A tax of one-half of one percent (½%) was levied on the value of houses and gardens adjoining them: and another, of one percent (1%) on fields, vineyards, and gardens not adjoining the owner's house. There was a tax of one and one half percent (1½%) on the amounts of direct loans of money and of commercial credits (*commendae*) in kind – grain, oil, honey, textiles, etc. – extended to Christians and Muslims. The tax on loans to fellow Jews was much lower, only five-twelfths of one percent ($\frac{5}{12}$%), since these bore no interest. Loans extended to aljamas, servants, and students and the sums involved in betrothal and marriage contracts and in wills went untaxed. There were taxes on mortgaged real estate, on rented homes and stores, on the purchase and sale of land, textiles, grain, foodstuffs, gold and silver, furs and other merchandise, as well as on the purchase of clothes and various other necessities. Finally the daily earnings of an artisan, if they were above a certain amount, were taxed. Teachers and the readers and sextons of the synagogues were exempted (Baer, *History of the Jews in Christian Spain*, 1 (1966), 206–7).

7

Market Days and Fairs

The nomadic nature of early medieval trade and the wide ranging contacts of Jewish merchants throughout the period made Jewish traders early and eager participants in market days and fairs, in spite of the religious and social problems attendant on such participation, especially in Christian countries. As merchants were prominent in European Jewish leadership and autonomy, fairs were suitable meeting places for deliberating Jewish affairs. Around 825 Archbishop Agobard complained that the day on which the Lyons weekly market was held had been changed from Saturday to suit Jewish traders. In the following three centuries there are many references in both Hebrew and Christian sources to Jews attending fairs, particularly in cities of the Rhineland such as Cologne and Treves. Gershom ben Judah (960—1028) mentions a fair at a sea or river port during which the assembled merchants from various communities enacted an ordinance. Champagne and Provence, believed to be where the fairs began, had many Jewish communities, whose members in all probability participated in them. Jewish attendance at markets and fairs decreased after the era of the Crusades when moneylending and pawnbroking became the major source of Jewish livelihood in northwestern and Central Europe. In other areas, where the trade in goods formed an important Jewish occupation, their attendance continued.

The 16th century, in Eastern and subsequently in Central Europe, witnessed the creation of economic and social patterns adapted to the attendance of large numbers of Jews of various fairs and markets. In Poland-Lithuania it was expressly forbidden to fix the dates of fairs and markets on the Sabbath or Jewish holidays. The Jews' commercial rights at fairs and markets were the only ones not challenged by competing Christian merchants. When persecution in 1539—40 resulted in Lithuanian Jews ceasing to travel to fairs, the nobility appealed to the king to suppress the persecutions at once. One of the most important fairs was the "Gromnice" (February 2), when many Jewish merchants and heads of communities convened at Lublin; much trade was done and debts and taxes were gathered. Other fairs took place in Brody, Gniezno, Gdansk (Danzig), Torun, Lvov, and Cracow, and there were innumerable lesser ones as well. As the fairs bore the names of their patron Christian saints, these became common usage and were inscribed on official and business documents. The distinctive creation of Polish Jewry, the Councils of the Lands, was an outgrowth of a *bet din* which officiated at the Lublin fairs. Meetings of the Councils took place there regularly, twice a year, during the 16-day spring and summer fairs; sometimes they were held during the Jaroslaw fairs in the fall. The Lithuanian Council also convened during fairs, and common sessions took place at Leczyna. One of the tasks of the Councils was regulating the nomination of a *parnas* and *dayyan* (see below) for the duration of the fair. As both positions carried wide powers, they had to be judiciously distributed among the contending lands. In Poland-Lithuania the social aspects of the fair were as significant as the economic and communal leadership ones. N. N. Hannover described a mid-17th-century fair: "the head of the yeshivah journeyed with all his pupils to the fair on market day . . . and at each fair there were hundreds of heads of yeshivot, thousands of pupils, and tens of thousands of youths and Jewish merchants . . . And whoever had an eligible son or daughter went to the fair and arranged a match, for everyone could find one to his liking. And at every fair hundreds of matches were made, and sometimes thousands; and the children of Israel, men and women, wore kingly vestments at the fair" (*Yeven Meẓulah*, 1966, 86 f.). Meir b. Gedaliah (Maharam) of Lublin (1558–1616) described another aspect of Jewish life at the fairs: "It is a regular custom that at every fair a place is determined as a synagogue for daily prayer, and every Sabbath scholars and yeshivah students and leaders of the land and people congregate there and read the Torah" (Responsa, 84).

Jews had been expelled from Breslau in 1455, but they were never absent from the fairs. In 1537 the municipal council opposed an attempt by Ferdinand I to levy a special poll tax on Jewish visitors to the fairs. A century later, at the request of the textile guilds and the imperial authorities and despite the opposition of the local merchants, Jews were permitted to be in the town a few days before and after the fairs. In 1697 the authorities divided the Jews into five categories whose duration of stay depended on the scope of their economic transactions.

Jews attended the fairs as a corporation of merchants based on their communities or countries or origin. These corporations were also responsible for nominating their officials: a *parnas ha-yarid*, in charge of keeping order and representing the fair corporations; a *dayyan ha-yarid*, who held regular judicial authority and was empowered by the chief rabbi of the land (first mentioned in 1698); supervisor of ritual law; and *shames* (*shammash*), the distinctive Breslau functionary, who was permitted to remain between the fairs and guarantee the continuity of business transactions. First mentioned in 1673, he was elected by the *Judenschaft*, authorized by the Councils of the Lands, recognized by the

Breslau municipal council, sworn in, and allowed to wear a sword. In 1696 there were ten *shamosim* at the fair, one each for the four Polish lands and one for Bohemia, Moravia, Glogau, Posen, Leczno, and Zuelz. The number of Jewish visitors at a fair in 1685 was 332, and they practically monopolized Polish trade, particularly in textiles, silks, spices, tobacco, and above all in furs.

Jewish attendance at fairs within the Austrian Empire was encouraged by Emperor Maximilian I, who in 1494 permitted Jews to attend markets in the imperial cities from which they had been expelled on payment of three florins *Mautgeld* ("body tax"). This right, confirmed by his successors in return for extraordinary taxation, became the legal cornerstone of Jewish economic activity. Joseph II eventually abolished the *Leibzoll* and declared all markets open to Jews (1782/83). In practice, however, many restrictions remained in force until 1848. At Brno, for example, the Jews were allowed to enter through only one gate (*Judentor*) at fixed hours, were restricted to one market, and forced to lodge in one inn, the *Neue Welt* in the Krona suburb. They struggled for many years for the right to erect stalls. Complaints by Christian merchants against underselling and inferior wares were continuously raised, and peddlers (called *pinkerljuden*) were particularly harassed at the Brno fairs. The Council of Moravia regulated the supervision of dietary laws at the fairs, distributed stalls before the fairs commenced, and prohibited the Jews from being at the fair on the day before it opened. There was a tendency to establish Jewish communities near locations of major and minor markets and fairs.

There were a great many fairs in Central Europe. Many Jewish calendars recorded dates of fairs, which Jews attended as peddlers who both bought and sold wares, as merchants buying goods wholesale for retailing, and sometimes as popular performers like jugglers. Registers of the special scales for weighing feathers at the Linz markets of 1594 and 1603 show that there were 131 Jewish traders in feathers and only 12 Christian dealers. Other important commodities were leather, skins, old clothes, and new clothes and textiles imported from Bohemia. In 1714 Bohemian *"Federjuden"* (feather merchants) had to have special permission to attend because of the plague. About 300 Jews dealing in similar articles attended the Krems fairs annually; in 1701 the Moravian Jews boycotted it because a Jew had been arrested as a thief.

The records of Zurzach fairs in Switzerland mention the *Judengeleit*, a tax of between 7 and 19 batzen according to age and wealth which was a considerable source of income. The number of Jews attending grew from about 150 in the mid-18th century to about 200 at its close; most foreign Jews were from Gailingen, Hohenems, and communities in Baden, Alsace, and Swabia, which were composed primarily of peddlers and merchants. More than three-quarters of the households of the nearby communities of Endingen and Lengnau attended these fairs. Although Jews were not tolerated throughout most of Switzerland they were allowed and encouraged to attend the fairs, particularly the livestock merchants. In France in 1741, the controller-general of finances wrote a circular letter to all provincial governors asking them about the commercial activities of the Jews. Unanimously they replied that Jews should not be excluded from the fairs and markets because they helped keep down prices. The monopolistic guilds were forcing up prices, while the outside merchants, who came for the duration of the fair, forced them down. An endemic source of strife and litigation between Jews and local merchants and the authorities was the constant attempt to sell outside the market, or not on market days, or on the way to or back from markets, or to remain in the area after the fair was over. In Italy Jews were to be found at the major fairs and often participated in the festive processions which inaugurated them. The community of Mantua bought and erected stalls at the fairgrounds for its members; there was an unsuccessful attempt to prohibit their use in 1740. A Jewish community had the right to tax Jewish merchants attending the fairs for the use of communal amenities. In 1720 the Jewish communities of the duchy of Parma tried, without success, to tax Jewish merchants attending the Parma city fairs (where there was no community). A long dispute (1748–51) between the community of Verona, which had attempted to exact a business tax from foreign visitors at the fairs, and the communities of Mantua, Ferrara, and Modena ended with rabbinical authorities in Italy and Germany deciding against Verona's action.

European rulers were aware of the economic benefits resulting from Jewish participation in fairs. Joachim II, elector of Brandenburg, expelled the Jews in 1510 but subsequently allowed them to attend fairs. After the 1573 expulsion from Brandenburg, Posen Jews regularly received permission to attend the Frankfort on the Oder fairs. Elector Frederick William (1640–88) encouraged Polish Jews to attend fairs in his realm long before he admitted 50 Jewish families from Austria to settle and trade freely throughout his lands (1671). Though Jews were rigorously excluded from Saxony, the internationally important Leipzig fairs needed Jews to participate in large numbers. Between 1675 and 1764, 82,000 Jews attended the biannual Leipzig markets; their number fluctuated according to political and economic factors, but grew steadily from about 400 a year in the mid-17th century to twice that amount by the end of the century and continued to grow; they generally constituted about one-fifth of the total attendance. Their number increased from an average of 1,073 in the 1780s to 3,370 in the 1800s and 6,444 in the 1830s, when they formed around one-quarter of the participants. Between 1675 and 1764 the majority of Jewish participants came from Central Europe, though the number of East European Jews was increasing slowly, eventually amounting to one-third of the total

Three Jews (with beards, right) in a Tatar market in the Crimea. Drawing by the Leipzig engraver, Geissler, 18th century.

Jewish attendance in the early 19th century. The attendance lists of the fairs offer a true mirror of 18th-century Jewish society. Members of the leading families attended. The leading Court Jews of the day were also present. Jewish visitors to Leipzig congregated in the Bruehl, which became in effect a Jewish quarter for the duration of the fairs. The *Landrabbiner* of Anhalt had rabbinical jurisdiction there and those who died at the fair were buried in Dessau. At Leipzig Jews bought wares worth about half a million thalers annually between 1773 and 1775, primarily textiles. Officially they sold wares worth one-fifth of that amount, but the sales figure was not the true one, for the "scales tax" (*Wagegold*) was 1% of all sales; it was not until 1813 that it was reduced to 0.5%, the same as the Christian tax. In addition the city exacted a high entrance fee. "*Volljuden,*" who did not enjoy special privileges and protection and were the majority, paid six thalers each and three for a wife or servant. Jewelers paid eight thalers and cooks ten thalers and 12 groschen.

In the Pale of Settlement and Austrian Galicia the market square and the regular market days became the center of the *shtetl* and the heart of its economy. To a large extent the economic and social life in these townships was regulated by buying from peasants and selling to them on the fixed market day

Market day in Utena, Lithuania, 1937—38.

in the appointed place; taverns were therefore erected around the market square. Jewish emigrants carried over this type of market (with some changes) into large cities in Western Europe; an example is the Petticoat Lane Market in London.

8

Mintmasters and Moneyers

In the Middle Ages rulers tended to lease the right of minting coins to mint-masters or to grant and sell the right to their territorial vassals, who themselves employed such mintmasters. Jews carried out this prestigious and profitable enterprise mainly either as suppliers of precious metals for minting purposes or as distributors of coins; very rarely were they the actual craftsmen. In general, in the later Middle Ages, the Jewish master of the mint or purveyor was superseded by a Christian.

The Jew Priscus was probably master of the mint for King Clotaire of the Franks and issued the royal coins at Chalon-sur-Saône around 555 C.E. Some Czech numismatists consider that Omeriz, Mizleta, and Nacub, moneyers for Duke Boleslav II in Prague toward the end of the tenth century, were Jews. This is also true of Zanta and Noc, who worked at the Vysehrad mint (near Prague). Ladislaus II of Bohemia (1158–73) had a Jewish mintmaster in his province of Lusatia. In the 13th century a cleric complained that the Jews were still lessees of the mint and customs. For much of the 12th and 13th centuries the coinage of some Polish rulers was issued by Jewish mintmasters and often had Hebrew inscriptions on the coins. Boleslav IV (1146–73) used Jews to mint and distribute his currency. Shortly after, Casimir II (1177–94) allowed a Hebrew inscription to appear on state coins. Mieszko III (1173–77, 1195–1202) gave a life grant to the Jews to lease the state mint, and Polish currency in the last two decades of the 12th century was stamped solely in Hebrew. Most of the inscriptions were various dedications to Mieszko. Boleslav of Kujawy and Mieszko the Younger imitated their father. Boleslav permitted his own name to be stamped in Hebrew, while Mieszko the Younger allowed the names of Jewish mintmasters, such as Ben Jacob and Joseph ha-Kohen, to be inscribed; sometimes the names covered the entire face of the coin, as in the case of Rabbi Abraham b. Isaac Nagid. Przemyslav I later continued this practice some 40 years, as did his son Przemyslav II; Menahem, Jacob, and Abraham were mintmasters whose names were stamped on coins.

In later Polish history, Jews continued to be mintmasters, although no Hebrew appeared on their coins. In 1360 the Cracow mint was transferred to Lewko, an important Jewish financier. Under Sigismund I, between 1509 and 1518, Abraham Ezofowitz was minister of the exchequer and in charge of minting coins. In 1555 Sigismund II leased the mint in his Lithuanian province of Poland for three years to a Jew in Vilna. He again gave the Vilna concession to the Jews Felix and Borodavka in 1560. Because of their prominence in the fields of money changing, moneylending, and finance, Jews participated in minting activities in Poland almost without interruption from the early stages of the kingdom until its partition. From the 17th century, the Councils of the Lands, both in Poland and Lithuania, showed much concern and great reservation about coin minting and the coin trade.

Jews leased mints in Christian Spain as early as the 11th century. Bonnom (Shem Tov) made gold coins under the authority of Count Ramón Berenguer I of Barcelona. In 1066 the count's son sold the right to mint coinage to a syndicate which included David b. Jacob ha-Ivri. Benveniste de Porta (d. 1268) leased the mint of Barcelona from James I of Aragon. Sancho IV of Castile gave a similar concession to Abraham el Barchilon in 1287. A century later, in 1331, Alfonso XI of Castile repeated this with Samuel ibn Waqar (Aben Huacar); Pedro IV of Aragon gave control of the royal mint to a Jewish company at about the same time.

As early as 1063 Queen Anastasia of Hungary permitted a Jew to mint his own coins at the royal mint. Hebrew appears on a coin of Andrew II in the early 13th century. Andrew's Golden Bull of 1222 excluded Jews and Muslims from the office of mintmaster, but the prohibition was disregarded, for the coins of his son Bela IV and his grandson Stephen V bear Hebrew letters, apparently standing for the initials or signs of Jewish mintmasters.

The first Jew recorded by name in Austria was Shlom the mintmaster, massacred by crusaders in 1195. The nobility obtained a decree in 1222 specifically excluding Jews from the post, but Jews were again employed in this capacity some 40 years later. Jewish mintmasters were found in other German states and principalities, particularly in the 12th century, though their role was much less significant in the centuries that followed. In the Wetterau region, thin coins stamped on one side only, known as bracteates, were issued between 1170 and 1180, with the name David ha-Kohen imprinted in Hebrew. In this same period Otto the Rich, margrave of Meissen, employed Gershon, who also struck his name in Hebrew on bracteates. Nearby, at Lausitz and Pegau, Jews operated mints for the local nobility. Twelfth-century bracteates from Saxony, made under both Count von Mansfeld and Duke Bernhard I, show Hebrew letters. Similarly Jehiel, the name of a Jewish mintmaster at Wuerzburg in the early 13th century, is clearly marked in Hebrew on numerous bracteates. The question of whether a Jewish mintmaster might operate on the Sabbath appears twice in contemporary responsa; he might do so only if he had a Christian partner. The number of Jewish mintmasters was restricted, however, both by the appearance of Christian symbols and formulas on coins and by guild regulations.

The 16th and 17th centuries witnessed political and economic developments in Central Europe which enabled Jews to play an unprecedented role in purveying. The growing independence of the many petty Germany states, the mercantilist theory of the supreme value of precious metals for state economy, as well as the readiness of the unprincipled rulers to issue debased coin, combined to create a need for expertise and initiative. The increased demand for currency was thwarted by the depletion of the silver mines; the metals had to be imported from the Americas or bought at the entrepôts of Amsterdam, London, and Hamburg, where Sephardi Jews were prominent in the bullion trade. In Poland, too, Jews were experts in all aspects of the coin trade. The princes and rulers of the petty and larger states of the Holy Roman Empire and elsewhere turned to them for purveying, minting, and distributing currency. This was done by means of contracts between the ruler and his *Muenzjude* ("mint Jew"), who was to be found at virtually every court. The purveying of silver was conducted by a sophisticated network of contractors and subcontractors reaching down to the level of the peddler, entrusted with the task of buying up foreign coinage, silver and copper wares, and anything else suitable. The actual minting was supervised by Jews, contractors of the mint. The coin dies were often made by Jewish seal engravers, a profession which Jews tended to monopolize, by virtue of its being free of medieval guild restrictions. The distribution of the freshly minted, frequently inferior quality coinage was often entrusted to military contractors, frequently Jews. While *Muenzjuden* were active throughout the 17th and 18th centuries, their activity increased even further during the unstable periods of intensive monetary activity, especially so from 1618 to 1623, the 1670s and 1680s, from 1756 to 1763, and at all times during war and turmoil. During these crucial phases the activity of the *Muenzjuden* brought them into a disrepute that aroused anti-Jewish feelings, reaching a peak during the Seven Years' War.

Among the more prominent Jewish mintmasters of the 16th century were Phybes of Hanover, a lessee of the mint at Wunstorf, Brunswick, in 1566, and Isaac Meir (Mayer) of Prague, who administered the mint from 1546 to 1549. The most famous was Lippold, the mintmaster of Brandenburg, who ruled the electorate's Jewry with an iron hand. In Breslau Manasseh of Hotzenplotz gained a foothold to power through his services to the mint, and the number of Jewish silver purveyors in other minting centers in Austria and southern Germany was large. In 1627 they supplied 29% of the silver to the Breslau imperial mint and 50% in 1656. The dependence of the government on such purveyors increased in the 18th century to 78% in 1704, and to 94% in 1720. In the crisis of the 1670s and 1680s Jews were less prominent, although some Court Jews were active in the precious metals and coin trades. Jewish mintmasters reestablished communities in Saxony, from which Jews had been expelled. The nuclei of the Jewish communities of Leipzig and Dresden were formed by the *Muenzjuden*. Gerd Levi (1659–1739) received a licence to buy and supply silver (1710) to the Leipzig mint; his son, Levi Gerd, continued in his father's footsteps.

The classical country of Jewish minting activity, however, was Prussia. Throughout most of the 17th and 18th centuries the *Muenzjuden* constituted the leadership of the Berlin community. Israel Aron, first head of the newly reconstituted (1671) community of Viennese exiles, was purveyor to the Berlin mint. His widow, Esther, married the court jeweler Jost Liebmann and received (between 1700 and 1713) permission to mint large series of small coins as payment for the precious stones which she had supplied to the court. Levin Veit monopolized the purveying of silver in the years 1717 to 1721 and received permission to smelt and refine silver. In the 1750s two firms, that of Daniel Itzig and members of the Gomperz family, and that of V. H. Ephraim and members of the Fraenkel family, competed fiercely, one outbidding the other for the state minting contract. Frederick II's growing and urgent demands for funds during the war forced the competing firms into a partnership (in 1758), which leased all Prussian and Saxon mints. The Saxon mints of Leipzig and Dresden had been occupied by Frederick, who turned them over to his entrepreneurs, who then issued successive series of millions of more debased Saxon coins. These were known as "Ephraimiten" and gave rise to the bitter popular refrain: "Pretty on the outside, worthless within; on the outside Frederick, Ephraim within." Frederick instituted similar proceedings with the currency of Mecklenburg-

Coin minted in Wroclaw, Poland, by Isaac Meir, 16th century.

Schwerin, Anhalt-Zerbst, and Anhalt-Dessau, and he was also forced to debase Prussian currency. The last Ephraim-Frederick contract was signed on Dec. 17, 1762. After the war *Muenzjuden* were employed in buying up the corrupt coinage and in supplying silver for the reconstituted currency. Ephraim and his sons were gradually overshadowed by the Itzig family, who were sole purveyors of precious metals between 1771 and 1786. One of Itzig's many agents was Joachim David Friedlaender of Koenigsberg and his sons (David was the most talented). The last important mint entrepreneur was Liepmann Meyer Wulff of Berlin, who supplied the mint between 1799 and the Prussian debacle of 1806, after which thorough governmental reforms were introduced which abolished the need for the services of private silver and gold purveyors.

The tradition of Jewish moneyers and mintmasters in the Muslim world goes back to the Middle Ages. A certain Sumayr was die cutter and mintmaster for Abdalmalik (685–705), the Ummayyad caliph at Damascus. Since the earliest Muslim coins were struck at this time, Sumayr was one of the technical founders of Islamic coinage. Jewish moneyers were known in Cairo from earliest times, possibly being successors to those previously operating in Alexandria. Japheth b. Abraham, in partnership with two other Jews, was administrator of the Fostat mint (Cairo) in about 1086. A brief mention is made in a document from the Cairo *Genizah* of two Jewish partners working the caliphate mint in the second half of the 12th century. The most noted Cairo mintmasters were Isaac Sholal and Abraham Castro, who was appointed to the position after the conquest of Egypt by Sultan Selim (c. 1520). When the Egyptian viceroy, Ahmed Pasha, plotted independence, it was Castro who informed Constantinople. He was reinstated after Ahmed's defeat in 1524. In the 1660s this same position was held by the court banker Raphael Joseph, known as Chelebi. Under Murad III (1574–95) the director of the Turkish mint was a Jew, Hodja Nessimi (or Nissim). In this same period, Moses Benveniste – known to the Turks as Hodja Moussahibi – was involved in the currency "reform" which led to a revolt of the janissaries against "Jews' Money" in 1589. Samuel b. Abraham, head of the Crimean Karaites, was moneyer to the last Tatar khan in the mid-18th century. As the treasury minister, he held the official title of Aga. His son Benjamin succeeded him in both position and title. When the Crimea was conquered by Russia in 1783, Benjamin was permitted to retain his title. Yaḥyā b. Judah Badiḥi (1810–1888) was minter for the imam of Yemen in the mid-19th century.

9
Moneylending

With the development of an urban economy in the caliphate of the ninth century, the financing of the ever-growing needs of trade, of crafts, and of the state, became a pressing need. Jews financed the business of their coreligionists through participating in various ways as partners, both in financing and in profits. While some of these means of participation were actual, others were formal only, devised to evade the prohibitions on usury. In the tenth century, large-scale Jewish financiers appear, like the Netira family, who loaned large sums to the state on interest, against the collateral of state incomes. These loans were evidently the accumulated savings of middle- and small-scale Jewish merchants, deposited with Jewish state bankers for greater income and security. When (up to the 15th century) the majority of the Jewish people lived in Islamic lands and in Christian Spain, moneylending was one of the occupations of Jews, as of other city dwellers. While Jews first came to Northwestern Europe mainly as international traders, when some of them later turned to local trade (1000 C.E.), they engaged in credit operations. The impact of the First Crusade (1096–99) on the status and livelihood of the Jews in France, Germany, and England drove them out of trade through the lack of security arising from the inimical attitude of society in general; at the same time, Jewish merchants and craftsmen were denied any share in the Christian towns and guilds which were rapidly evolving as the only social framework for trade and crafts in those countries. This crystallized at a time when European trade, agriculture, and building were expanding and in need of financing. Ready cash – which then meant precious metals – was scarce. Available means in Christian hands were channeled into credit for merchant ventures and other relatively creative loans, in which it was also easier to formulate partnerships that evaded the stigma of usury. Under such circumstances the Church found it easy to act in accordance with the agricultural ethos of its upper strata, and to insist on the prohibition of usury. There remained the field of loans for consumption – the need for which arose in cases of illness, litigation, and unforeseen expenses – for which Christian capital was not readily available and where usury was least avoidable. Deprived of its former uses, Jewish capital entered this field, as well as granting any other possible loan.

Hence among the Jews of the region between the Pyrenees and Scotland, between the Atlantic and the Elbe, usury became the main source of livelihood from about the 12th to the 15th centuries. They were not the only people to lend money on interest in that region: there were also the Cahorsins of southern France, the Catalans, and the Lombards. But religious enmity, the social separateness of the Jews, and their hateful image, combined to identify Jew with usurer in the western Christian imagination. In those countries Jews sometimes lent on a debt deed only, without surety. Medieval Hebrew sources from those regions described this kind of loan as *be-emunah* ("on trust"), a practice usually reserved for established and proved clients. Most loans were given on the double surety of a written deed and a collateral (Heb. *mashkon*). Since repayment of a loan for consumption was often difficult, the needy debtor came to hate the infidel Jewish creditor who, out of his own need, had helped him. Many anti-Jewish persecutions hence acquired an economic as well as a religious character, the instigators being no less anxious to destroy incriminating bonds than to eliminate accursed infidels.

In England the extent as well as the problems of Jewish moneylending were seen at their clearest. The most common interest rate was twopence in the pound a week (43⅓% annually), though half and twice as much were also common. There were many partnerships, often between members of the same family; this form was utilized by the extremely wealthy Aaron of Lincoln. To supervise Jewish lending, to insure maximum tax exactions from the Jewish lenders, and to make certain that debt deeds would not be lost even in times of massacres, the Archa system was introduced. In the 13th century Jewish moneylending was conducted through tenants of the commons and of the middle class, whose bonds were bought up, on default, by the nobility and ecclesiastical institutions. This too, aroused the enmity of the commoners toward the Jews. In 1275 Edward III passed severe anti-usury laws, at the same time exacting extremely high tallages and calling in Italian moneylenders to replace the Jews. Some of the latter turned to coin-clipping, which led in part to the total expulsion in 1290.

Though in the heterogeneous Holy Roman Empire moneylending practices varied greatly according to time and place, the history of Jewish moneylending in Regensburg may be typical of Rhenish and south German cities. Until about 1250 the municipality was the chief beneficiary of Jewish loans; until about 1400 the nobility and clergy were the main recipients; while after 1400 knights, burghers, and artisans pawned objects for short terms, and borrowed small sums at high rates of interest. This latter situation eventually became the focus of lower-class enmity toward the Jews and contributed to their expulsion in 1519.

Interest rates in Germany fluctuated greatly in practice and even in their legal norms. Frederick II of Austria fixed the Jews' maximum interest rate at 173⅓% in 1244; in the more developed cities of the Rhineland and south Germany 43⅓% was more common, though this rate did not apply in the case of foreigners or peasants; 86⅔% was also common and acceptable. An investigation in 1676, motivated by anti-Jewish feeling, in the electoral Palatinate in western Germany, showed that an interest rate of 14.5% was honored there by the Jewish moneylenders. The Christian rulers who exploited Jews as their agents for usury — and then extorted from them a large part of their usurious gains, especially when the Jews became impoverished — used to proclaim moratoriums on the individual, partial, or total debts to Jews. The respective treasuries all profited by such measures, the best known being those of Emperor Wenceslaus in 1385 and 1390, which utterly impoverished the Jews while barely alleviating the burdens of the treasury. Likewise, total and bare-faced confiscation was often resorted to, as was expulsion, which left the field open to the Jews' remaining competitors. Because of the collateral in their hands Jewish moneylenders frequently engaged in related occupations, such as the repair and upkeep of clothes, armor, and precious objects, and in their sale when pledges were not redeemed, a frequent occurrence. Hence the rudiments of certain crafts, as well as the sale of secondhand goods, were an integral part of this occupation. Articles regulating moneylending constituted the core of all charters issued to Jews in medieval Germany from the 12th century. They determined not only the rates of interest, but also ensured the rights of the creditor to the collateral, even if it had been stolen. The moneylender had to take an oath that he had received it in good faith and in daylight whereupon the legal owner of the collateral had to repay him the amount loaned on the pledge. This right clashed with Germanic legal conceptions, which demanded the return of the object to the rightful owner without any payment; hence the misconception that the charters allowed the Jews to act as fences.

When it became apparent in Italy that the citizens had need of cash loans, the activities of Jewish moneylenders were regulated by means of the *condotta*, conditions set out in charter treaties between municipalities or rulers and Jewish moneylenders, first signed in the late 13th century in Umbria. The interest rate varied between 15% and 25% and was never to exceed the value of the pledge. The profit of the loan-banks in 15th-century Florence was approximately 4%.

The first privilege granted to Jews in Poland in 1264 regarded them mainly as moneylenders. However, under favorable conditions, Jews soon took part in other economic activities, so that within a century moneylending became only one of their many-sided economic functions in the Polish cities and countryside. The Arenda system, for example, stems from a change from lending to leasing. By the end of the 16th century, Jewish trade demanded more capital than the

A Jewish moneylender with his family in the background negotiating with a peasant and a townsman. Woodcut from Nuremberg, Germany, 1491.

Jews themselves possessed, so that many Jewish traders became indebted to Christians. Lending on interest between Jews was explicitly initiated and legalized there, in the institution *hetter iska*, a legal device which created a formal partnership between creditor and debtor. Interest rates inside the Jewish business community in the latter half of the 17th century were between 25% and 33⅓%, whereas the Christians loaned at 6%–10%, and interest rates between Jews and Christians ranged between these two figures. Jews also developed their own system of credit bonds – the *mamran* (*membranum*) – used mainly at the great fairs of Poland-Lithuania. With the rise of modern banking, Jewish moneylending of the conventional type gradually decreased in importance, though in Western Germany and in Alsace-Lorraine it was sufficiently widespread to be detrimental to emancipation of the Jews during the French Revolution, and later on to influence the attitude of Napoleon Bonaparte to Jewish emancipation. It likewise was one of the causes of the anti-Jewish Hep! Hep! disturbances of 1819, as well as 1830 and 1848.

When Jews moved to western countries in the late 19th–early 20th centuries, moneylending was a frequent occupation, especially in the first and second generation, and the Jewish moneylender became a familiar stereotype.

10

Peddling

Peddling can be defined as the retail sale of wares or trade services and the buying up of agricultural and village produce by an itinerant seller, craftsman, or buyer who made relatively short trips, usually recurrent, to the places where his clients or employers lived. From the Middle Ages it was an important source of livelihood for Jews in many countries. In the Muslim Near East many Jews were engaged either in peddling their crafts, as shown by the evidence of the ninth-century Karaite Benjamin Nahawendi, or in peddling wares, e.g., in 12th-century Egypt. Peddling wares and crafts remained the source of income for many Jews up to the 20th century. It is difficult to determine to what extent the traders buying from and selling to feudal lords in 11th-century Western Europe could be considered as peddlers. With the predominance of moneylending there from the 12th century onward, the Jews ceased to engage in peddling until the 15th century; a new situation then obtained, a combination of general economic trends, the tendency of Jews expelled from cities to settle in nearby villages and estates, and the movement of Jews from the west eastward. Expulsions and the development of an economy based on great landed estates created similar conditions for peddling in Bohemia. Jews were permitted to settle on these estates, the express condition of this settlement being the *"Versilbern,"* i.e., their obligation to purchase, at a fixed price, the total agricultural produce of the estate. The Jewish leaseholder would pass on the produce to customers through Jewish peddlers, who also sold spices, tobacco, textiles, and manufactured utensils — again supplied to them by the leaseholder — to the peasants. The leaseholder often maintained a warehouse and processing plant and concentrated on wholesale commerce. The peddler was thus dependent, economically, legally, and socially, on the wholesaler from whom he received and offered wares on credit. By means of this system Court Jews, who were often military contractors as well, were able to tap the economy of the country at its roots to supply immense amounts of grain, fodder, and livestock for the army. The Jewish peddler was a fixture of Bohemian rural life until well into the 19th century, when his role as intermediary in the purchase of agricultural produce declined: he sold hardware, haberdashery, sewing articles, and trinkets, and bought the peasants' by-products: feathers, furs, and hides. Poorer peddlers also bought old clothes, rags, bones, and junk. The peddler lived amicably among his Christian neighbors, to whom he was identical in dialect, dress, and manners. Generally a strict observer of the dietary laws, he adopted a special diet of eggs, cheese, onions, and bread on his Sunday-till-Friday peddling excursions. Many Bohemian and Moravian communities were founded by peddlers, a prominent example being that of Carlsbad. There were communities in the south of Bohemia and Moravia, such as Kolodeje, which consisted mainly of peddlers doing business in upper and lower Austria, where Jews were not permitted to settle.

In Germany, following the expulsions of the 15th and 16th centuries, many Jews settled in villages and on estates of the gentry where they gradually adapted themselves to peddling from house to house (known in German as *hausieren*), becoming to a certain degree the itinerant middlemen between estates and villages on the one hand and towns on the other. The large estate (*Gut*) looked for intermediaries to bring its increasing amount of produce to the townspeople free of the limitations imposed by town and guilds. The activity of the Jewish peddlers was viewed with suspicion and animosity by feudal circles and townsfolk, who were wary of the changes the proliferation of peddlers was making in the relationship between the town and its surroundings. Legislation was enacted against the peddlers in several German principalities. From the second half of the 17th century the situation was exacerbated by the continous emigration of Jews from Poland to Germany, many of whom turned to peddling. The traveling peddler was sometimes identified with wandering Jewish beggars (*Betteljuden*), as well as with vagabonds in general; smuggling also came naturally to be associated with his mobility, in particular near borders. Frequently *Schutzjuden* employed their unlicensed brethren as peddlers, thereby offering them legal protection and security. Thus, in Luebeck (1658) the first of a continuous series of complaints lodged against Jewish *Hausieren* accused them of buying up precious metals, probably for reminting by the *Schutzjuden* mintmasters. When the Jews were compelled to leave Luebeck in 1699, they settled in nearby Moisling, but complaints against the activity of Jewish peddlers in the city of Luebeck continued to be made up to the mid-19th century.

In Prussia it was objected in 1672 that Jewish peddlers "are not ashamed to go around buying and selling on holy Sunday, going to villages and entering the public houses offering their wares" (S. Stern, *Der Preussische Staat und die Juden*, I Akten, p. 29). Innumerable laws prohibiting all forms of *hausieren* were passed in many German principalities and towns. Measures taken against peddling in 1819 were one cause for thousands of Jews to emigrate from Bavaria to the U.S. Similar laws against peddling were enacted in Baden, Hesse, and Wuerttemberg. In these states emancipation was made conditional on the Jews abandoning peddling. The rapid development of 19th-century Germany gradually made the peddler's role obsolete, though he persisted in agricultural or remote regions. In the main, Alsace-Lorraine was similar to Germany, and from there peddlers penetrated into those parts of France prohibited to Jews. The rural peddler, who was found mainly in southern Germany in the middle and late 19th century, generally lived amicably among his Christian neighbors. A staunch upholder of Orthodoxy, he often had special cooking utensils, inscribed *"kasher,"* reserved for his use in the local inns.

In the variegated Jewish economic life of Poland-Lithuania, various forms of peddling were common, including market hawkers and rural peddlers engaged in buying and selling; women were often found among them. In Lvov there was even a guild of Jewish street vendors. However, major cities passed laws prohibiting peddling, which was blamed for unbusiness-like practices and regarded as endangering the livelihood of Christians. Established Jewish traders, too, often opposed the competition of the mobile peddlers. In the Pale of Settlement of Czarist Russia peddling was an important means of livelihood up to 1917, particularly in the eastern part of the region. A rapidly growing population in the townlets and expulsion from the villages led many to take up peddling. Numerous Jewish craftsmen left their homes on Sunday, worked all week in villages, and returned home on Friday; because of this they were known as *Wochers*. More important than the peddler who brought wares to sell was the one who bought up agricultural produce, in particular goods (like flax and hemp) which could be supplied to industrial centers at home or exported to Germany. In the large cities there were also many Jewish hawkers. Peddling could not, of course, survive in a Communist economy, but in Poland and the Baltic states it continued up to the Holocaust.

Jewish rural peddlers, immigrants from Alsace-Lorraine and the Rhineland, began to appear in England toward the middle of the 18th century, becoming common in most of southern England in the late 18th and early 19th century. The poet Robert Southey stated in 1807: "You meet Jew peddlers everywhere, traveling with boxes of haberdashery on their backs, cuckoo-clocks, sealing wax . . . miserable prints of King and Queen . . . even the Nativity and Crucifixion." Some Jews were also street vendors in London and other large cities. The influx of East European Jews in the 1880s caused a sudden resurgence in street vending in London and other major cities. Penniless immigrants, immediately off the boat, began hawking wares bought on credit; in 1906, 600 of Glasgow's 6,000 Jews were engaged in peddling and the percentage in Edinburgh was even higher. Street vending was the springboard to other commercial occupations; the father of Simon Marks, founder of Marks and Spencer's, proudly exhibited the cart from which he conducted his first business.

In the Netherlands peddling and street vending received a fresh impetus with the arrival of Ashkenazim in the early 20th century. In 1921 31.6% of Amsterdam's 6,500 peddlers were Jews. The situation was identical in Belgium where there were about 1,600 Jewish market vendors in 1937, primarily in Brussels.

The vast areas of North America made peddling important generally till about the middle of the 19th century. Sephardi peddlers appeared as early as 1655. Of licenses granted to peddlers in Pennsylvania, one out of 18 was to a Jew in 1771, five out of 49 in 1772, and four out of 27 in 1773. Trade in calico, cutlery, snuff, and similar goods was often conducted by barter in return for skins and furs. Peddlers frequently traded with Indians, who learned to respect the peaceful and peculiar Jewish peddler with his strange dietary laws: some Cherokees named one "the eggeater." The wares of the peddler, those he sold and those he purchased for sale, were generally handled by a wealthy wholesale trader with sufficient capital, like David Franks, Joseph Simon, or the Gratz family. Business was conducted through frontier entrepôts where furs and skins were exchanged for cash and additional negotiable goods. Occupational hazards were financial failure and murder on the highway.

In the second and third decades of the 19th century mass emigration of Jews from southern Germany and Prussian Poland brought many of them to peddling in the United States. They dealt mainly in consumer goods, haberdashery, trinkets, and jewelry. Carrying a pack sometimes weighing around 100 lb., the peddler served the farmers' stores and sold to them at their home. About one-half of all Jewish peddlers in the period 1820–80 arrived in this immigration wave, settling predominantly in the west, beyond the Appalachians in the Middle West, and after 1865 in the Far West. Many new colonists knew German, which helped the German-Jewish peddler. In order to operate properly in these newly developed areas, the peddler needed a store to replenish his supplies, but here the functions were complementary, unlike in Europe where they were fiercely competitive. An enterprising peddler, often the first in the vicinity, opened a store to supply fellow peddlers, thus moving up economically and socially. After settling, peddlers became the nucleus of a community. The Jewish population of Cincinnati grew from a handful in 1818 to 3,300 in 1850, a large percentage of whom were peddlers, future peddlers, and former peddlers. Immediately after the 1849 gold rush Jewish peddlers arrived to ply the mines, and communities were soon founded in San Francisco and Sacramento, the supply center for the mining area. One such man was Levi Strauss, manufacturer of the original blue jeans; many others founded stores. The Jewish peddler was present throughout the Far West: the Goldwater department stores of Arizona were founded by a peddler: Meyer Guggenheim began his meteoric career as a peddler in the west. The Seligman family of New York were peddlers from Baiersdorf, Bavaria. Other successful peddlers were Adam Gimbel, Moses and Caesar Cone, and Nathan Straus.

The Chicago Jewish community leader Abraham Kohn (d. 1871) described in his diary his way of life on becoming a peddler within a week of his arrival from Bavaria: "Leading such a life that none of us is able to observe the smallest commandment. Thousands of peddlers wander about America: young, strong men, they waste their strength by carrying heavy loads in the summer's heat; they lose their health in the icy cold of winter. And thus forget completely their Creator. They no longer put on the phylacteries; they pray neither on working day nor on the Sabbath. In truth, they have given up their religion for the pack which is on their backs" (AJA, 3, (1951) p. 99). He found consolation in the many acquaintances from Bavaria he encountered in his rise to financial success – within two years he owned a store in Chicago. The turnover in the profession was rapid, the average peddling term being between one and five years and the average age 18–25. Unlike in Europe, where peddling was a traditional continuous occupation, in the U.S. the individual Jew used peddling as a short-term step to more stable commercial ventures. After amassing some capital he tended to enter into a partnership with a compatriot, being especially inclined to enter the clothing trade and open a shop. Country peddling became obsolete with the growth of retail trade. The mail-order business, developed especially by Julius Rosenwald's Sears-Roebuck Co., struck hard.

Jewish vendors appeared in strength on American streets with the mass emigration from Eastern Europe in the late 19th and early 20th centuries. The Lower East Side of New York witnessed the emergence of open air markets and pushcart traders and peddlers offering every conceivable type of merchandise. The situation in Chicago was similar. In 1890–93 a census conducted in New York among 23,801 Jewish families revealed that peddling was the second most common occupation (after tailoring), with 2,440 full-time peddlers. Their ranks were swelled in times of economic crises and unemployment. The great number of peddlers at any one given moment barely suggested the multitudes who had passed through this apprenticeship.

11
Secondhand Goods

In Western and Central Europe and Italy trade in secondhand goods and old clothes was an integral part of moneylending against pledges, as the pawned and forfeited articles (jewelry, clothing, etc.) had to be sold. As many of the goods had to be refurbished or repaired, dyeing, tailoring, and mending became ancillary occupations. Later it became a separate trade which, until the spread of the industrial and technological revolutions, catered to the needs of large sectors of the population.

The trade in old clothes in Italy, known as *strazzaria* (from *straccio, strazzo,* "rag"), was conducted mainly through peddling and eventually came to include trade in new garments and cloth as well. From the 16th to the 18th centuries it was the most important Jewish occupation after moneylending. The *strazzaiuoli* often dealt in imported wares, thereby angering the local textile and clothing manufacturers. A 1667 list of 112 Jewish households in Mantua (about one-half of the community) included eight traders in secondhand goods, five tailors, three renovators of clothes, two clothing shops, three scrap-iron traders, and 15 "general" merchants. Fifty years later there were 25 dealers in old clothes and secondhand goods, 19 textile and cloth merchants, and nine traders in scrap iron. *Strazzaria* was a major and characteristic occupation of Roman Jewry even before the issue of Pope Paul IV's extremely restrictive and discriminatory bull of 1555, *Cum nimis absurdum*, which made it the sole trade permitted to them. In the mid-19th century the historian F. Gregorovius reported:

> If we now enter the streets of the ghetto itself we find Israel before its booths, buried in restless toil and distress. They sit in their doorways or outdoors on the street which affords scarcely more light than their damp and dismal rooms, and tend their ragged merchandise or industriously patch and sew ... The daughters of Zion sit upon these rags and stitch anything than can be stitched. They have a reputation for great art in patching, darning, and piecing, and it is said that no rent in any sort of drapery or fabric can be so fearful that these Arachnes cannot make it invisible and untraceable ... It was frequently with painful sympathy that I looked upon them, pale and exhausted and stooped, as they diligently

plied their needles, men as well as women, girls, and children (*The Ghetto and the Jews of Rome* (1966), 66f.).

Their lot and vocation continued well into the 20th century though many branched off into the antiques trade and the clothing industry. In 1940 the licenses of the street vendors of old and new clothes were revoked and in the subsequent persecutions they were particularly hard hit.

Elsewhere in Europe Jews frequently traded in old clothes, at first in association with moneylending and later, in conjunction with related crafts, peddling, and textile trading. In the Netherlands and England, as well as other countries with large numbers of Jewish immigrants, Jews were active in the trade in secondhand goods. In Amsterdam poor Ashkenazi Jews were officially designated as "repairers of old clothes." The mended clothes were exported in large quantities to various destinations. One of the richest merchants in Amsterdam was instructed by a Jew in Poland to pay a Polish Jew in Amsterdam a sum of 10,000 to 12,000 guilders for the sale of rags. These may have been utilized for paper production. In London the old clothes trade was situated in the "Rag Fair," in Rosemary Lane (Royal Mint Street), where there were about 500 to 600 Jewish old-clothes dealers in 1850 (in 1800 there had been about 1,000). The "old clo" men, as they were called after their traditional call, brought their wares to two exchanges, Isaacs & Simmons and Levy, from where they were resold either to wholesale merchants or to retail dealers for a variety of purposes. The German and Dutch Jews who entered the secondhand-clothing and rag dealers' markets at Houndsditch in the East End in the 18th century, later dominated the trade and thereby fixed the area of future Jewish settlement in London. The rag trade became obsolete with the rise in the standard of living of the masses and the introduction of Singer's sewing machine and modern methods of mass production of ready-made clothing. In different countries and at various times when traditional Jewish occupations were attacked (as in Prussia in the 18th century) the trade in secondhand goods also came under pressure. In Paris in 1911 there were about 1,500 Jewish old clothes dealers (*brocanteurs*) and 400 ragpickers (*chiffonniers*); in 1941, 2,533 traders in secondhand goods were recorded. Their real number on both dates was probably larger; the majority were impecunious immigrants from Eastern Europe.

Both in England and the U.S. some Jews extended their activities from the secondhand goods trade to buying and selling waste products in general. A study in Detroit by J. S. Fauman (*Jewish Journal of Sociology*, 3, (1941), 41 ff.) revealed that while there had been no Jewish dealers in waste products (paper, scrap metal) there until 1870, from 1880 Jews were predominant, and the location of the lots and junkyards moved in relation to the areas of Jewish residence. "The waste industry, low in status, poorly organized, requiring little

Monmouth Street, a hub of London's old clothes trade in the 19th century, as depicted by the caricaturist George Cruikshank.

capital and unattractive to other groups, was easily accessible to Jews." Enterprises of this kind attracted and held Jews because of resemblances to their traditional commercial activities, because of strong familial ties, and because the independence of this type of trade enabled them to close their businesses on the Sabbath and festivals. The Detroit pattern prevailed in many other cities. An economic survey made by *Fortune* magazine ("Jews in America" (1936), 43) estimated that 90% of the scrap-iron and steel industry in the U.S. (worth half a billion dollars in 1929) was Jewish-owned. Through trade in waste materials and particularly in ferrous and non-ferrous metals many Jews entered the metal industry, especially in Germany (see Metals and Mining, p. 173).

12
Slave Trade

Jews engaged in the slave trade — although they never played a prominent role in it — from the early Middle Ages to the early modern period. While it was not proscribed to pagans, none of the three monotheistic religions either prohibited slavery or trade in slaves except insofar as converts to a particular religion were concerned. It was as if three circles were drawn, each opposing only the enslavement of its own members by a member of one of the other two. Thus the only legitimate objects of slavery and the slave trade were pagans and Jews, Christians, and Muslims captured in war by victors of either of the other religions. In Europe, aside from the Nordic countries, in the early Middle Ages there remained pagans in the Slav countries only (and their generic name, or variations thereof, became the appellation for the slave throughout Western Europe). Slaves were needed for agriculture, domestic service, and as eunuchs in Muslim harems. They were one of the few "commodities" that Europe could export to the Byzantine and later Muslim Mediterranean, from which it imported so much, thus restoring to some extent the balance of payments. The Jewish slave owner, however, was expected by the Church to release his slave the moment the latter converted to Christianity, sometimes by inducement. Jews also used slaves in their vineyards, and a forced conversion of a slave was a loss to them. As each slave owner in all religions considered himself responsible for the soul and behavior of his slaves, he felt in duty bound to convert them to his faith; in the case of the Jews, who were in a minority everywhere, this caused friction and problems for the Jewish owners. Thus tension colored the attitude to Jewish ownership of slaves and participation in the slave trade in Christian countries.

Under the Muslim rule in Spain, where there was a slave market in Baena in the ninth century, Jews owned slaves without hindrance as long as the slaves were not Muslims. However, there is no evidence of a slave trade carried on by Jews in Christian Spain (Baer, Spain, 1 (1961), 417). Slaves were employed primarily for domestic and agricultural service in the households of the Jewish upper classes, and this situation persisted for some time under Christian rule, especially in Majorca, where Jews owned large estates and many slaves; in the middle of the 13th century James I put obstacles in the path of Jewish ownership of Moorish slaves in Majorca, who wished to be baptized and thereby freed. In late Roman Spain and Frankish Gaul, Church opposition to Jewish ownership of slaves was much in evidence. Church councils repeatedly denounced Jewish ownership of Christian slaves and of those slaves who wished to convert to Christianity; but these denunciations remained ineffectual. Pope George the Great (sixth century) inveighed against a Jewish merchant, because his import of slaves from Gaul into Italy included some Christians. The Muslim conquest of Spain created a nearby market for slaves, to which Jews were accused of catering. Emperor Louis I the Pious granted a number of Jews (c. 825–8) the right to import foreign slaves and sell them within the confines of the empire. Archbishop Agobard of Lyons claimed that royal officials in Lyons accepted the Jewish traders' view that heathen slaves who requested baptism should be considered as doing this solely in order to gain their freedom, and that this should not be granted unless the owner was paid the sum he demanded. Agobard denounced this view, claiming in the course of his arguments that in some cases Jews even sold people born Christian into slavery.

Jewish slave traders (among others) are recorded in the custom dues rolls of Raffelstetten on the Danube, in 906, a major interregional market in the early Middle Ages. The Arab geographer Ibn-Khurdadbah (c. 870–92) includes slaves (eunuchs) among the many articles sold by the Radhanites, said to have traveled from Franconia to China by sea or land. Ibrahim ibn Ja'qub, the Jewish traveler, recorded the presence of Jewish slave traders in Prague around 970 (alongside Muslims and Turks), and Bishop Adalbert of Prague resigned in 988 after failing to buy the freedom of a group of slaves bought by a Jewish trader. The Jews of that period regarded the Slavic east as the land of slaves par excellence – "Canaan" (see Gen. 9:25 and Midrashim to this verse). Jewish slave traders appear in the Koblenz custom rolls of 1004; they are mentioned in 1009, when the margrave of Meissen was accused of selling slaves to Jews, and in 1085, when a Polish princess in Silesia was praised for buying up Christian slaves from Jews and freeing them. With the Christianization of most of the Slavs, this trade ceased as far as Jews in Christian Europe were concerned.

While responsa and deeds of manumission indicate the frequency of slaves, mainly women employed as housemaids and occasionally men who were business agents in personal service in Jewish households in Muslim lands, a thorough study of conditions in Egypt in the 11th–13th centuries reveals that "during the classical *Genizah* period the Jews had no share in the slave trade" (S. D. Goitein, *A Mediterranean Society* (1967), 140), in particular after Maimonides' time. Slave ownership in Muslim lands raised the problem of responsibility for the slaves' conversion to Judaism and, frequently, that of sexual relations between the owner and his female slave. Marriage contracts quoted in Maimonides'

Slaves being redeemed from Jewish traders by Bishop Adalbert of Prague. Detail from the bronze door of the 12th-century Cathedral of Gniezno (Gnesen), Poland.

responsa include the condition that the husband promise not to buy a female slave without his wife's consent, parallel to his promise not to take a second wife against his first wife's will. He also referred to the question of castration (forbidden in Jewish law) and the sale of eunuchs.

In the Ottoman Empire slavery flourished through the wars of expansion. Most wealthy Jewish families owned one or more slaves for domestic purposes. The Marrano Diaspora in the New World (particularly in the Carribean) became both customer for, and trader in, African and Indian slaves. Slave-owning Marranos settling in Protestant countries created serious legal difficulties (as in London and Hamburg); a Portuguese relative of Albertus Denis was forced to leave Danzig because of public indignation at his treatment and ownership of slaves. The Ottoman authorities opposed Jewish participation in the slave trade, but one exception occurred during the 1571 war against Cyprus when Jewish slave traders were required to pay a special state tax. Toward the end of the 16th century the sultan decreed also that a special tax be paid by Jews who owned slaves. Subsequently, slaves and slavery gradually disappeared from Jewish life. Modern European and U.S. historians up to the mid-1950s (including Jewish historians) confused the ownership of slaves by Jews with their part in the slave trade. The role of the Jews in the slave trade was also vastly exaggerated. This was done either to overemphasize the importance of Jews in early medieval trade or to put the odium of this trade onto the Jews (according to modern views – in disregard of the acceptability of slavery during the period of Jewish participation in it). This tendency was reinforced by anti-Semitic prejudices.

In the Americas. Until 1730 the Dutch West India Company maintained a monopoly on the importation of slaves into all the Dutch colonies in the Americas, but Jews appear to have been among the major retailers of slaves in Dutch Brazil (1630–54), because Jews possessed ready money and were willing to trade slaves for sugar. The bylaws of the Recife and Mauricia congregations (1648) included an *imposta* (Jewish tax) of 5 soldos for each slave which a Brazilian Jew purchased from the West Indies Company. In Curaçao, the Dutch occasionally gave permission to a merchant to conduct independent transactions in slaves; two such Jewish entrepreneurs were the brothers David and Jacob Senior, who came to the island from Amsterdam about 1685. Another Curaçao Jew, Manuel Alvares Correa (1650–1717), who was active in the local slave trade for many years, served in 1699 as an intermediary between the Dutch and Portuguese West Indies companies for the transfer of a shipment of slaves from Africa to Mexico via Curaçao.

In all of the American colonies, whether Dutch, French, or British, almost every merchant or trader had dealings in slaves: when he acted as auctioneer or agent for the sale of an estate, when he served his planter clients in the sale or purchase of slaves or in the pursuit of runaways. In the Barbados, until 1706, Jews were limited by law in the number of slaves they themselves could own, but in Jamaica there was no such restriction. Among the Jamaican Jewish merchants who seem to have specialized in the slave trade were David Henriques, Hyman Levy, and especially Alexander Lindo, who was a major importer of slaves during the period 1782–92. During an investigation of slave mortality conducted in Jamaica in 1789, Lindo testifies that 150 slaves on a ship "consigned to" him had died in the Middle Passage and that another 20 perished after their arrival in Jamaica, but it is unclear whether he owned this slave shipment or any of the others in which he was involved. Members of the well-known Gradis family of Bordeaux were active in the shipment of slaves from West Africa to such French colonies as Santo-Domingo (Dominican Republic).

On the North American mainland, a number of Jews were active participants in the infamous triangular trade, which brought slaves from Africa to the West Indies, where they were exchanged for molasses, which was in turn taken to New England and converted into rum for sale in Africa. David Franks of Philadelphia was in this business during the early 1760s; Aaron Lopez and Jacob Rodriguez Rivera of Newport, Rhode Island, had at least one slaver on the high seas each year after 1764, and in 1772 and 1773 had a total of eight such ships under sail. Isaac Da Costa of Charleston was another large-scale importer of slaves. In Louisiana, under both French and Spanish rule, the Monsanto brothers made frequent transactions in slaves; during 1787 they purchased 44 Negroes.

Although Jews in Philadelphia and New York City were active in the early abolition movement, Jewish merchants, auctioneers, and commission agents in the Southern states continued to buy and sell slaves until the end of the Civil War. The fact that Jacob Levin of Columbia, South Carolina, and Israel I. Jones of Mobile, Alabama, two merchants who often dealt in slaves, were leaders of their Jewish communities in the 1850s is evidence that at no time did Southern Jews feel tainted by the slave trade. Levy Jacobs was an active trader in slaves both in New Orleans and in Mobile during the 1820s; Ansley, Benjamin, George, and Solomon Davis of Richmond and Petersburg, Virginia, went on the road to sell gangs of slaves in the states of the lower South beginning about 1838; B. Mordecai of Charleston had large slave pens alongside his warehouses and purchased $12,000 worth of slaves at one sale in 1859. But the total business activity of all the Southern Jews who dealt in slaves in any way probably did not equal the turnover of the largest single non-Jewish firm which specialized in slaves, Franklin and Armfield.

13

Spice Trade

In their original settlements in the East Mediterranean and Near East, Jewish merchants traded in luxury goods, including spices. This latter trade became more evident in the Diaspora era, when Jews, along with Greeks and Syrians, appeared as traders in Western Europe. Because of their relationship with the Orient, they were able to supply these products, which were grown mainly in the countries from southern Arabia to the Moluccas and were used for medicinal purposes, in the preparation of food and beverages, and in perfumes. At first the Syrians led this trade, losing their position to the Jews only after the conquest of the Syrian coast by the Arabs. Writing on the trade routes in the years between 854 and 874, Ibn Kordabheh, postmaster of the caliph of Baghdad, mentioned that the Jewish Radhanites traded in musk, aloes, camphor, cinnamon, and other commodities between France and China. From the tenth century the northern route through the Slav countries became increasingly important to Jewish traders as they were displaced in the Mediterranean by Italian merchants. When visiting Mainz around 978, Ibrahim Tartuschi, an Arab from the Iberian Peninsula, was astonished to find the markets filled with large quantities of spices which could only be found in the Far East; it was generally believed that these were brought by Jewish merchants from the Orient by way of Kiev. The activities of Jewish traders on the Mediterranean and Indian Ocean trade routes and ports are revealed in 11th- to 13th-century *Genizah* documents and responsa. The disuse of the Eastern routes with the expansion of Tatar and Turkish conquest added to the increased Christian participation in overseas trade and the restriction of Jewish commercial activities, and caused the Jews to lose their position as intermediaries with the Orient, being replaced by the Italians and especially the Venetians.

Jewish merchants once more played a part in the spice trade with the opening of the direct route to East India by the Portuguese. Prominent among these merchants was the New Christian Mendes family, probably descendants of the Spanish Benveniste family. Rui Mendes (de Brito) sent a ship to East India with Vasco da Gama's second voyage in 1502, and in 1505, in association with the German Lucas Rem, armed three ships for East India. He was probably a close relative of the brothers Francisco and Diogo Mendes who, the former in Lisbon and the latter in Antwerp, controlled a major part of the commerce in pepper and other spices in northern Europe, the largest market at that time. After the death of Diogo Mendes (1542 or 1543), Francisco's widow, Beatrice de Luna, carried on the Antwerp branch of the enterprise. About 12 other New Christians in Antwerp were engaged in the spice trade, on the basis of annual contracts made with the king of Portugal. For some time the Perez family and other Spanish merchants, who were probably also New Christians, were the representatives of these *contractadores*. When Philip II succeeded to the throne of Portugal, he tried to renew the system of contracts, which had been in the hands of the German Konrad Rott during the last years of Portuguese independence. After Rott's bankruptcy, the Lisbon and Antwerp branches of the Ximenes and D'Evora families participated in the European contract. From 1592 to 1596 the Indian contract was in the hands of a consortium of New Christians: Tomáz and André Ximenes, Duarte Furtado de Mendoza, Luis Gomes d'Elvas, Heitor Mendes, and Jorge Rodriguez Solis. Attacks on Portuguese ships by English pirates, the revival of the Levantine spice trade from Alexandria and Syria to the Mediterranean ports, and the opening of East Indian navigation by the Dutch and English, all contributed to the decline of the Portuguese monopoly and thus of the activities of the New Christian groups. However, their participation in the spice trade in Hamburg and Amsterdam remained prominent. Among the 16 spice importers in Amsterdam in 1612, 11 were "Portuguese," i.e., Sephardim. In the first part of the 18th century the spice trade still represented a considerable proportion of the commercial activities of the Sephardi community in Amsterdam.

14
Stock Exchanges

Jews came to the stock exchange by way of their medieval occupation of moneylending and their activity in the modern period as Court Jews and in banking. Soon after the founding of the first European international exchange at Antwerp (1536), *anusim* arrived there and for a short time played a prominent role in it until their expulsion by Charles V. Many of them then moved to Amsterdam, the economic capital of Europe in the 17th and early 18th centuries. By 1674, 13% of the total number of investments on the stock exchange was in "Portuguese" Jewish hands, though the size of their individual investments was not great. A contemporary noted that many brokers refrained from visiting the stock exchange on Saturday, when the Jews were absent. The first book to describe the practices of the Amsterdam stock exchange was published in Spanish by Joseph Penso de la Vega in 1688. Jews were excluded from most of the commodity exchanges in Germany. Benjamin and Abraham Goldsmid were prominent on the Royal Exchange in London at the end of the 18th and the beginning of the 19th centuries, and after the Napoleonic Wars they were eclipsed by N. M. Rothschild who was the dominant figure on the London Exchange.

In the United States Ephraim Hart was among the 22 founders of the first board of stockbrokers in New York in 1792. August Belmont was the representative of the Rothschilds in the 19th century. In the mid- and late 19th century a number of German-Jewish underwriting firms were prominent on the board: J. and W. Seligman and Co., run by the eight Seligman brothers and led by Joseph Seligman, and Kuhn, Loeb, and Co., which was raised to international repute by Jacob Schiff, Otto Kahn, and Paul M. Warburg. The battle between Hill-Morgan and Harriman-Schiff for control of the Northern Pacific railway stocks resulted in the stock exchange crash known as "Black Thursday."

Even at the height of their activity, Jews were never the largest nor the most prominent group on the exchanges in England and the United States; by the mid-20th century their number and proportion had declined considerably. In Continental Europe Jews were more prominent on the stock exchange. Jews attended the exchanges of Lyons and Paris as early as the 18th century but it was only with the rise of the house of Rothschild in the post-Napoleonic era that they became prominent there; the initiative of this house in floating railroad stocks was followed by the Fould house and others. The Pereire brothers founded the Crédit Mobilier, the first joint-stock bank. In the aftermath of the Panama Canal stock scandal (1892–93), in which Baron Jacques Reinach was incriminated, anti-Semitic attacks were made on Jewish activity on the exchanges.

Jews were not allowed into the Frankfort stock exchange, the most important in Germany at the time, until 1811, but from then until the Nazi regime they played a dominant and later a leading role, partly attributable to the activity of the house of Rothschild and other Jewish financial magnates. The stock exchange of Berlin was a relative latecomer. The patrician Jewish families of Berlin – Gomperz, Veit, Ephraim, Riess, and Wulff, who had amassed wealth as court jewelers, army contractors, and mint purveyors – played a predominant part from its foundation. The statutes of the bourse corporation of 1805 found it necessary to lay down that two of the four chairmen must be Christians. In 1807, 159 of the 174 member firms were Jewish. Such marked preponderance of Jewish firms continued for a short period only. As in banking, the role of the Jews on the stock exchanges declined rapidly with the founding of public banks. In 1882 there were 2,908 Jews in Prussia engaged in stocks and banking, 22% of the total; by 1925 the absolute number of Jews in these fields had increased to 5,620 but their percentage of the total was only 3.84%, although many of this small ratio were in key positions. The economic recession of 1873–76 was blamed on stock speculators, some of whom were Jews, and this was one of the factors behind the anti-Semitic movement led by A. Stoecker. In Vienna H. Todesco and other leading Jewish financiers were prominent from the foundation of the exchange, on which a Rothschild soon came to play a leading role. The number of Jewish stockbrokers was also high. In the stock exchanges of Budapest, Prague, and Bucharest, Jews filled important positions in the 19th and early 20th centuries. The Jewish role decreased as a result of anti-Semitic economic nationalism.

It was not only in times of economic crisis and financial speculation that the activity of Jews on the stock exchange was seized on as a pretext for anti-Semitic outbursts; anti-Jewish agitators magnified their influence out of all proportion, creating an anti-Jewish stereotype out of "Jewish mastery" over the stock exchange. In this they were aided by the theories of men like Werner Sombart, who ascribed the creation and workings of the stock exchange to the "capitalist Jewish spirit."

GLOSSARY

Aliya, (1) immigration to Erez Israel; (2) one of the waves of immigration to Erez Israel from the early 1880s.

Ashkenaz, name applied generally in medieval rabbinical literature to Germany.

Ashkenazi (pl. **Ashkenazim**), German or West-, Central-, or East-European Jew(s), as contrasted with Sephardi(m).

Crypto-Jew, term applied to a person who although observing outwardly Christianity (or some other religion) was at heart a Jew and maintained Jewish observances as far as possible (see Converso; Marrano; Neofiti; New Christian; Jadīd al-Islām).

Diaspora, Jews living in the "dispersion" outside Erez Israel; area of Jewish settlement outside Erez Israel.

Erez Israel, Land of Israel; Palestine.

Exilarch, lay head of Jewish community in Babylonia and elsewhere.

Gabbai, official of a Jewish congregation; originally a charity collector.

Gaon (pl. **geonim**), head of academy in post-talmudic period, especially in Babylonia.

Genizah, depository for sacred books. The best known was discovered in the synagogue of Fostat (old Cairo).

Ḥalakhah (pl. **halakhot**), an accepted decision in rabbinic law. Also refers to those parts of the Talmud concerned with legal matters. In contradistinction to *aggadah.*

Hazakah, presumption of legal tithe to possession or tenant rights.

Ḥevra kaddisha, title applied to charitable confraternity now generally limited to associations for burial of the dead.

Histadrut (abbr. for Heb. **Ha-Histadrut ha-Kelalit shel ha-Ovedim ha-Ivriyyim be-Erez Israel**), Erez Israel Jewish Labor Federation, founded in 1920; subsequently renamed Histadrut ha-Ovedim be-Erez Israel.

Holocaust, the organized mass persecution and annihilation of European Jewry by the Nazis (1933–1945).

ICA, Jewish, Colonization Association.

Karaite, member of a Jewish sect originating in the eighth century which rejected rabbinic (Rabbanite) Judaism and accepted only Scripture as authoritative.

279

Kasher, ritually permissible food.

Kristallnacht (Ger. "crystal night," meaning "night of broken glass"), organized destruction of synagogues, Jewish houses, and shops, accompanied by mass arrests of Jews, which took place in Germany and Austria under the Nazis on the night of Nov. 9–10, 1938.

Marrano(s), descendant(s) of Jew(s) in Spain and Portugal whose ancestors had been converted to Christianity under pressure but who secretly observed Jewish rituals.

Nagid (pl. **negidim**), title applied in Muslim (and some Christian) countries in the Middle Ages to a leader recognized by the state as head of the Jewish community.

New Christians, term applied especially in Spain and Portugal to converts from Judaism (and from Islam) and their descendants; "Half New Christian" designated a person one of whose parents was of full Jewish blood.

ORT, organization for development of skilled trades and agriculture among Jews.

Pale of Settlement, 25 provinces of czarist Russia where Jews were permitted permanent residence.

Pinkas, community register or minute-book.

Responsum (pl. **responsa**), written opinion (*teshuvah*) given to question (*she'elah*) on aspects of Jewish law by qualified authorities; pl. collection of such queries and opinions in book form (*she'elot u-teshuvot*).

Sha'atnez, ritually prohibited mixture of wool and linen.

Shtadlan, Jewish representative or negotiator with access to dignitaries of state, active at royal courts, etc.

Shtetl, Jewish small-town community in Eastern Europe.

Takkanah (pl. **takkanot**), regulation supplementing the Law of the Torah; regulations governing the internal life of communities and congregations.

Tanna (pl. **tannaim**), rabbinic teacher of mishnaic period.

Yishuv, settlement; more specifically, the Jewish community of Erez Israel in the pre-State period. The pre-Zionist community is generally designated the "old yishuv" and the community evolving from 1880, the "new yishuv."

BIBLIOGRAPHICAL ABBREVIATIONS

a) General

AJA	*American Jewish Archives* (1948 ff.).
AJHSP	*American Jewish Historical Society–Publications* (after vol. 50 = AJHSQ).
AJHSQ	*American Jewish Historical* (Society) *Quarterly* (before vol. 50 = AJHSP).
AJYB	*American Jewish Year Book* (1899 ff.).
Aronius, Regesten	I. Aronius, *Regesten zur Geschichte der Juden im fraenkischen und deutschen Reiche bis zum Jahre 1273* (1902).
Ashtor, Korot	E. Ashtor (Strauss), *Korot ha-Yehudim bi-Sefarad ha-Muslemit*, 1 (1966²), 2 (1966).
Ashtor, Toledot	E. Ashtor (Strauss), *Toledot ha-Yehudim be-Miẓrayim ve-Suryah Taḥat Shilton ha-Mamlukim*, 3 vol. (1944–70).
Baer, Spain	Yitzhak (Fritz) Baer, *History of the Jews in Christian Spain*, 2 vols. (1961–66).
Baron, Social	S. W. Baron, *Social and Religious History of the Jews*, 3 vols. (1937); enlarged, 1–2 (1952²), 3–14 (1957–69).
BŻIH	*Biuletyn Żydowskiego Instytuto Historycznego* (1950 ff.).
Dubnow, Hist. Russ.	S. Dubnow, *History of the Jews in Russia and Poland*, 3 vols. (1925–29).
Fischel, Islam	W. J. Fischel, *Jews in the Economic and Political Life of Medieval Islam* (1937; reprint with introduction "The Court Jew in the Islamic World," 1969).
Halpern, Pinkas	I. Halpern (Halperin), *Pinkas Va'ad Arba Araẓot* (1945).
Hirschberg, Afrikah	H. Z. Hirschberg, *Toledot ha-Yehudim be-Afrikah ha-Ẓefonit*, Zools. (1965).
HJ	*Historica Judaica* (1938–61).
IEJ	*Israel Exploration Journal* (1950 ff.).

JAOS	*Journal of the American Oriental Society* (c. 1850 ff.).
JGGJC	*Jahrbuch der Gesellschaft fuer Geschichte der Juden in der Cechoslovakischen Republik* (1929–38).
JHSEM	Jewish Historical Society of England, *Miscellanies* (1925 ff.).
JHSET	Jewish Historical Society of England, *Transactions* (1893 ff.).
Jos., Ant.	Josephus, *Jewish Antiquities.*
Jos., Was	Josephus, *Jewish Wars.*
JSOS	*Jewish Social Studies* (1939 ff.).
Kisch, Germany	G. Kisch, *Jews in Medieval Germany* (1949).
Krauss Tal Arch	S. Krauss, *Talmudische Archaeologie,* 3 vols. (1910–12; reprinted 1966).
KS	*Kirjath Sepher* (1923/4 ff.).
MGJV	*Mitteilungen der Gesellschaft fuer juedische Volkskunde* (1898–1929); title varies, see also JJV.
MGWJ	*Monatsschrift fuer Geschichte und Wissenschaft des Judentums* (1851–1939).
Milano, Italia	A. Milano, *Storia degli Ebraim Italia* (1963).
Neuman, Spain	A. A. Neuman, *The Jews in Spain, their Social, Political, and Cultural Life During the Middle Ages,* 2 vols. (1942).
Pritchard, Pictures	J.B. Pritchard (ed.), *Ancient Near Eastern Pictures* (1954, 1970).
REJ	*Revue des études juives* (1880 ff.).
Roth, Art	C. Roth, *Jewish Art* (1961).
Roth, England	C. Roth, *History of the Jews in England* (1964[3]).
Roth, Italy	C. Roth, *History of the Jews in Italy* (1946).
Roth, Marranos	C. Roth, *History of the Marranos* (2nd rev. ed. 1959; reprint 1966).
Tcherikower, Corpus	V. Tcherikower, A. Fuks, and M. Stern, *Corpus Papyror 'n Judaicorum,* 3 vols. (1957–60).
YIVOA	*YIVO Annual of Jewish Social Studies* (1946 ff.).
YLBI	*Year Book of the Leo Baeck Institute* (1956 ff.).
ZGJD	*Zeitschrift fuer die Geschichte der Juden in Deutschland* (1887–92).

b) Biblical and rabbinic

BB.	*Bava Batra* (talmudic tractate)
Ber.	*Berakhot* (talmudic tractate)
BM.	*Bava Meẓia* (talmudic tractate)
Ḥag	*Ḥagigah* (talmudic tractate)
Ḥul	*Ḥullin* (talmudic tractate)
Josh.	Joshua (Bible)
Ket.	*Ketubbot* (talmudic tractate)
Men.	*Menaḥot* (talmudic tractate)
Pes.	*Pesaḥim* (talmudic tractate)
Ps.	Psalms (Bible)
Sanh.	*Sanhedrin* (talmudic tractate)
Yad.	Maimonides, *Mishneh Torah* (*Yad Ḥazakah*)

BIBLIOGRAPHY
(arranged according to chapter order)

AGRICULTURE: MIDDLE AGES: S. D. Goitein, *A Mediterranean Society*, 1 (1967), 116–27, 425–30; G. Caro, *Sozial- und Wirtschaftsgeschichte der Juden im Mittelalter und der Neuzeit*, 2 vols. (1920–24); Ashtor, Korot; Baer, Spain; Baron, Social; B. Blumenkranz, *Juifs et Chretiens dans le monde occidental* (1960); H. Z. Hirschberg, *Yisrael be-Arav* (1946); Hirschberg Afrikah; A. Milano, *Vicende economiche degli Ebret nell Italia meridionale ed insulare durante il Medioevo* (1954); Neuman, Spain; S. Saige, *Les Juifs du Languedoc* (1881); O. Stobbe, *Die Juden in Deutschland* (1866). TRADE IN AGRICULTURAL PRODUCTS: Baer, Spain, index, s.v. *Commerce*; G. Caro, *Sozial- und Wirtschaftsgeschichte der Juden im Mittelalter und in der Neuzeit*, 2 vols. (1908–20); Kosover, in: *YIVO Bleter*, 12 (1937), 533–45; I. Schipper (ed.), *Dzieje handlu zydowskiego na ziemiach polskich* (1938); Roth, England 73, 115; H. G. Richardson, *English Jewry under Angevin Kings* (1960), index, s.v. *Corn dealing*; S. D. Goitein, *A Mediterranean Society* (1967), 116–26, 265. MODERN EUROPE: V. Niktin, *Yevreyskiya poseleniya severo i yugozapadnogo kraya* (1894); Yevreyskoye kolonizatsionnoye obshchestvo, *Sbornik ob ekonomiches-komu polozheniyu Yevreyev v Rossii* (1904); S. Y. Borovoi, *Yevreyskaya zem-ledelcheskaya kolonizatsiya v staroy Rossii* (1928); B. Brutzkus, *Di Yidishe Landvirtshaft in Mizrakh-Erope* (1926); Jewish Agricultural Society *Der Yid-isher Landvirt* (1932–39); S. Tapuach, in: *YIVO Bleter*, 10 (1936), 19–25; idem, in: *Przeglad Socjologiczny*; 5 (1937); I. Schipper et al. (eds.), *Zydzi w Polsce odrodzonej*, 2 vols. (1932–33), index; J. Babicki, *Yidishe Landvirtshaft in Stanislaver Voyevodshaft* (1948[2]); idem in: *Yidishe Ekonomik*, 1–3 (1937–39); L. Babicki, in: *Sprawy Narodowościowe*, no. 4–5 (1932); Bartis, in: *Zion*, 32 (1967), 46–75; A. Tartakower, *Megillat ha-Hityashevut* (1958); Kh. Schmeruk *Ha-Kibbutz ha-Yehudi ve-ha-Hityashevut ha-Hakla'it be-Byelorusyah ha-Sovyetit 1918–32* (1961); *Hakla'im Yehudim be-Arvot Rusyah* (1965). UNITED STATES: H. J. Levine and B. Miller, *American Jewish Farmer in Changing Times* (1966); E. Lifshutz, in: AJHSQ, 56 (1966), 151–62. CANADA: Belkin, in: A. D. Hart (ed.), *Jew in Canada* (1926); Sack, *ibid.*; A. Rhinewine, *Looking Back a Century* (1932); L. Rosenberg, Agriculture in Western Canada (1932); idem, *Canada's Jews* (1939); A. A. Chiel, *Jewish Experiences in Early Manitoba* (1955); idem, *Jews in Manitoba* (1961).

ARENDA: Dubnow, Hist Russ, 3 (1920), index, s.v. *Arendar*; idem, *Pinkas Va'ad ha-Kehillot be-Medinat Lita* (1925); R. Mahler, *Toledot ha-Yehudim be-*

Polin (1946), index; idem, *Yidn in Amolikn Poyln in Likht fun Tsifern* (1958), index; S. B. Weinryb, *Neueste Wirtschaftsgeschichte der Juden in Russland und Polen* (1934), index; I. Schiper, *Dzieje handlu żydowskiego na żiemiach polskich* (1937); Halpern, Pinkas, index, s.v. *Arenda;* H. H. Ben-Sasson, *Hagut ve-Hanhagah* (1959); idem, in: *Zion*, 21 (1956), 183–206; Ettinger. *ibid.*, 20 (1955), 128–52; 21 (1956), 107–42.

LIVESTOCK: A. Kapp, *Die Dorfjuden in der Nordpfalz* (1968), 257 ff.; U. Jeggle, *Judendoerfer in Wuerttemberg* (1969), index, s.v. *Viehhandel;* J. Picard, *The Marked One* (1956); F. Guggenheim-Grunberg, in: *The Field of Yiddish*, 1 (1954), 48–62; P. J. Diamant, in: *Zeitschrift fuer die Geschichte der Juden*, 1 (1964), 79–83; M. Shahaf, in: *Yeda Am*, 2 (1954), 42–46; B. Brilling, *ibid.*, 3 (1955), 15 ff.; H. Bloom, *The Economic Activities of the Jews of Amsterdam* (1935), index, s.v. *Livestock;* H. Genschel, *Die Verdraengung der Juden aus der Wirtschaft im dritten Reich* (1966), index, s.v. *Viehhandel;* B. Rosenthal, in: MGWJ, 79 (1935), 443–50; M. Grunwald, *Samuel Oppenheimer und sein Kreis* (1913); Z. Szajikowski, *Franco-Judaica* (1962), index, s.v. *Horses, Cattle;* L. Davidsohn, *Beitraege . . . Berliner Juden . . .* (1920), 52–56; G. L. Weisel, *Aus dem Neumarker Landestor* (1926), 105 f; O. Donath, *Boehmische Dorfjuden* (1926); A. Weldler-Steinberg, *Geschichte der Juden in der Schweiz* (1966); A. Hertzberg, *The French Enlightenment and the Jews* (1968), index, s.v. *Horses, Cattle, Alsace;* S. Ettinger, in: *Zion*, 21 (1956), 107–42; H. H. Ben-Sasson, *ibid.*, 183–206.

WINE AND LIQUOR TRADE: S. B. Weinryb, *Neueste Wirtschaftsgeschichte der Juden in Russland und Polen* (1934); J. Hessen, *Istoriya Yevreyskogo naroda v Rossii* (1925); R. Mahler, *Yidn in Amolikn Poyln in Likht fun Tsifern* (1958); I. Rychlikowa, *Studia nad towarowa produkcja wielkiej własności w Małopolsce w latach 1764–1805* (1966); J. Burszta, *Społeczeństwo i karczma* (1951); R. Rozdolski, *Stosunki poddańcze w dawnej Galicji*, 2 vols. (1962), Ringelblum in; *Sprawy narodowościowe*, 8 (1934); I. Schiper, *Dzieje handlu żydowskiego na żiemiach polskich* (1937); Ettinger, in: *Zion*, 20 (1955), 128–52; 21 (1956), 107–42; H. H. Ben-Sasson, *ibid.*, 21 (1956), 83–206; Goldberg, in: BŻIH, 59 (1966); C. Roth, in: JHSET, 17 (1953), 39–43; J. Katz, *Tradition and Crisis* (1961), index.

CONSTRUCTION: G. Cohen, *The Jews in the Making of America* (1924), 127 ff.; S. D. Goitein, *A Mediterranean Society*, 1 (1967), s.v. *Carpenters, Masons, Stonecutters;* L. Rosenberg, *Canada's Jews* (1939), 202 ff.; M. U. Schappes, *The Jews in the U.S.* (1958), 197; B. Brutzkus in: *Zeitschrift fuer Demographie und statistik der Juden*, 4 (1908), 84; M. Rischin, *The Promised City* (1962), 27, 59 f., 188 f.; S. Kaznelson (ed.), *Juden im deutschen Kulturbereich* (1959), 84–86; R. Mahler, *Yehudei Polin bein Shetei Milḥamot Olam* (1969), 76 f., 102 f.; H. Kahn, *Die juedischen Handwerke in Deutschland* (1936).

CRAFTS: M. Wischnitzer, *History of Jewish Crafts and Guilds* (1965); Krauss,

Tal Arch; A. Ruppin, *The Jew in the Modern World* (1934), 182–204; J. Lestschinsky, *Das wirtschaftliche Schicksal des deutschen Judentums* (1936; *Goralah ha-Kalkali shel Yahadut Germanyah*, 1963); E. Tcherikower (ed.), *Geshikhte fun der Yidisher Arbeter Bavegung in die Fareynigte Shtatn*, 2 vols. (1943–45); C. Singer et al. (eds.), *A History of Technology*, 1 (1954); Pritchard, *Pictures*, 305.

DIAMONDS: S. D. Goitein, *A Mediterranean Society*, 1 (1967), s.v. *Jewelry*, *Pearls*; W. J. Fischel, *Ha-Yehudim be-Hodu* (1960), 41, 146–75; idem, in: *Sefunot*, 9 (1965), 249–62; idem, in: *Journal of Economic and Social History of the Orient*, 3 (1960), 78–107, 175–95; idem in: *REJ*, 123 (1964), 433–98; Fischel, *Islam*, 72–78; H. Kellenbenz, *Sephardim an der unteren Elbe* (1958), 113, 133, 165, 168, 177, 191–8, 195, 458 f.; S. Stern, *The Court Jew* (1950), 42–59; H. Schnee, *Die Hoffinanz und der moderne Staat*, 1 (1953), 38 ff., 54, 59 ff., 88 ff., 146 ff., 180, 244–53; 2 (1954), 19 ff., 61 f., 93 f., 156 f., 183 ff.; 3 (1955), 23, 35 f., 38 f., 50, 75, 182 ff., 194 f.; 44 (1963), 124 ff., 192, 188 f.; C. Roth, *Venice* (1933), 182 f.; JHSEM, 3 (1937), 100–3; R. J. D'Arcy Hart, *ibid.*, 57–75; L. Wolf, *ibid.*, 1 (1925), XXVI–XLI; H. Heertje, *De diamantbewerkers van Amsterdam* (1936); H. I. Bloom, *The Economic Activities of the Jews of Amsterdam* (1937); S. Kleerekoper, in: *Studia Rosenthaliana*, 1 (1967), 75–80; K. Liberman, *L'Industrie et le commerce diamantaires belges* (1935); P. H. Emden, *Randlords* (1935); L. Hermann, *A History of the Jews in South Africa* (1935), 226–36; E. Rosenthal, in: G. Saron and L. Hotz (eds.), *The Jews of South Africa* (1955), 105–20; N. Shapira, in: *Gesher*, 2 (1956), no. 2, 84–104; J. Gutwirth, in: JJSO, 10 (1968), 121 ff.

DYEING: Demsky, in: IEJ, 16 (1966), G. Caro, *Sozial- und Wirtschaftsgeschichte der Juden*, 2 vols. (1908–20), index, s.v. *Farben*; R. Strauss, *Die Juden in Koenigreich Sizilien . . .* (1910), 66 ff.; A. S. Hershberg, *Ḥayyei ha-Tarbut be-Yisrael bi-Tekufat ha-Mishnah ve-ha-Talmud*, 1 (1924), 207–316; I. S. Emmanuel, *Histoire de l'industrie des tissus des Israélites de Salonique* (1935), 16 ff.; J. Starr, in: *Byzantisch-Neugriechische Jahrbuecher*, 12 (1936), 42–49; Ashtor, *Toledot*, 1 (1944), 176 ff.; R. S. Lopez, in: *Speculum*, 20 (1945), 23 f. (Eng.); Roth, *Italy*, index; J. R. Marcus, *Early American Jewry*, 2 vols. (1951–53), index, s.v. *Dyeing Industry*, *Indigo*; S. Avitsur, in: *Sefunot*, 6 (1962), 58 ff.; Hirschberg, *Afrikah*, 1 (1965), 200 ff.; M. Wischnitzer, *History of Jewish Crafts and Guilds* (1965), 127 ff., 203 f., and index; S. D. Goitein, *A Mediterranean Society*, 1 (1967), index.

GOLDSMITHS AND SILVERSMITHS: L. A. Mayer, *Bibliography of Jewish Art* (1967), index, s.v. *Goldsmith* and *Ceremonial Art*; A. Wolf in: MGJW, 9 (1902), 12–74; 15 (1905), 1–58; 24 (1907), 103–17; M. Gruenwald, *ibid.*, 74 (1925), 419 f.; Y. Bronner, in: *Zeitschrift fuer die Geschichte der Juden in der Tschechoslowakei*, 1 (1931), 243–7; H. Flesch, in: *Die juedischen Denkmaeler in der Tschechoslowakei* (1933), 32–33; Baer, *Urkunden*, index; Baer, *Spain*, index; Y. W. Rosenbaum, *Myer Myers, Goldsmith* (1954); A. G. Grimwalde, in: JHSET, 18 (1953–55), 113–26; C. Roth, *The Jews in the Renaissance* (1959),

195–8, S. Simonsohn, *Toledot ha-Yehudim be-Dukkasut Mantova*, 2 vols. (1962–64) index, s.v. *Zorefim*; M. Wischnitzer, *A History of Jewish Crafts and Guilds* (1965); A. Ben-Yakob, *Yehudei Bavel mi-Sof Tekufat ha-Ge'onim ad Yamenu* (1965), index, s.v. *Zorefim*; O. Muneles (ed.), *Prague Ghetto in the Renaissance Period* (1965), 108–25; Ashtor, Korot, 1 (1966), 180; J. Hrasky, in: *Judaica Bohemiae*, 2 (1966), 19–40; 97–106; H. Bentov, in: *Sefunot*, 10 (1966), 413–83; J. M. Landau, *Ha-Yehudim be-Miẓrayim ba-Me'ah ha-Tesha-Esreh* (1967); S. D. Goitein, *A Mediterranean Society* (1967), index; W. Pillich, in: *Zeitschrift fuer die Geschichte der Juden*, 4 (1967), 79–82; B. Brilling, *ibid.*, 5 (1968), 21–26; 6 (1969), 137–46; idem, *Geschichte der juedischen Goldschmiedwerke in Schlesien* (1969); I. Roukhomovsky, *Zikhroynes fun mayn Leybn un fun mayn Shtetl* (1930); A. Kanoff, *Jewish Ceremonial Art* (1970).

METALS AND MINING: Baer, Urkunden, index; I. Abrahams, *Jewish Life in the Middle Ages* (1917, repr. 1960), 221, 226 ff.; G. Caro, *Sozial- und Wirtschaftsgeschichte der Juden im Mittelalter und in der Neuzeit*, 2 (1920), index, s.v. *Metall*; Baron, Social[2], 273; L. Hermann, *A History of the Jews in South Africa* (1935), 226–40; L. Berger, in: I. Halpern (ed.), *Beit Yisrael be-Polin*, 1 (1948), 211–3; A. Marcus, in: YIVOA, 7 (1952), 176–81; M. Hendel, *Melakhah u-Va'alei Melakhah be-Am Yisrael* (1955); M. Wischnitzer, *A History of Jewish Crafts and Guilds* (1965), index, s.v. *Blacksmiths, Coppersmiths*, etc.; I. M. Dijur, in: J. G. Frumkin et al. (eds.), *Russian Jewry* (1966), 140 ff.; G. Saron and L. Hotz (eds.), *The Jews in South Africa* (1955), passim; *The Jews of Czechoslovakia*, 1 (1968); 371–7; S. M. Auerbach, in: YLBI, 10 (1965), 188–203; J. Jaros, in: BZIH, no. 35 (1960), 87–99.

PETROLEUM AND OIL PRODUCTS: N. Shapira, in: *Gesher*, 5 (1959), 122–9; H. Landau, in: *YIVO Bleter*, 14 (1939), 269–85; I. M. Dijur, in: J. G. Frumkin et al. (eds.), *Russian Jewry; 1860–1917* (1966), 140 ff.; J. C. Pick, in: *Jews of Czechoslovakia*, 1 (1968), 375; R. Mahler, *Yehudei Polin Bein Shte Milḥamot ha-Olam* (1968), 107.

RAILROADS: K. Grunwald, in: YLBI, 12 (1967), 163–212; 14 (1969), 119–61; idem, *Tuerkenhirsch* (1966); R. E. Cameron, *France and the Economic Development of Europe, 1880–1914* (1961); E. C. Corti, *Rise of the House of Rothschild* (1928); idem, *Reign of the House of Rothschild* (1928); P. H. Emden, *Money Powers of Europe* (1937); J. Plenge, *Gruendung und Geschichte des Crédit Mobilier* (1903); AJYB, 23 (1921).

SHIPS AND SAILING: S. Tolkowsky, *They Took to the Sea* (1964; incl. bibl.); R. Patai, *Ha-Sappanut ha-Ivrit* (1938; incl. bibl.); idem, in: JQR, 32 (1941/42), 1–26: C. Roth, *Venice* (1930), 175–80; H. I. Bloom, *The Economic Activities of the Jews of Amsterdam* (1937), index; A. L. Lebeson, in: HJ, 10 (1948), 155–74; Tcherikover, Corpus, 1 (1957), 105; Baron, Social[2], 4 (1957), 183 f.; 12 (1967), 46, 100 f., 104 ff.; E. Rosenbaum, in: YLBI, 3 (1958), 257–99; H. Kellenbenz, *Sephardim an der unteren Elbe* (1958); J. Frumkin et al. (eds.), *Russian Jewry* (1966), 139–40; S. D. Goitein, *A Mediterranean Society*, 1 (1967), passim; M.

Grunwald, *Juden als Rheder und Seefahrer* (1902); idem, in: *Mitteilungen fuer juedische Volkskunde* (1904), no. 14, 82–84; W. J. Fischel, in: A.A. Neumann and S. Zeitlin (eds.), *The Seventy-Fifth Anniversary Volume of the Jewish Quarterly Review* (1967), 192–210; idem, in: JQR, 47 (1956/57), 37–57; M. A. Gutstein, *The Story of the Jews of Newport* (1936); D. Corcos, in: *Zion*, 25 (1960), 122–33.

SUGAR TRADE AND INDUSTRY: S. D. Goitein, *A Mediterranean Society*, 1 (1967), index; H. Landau, in: *Shriften far Ekonomik un Statistik*, 1 (1928), 98–104 (Yid.), 16–17 (Ger.); E. O. von Lippman, *Geschichte des Zuckers* (1929²); B. D. Weinryb, *Neueste Wirtschaftsgeschichte der Juden in Russland und Polen* (1934), index, s.v. *Zucker*; P. Friedmann, in: *Jewish Studies in Memory of G. A. Kohut* (1935), 231–2, 241 (Ger.); H. J. Bloom, *The Economic Activities of the Jews of Amsterdam* (1937), index; N. Deerr, *History of Sugar*, 2 vols. (1949–50); H. Kellenbenz, *Sephardim an den unteren Elbe* (1958); N. Shapira, in: *Gesher*, 4 (1958), no. 3, 101–12; Roth, Marranos.

TAILORING: M. Wischnitzer, *A History of Jewish Crafts and Guilds* (1965); M. Hendel, *Melakhah u-Va'alei Melakhah be-Am Yisrael* (1955), index. ORIENT: S. D. Goitein, *A Mediterranean Society* (1967); idem, in: JSOS, 17 (1955), 3–26; A. Bauer, *Yehudei Kurdistan* (1948), 183; H. Bentov, in: *Sefunot*, 10 (1966), 431 f.; M. S. Goodblatt, *Jewish Life in Turkey* (1952). ITALY: M. A. Shulvass, *Ḥayyei ha-Yehudim be-Italyah* (1955), 130–2; J. Donath, in: MGWJ, 72 (1928), 574 f.; Roth, Italy; idem, *History of the Jews in Venice* (1930), index; S. Simonsohn, *Toledot ha-Yehudim be-Dukkasut Mantovah* (1964), index, s.v. *ḥayyatim*. CZECHOSLOVAKIA: H. Flesch, in: MGWJ (1930); B. Heilig, in: JGGJC, 3 (1931), 307–448; idem, in: *Zeitschrift des deutschen Vereins fuer die Geschichte Maehrens und Schlesiens*, 31 (1929); idem, *Urkundliches zur Wirtschaftsgeschichte der Juden in Prossnitz* (1929); T. Jakobovitz, in: JGGJC, 8 (1936), 108–11; R. Kestenberg-Gladstein, in: *Zion*, 9 (1944), 1–26; 12 (1947), 47–65; J. Pick, in: *Jews in Czechoslovakia* (1968). POLAND: J. Jacobson, in: MGWJ, 65 (1921), 43 ff.; I. Halpern, in:*Zion*, 2 (1937), 72 ff.; idem, *Yehudim ve-Yahadut be-Mizraḥ Eiropah* (1969), passim; I. Goldberg and A. Wajn, in: *Bleter far Geshikhte*, 15 (1962/3), 155–205; M. M. Zarchin, *Jews in the Province of Posen* (1939), 31–42; idem, in: JQR, 27 (1937/38), 47–56; M. Hendel, in: *Reshumot*, 5 (1953), 131–45; E. Ringelblum, in: *Ekonomishe Shriften*, 2 (1932), 20–31; M. Balaban, *Der Judenstaat von Lublin* (1919), 63 ff.; R. Mahler, *Yehudei Polin Bein Shetei Milḥamot Olam* (1968). LITHUANIA: *Di Yidishe Hantverker in Lite in Tsifern* (1938); M. Linder, in: *Yidishe Ekonomik*, 3 (1939), 1–18; *Der Shnayder*, 1, 1936. GERMANY AND AUSTRIA: A. Marcus, *Die Wirtschaftliche Krise der deutschen Juden* (1935), 70–96; idem, in: *YIVO Annual*, 7 (1952), 195–9; J. Lestschinsky, *Das Wirtschaftliche Schicksal des deutschen Judentums* (1932); B. Daehn, *Berlin Hausvogteiplatz* (1968); E. Landsberg, in: *Der Morgen*, 3 (1927), 111–3; S. Mayer, *Die Wiener Juden* (1912). FRANCE: M. Lanzel, *Ouvriers juifs de Paris: Les·Casquettiers* (1912); M. Roblin, *Les Juifs de Paris* (1952), 97 ff.; A. Hertzberg, *The French Enlightenment and the Jews* (1968), index; Z. Szajkowski, in: *Yidishe Ekonomik*, 2 (1938), 232–49; J. Klatzmann, *Le Travail* *à domicile dans l'industrie parisienne des vêtements* (1957); *Der Trikofabrikant*, 1 (1958–); S. Friedmann, *Etuden tsu der Geshikhte fun Eyngevanderten Yidishn Yishuv in Frankraykh* (1936); idem, *Di Profesionale Bevegung Tsvishn di Yidishe Arbayter in Frankraykh biz 1914* (1937). ENGLAND: V. D. Lipman, *Social History of the Jews in England 1850–1950* (1954); idem, in: JJSO, 2 (1960), 202–18; L. P. Gartner, *The Jewish Immigrant in England 1870–1914* (1957); M. Freedman (ed.), *A Minority in Britain* (1955); J. Gould and S. Esh (eds.), *Jewish Life in Modern Britain* (1964). U.S.: O. Schmelz, *Jewish Demography and Statistics Bibliography for 1920–1960* (1961); L. Levine, *Women's Garments Workers* (1924); J. M. Budish and G. Soule, *New Unionism in the Clothing Industry* (1920); J. Seidman, *Needle Trades* (1942); M. Epstein, *Jewish Labor in U.S.A.*, 2 vols. (1950–53); M. Rischin, *The Promised City* (1962); R. Glanz, *Jews in American Folklore* (1961), chap. 16; idem, in: *YIVO Annual*, 9 (1954), 308–31; J. Greenfeld, *ibid.*, 2/3 (1947/48), 180–204; E. Feldman, in: AJA, 12 (1960), 3–14; N. Goldberg in: *YIVO Bleter*, 23 (1944), 178–205; *Jews in America* (1938), 50–52; J. Loft, in: JSOS, 2 (1940), 61–78; W. Herberg, in: *Jewish Frontier*, 20 (1953), 24–29; M. Josephson, *Sidney Hillman: Statesman of American Labor* (1952), index; M. Hall (ed.), *Made in New York: Case Studies in Metropolitan Manufacturing* (1959).

TEXTILES: OTTOMAN EMPIRE: S. Avizur, in: *Sefunot*, 6 (1962), 41–71; 8–12 (Eng.); idem, in: *Oẓar Yehudei Sefarad*, 5 (1962), 101–8; S. A. Rosanes, *Korot ha-Yehudim be-Turkiyyah*, 3 (1938), 384–96; I. S. Emmanuel, *L'Histoire de l'Industrie des Tissus des Israélites de Salonique* (1935); M. S. Goodblatt, *Jewish Life in Turkey* (1952), 47 ff.; M. Benayahu, in: *Oẓar Yehudei Sefarad*, 5 (1962), 101–8; S. Schwarzfuchs, in: REJ, 121 (1962), 169–79; Y. Kena'ani, *Ha-Ḥayyim ha-Kalkaliyyim bi-Zefat* (1935). POLAND: P. Friedmann, in: S. W. Baron and A. Marx (eds.), *Jewish Studies in Memory of George A. Kohut* (1935), 178–247; idem, in: *Lodzer Tagblatt* (1931), nos. 204, 210, 216, 222, 228, 234, 240, 246, 252; idem, *Lodzer Visenshaftlikhe Shriftn*, 1 (1938), 63–132; R. Mahler, *Yehudei Polin Bein Shetei Milḥamot Olam* (1968), 69–113; W. M. Glicksman, *In the Mirror of Literature* (1966), 43 f., 55 f., 130–43; A. Yasny, *Geshikhte fun der Yidisher Arbeter Bavegung in Lodz* (1937); B. D. Weinryb, *Neueste Wirtschaftsgeschichte der Juden in Russland und Polen* (1934), index, s.v. *Textil, Weber, Tuchmacher*; D. Boim, in: *Yidishe Ekonomik*, 1 (1937), 34–43; 83–91; S. E., *ibid.*, 199–201; M. Linder, *ibid.*, 149–57, 240–51; M. Ashkewitz, *Zur Geschichte der Juden in Westpreussen* (1967), 69 ff.; D. Avron (ed.), *Pinkas Hekhsherim shel Kehillat Pozen*, index, s.v. *Soḥer Ẓemer*. CENTRAL EUROPE: S. Mayer, *Die Wiener Juden* (1917); J. Pick, in: *The Jews of Czechoslovakia* (1968), 409–16; E. Hofmann, in: H. Gold (ed.), *Juden und Judengemeinden Boehmens* (1934), 529–69; R. Kestenberg-Gladstein, in: *Zion*, 12 (1947), 49–65, 160–89; B. Heilig, in: BLBI, 3 (1960), 101–22. GERMANY: A. Marcus, *Die Wirtschaftliche Krise des deutschen Juden* (1931), 70–96; idem, in: *YIVO Annual*, 7 (1952), 189–99; S. Stern-Taeubler, in: JSOS, 11 (1949), 129–52; E. Landsberg, in: *Der Morgen*, 3 (1927), 99–113; A. Cohn, *Beitraege zur Geschichte der Juden in Hessen-Kassel* (1933), 41–50; M. Zelzer, *Weg und Schicksal der Stuttgarter Juden* (1965), 32 ff., 472–7; A. Taenzer, *Die*

Geschichte der Juden in Jebenhausen und Goeppingen (1927), 109–50, 431–69; J. Jacobson, in: ZGJD, 1 (1929), 152–62; F. v. Gruenfeld, *Das Leinenhaus Gruenfeld* (1967); I. M. Kulisher, in: *Yevreyskaya Starina*, 11 (1924), 129–61. GREAT BRITAIN: A. R. Rollin, in: JHSET, 17 (1951–2), 45–53; C. C. Aronsfeld, in: YLBI, 7 (1962), 315 ff.; V. D. Lipman, *Social History of the Jews in England, 1850–1950*, 1 (1954); idem, in: JJSO, 2 no. 2 (1960); M. Freedman (ed.), *A Minority in Britain* (1955); L. P. Gartner, *The Jewish Immigrant in England 1870–1914* (1960); J. Gould and S. Esh, *Jewish Life in Modern Britain* (1964); A. R. Rollin, in: JHSET, 15 (1946).

TOBACCO TRADE AND INDUSTRIES: M. Hainisch, in: *Vierteljahrschrift fuer Sozial- und Wirtschaftsgeschichte*, 8 (1910), 394–444; W. Stieda, *Die Besteuerung des Tabaks in Ansbach-Bayreuth und Bamberg-Wuerzburg im achtzehnten Jahrhundert* (1911); M. Grunwald, *Samuel Oppenheimer* (1913), 295–300; A. D. Hart, *The Jew in Canada* (1926), 324–5, 337; S. B. Weinryb, *Neueste Wirtschaftsgeschichte der Juden in Russland und Polen* (1934), index, s v. *Tabakindustrie*; P. Friedmann, in: *Jewish Studies in Memory of G. A. Kohut* (1935), 196, 232–3 (Ger.); H. I. Bloom, *The Economic Activities of the Jews of Amsterdam* (1937); H. Rachel et al., *Berliner Grosskaufleute und Kapitalisten*, 2 (1938), 50–52; J. Starr, in: JSOS, 7 (1945), 323–6; M. Epstein, *Jewish Labor in U.S.A.* (1950), 76–78; J. Shatzky, *Geshikhte fun Yidn in Varshe*, 3 (1953), 37, 43–46; H. Schnee, *Die Hoffinanz und der moderne Staat*, 1 (1953), 89, 185; 2 (1954), 88 f., 294 ff.; 3 (1955), 123 ff.; 4 (1963), 219–22, 239–41; S. Gompers, *Seventy Years of Life and Labour* (1957[2]); H. Kellenbenz, *Sephardim an der unteren Elbe* (1958), 205, 436–46; J. Frumkin et al., *Russian Jewry* (1966), 130–1; V. Kurrein, in: *Menorah*, 3 (1925), 155 f.; A. Mueller, *Zur Geschichte der Judenfrage in . . . der Landgrafschaft Hessen-Darmstadt* (1937), 54–56; S. Simonsohn, *Toledot ha-Yehudim be-Dukkasut Mantovah*, 2 vols. (1962–64); Z. Kahana, in: *Kol Torah*, 3 (1949/50), 55–61; L. P. Gartner, *The Jewish Immigrant in England 1870–1914* (1960), 73–75; V. D. Lipman, *Social History of the Jews in England* (1954), index.

BANKING AND BANKERS: MIDDLE AGES–18TH CENTURY: I. Schipper, *Toledot ha-Kalkalah ha-Yehudit*, 2 vols. (1935–36); W. Sombart, *Jews and Modern Capitalism* (1951); J. Guttmann, *Die Juden und das Wirtschaftsleben* (1913), review of W. Sombart; M. Hoffmann, *Geldhandel der deutschen Juden waehrend des Mittelalters* (1910); G. Caro, *Sozial- und Wirtschaftsgeschichte der Juden*, 2 vols. (1908–20), index, s.v. *Bankiers*; H. Waetjen, *Das Judentum und die Anfaenge der modernen Kolonisation* (1914); H. Schnee, *Hoffinanz und der moderne Staat*, 6 vols. (1953–67); S. D. Goitein, *A Mediterranean Society*, 1 (1967); L. Poliakov, *Les Banchieri juifs et le Saint-Siège du XIIIe au XVIIe siècle* (1965). 19TH AND 20TH CENTURIES: P. Emden, *Money Powers of Europe . . .* (1938); M. Lévy-Leboyer, *Les banques européennes . . .* (1964); J. Wechsberg, *Merchant Bankers* (1966); J. Riesser, *German Great Banks* (1911[3]); A. Marcus, *Die Wirtschaftliche Krise der deutschen Juden* (1931); idem, in: YIVOA, 7 (1952), 175–203; Goldberg, in: *Yivo Ekonomishe Shriftn*, 2 (1932), 56–92; S. Birmingham, *Our Crowd* (1967); K. Zielenziger, *Juden in der deut-*

schen Wirtschaft (1930); B. E. Supple, in: *Business History Review*, 31 no. 2 (1957); E. O. Eisenberg, in: *The National Jewish Monthly*, 53 no. 6 (Feb., 1939); Milano, in: JQR, 30 (1939/40), 149–86; Giuseppi, in: JHSEM, 6 (1962), 143–74; G. Myers, *History of the Great American Fortunes* (1910, 1937^2); D. S. Landes, *Bankers and Pashas . . . in Egypt* (1958); K. Grunwald, *Hamizraḥ ha-Ḥadash: Ha-Banka'im ha-Yehudim be-Iraq* 1 (1960), 160–5; H.-D. Kircholtes, *Juedische Privatbanken in Frankfurt/M.* (1969).

BROKERS: M. Breger, *Zur Handelsgeschichte der Juden in Polen waehrend des 17. Jahrhunderts* (1932), 13 ff., 23 f.; S. B. Weinryb, *Neueste Wirtschaftsgeschichte der Juden in Russland und Polen* (1934); H. I. Bloom, *The Economic Activities of the Jews of Amsterdam* (1937); H. Gousiorowski, *Die Berufe der Juden Hamburgs* (1927), 20–23, 31–32, 45–46, 78–79; D. Abrahams, in: JHSEM, 3 (1937), 80–94; Halpern, Pinkas, index, s.v. *Sarsarut*; R. Mahler, *Toledot ha-Yehudim be-Folin* (1946), index, s.v. *Sarsurim*; A. Marcus, in: YIVOA, 7 (1952), 175–203; H. Kellenbenz, *Sephardim an der unteren Elbe* (1958); Baer, Spain; W. Harmelin, in: YLBI, 9 (1964), 243 ff.; D. Avron (ed.), *Pinkas ha-Kesherim shel Kehillat Pozna* (1966), index, s.v. *Sarsurim*; S. D. Goitein, *A Mediterranean Society*, 1 (1967), index; A. S. Diamond, in: JHSET, 21 (1968), 53 f; J. Jacobson, in: MGWJ, 64 (1920), 293 ff.; S. Mayer, *Die Wiener Juden* (1917), 220 ff., 264 f., 453 f.; W. M. Glicksman, *In the Mirror of Literature* (1966), 203–8.

CONTRACTORS: M. Grunwald, *Samuel Oppenheimer und sein Kreis* (1913); H. I. Bloom, *The Economic Activities of the Jews of Amsterdam* (1937), index; B. G. Sack, *History of the Jews in Canada*, 1 (1945), 27 ff.; Kisch, Germany, 115, 414 ff.; S. Stern, *Court Jew* (1950), 38–59; idem, *Der preussische Staat und die Juden*, 2 vols. (1962); J. R. Marcus, *Early American Jewry*, 2 vols. (1951–53), index, s.v. *Army purveyors*; idem, *American Jewry Documents* (1959), index, s.v. *Army purveyors*; H. Schnee, *Die Hoffinanz und der moderne Staat*, 6 vols. (1953–67); Baron, Social, index; W. Sombart, *Jews and Modern Capitalism* (1962), 68–70; Roth, England, index, s.v. *Army contractors*; A. Hertzberg, *French Enlightenment and the Jews* (1968), index, s.v. *Army*.

COURT JEWS: S. Stern, *Court Jew* (1950); idem, *Der preussische Staat und die Juden*, 4 vols. (1962); H. Schnee, *Die Hoffinanz und der moderne Staat*, 6 vols. (1953–67); J. R. Marcus, *Jews in the Medieval World* (1938, paperback 1965), 291, 415 ff.; H. Kellenbenz, *Sephardim an der unteren Elbe* (1958); C. Roth, *Essays and Portraits in Anglo-Jewish History* (1962); idem, in: JSOS, 5 (1943), 355–66; R. Straus, *ibid.*, 3 (1941), 15–40; F. Redlich, in: *Explorations in Entrepreneurial History*, 3 (1951); Carsten, in: YLBI, 3 (1958), 140 ff.

DEPARTMENT STORES: H. Uhlig, *Die Warenhaeuser im Dritten Reich* (1956), incl. bibl.; G. Tietz, *Hermann Tietz* (Ger., 1965); K. Zielenziger, *Juden in der deutschen Wirtschaft* (1930), 206–20 (on Tietz); Reissner, in: YLBI, 3 (1958), 227–56 (on N. Israel); Moses, *ibid.*, 5 (1960), 73–104 (on Schocken); G. Rees, *St. Michael: a History of Marks and Spencer* (1969); M. C. Harrimann, *And the Price is Right* (1958); A. Marshall, *The Gay Provider* (1961); A. Briggs, *Friends of the People* (1956).

JEWISH AUTONOMOUS FINANCE: Baron, Social[2], index; Baron, Community, index, s.v. *Financial administration*; Baer, Spain, index; H. H. Ben-Sasson, *Hagut ve-Hanhagah* (1959), 147, 158, 229–32, 239; Roth, England, index, s.v. *Taxation*; Roth, Italy, index; Milano, Italia, 485–514.

MARKETDAYS AND FAIRS: R. Mahler, *Toledot ha-Yehudim be-Polin* (1946), index, s.v. *Yarid*; M. Breger, *Zur Handelsgeschichte der Juden in Polen im 17. Jahrhundert* (1932), 15 ff.; B. D. Weinryb, *Neueste Wirtschaftsgeschichte der Juden in Russland und Polen* (1934), index, s.v. *Messe*; S. Dubnow, *Pinkas ha-Medinah* (1925), index, s.v. *Yarid*; Halpern, Pinkas, s.v. *Yarid*; D. Evron, *Pinkas ha-Kesherim shel Kehillat Pozna* (1967), index, s.v. *Yarid*; S. Simonsohn, *Toledot ha-Yehudim be-Dukkasut Mantovah* (1964), index, s.v. *Yarid*; I. Halpern, *Takkanot Medinat Mehrin* (1952), index, s.v. *Yarid*; H. Gold (ed.), *Die Juden und Judengemeinden Maehrens* (1929), 144 ff.; F. Guggenheim-Gruenberg, *Die Juden auf der Zurzacher Messe im 18. Jahrhundert* (1957); A. Hertzberg, *The French Enlightenment and the Jews* (1968), index, s.v. *Fairs*; Z. Szajkowski, *Franco-Judaica* (1962), index, s.v. *Markets*; A. F. Pribram, *Urkunden und Akten zur Geschichte der Juden in Wien* (1918), index, s.v. *Markt, Jahrmarkt*; L. Moses, *Die Juden in Niederoesterreich* (1935), 91–94; idem, in: A. Engel (ed.), *Gedenkbuch . . . Kuratoriums* (1936), 90–101; V. Kurrein, *Die Juden in Linz* (1927), 26–38; idem, in: JGGJČ, 4 (1932), 481–4; A. Weldler-Steinberg and F. Guggenheim-Gruenberg, *Geschichte der Juden in der Schweiz* (1966), 21–86; B. B. Brilling, *Geschichte der Juden in Breslau von 1454 bis 1702* (1960); R. Markgraf, *Zur Geschichte der Juden auf den Messen im Leipzig* (1894); M. Freudenthal, *Leipziger Messgaeste* (1928); W. Harmelin, in: YLBL, 9 (1964), 239–66.

MINTMASTERS AND MONEYERS: MEDIEVAL EUROPE: P. Grierson, *Bibliographie Numismatique* (1966); S. Stern, *Court Jew* (1950), 47, 157, 162–76, 211, 218; M. Hoffmann, *Geldhandel der deutschen Juden* (1910); S. Katz, *Jews in the Visigothic and Frankish Kingdoms of France and Gaul* (1934), 122 f.; d'Amecourt, in: *Annuaire de la Société française de Numismatique et d'Archéologie*, 4 (1873), 128–31; J. Cahn, in: *Zeitschrift fuer Numismatik*, 33 (1922); *Biographical Dictionary of Medalists*, 8 vols. (1902–30); Baer, Spain, 1 (1961), 146, 327, 131–2; 2 (1966), 29; Neuman, Spain, 2 (1942), 237, 245, 252; D. M. Friedenberg, in: *Numismatist*, 130 (1967), 1515–28; W. Gumowski, *Handbuch der polnischen Numismatik* (1960), 91–96; I. Schiper, *Di Virtshaft Geshikhte fun di Yidn in Polyn Beysn Mittelter* (1929), 235 ff.; A. Wolf, in: MGJV, 9 (1902), 24–25; L. Réthy and G. Probszt, *Corpus Nummorum Hungariae*, 71, 74, 77, 89. CENTRAL EUROPE AND MODERN ERA: H. I. Bloom, *The Economic Activities of the Jews of Amsterdam* (1933); B. Brilling, *Geschichte der Juden in Breslau 1754–1802* (1960); idem, in: JGGJC, 7 (1935), 387–98; F. Redlich, in: *Explorations in Entrepreneurial History*, 3 (1951), 161–98; H. Kellenbenz, *Sephardim an der unteren Elbe* (1958), 210–44; H. Schnee, *Die Hoffinanz und der moderne Staat*, 6 vols. (1953–67); A. Pribram, *Urkunden und Akten zur Geschichte der Juden in Wien* (1918), index, s.v. *Muenzjuden*; M. Koehler, *Juden in Halberstadt* (1927), 41–48; S. Stern, *Der preussische Staat und die Juden*, 2

(1962), Akten: no. 46–71; no. 124–8; no. 144–69; no. 177; M. Grunwald, *Samuel Oppenheimer und sein Kreis* (1913), index. MUSLIM COUNTRIES: S. D. Goitein, *A Mediterranean Society*, 1 (1967), 362, 365; S. Proznański, *Babylonische Geonim* (1914), 133; S. Assaf, in: *Zion*, 1 (1937), 256 f.; A. N. Pollak, *ibid.*, 24–30.

MONEYLENDING: S. Stein, in: *Essays . . . J. H. Hertz* (1942), 403 f.; idem, in: JTS, 4 (1953), 161–70; idem, in: HJ, 17 (1955), 3–40; idem, in: JSS, 1 (1956), 141–64; 2 (1957), 94; idem, in: JJS, 10 (1959), 45–61; idem, *Jewish-Christian Disputations in 13th Century Narbonne* (Inaugural Lecture, University College, London, 1969), 1–27; D. Tama, *Transactions of the Parisian Sanhedrin* (1807); W. Sombart, *Die Juden und das Wirtschaftsleben* (1911); Roth, Italy; J. T. Noonan, Jr., *Scholastic Analysis of Usury* (1957); R. W. Emery, *Jews of Perpignan in the 13th Century* (1959); J. Katz, *Exclusiveness and Tolerance* (1961); Baer, Spain; S. Stern, *Der preussische Staat und die Juden*, 2 vols. (1962); J. Parkes, *Jew in the Medieval Community* (1938), index, s.v. *Usury*; B. N. Nelson, *Idea of Usury* (1949), index, s.v. *Jews*; L. Poliakov, *Les banchieri juifs et le Saint-Siège* (1965); M. Neumann, *Geschichte des Wuchers in Deutschland* (1865), 292–347; J. E. Scherer, *Die Rechtsverhaeltnisse der Juden in den deutsch-oesterreichischen Laendern* (1901), 185–96; G. Caro, *Sozial- und Wirtschaftsgeschichte der Juden im Mittelalter*, 2 vols. (1908–20), index, s.v. *Wucher*; M. Hoffmann, *Der Geldhandel der deutschen Juden waehrend des Mittelalters* (1910); R. Straus, *Die Judengemeinde Regensburg* (1932); idem, *Regensburg und Augsburg* (1939); idem, *Die Juden in Wirtschaft und Gesellschaft* (1964); Kisch, Germany, index; M. Breger, *Zur Handelsgeschichte der Juden in Polen im 17. Jahrhundert* (1932); W. J. Fischel, *Jews in the Economic and Political Life of Medieval Islam* (1937); Z. Szajkowski, *Agricultural Credit and Napoleon's Anti-Jewish Decrees* (1953); idem, *Economic Status of the Jews in Alsace, Metz and Lorraine* (1954); H. H. Ben-Sasson, *Hagut ve-Hanhagah* (1959); idem, *Toledot Am Yisrael*, 2 (1969), 92–98; S. Simonsohn, *Toledot ha-Yehudim be-Dukkasut Mantovah*, 2 vols. (1962–64), index, s.v. *Halva'ah u-Malvim be-Ribbit*; H. G. Richardson, *English Jewry under Angevin Kings* (1960), index, s.v. *Usury*; S. Grayzel, *The Church and the Jews in the XIIIth Century* (1966²), index; S. D. Goitein, *A Mediterranean Society*, 1 (1967), index, s.v. *Loans on interest*; F. R. Salter, in: *Cambridge Historical Journal*, 5 (1935–37), 193–211; P. Elman, in: *Economic History Review*, 7 (1936–37), 145–54.

PEDDLING: BOHEMIA: R. Kestenberg-Gladstein, in: *Zion*, 12 (1947), 49–65, 160–185; idem, *Neuere Geschichte der Juden in den boehmischen Laendern* (1969), 96 ff., 350 f.; S. H. Lieben, in: *Afike Jehuda Festschrift* (1930) 39 ff.; O. Donath, *Boehmische Dorfjuden* (1926); I. Ziegler, *Dokumente zur Geschichte der Juden in Karlsbad* (1913). GERMANY: M. Grunwald, *Hamburg's deutsche Juden bis zur Aufloesung der Dreigemeinden* (1904), 23, 57, 60, 150; F. Nienhaus, *Die Juden im ehemaligen Herzogtum Cleve* (1914), 24–28, A. Mueller, *Geschichte der Juden in Nuernberg* (1968), 61, 105 ff., 123 ff.; S. Stern, *Der preussische Staat und die Juden*, 1 (1962), Akten, no. 2, 23, 27, 28, 144, 156,

165, 213, 377, 419, 441, 455; 2 (1962), Akten no. 187, 201, 549, 551, 553, 602, 609, 611, 660; A. Kapp, in: ZGJD, 6 (1935), 45–47; H. Schwab, *Jewish Rural Communities in Germany* (1956); E. Baasch, in: *Vierteljahreshefte fuer Sozial- und Wirtschaftspolitik*, 16 (1922), 370–98; D. A. Winter, *Geschichte der juedischen Gemeinde in Moisling/Luebeck* (1968), 1–85; S. Schwarz, *Die Juden in Bayern* (1963), 125, 195–205; H. Gonsiorowski, *Die Berufe der Juden Hamburgs* (1927), 39 f., 48 ff., 65 f., 74–77; L. Kahn, *Geschichte der Juden in Sulzburg* (1969); C. Rixen, *Geschichte und Organisation der Juden im ehemaligen Stift Muenster* (1906), 52–57; A. Taenzer, *Die Geschichte der Juden in Jebenhausen und Goeppingen* (1927), 102–43; A. Welder-Steinberg, *Geschichte der Juden in der Schweiz* (1966); M. Aschkewitz, *Zur Geschichte der Juden in Westpreussen* (1967), 85 ff., 95 f.; T. Oelsner, in: JSOS, 4 (1942), 241–68, 349–98; B. Brilling, *Geschichte der Juden in Breslau* (1960), 22 f.; F. Kynass, *Der Jude im deutschen Volkslied* (1934), 84 f., 90 f., 135–8; A. Blum, *Die wirtschaftliche Lage der juedischen Landbevoelkerung im Grossherzogtum Baden* (1901), 31 f. AUSTRIA: D. Herzog, *B'nai B'rith Mitteilungen fuer Oesterreich*, 33 (1933), 341–6; L. Moses, *Geschichte der Juden in Niederoesterreich* (1935), 91 ff.; G. Wolf, in: *Neuzeit*, 27 (1887), 87 f. POLAND: R. Mahler, *Toledot ha-Yehudim be-Polin* (1946), index, s.v. *Rokhelim*; S. Dubnow (ed.), *Pinkas ha-Medinah* (1925), 60, 70, 258 f.; W. H. Glicksman, *In the Mirror of Literature* (1966), 170 ff., 189 ff., 192, 198; J. Jacobson, in: MGWJ, 64 (1920), 222 ff.; L. Shelomowitch, in: *Yidishe Ekonomik*, 3 (1939), 194–209; I. Schiper (ed.) *Dzieje handlu zydowskiego na ziemiach polskich* (1937). THE LOW COUNTRIES: K. Liberman, in: *Yidishe Ekonomik*, 2 (1938), 250–65; S. Kleerekoper, in: *Studia Rosenthaliana*, 1 (1967), 73 ff.; H. I. Bloom, *The Economic Activities of the Jews of Amsterdam* (1937), index. FRANCE: Z. Szajkowski, *Poverty and Social Welfare among French Jews (1800–1880)* (1954), 30 f.; idem, *The Economic Status of the Jews in Alsace, Metz and Lorraine (1648–1789)* (1954), 62 ff.; idem, *Franco-Judaica* (1962), index; idem, in: JSOS, 8 (1946), 307 f. ENGLAND: A. M. Jacob, in: JHSET, 17 (1953), 63–72; J. Rumney, *ibid.*, 13 (1936), 336 ff.; V. D. Lipman, *Social History of the Jews in England, 1850–1950* (1954), 28–32; L. P. Gartner, *The Jewish Immigrant in England, 1870–1914* (1960), index; C. Roth, *Essays and Portraits in Anglo-Jewish History* (1962), 130–9; A. Rubens, in: JHSET, 19 (1960), U.S.: M. Whiteman, in: JQR, 53 (1963), 306–21; idem, in: *Studies and Essays in Honor of A. A. Neuman* (1962), 503–15; F. S. Fierman, in: *Password*, 8 (1963), 43–55; O. Handlin, *Adventure in Freedom* (1954), index; R. Glanz, *The Jew in Old American Folklore* (1961), 122–46; idem, in: JSOS, 7 (1945), 119–36; idem, *The Jews of California* (1960); W. J. Parish, in: *New Mexico Historical Review*, 35 (1960), 1–29; M. Freund, *Jewish Merchants in Colonial America* (1939); S. Stern, in: E. E. Hirschler (ed.), *Jews from Germany in the United States* (1955), 36–39; H. L. Golden, *Forgotten Pioneer* (1963); M. Rischin, *The Promised City* (1962), index; A. Schoener (ed.), *Portal to America: The Lower East Side 1870–1925* (1967); AJA, 8 (1956), 87–89; 19 (1967), 6–8; A. V. Goodman, *ibid.*, 3 (1951), 81–111; W. L. Provol, *ibid.*, 16 (1964), 26–34; L. M. Friedman, in: AJHSP, 44 (1955/56), 1–7; AJHSP, 38 (1948/49), 22 ff.; 40 (1950/51), 59 ff., 327; 53 (1963/64), 271; 54 (1964/65), 488–90; 56

(1966/67), 296–300; L. Berg, in: *Commentary* (July 1965), 63–67; J. R. Marcus (ed.), *Memoirs of American Jews*, 3 vols. (1955).

SECONDHAND GOODS: R. Glanz, *The Jew in Old American Folklore* (1961), 147–65; S. Simonsohn, *Toledot ha-Yehudim be-Dukkasut Mantovah* (1964), index, s.v. *Mishar Sehorot Meshummashot*; V. D. Lipman, *Social History of the Jews in England* (1954), 13, 31 ff.; Roth, Italy, index, s.v. *Ragpickers* and *Second-hand dealers*; idem, in: HUCA, 5 (1928), 353 ff.; idem, *History of the Jews in Venice* (1930), 173 ff.; Z. Szajkowski, *Franco-Judaica* (1962), nos. 48, 191, 309, 1395–493; H. Heilig, in: JGGJC, 3 (1931), 307–448; H. I. Bloom, *The Economic Activities of the Jews of Amsterdam* (1935), index, s.v. *Old clothes*; J. Rumney, in: JHSET, 13 (1932–35), 332 ff.; L. P. Gartner, *The Jewish Immigrant in England, 1914–1970* (1960), 82–84; W. M. Glicksman, *In the Mirror of Literature* (1966), 195 f.

SLAVE TRADE: S. D. Goitein, *A Mediterranean Society*, 1 (1967), index; T. Oelsner, in: YIVOA, 12 (1958/59), 184 f.; idem, in: YLBI 8 (1962), 188 f.; Baron, Social², 3 (1956), 30 f., 243 f.; 4 (1956), 187–96; 332–8; idem, in: *Essays on Maimonides* (1941), 229–47; Roth, *Dark Ages*, 27 f., 306–10, 386, 410; S. Assaf, *Be-Oholei Ya'akov* (1943), 223–56; idem, in: *Zion*, 4 (1939), 5 (1940); M. S. Goodblatt, *Jewish Life in Turkey* (1952), 125 ff.; A. S. Diamond, in: JHSET, 21 (1962–67); J. Starr, *Jews in the Byzantine Empire* (1939), index; D. B. Davis, *Problem of Slavery in Western Culture* (1966), 98 ff.; S. Grayzel, *The Church and the Jews in the XIIIth Century* (1966²), index; J. Parkes, *Church and Synagogue* (1934), index; M. Hoffman, *Der Geldhandel der deutschen Juden waehrend des Mittelalters* (1910), 15 ff.; Baer, Spain, index; B. Z. Wacholder, in: HJ, 18 (1956), 89–106; I. A. Agus, *Urban Civilization in Pre-Crusade Europe* (1965), index; A. Hertzberg, *The French Enlightenment and the Jews* (1968), index; E. Taeubler, in: *M. Philippson Festschrift* (1916), 381–92; B. Blumenkranz, *Juifs et Chrétiens dans le Monde Occidental 430–1096* (1960), 18–55, 107, 190 f., 337; C. Haase, in: *Die Staedte Mitteleuropas im 12. und 13. Jahrhundert*, ed. by W. Rauch (1963), 133 and n. 50; C. Cahen, in: REJ, 123 (1964), 499–504. IN THE AMERICAS: F. Bancroft, *Slave Trading in the Old South* (1931); Chyet, in: AJHSQ, 52 (1962/63), 295–300; I. S. Emmanuel, *Precious Stones of the Jews of Curaçao* (1957), 304; idem, *History of the Jews of the Netherlands Antilles* (1970), index; Friedenwald, in: AJHSP, 5 (1897), 60–97; B. W. Korn, *Early Jews of New Orleans* (1969); idem, *Jews and Slavery in the Old South* (1961); *Report, Resolution and Remonstrance of the Honourable the Council and Assembly of Jamaica at a Joint Committee on the Subject of the Slave Trade* (London, 1790); A. Wiznitzer, *Jews in Colonial Brazil* (1960), 72–73; idem, *Records of the Earliest Jewish Community in the New World* (1954), 28, 74; *Jamaica Royal Gazette* (March 30, 1782; Apr. 12, 1806); *Kingston Journal* (July 28, 1787; Nov. 10, 1787); H. M. Alvares Correa, *Alvares Correa Families of Curaçao and Brazil* (1965), 10–11.

SPICE TRADE: W. Heyd, *Geschichte des Levantehandels im Mittelalter* (1879); P. Lambrechts, in: *Antiquité Classique*, 6 (1937), 357 ff.; J. Brutzkus, in: ZGJD,

3 (1931), 97 f.; L. Rabinowitz, *Jewish Merchant Adventurers, a Study of the Radanites* (1948); S. D. Goitein, *A Mediterranean Society*, 1 (1967), index; Roth, Marranos, index; C. Roth, *House of Nasi, Doña Gracia* (1947); J. A. Goris, *Etude sur les colonies marchandes méridionales à Anvers de 1488 à 1567* (1925); Brugmans-Frank, 1 (1940); D. Gomes, *Discursos sobre los comercios de las dos Indias*, ed. by M. B. Amzalak (1943); J. G. da Silva, in: *XIII Congresso Luso-Espanhol para o Progresso das Ciências*, Lisbon, 1950; J. L. de Azevedo, *Epocas de Portugal Economico* (1947²); H. I. Bloom, *The Economic Activities of the Jews of Amsterdam* (1937); C. von Rohr, *Neue Quellen zur zweiten Indienfahrt Vasco da Gamas* (1939); J. Polišenský and P. Ratkoš in: *Historica*, 9 (1964), 53–67; H. Kellenbenz, in: *Monumenta Judaica* (1963), 199 f.; idem, *Sephardim an der unteren Elbe* (1958); idem, *La participation des capitaux de l'Allemagne Méridionale aux entreprises portugaises d'Outre-Mer au tournant du XVe siècle et XVIe siècle* (1966).

STOCK EXCHANGE: G. N. Hart, in: AJHSP, 4 (1896), 215–8; S. Mayer, *Die Wiener Juden* (1917); R. Lewinsohn, *Juedische Weltfinanz?* (1925); H. Goslar, in: *Gemeindeblatt der juedischen Gemeinde zu Berlin*, 21 (1931), 14–18; J. Lestschinsky, *Das wirtschaftliche Schicksal des deutschen Judentums* (1932); H. I. Bloom, *The Economic Activities of the Jews of Amsterdam* (1937); P. H. Emden, *Money Powers of Europe* (1938); H. Rachel, *Berliner Grosskaufleute und Kapitalisten*, 2 (1938), 541 ff.; R. Strauss, in: JSOS, 3 (1941), 15–40; D. Bernstein, in: S. Kaznelson (ed.), *Juden im deutschen Kulturbereich* (1959²), 720–59; E. V. Morgan and W. A. Thomas, *The Stock Exchange* (1962); R. Glanz, *The Jew in Old American Folklore* (1961), 166 ff.; R. Sobel, *The Big Board* (1965); A. Hertzberg, *French Enlightenment and the Jews* (1968), 74 ff., 143–4, 146–7; S. Birmingham, *Our Crowd* (1968).

ILLUSTRATION CREDITS

Jerusalem, Israel Department of Antiquities and Museums: p. 6.

Jerusalem, Israel Museum Department of Ethnography Photo Collection: pp. 33, 151, 178.

Cecil Roth Collection: pp. 65, 213, 227, 268.

Ein Harod, Mishkan LeOmanut, Museum of Art: pp. 66, 145.

Jerusalem, Jewish National and University Library Photo Collection, Schwadron Collection: pp. 117, 219, 234, 249.

Courtesy Dr. Joseph Brandes, New Jersey: p. 120.

Jerusalem, Central Archive for the History of the Jewish People: p. 122.

Tel Aviv, Israel Government Press: pp. 124, 140, 146, 161, 165.

London, Jewish Colonization Association: p. 131.

Tel Aviv, Einhorn Collection: p. 134.

Munich, Bayerische Staatsbibliothek, Cod. Heb. 200 fol. 11r: p. 143.

Courtesy YIVO, New York: pp. 154, 193.

Albright-Kelso in AASOR: p. 162.

INDEX